WHAT WOULD YOU DO ALONE
IN A CAGE WITH NOTHING
BUT COCAINE?

What Would You Do Alone in a Cage with Nothing but Cocaine?

A PHILOSOPHY OF ADDICTION

HANNA PICKARD

ILLUSTRATED BY
MARCO VENNIRO

PRINCETON UNIVERSITY PRESS
PRINCETON & OXFORD

Published by Princeton University Press

41 William Street, Princeton, New Jersey 08540
99 Banbury Road, Oxford OX2 6JX

press.princeton.edu

"Wanting to Die" from The Complete Poems by Anne Sexton. Copyright © 1981 by Linda Gray Sexton and Loring Conant, Jr., executors of the will of Anne Sexton. Used by permission of HarperCollins Publishers and of Sterling Lord Literistic, Inc.

GPSR Authorized Representative: Easy Access System Europe - Mustamäe tee 50, 10621 Tallinn, Estonia, gpsr.requests@easproject.com

All Rights Reserved

ISBN 9780691253534
ISBN (e-book) 9780691253558

Library of Congress Control Number: 2025944743

British Library Cataloging-in-Publication Data is available

Editorial: Rob Tempio and Chloe Coy
Production Editorial: Nathan Carr
Jacket/Cover Design: Karl Spurzem
Production: Erin Suydam
Publicity: Maria Whelan and Carmen Jimenez
Copyeditor: Natalie Jones

Jacket/Cover Credit: Jacket illustration by Marco Venniro

This book has been composed in Arno

10 9 8 7 6 5 4 3 2 1

For Ian

CONTENTS

NOTE TO READERS

THIS BOOK proposes a new paradigm for addiction. It draws from a broad range of disciplines and sources, and my hope is to engage a broad range of readers. It also has a strong overarching narrative, meaning that the chapters are best read in order. But this does not mean that every chapter must be read with care—or even at all. I have tried to make the book accessible to readers no matter their background and interests, but it moves between philosophy, psychology, science, ethics, clinical materials, memoirs and more, so it is inevitable that readers will differ in which parts they find more approachable, and which parts harder work. If you get stuck with a chapter, feel free to skim it or skip it. It should still be possible to follow the narrative. The introduction to the book launches the paradigm. The introductions to parts II, III, and IV serve as stopping points to remind you of where you have got to in the book and preview what is to come. The conclusion summarizes the main themes. The map is so that you know (more or less) the kind of writing and material you can expect from each chapter, to better navigate your way.

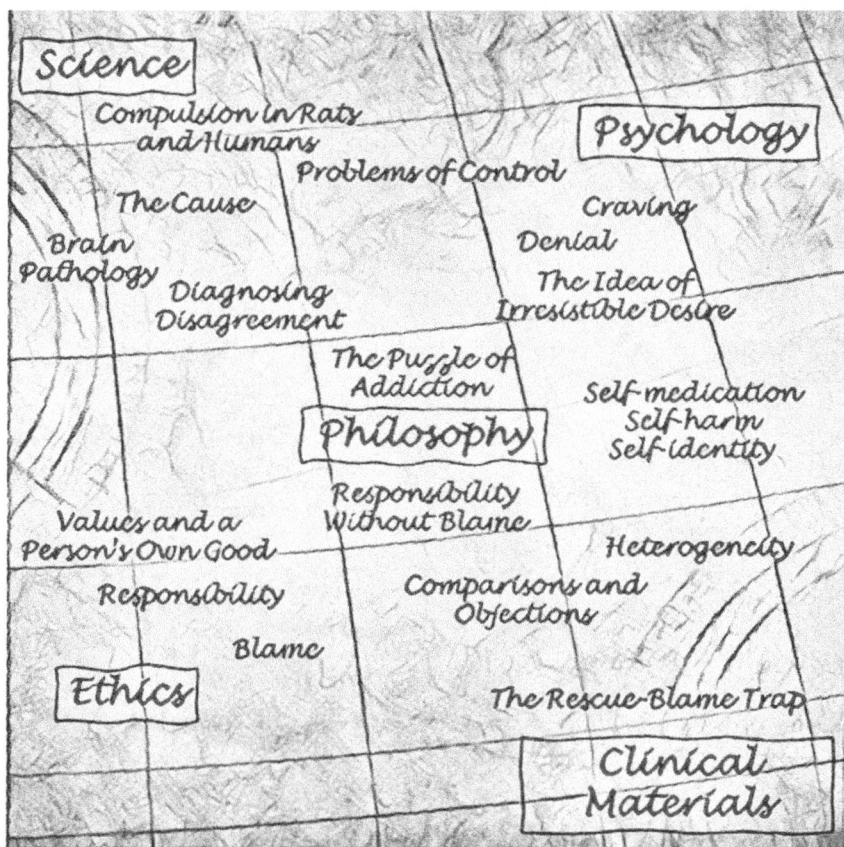

Science

Compulsion in Rats
and Humans
Problems of Control
The Cause
Brain
Pathology
Diagnosing
Disagreement

Psychology

Craving
Denial
The Idea of
Irresistible Desire

The Puzzle of
Addiction

Philosophy

Self-medication
Self-harm
Self-identity

Responsibility
Without Blame
Values and a
Person's Own Good
Heterogeneity
Responsibility
Comparisons and
Objections
Blame

Ethics

The Rescue-Blame Trap

Clinical
Materials

Introduction

WHAT WOULD YOU DO alone in a cage with nothing but cocaine? In a seminal study published in 1985, the animal experimentalists Michael Bozarth and Roy Wise asked this question of rats.[1] The rats learned to press a lever to get a dose of cocaine, delivered immediately and intravenously. They were then permanently housed in an experimental chamber containing only food, water, and the lever, which they could press for as much cocaine as they wanted. You will not be surprised at the answer to the question. The rats in this experiment took a lot of cocaine. They also stopped eating and drinking. Within a month, 90 percent had died, from exhaustion, starvation, and dehydration. This image of a rat in a cage pressing a lever again and again—abandoning itself to cocaine at the expense of food and water—is strikingly evocative of the nineteenth-century writer Oscar Wilde's chilling description of human addiction: "Men and women at such moments lose the freedom of their will. They move to their terrible end as automatons move."[2]

The rat relentlessly pressing the lever, the human whom drugs have made into a walking zombie—these are the poster children of the currently dominant scientific paradigm of addiction, which sees it as a brain disease causing compulsive drug use. In 1984, the biological psychiatrist Nancy C. Andreasen published her book *The Broken Brain*, capturing in that turn of phrase a way of thinking about mental disorder that had been gaining popular and scientific ground since the nineteenth century, buoyed by progress in brain-imaging techniques and increasing use of animal experimentation.[3] In 1997, Alan L. Leshner, then director of the US National Institute on Drug Abuse (NIDA), published his seminal article "Addiction Is a Brain Disease, and It Matters," cementing a broken brain model of addiction as scientific orthodoxy.[4] Since then, the brain disease model has grabbed the spotlight, claiming by far the lion's share of funding and credibility, and putting neuroscience and animal

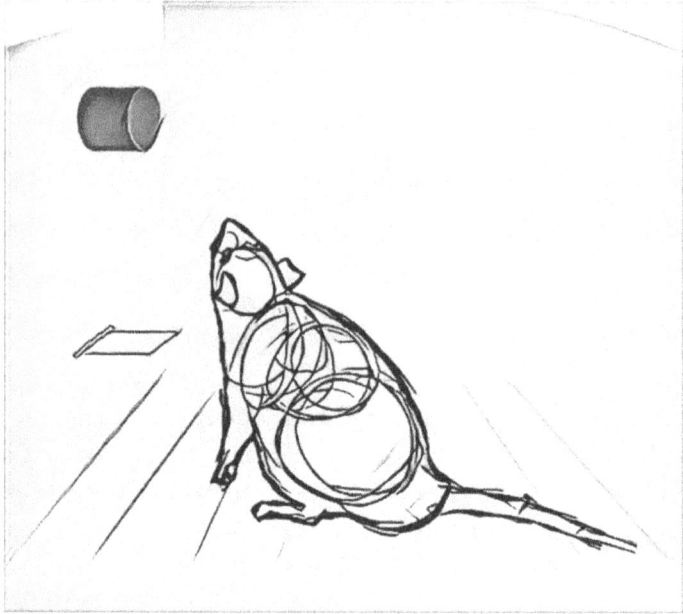

models at the center of addiction research. Dissent is heresy. Junior scientists would be foolish to question the paradigm, while senior scientists have built their labs and legacies within it.

The core idea of the model is as gripping as it is familiar. After prolonged drug use, "a metaphorical switch in the brain" is flicked and the brain is "hijacked" by drugs.[5] In keeping with Wilde, the brain disease model treats addiction as occurring when the kind of freedom of will that we normally take for granted is lost: The ordinary, voluntary behavior of a rat or a person—pressing a lever, downing a drink, swallowing a pill, injecting, inhaling or snorting a substance—becomes compulsive, transformed into a passive, involuntary symptom of a brain disease.[6]

Yet hidden behind the party line, models of addiction within neuroscience—as well as models stemming from adjacent disciplines and those at greater remove—are multiplying and competing, fomenting disagreement about something as basic as what addiction is (see chapters 1 and 2). Meanwhile, translational results issuing from the brain disease model—that is, the discovery of new and effective clinical treatments, which virtually all scientific funding applications claim as their justification and aim—are shockingly meager.[7]

The most effective medications for opioid addiction are methadone and buprenorphine. These are themselves psychoactive opioids, typically taken in liquid form or as tablets or strips that are dissolved in the mouth. Together with naltrexone—an anti-craving drug used for both opioid and alcohol addiction—they were discovered in the 1960s and 1970s, before the ascendency of the brain disease model.[8] The go-to pharmacological treatment for alcohol addiction is disulfiram, marketed under the brand name Antabuse, and discovered in the 1940s.[9] It produces a host of unpleasant symptoms if combined with ethanol and so discourages drinking.

Perhaps even more surprisingly given the dominance of the brain disease model, the most effective treatment for cocaine and some polydrug addictions is not pharmacological but behavioral. Contingency management treatment reliably delivers small rewards, such as prizes, money, and vouchers for meals or movies—or, in the behavioral psychologist Kenneth Silverman's inspired innovation of a *therapeutic workplace*, skills training and employment—on condition of drug abstinence.[10] It is based on operant conditioning principles, a form of reinforcement learning originating in the psychologist Edward Thorndike's discovery of the law of effect at the end of the nineteenth century, and elaborated by B. F. Skinner in the 1930s and 1940s.[11]

These principles are in fact the foundation for a series of animal experiments conducted over the past two decades that require reinterpretation of Bozarth and Wise's 1985 seminal finding. In 2005, the animal experimentalist Serge H. Ahmed published the first results from a forced-choice rodent study paradigm. Ahmed pioneered a simple but ingenious innovation. He introduced a second lever into the experimental chamber, thereby making it possible to give rats an either-or choice between cocaine and an alternative reward. Over a series of studies, he and his colleagues found that, in controlled conditions, when given a choice between pressing a lever for cocaine or pressing a lever for water sweetened with saccharin, 90 percent of the rats—including those who showed every indication of addiction-like behavior and none of whom was water or food deprived—chose the saccharin water, forgoing cocaine.[12] Then, in 2018, the animal experimentalists Marco Venniro, Yavin Shaham, and their colleagues published findings from a series of studies that extended Ahmed's paradigm by switching the alternative from saccharin water to social reward. They found that, when given a choice between pressing a lever for methamphetamine or heroin or pressing a lever to get one minute of playtime with another rat, almost 100 percent of the rats—including those who showed every indication of addiction-like behavior and none of whom

was socially deprived—chose to press for playtime with the other rat, thereby forgoing the drug.[13] Indeed, in a follow-up study, it transpired that rats will even forgo cocaine for the lingering scent of another rat in an empty experimental chamber.[14] So much for the idea that rats are compelled by their cocaine-broken brains to keep pressing the lever for more, when all it takes to lure them away is a drink of saccharin water, a minute of playtime, or the whiff of a buddy (see chapters 6 and 7). Why then did they take so much cocaine in Bozarth and Wise's 1985 experiment, when they were alone in a cage with nothing but cocaine? Presumably, because they were alone in a cage with nothing but cocaine.

The currently dominant scientific paradigm is broken. It is time for heresy.

Although I have collaborated with addiction scientists and animal experimentalists, I am not one. I am a philosopher. But I also spent a decade from 2007 to 2017 working part-time as an assistant team therapist in the United Kingdom, in a National Health Service (NHS) therapeutic community for people with personality disorder and complex needs, many of whom struggled with drug and behavioral addictions. UK therapeutic communities (TCs) are distinctive care environments, different from what often falls under this label in the United States as well as from more conventional medical contexts. They are informal and nonhierarchical, requiring genuine, sustained relationships between clinicians and patients, as well as between patients themselves. Medication is of course part of treatment if appropriate, but a great deal of time is spent not merely in therapy together but as a community: cooking, eating, playing games, going on outings, running the business of the group. Relationships are considered the crucial mediators of psychological and behavioral change and recovery, and thus integral to therapeutic success. Indeed, at the therapeutic community where I worked, patients typically arrived at our door taking a staggering number of medications that did them little if any good while having many negative side effects, which we then worked to help them come off. We also typically helped those patients whose identity revolved around having a brain disease to reflect on its meaning in their lives—what it did for them and how it limited them. A willingness at least to question, if not indeed abandon, this identity—and, with it, the idea that fundamentally their problems stemmed from a broken brain—was often an essential step toward recovery. So too, unquestionably, was the social support and sense of belonging provided by the group.[15]

I begin this book with the juxtaposition of experiments with rats and my own experience of working in a therapeutic community—an experience that is certainly atypical for a philosopher, but atypical even for clinicians—because where ideas come from matters. I have spent years studying addiction by drawing on a wide range of perspectives, including animal models but also neuroscience, cognitive science, social psychology, cultural anthropology, behavioral economics, public health, psychiatry, law, literature and addiction memoirs—all of which inform this book. But my understanding of addiction is both anchored in philosophy and has its origins in my own experience of working clinically with people with personality disorder in a therapeutic community in the UK. That is, with a patient group whose primary diagnosis is most certainly considered a mental disorder, but is not considered a brain disease, and in a clinical context where the primary orientation to understanding and addressing mental disorder is not neurobiological, but social and psychological. No surprise, then, that I am a broken brain heretic. I believe we need a new paradigm for understanding addiction that jettisons what is wrong with the brain disease model but retains what is right. This book hopes to provide one.

The paradigm I develop in the pages that follow can be distilled into two core and connected characteristics: *humanism* and *heterogeneity*. Although it will take a book to complete the presentation of the paradigm, I introduce these characteristics here. I also begin the task of uprooting some of the dogma, fear, and moralism that infects so much of our thinking about drug use and addiction—a clearing of the ground, so to speak, so the paradigm I go on to present can be considered with a more open mind.

To begin, then, with humanism. What I mean by this idea can be summed up in a single, foundational principle for explaining human behavior. *Psychology first.*

Psychology is our most basic, powerful tool for understanding ourselves and others.[16] Humans are self-conscious and self-reflective beings. We understand ourselves to act for reasons, both good and bad. We take our actions to be explained by our thoughts and feelings, beliefs and desires, pleasures and pains, hopes and fears, plans and intentions. In other words, we take our actions to be explained by our psychological states. We act in order to express, communicate, and satisfy our psychological states: to show what we think and how we feel, to get what we want, to avoid what we don't, to further what we hope for and make good what we intend. We begin to master the art of psychological explanation in the cradle, and we carry it with us to the grave. But it is neither fixed for all humans for all times, nor simple and easy to codify.

On the one hand, the psychology that we use in our day-to-day lives shifts and deepens as we study it. Philosophical and scientific psychology can come to inform ordinary psychology. This happened in our culture at large with Sigmund Freud and the advent of psychoanalysis, B. F. Skinner and the coming of the behaviorists, and Noam Chomsky and the cognitive revolution; it happens if you read (or write) an article or a book, and rethink or refine your individual understanding of some aspect of our minds that you previously hadn't given much attention to.

On the other hand, to be powerful and generative, the psychology that we use in our day-to-day lives must take not only individual history and personality into account, but also the social, cultural, and economic circumstances within which each person finds themself and fashions a life. Psychology and psychological explanation are inextricably linked with life circumstances. This is why pointing out that a rat is literally alone in a cage with nothing but cocaine (or, as we shall see in some of the chapters that follow, that this is metaphorically true of a person) can be explanatory of why the rat (or the person) might take a lot of drugs. We imagine the psychological impact of being trapped in isolation and emptiness; we imagine the boredom, the loneliness, the misery and the suffering. And we note that, in this cage, literal or metaphorical, there is only one thing that offers any relief. *Cocaine.*

If you pick up any addiction memoir or listen to how people with addiction speak about it, you cannot help but see that, on the whole, they both describe their use of drugs in psychological terms and weave it into the story of their lives. Here is how the writer and journalist Pete Hamill introduces his memoir *A Drinking Life*:

> This is a book about my time in the drinking life. It tells the story of the way one human being became aware of alcohol, embraced it, struggled with it, was hurt by it, and finally left it behind. The story has no hero.
>
> The culture of drink endures because it offers so many rewards: confidence for the shy, clarity for the uncertain, solace to the wounded and lonely, and above all, the elusive promises of friendship and love. From almost the beginning of awareness, drinking was a part of my life; there is no way that I could tell the story of the drinking without telling the story of the life. Much of that story was wonderful. In the snug darkness of the saloons, I learned much about being human and about mastering a craft. I had, as they say, a million laughs. But those grand times also caused great moral, physical, or psychological damage to myself and others. Some of that harm was probably permanent. There is little to be done now but take responsibility.[17]

As Hamill does in his memoir, people with addiction tend to speak of when and why they first started using; where they use; who they use with; what makes them want to use; what drugs do for them; what drugs mean to them; how they crave them, love them, need them, hate them; how they feel when they use; how they feel when they don't use; how they feel about the fact that they use; and even, for some people, how their use is part of their identity—their sense of who they are. Often, although not always, they also express uncertainty about the brain disease model, which sits uneasily with their own experience of addiction.[18] This idea—of a psychological relationship to drugs and how that relationship is linked to a person's life circumstances and identity—is crucial to understanding and treating human addiction.[19] It is explored in many of the chapters that follow (see especially chapter 4, and parts III and IV).

Two clarifications of the *psychology first* principle are in order. First, psychology *first* does not mean psychology *exclusively*. On the one hand, even when psychological explanation is successful, both neuroscience and cognitive science can supplement it, identifying physical states and computational processes that underpin psychological states and psychological processes. But supplementation is not the same as supplantation. The philosopher and ex-addict (his preferred term) Owen Flanagan puts the point thus in his book *What Is It like to Be an Addict?*: "When we identify genes behind susceptibility or brain circuits that subserve craving we explain susceptibility and craving, we don't explain them away."[20] Nor does an appeal to neuroscience and cognitive science to supplement psychological explanation depend in any way on the presence of pathology—understood in the most basic sense as the idea that something is neurobiologically or cognitively *wrong* (see chapter 8). Studying the brain at either the neurobiological or the cognitive level can illuminate addiction—as it can illuminate all forms of human behavior—whether or not addiction is a brain disease. Put otherwise, the fact that neuroscience and cognitive science can contribute to an understanding of addiction in no way shows that addiction is a brain disease—on pain of the consequence that all human behavior is a brain disease.

On the other hand, when psychological explanation fails—when we simply cannot make sense of ourselves and others in psychological terms—neuroscience and cognitive science may sometimes step in and take over, supplanting rather than supplementing psychology. Indeed, some people with addiction experience a kind of self-opacity—a failure, at least some of the time, to fully understand themselves or to be able to explain their drug use in psychological terms without remainder—inviting us to look beyond psychology and life circumstances for explanations (see chapters 9, 14, and 15). But if you want to understand a self-conscious and self-reflective being, the place to start is to consider how they understand themself. This is as true of a person in the grip of addiction as of anyone.

Second, psychology *first* does not mean treating what people say about themselves as infallible or beyond question. No doubt, there are aspects of our minds—most notably, what our current conscious experience is subjectively like for us—where we have a great deal of authority. But we can all be wrong about why we do what we do—about what explains our behavior—even if we have made serious and sincere efforts at self-understanding.[21] There are many reasons why this is true in general; here are two reasons that bear on addiction in particular. The first is the possibility of denial and self-deception: psychological processes whose function is to block self-knowledge. This possibility can at times provide a reason to question what people with addiction say about their drug use, both to others and to themselves. This fallibility does not, however, require us to abandon psychology for neuroscience or cognitive science. Quite the contrary. Denial and self-deception lie at least partly outside of our conscious awareness, but they are fundamentally psychological processes that serve to protect us from the pain of facing up to certain truths (see chapter 13). They are psychologically motivated. And it is typically through a conscious, painful process of psychological reflection that they are overcome. The second is that, as the philosophers and qualitative researchers Doug McConnell and Anke Snoek have emphasized in their work on addiction, culture shapes self-understanding by providing us with interpretive tools: ideas, tropes, schemas, archetypes, narratives.[22] If these are misguided—as I believe the brain disease model in many respects to be—then so too is any self-understanding shaped by them.

The paradigm proposed in this book is therefore humanistic in that it aims to counter the brain disease model's persistent sidelining of psychological explanations of addiction in favor of explanations that are both neurobiological and pathological. The paradigm does not thereby reject the scientific study of addiction: The supplementation of psychology by neuroscience and cognitive science can be important and illuminative. Nor does it pretend that self-report is infallible. It does, however, thereby raise a serious concern about the scope of the relevance of animal models to human addiction[23]—one of the experimental methods most central to addiction neuroscience, and from which I, myself, have learned a great deal. For nothing about a person's own understanding of their relationship to drugs and the role of this understanding in forming and maintaining their addiction can be modeled in animals who, like rats and most other nonhuman animal subjects, are not self-conscious or self-reflective beings.

Let us now turn to the second core characteristic of the paradigm: heterogeneity. What I mean by this is that there is no one-size-fits-all explanation or theory of addiction.

Different cultures sanction and condemn different drugs. For example, in our society, alcohol and prescription drugs are generally culturally sanctioned, while MDMA (methylenedioxymethamphetamine—colloquially known as molly or ecstasy) and heroin are generally culturally condemned; but other societies condemn alcohol, while some subcultures within our society sanction MDMA and heroin. The importance of cultural attitudes to how and why people become addicted cannot be exaggerated. Meanwhile, different drugs act differently on the brain and have different psychoactive effects. People, of course, are also different: their histories, their personalities, their life circumstances. And the ways they understand themselves are different too. One person is in denial, another is not. One person's identity is wrapped up in their addiction, another's is not. One person is obsessed with drugs and constantly craving them, another is not. One person is alone in a metaphorical cage with their grief, anxiety, anger, shame, despair, and self-loathing, while another is defiant, reckless, impulsive—something of a thrill seeker. Actions—including drug use—that appear similar on the surface may have different explanations in different people when we dig deep. As the philosopher Jenann Ismael succinctly puts the general point, "human beings are all specificity."[24] Explaining behavior by appeal to psychology opens the door to heterogeneity, allowing different cases of addiction to be explained by appeal to different psychologies and life circumstances. Heterogeneity is in this way connected to humanism. But, once this door is open, heterogeneity also allows some cases of addiction to be explained less by ordinary psychology than by neuroscience or cognitive science—that is, it allows for supplantation, not just supplementation, in some cases. Indeed, the paradigm put forward in this book allows that some cases of addiction may be explained by brain pathology—even if others are not. Why not, if addiction is heterogeneous?[25]

Recognizing the heterogeneity of addiction therefore holds tremendous promise as a way of moving beyond the deep disagreement currently found between models of addiction, as well as aligning addiction science with good clinical care—care that, to count as good, must be attentive to individual differences and tailored to individual needs (see chapter 3). But this promise is predicated on heterogeneity: on relinquishing the idea of a universal explanation of addiction or underlying "essence" that makes it what it is, and which every case of addiction must have, and no case of addiction can lack. As we shall see, the brain disease model is committed to such an essence, namely brain pathology (chapter 2).

Here, then, are the bare bones of the paradigm to come. I shall argue that addiction is a pattern of drug use that persists despite evident and severe costs such that it counts profoundly against a person's own good—that is, addiction is a pattern of *behavior* (chapter 1). To identify cases of addiction, we need to think about what it means for drug use to be—or not be—*good* for a person (chapter 4). To explain addiction, we need to explain *why* a person would persist in using drugs given that doing so is *not* good for them. The explanations canvassed over the course of this book include the possibility of brain pathology (chapters 8 and 9) but also self-medication and a person's social, cultural, and economic circumstances (chapter 10); the development of a security-based attachment to drugs (chapter 10); self-harm and a desire to die (chapter 11); an "addict" identity (chapter 12); denial and cognitive difficulties (chapter 13); problems of control (chapter 14); and cravings for drugs (chapter 15). Some of these explanations will apply to some people with addiction, while other explanations will apply to others; and sometimes more than one explanation will apply to one and the same person—potentially interacting in complicated ways—even though some are mutually incompatible. The paradigm is humanistic because most (albeit not all) of these explanations not only render drug use in addiction *psychologically* intelligible but are, in addition, deeply personal—as is the question of what is good for a person. The paradigm is heterogeneous because there is no universal explanation or underlying essence of addiction. Its explanations are varied (chapter 3 and part III). Its causes are diverse (chapter 9).

I am by no means the first to propose that these two characteristics—humanism and heterogeneity—are central to understanding addiction. The history of addiction research contains many heretics.[26] But despite this counter history, my experience is that the paradigm shift I propose in this book is often met with outrage, as if it demonstrated a total failure to understand addiction or to care about those who struggle with it. The paradigm must of course be judged on its intellectual merits, but I am writing this book because I believe the dominance of the brain disease model is not only stifling addiction research but failing people in need of help. I state this here, plainly, not to provoke, but to emphasize the common ground between many of us who think about addiction and want to understand it better: the desire to help those who struggle with it. Given this common ground, why then is critique of the brain disease model so often met with outrage—indeed, so readily characterized as heresy rather than simply as respectful disagreement? I believe part of the answer is an underlying fear on behalf of people with addiction: the fear that only the brain disease model can save us from what has come to be known as *the moral model* of addiction.

The moral model treats drug use in addiction as no different from ordinary drug use apart from addiction. According to the moral model, both kinds of drug use are voluntary and morally wrong. The brain disease model aims to counter the moral model by claiming that drug use in addiction is different from ordinary drug use. According to the brain disease model, only ordinary drug use is voluntary; drug use in addiction is compulsive and caused by brain disease. I know of no actual addiction researcher from any academic discipline who espouses the moral model. It is, rather, a picture of addiction associated with a kind of black-and-white, pulpit-thumping, puritanical morality that has seeped into our shared cultural understanding of drug use over the course of history—perhaps especially in the US.[27] But with the moral model contaminating the cultural air, it can seem as if the only reliable way to undermine the stigma surrounding addiction and stifle the tendency to blame and punish people who are addicted is to view them as victims of a brain disease that compels them to use drugs. This kind of motivation for the brain disease model is explicit in Leshner's seminal 1997 article and reaffirmed in an article published in 2021 by a group of distinguished neuroscientists led by Markus Heilig, "Addiction as a Brain Disease Revised: Why It Still Matters."[28] In other words, the brain disease model has become the scientific and public health orthodoxy in part out of faith that it, and only it, is capable of changing stigmatizing attitudes toward those with addiction, thereby countering the moral model and helping those in need. This faith in effect creates a dilemma: Either you commit to the brain disease model, or you fail to address stigma and adequately care about people with addiction.

The dilemma is false. The moral model and the brain disease model are not the only options. Although it will take the whole of the book to complete it, the paradigm developed here includes an ethics for addiction: a framework for addressing stigma, thinking about values, needs, differences, and responsibility, and supporting relationships with people with addiction (see part IV).[29] The dilemma also embodies two mistakes, one theoretical and one empirical, that are important to uproot at the outset.

The theoretical mistake is to allow the (real or imagined) ethical consequences of adopting a model to bear on the question of its scientific validity. The validity of any scientific model is established by considering confirming and disconfirming evidence—not by considering whether it does harm or good. A valid scientific model may, in certain circumstances, have terrible consequences. Think of the use of atomic theory in the development of the atomic bomb by the US and its subsequent deployment against Japan. These consequences are morally horrific. But they do not speak against the theoretical validity of atomic theory. Similarly, the dissemination of a scientific model that is not based on solid evidence but on mistake or even fancy may, in certain circumstances, have at least some consequences that are welcome. Think of the theory that the sun, moon, and stars all revolve around the earth, putting us at the center of the universe. Historically, belief in this theory may have bolstered religious conviction and a sense of humanity's importance, offering a kind of reassuring protection against the fear of death and meaninglessness that can overwhelm any of us. Needless to say, this silver lining, such as it is, does not confer theoretical validity. The bottom line is that ethics is one thing, science another. Ethics needs to govern how science is practiced and how scientific knowledge is used, and scientific models can do harm or good in light of how they are developed and used. But these points have no bearing on whether a model is supported by the evidence. Applying this lesson to the brain disease model: Whether it helps or hinders attempts to combat stigma and counter the moral model of addiction is irrelevant to its scientific validity.

The empirical mistake is to assume, from the armchair, that the ethical consequences of the brain disease model are plainly good: that it is successful in combating stigma and countering the moral model. Although more empirical research is needed, initial findings suggest that things are much more complicated. The effects of labeling addiction a brain disease are both good and bad—a "mixed blessing," as the sociologist Nick Haslam puts it.[30]

A caveat before presenting the relevant studies: It is in truth unclear how much real-world impact the brain disease model has had. Scientific support for it initially coincided with the American War on Drugs in the 1980s and 1990s. This kind of punitive policy was politically advantageous in the US and elsewhere because it appealed to a popular moralism about drugs and drug users, intersecting with discriminatory gender, race, and class stereotypes.[31] Indeed, this intersectional dynamic is arguably still present. The more recent push in the US to frame addiction as a public health rather than criminal justice problem coincides all too conveniently with the impact of the opioid epidemic on suburban and white communities.[32] Meanwhile, increased public acceptance of broken brain models of mental disorder was not associated with decreased stigma in the 1990s and 2000s.[33] Rather than itself shifting punitive and stigmatizing popular attitudes to addiction, the brain disease model may simply have functioned as a useful prop when these shifted for independent reasons.

Nonetheless, large-scale surveys and experimental vignette studies suggest that acceptance of the brain disease model has a variety of effects on people's attitudes. So let us begin with the effects that are good. The brain disease model—like other broken brain models of mental disorder—is associated with public support for research and treatment.[34] It can also have a positive impact on relationships between people with addiction and families, friends, and colleagues (but see chapter 16 for a fuller picture).[35] We are in general inclined to attribute responsibility and to blame people for actions only if they are voluntarily undertaken. Actions that are compelled are not voluntarily undertaken. By characterizing drug use in addiction as compulsive, the brain disease model undermines attributions of responsibility and the tendency to blame people with addiction for drug use and any associated wrongs or harms.

Turning now to the bad and with the proviso that cultural differences are under-studied yet likely to be significant:[36] Whatever its effects on personal relationships, the brain disease model—like other broken brain models of mental disorder—does not appear to combat addiction stigma, which remains high.[37] Indeed, there is evidence that it encourages social rejection and public perceptions of dangerousness and difference.[38] On reflection, this is hardly surprising. There is no reason to expect that labeling a condition a disease would be an antidote to stigma, for diseases are frequently associated with stigma. Think of cancer, leprosy, syphilis, or HIV/AIDS. People with diseases are often shunned and ostracized. To be pitied, yes, but as the acronym "NIMBY" says, "not in my backyard."

Relatedly, just as the brain disease model does not appear to decrease stigma in others, it does not appear to protect people with addiction from a kind of internalized stigma themselves. Even if they are not responsible or to blame for using drugs, they may yet feel that something is deeply wrong with them—deeply shameful.[39] After all, they have a brain disease. For this reason, the model can also impede people's ability to recognize that they have a problem with drugs and seek help. Broken brain models in effect divide people into two kinds: those whose brain is broken, and those whose brain is not. As the psychologist James Morris has argued, this may motivate denial and self-deception as a way of avoiding the stigma and threat to identity that the brain disease label creates.[40]

Lastly, the brain disease model may contribute to pessimism about recovery[41]—a mark of poor prognosis—and increase the likelihood of relapse.[42] In characterizing drug use as compulsive, the model undermines what is arguably a plank of all successful treatment, namely a sense of one's own agency and ability to do things differently. That is, an ability to change one's relationship to drugs and construct a life, an identity, where they play a less significant role.[43] To preview one of the core ideas of the ethical framework (see part IV): Because of its connection to voluntary agency, responsibility can have an important role to play in recovery if divorced from blame.

As I say, with respect to its ethical consequences, the brain disease model is a mixed blessing.

Three final introductory points of clarification and orientation, to finish clearing the ground for the paradigm to come.

First, I take it as a basic truth that there is nothing intrinsically morally wrong with using drugs. Most of us use drugs. We drink alcohol—beer, wine, whiskey, martinis, negronis. We drink caffeine—in coffee, tea, cola. We smoke cigarettes and vape. We use cannabis, opioids, amphetamines, benzodiazepines, Z-drugs (for example, the sedatives zopiclone, zolpidem, zaleplon)—prescribed or not. We use MDMA, psychedelics, ketamine, kratom. Meanwhile new drugs are always being created—by pharmaceutical companies as much as by drug cartels. There can no doubt be better or worse reasons for using drugs, as there can be better or worse reasons for anything we do. Equally, using drugs carries health risks—again, like other things we do. And in certain circumstances, namely those that straightforwardly involve or significantly risk seriously harming or violating the rights of others, using drugs is morally wrong. To take but a few examples: It is wrong to drink (or to use any drug) and drive, or to leave drug paraphernalia in public spaces, thereby putting others at risk. It is wrong to use drugs produced—as so many consumer goods in our society are—through exploitation, violence, and the destruction of communities in developing countries.[44] It is wrong to use drugs in ways and at times that compromise your ability to care for your children—whether you are addicted to drugs or not. But there is nothing intrinsically morally wrong with using drugs—nothing wrong with drug use *in itself*. Why would there be?

I do not believe there is any good answer to this question. If you disagree, I challenge you to provide it. I can see no moral principle that, for example, sanctions a bottle of beer or a glass of wine but condemns a line of cocaine or a tab of LSD or a joint. I can see no moral principle that permits opioids for pain relief when prescribed by a doctor as part of palliative care but forbids the use of heroin to escape from a life of misery and suffering on the streets. And, to address a common objection, let us be clear: The fact that a religion condemns the use of some drugs, or that a country criminalizes the possession of some drugs for some purposes, does not show that such use is *intrinsically* morally wrong.

The argument for this point originates in Plato's dialogue *Euthyphro*, written over two millennia ago.[45] The argument is beautifully simple. It cannot be that something is morally wrong because the gods proscribe it; rather, any gods worth worshipping as opposed to obeying merely for fear of their wrath—that is, any gods who are themselves morally good—will proscribe something only if it is morally wrong. Just so with the criminalization of conduct, as the philosopher Douglas Husak has in effect argued in his lifelong plea for drug decriminalization.[46] Although the principles by which conduct is legitimately criminalized are complex and contested,[47] the essence of Husak's argument mirrors Plato's *Euthyphro*. It cannot be that something is morally wrong because it is criminalized; rather, one of the most basic, agreed principles by which conduct is legitimately criminalized is that it is morally wrong—specifically, it involves or significantly risks seriously harming or violating the rights of others.

To help see the force of these arguments, let us take a concrete example: Think of how many religions and criminal codes have prohibited homosexual acts over the course of human history. Such prohibition did not make homosexual acts morally wrong. Quite the contrary. The fact that homosexual acts are in no way morally wrong makes it morally wrong to prohibit let alone punish them—a moral stain on religions and criminal codes that do. There are, inevitably, a host of reasons—religious, legal, political, social, cultural, prudential—to obey religious and criminal laws, even when these laws are bad, and so when there are, equally, moral reasons to resist, to revolt, to refuse to obey. The point here is not about whether, on balance, resistance or obedience is called for in whatever religious or legal circumstances we may find ourselves. The point is that, if conduct is not intrinsically morally wrong, religious and criminal law cannot make it so.

I believe it is imperative to state plainly the basic truth that there is nothing intrinsically morally wrong with using drugs, and to keep it clearly before our minds, if we are to be in any position whatsoever to address addiction stigma and reflectively consider what our attitudes to drugs and relationships with people with addiction ought to be like. I do not diminish the impact addiction can have on families, friends, colleagues, and communities. People with addiction sometimes wrong and hurt others—as well, of course, as harming themselves. (It bears saying immediately that so, too, do many people who are not addicted to drugs.) Thinking about how to reckon with this fact within our personal relationships is part of the project undertaken in this book (see part IV). Nonetheless, there are many occasions of drug use, in addiction as much as apart from it, where absolutely nothing is done that is morally wrong. Recognizing this helps us realize what should anyway be obvious: Addiction stigma comes from us. It comes from the cultural air we breathe, which is saturated with a history of religious moralism about drugs; from the criminalization of drug possession, which forges an invidious association between drugs, deviancy, and crime; and from the intersection of our ideas about drugs and drug users with discriminatory class, race, and gender stereotypes.

Demonizing drugs is the easy way out. It stops us, as individuals and as a society, from questioning, and thereby potentially changing, our own stigmatizing and stereotyping attitudes.

Notice that no matter the good intentions of its champions, the brain disease model implicitly demonizes drugs rather than encouraging such questioning. The brain disease model aims to address stigma and foster care for people with addiction by providing them with a simple, blanket excuse. Drug use is not voluntary in addiction, because people with addiction have a brain disease that compels them to use drugs. For this reason, no one is straightforwardly responsible or to blame for using drugs, once addicted. But here's the rub: We only need an excuse if we are doing something morally wrong. The felt need to provide an excuse for all drug use in addiction betrays an assumption that all drug use is morally wrong. Otherwise, we could proceed—as I argue we should at the end of this book—case by case (see chapter 19). First, simply by pausing, taking a breath, and reflecting on why we are inclined to blame someone and whether we are right to do so. Second, if indeed they have done something morally wrong—or if not morally wrong, then so upsetting to us personally that we can't pretend that nothing is wrong between us—only then by considering how we want to address what has occurred and relate to that person. As part of this, we can consider whether any of the wide panoply of reasons, excuses, justifications, and mitigating circumstances—including but by no means limited to compulsion—might reduce or even eliminate their responsibility or temper our tendency to blame. But this is hardly the only thing that matters when people hurt us and relationships go wrong.

The second clarificatory point pertains to the distinction between drug and behavioral addictions. In one sense, I reject this distinction: Using drugs is a behavior—something we do—just as much as is eating, gambling, exercising, working, watching porn, or having sex. I see no reason to think that people cannot be addicted to all these behaviors. Indeed, there is some reason to think that people can be addicted to just about any behavior, including, famously, eating carrots.[48] But the paradigm proposed in this book is intended as a paradigm for drug addiction, which is evidently different from other addictions given that—notwithstanding important differences between classes of drugs[49]—the ingestion of drugs typically affects the brain differently than, say, the ingestion of carrots. I would be delighted if the paradigm proved to offer insight into other behavioral addictions, and I will very occasionally discuss other forms of addiction, but I make no claim to offer a new paradigm for understanding all possible addiction. There are important differences between the many things to which we can become addicted—drugs, food, games of chance, exercise, work, porn, sex, and no doubt more—and each should be treated in its own right.

But that said, the third and final clarificatory point is that, despite proposing a new paradigm for drug addiction, I do not provide a watertight definition of "drug."

The *Oxford English Dictionary* (OED) defines "drug" thus:

a. Originally: any substance, of animal, vegetable, or mineral origin, used as an ingredient in pharmacy, chemistry, dyeing, or various manufacturing processes. In later use: *spec.* a natural or synthetic substance used in the prevention or treatment of disease, a medicine; (also) a substance that has a physiological effect on a living organism.[50]

b. A substance with intoxicating, stimulant, or narcotic effects used for cultural, recreational, or other non-medicinal purposes. In later use frequently: *spec.* a controlled substance used illegally and often habitually. Frequently in *plural*.[51]

A workable definition of "drug" for the purpose of understanding drug addiction can be extricated from the latter part of *a* combined with the first part of *b*. A drug is a substance with what we can summarily call a "psychoactive" effect on the mind and consequently the behavior of living organisms, at least in part because it has a physiological effect on bodies, in particular, brains; and which is typically used for cultural, recreational, and other nonmedicinal purposes as well as medicinal purposes. We need to specify that the psychoactive effect is due to a physiological effect to rule out pure placebos. But the caveat "in part" is essential since it is evident that much of the psychoactive effect of drugs is due to the expectation of the effect—hence not purely physiologically caused, but psychologically mediated.[52] Drugs can also clearly be used for medicinal and nonmedicinal purposes—in so far as the line between these can coherently be drawn at all. The scope of medicine is far from self-evident, including as it does conditions that are, or are caused by, diseases, and conditions that are not diseases at all, such as pregnancy and many natural effects of aging, like menopause—just to give some obvious examples. Doctors therefore routinely prescribe drugs for conditions that are not diseases, and people who are not doctors self-medicate with drugs for conditions that are. Importantly, however, the legality or habituality of use should be no part of the definition of "drug." Nothing becomes a drug through criminalization or ceases to be one through decriminalization, and drugs that are used infrequently or irregularly (say, because they are hard to produce, or only used by a culture as part of a yearly religious ritual) are no less drugs for that. This definition is potentially prey to counterexamples (for example, does it mean that sugar is a drug—and is that a problem?), so not watertight. But it is nonetheless a viable gloss on what we mean by "drugs" and will include all of the following common kinds: alcohol, amphetamines, ayahuasca, barbiturates, caffeine, cannabis, benzodiazepines, cocaine, fentanyl, GHB, heroin, inhalants, ketamine, khat, kratom, LSD, MDMA, mescaline, morphine, nicotine, PCP, psilocybin, Z-drugs, and many other kinds of prescription opioids, stimulants, and sedatives, as well as over-the-counter medicines, such as dextromethorphan and loperamide.

We know well enough what drugs are. Our problem is that we don't know what addiction is. This, then, is where the paradigm begins: by explicating addiction.

PART I

Explicating Addiction

1

The Puzzle of Addiction

WHAT IS ADDICTION?

Models of addiction are multiplying. Many fall under the umbrella of the brain disease model. These models agree that addiction is a brain disease but disagree about how exactly the addicted brain is broken. Examples include aberrant reinforcement learning models/habit models, emotional and motivational dysregulation models, pathological decision-making models, impaired cognitive control models, and impaired self-awareness/interoception models.[1] Other models reject the brain disease model, while yet disagreeing about what addiction is. Examples include rational choice models, behavioral economic models, nonpathological emotional and motivational self-regulation and psychological coping mechanism models, normal developmental learning models, social identity models, and models that see addiction as, metaphorically speaking, a *social* disease—an adaptative response to the cultural and material ills of contemporary society.[2] Academic presentations and research articles about addiction often begin by at least implicitly and often explicitly defining it in terms conducive to the model under investigation: Addiction *is* aberrant reinforcement learning or an impairment in cognitive control or a rational choice or a psychological coping mechanism or a social disease (and so on). Some of these models are mutually compatible, but many are decidedly not, and hence prone to view each other as rivals—sometimes, indeed, as worthy of contempt. This is particularly pronounced with respect to models on opposite sides of the brain-disease divide. Ultimately the cost of this impasse is born by people with addiction themselves.

How to move forward? The philosopher Owen Flanagan suggests interpreting these definitions as nominal only: "a form of rooting for the home team, and expressing unwarranted confidence that the part of reality that one's home team studies is where the main action is, not as plausible claims about what addiction *really is*."[3] But, as Flanagan would no doubt agree, words matter, and the proliferation of these definitions—nominal or real—gets in the way of what we need to move beyond the impasse. This is a shared understanding of what the object of study that models of addiction aspire to explain is, namely *addiction*. I therefore begin by putting all models to the side, to help us notice some considerations that are all too easily overlooked yet advance this understanding.

Let us begin with the fact that drug use is pervasive across human civilization, dating back millennia. Virtually all human cultures use drugs of some form. There is archaeological evidence of consumption of opium poppies in Britain and Europe from at least 5500 BCE, and of alcohol production around the world from at least 5000 to 7000 BCE, and possibly as early as 12,000 BCE. Peyote, mescaline, and other psychedelics have been used for thousands of years in Mexico, Central and South America; tobacco was cultivated in North America, kava in the Pacific, cannabis in Asia.[4] Now consider contemporary global rates. The United Nations World Drug Report 2022 estimates that one in seventeen people use what are conventionally called "illicit" drugs, such as heroin, fentanyl, opioids, cocaine, cannabis, amphetamines, and ecstasy; the World Health Organization Global Status on Alcohol and Health Report 2018 estimates that two in five people drink alcohol.[5] Approximately four in five people drink some form of caffeine daily and one in five use nicotine.[6] Meanwhile, the vast majority of people who use drugs of virtually all classes do not become addicted—presumably, this is just as true of drug use in the past as it is now.[7]

Look around at our communities, and you will find the ubiquity and mundanity of drug use anecdotally confirmed by a glance. A teenager who smokes to look edgy. A postoperative patient who takes opioids for pain. A student who takes MDMA to go clubbing, uses prescription amphetamines to study, and drinks alcohol at parties to feel less socially inhibited, more free. A truck driver who drinks coffee to stay awake. A couple who enjoy a bottle of wine as part of every meal. An artist who uses psychedelics for creativity. A sex worker who uses cocaine with their clients to heighten the sex. Friends who occasionally use heroin together for pleasure. A man who pours himself a drink to escape his boredom and loneliness. A woman who lights up a joint at the end of a long day to relax.

As a species, we have always used drugs, and most drug use does not lead to addiction. Yet, apart from the most exceptional of circumstances, all addiction originates with ordinary drug use. As the alcohol researcher Mark Keller puts it: "That drinking must precede alcoholism is obvious. Equally obvious, but not always sufficiently considered, is the fact that drinking is not necessarily followed by alcoholism."[8] Suppose, therefore, that we begin not with addiction but here, with ordinary drug use, and ask a simple question: Why do people use drugs?

From the basic, psychological perspective that we use to understand ourselves and others, the question is so easy to answer it hardly bears asking. The answer is that people use drugs because they have tremendous value. Drugs are means to many common and wholly intelligible ends. These include deep and varied forms of pleasure and euphoria, as well as other positive psychological states. Drugs give us energy. They make us sharper and more creative. They boost our confidence and help us feel connected to each other. They make sex more intense. They bring us feelings of peace and joy. They open us to nature, spirituality, our selves, the beauty of others and the world. But drugs also provide relief from negative psychological states such as pain, exhaustion, stress, insomnia, boredom, loneliness, and intense negative emotions—really all forms of misery and suffering. Sometimes they manage to do both. Indeed, most addiction memoirs emphasize how, when the author first took drugs, they were staggered at the feelings they induced—feelings of safety, security, control, power, of a profound transformation of mind and self.

Here is the addiction neuroscientist Judith Grisel describing her first drink:

> The first time I got drunk, at thirteen, I felt as Eve should have after tasting the apple. Or as a bird hatched in a cage would feel after being unexpectedly set free. The drug provided physical relief and spiritual antidote for the persistent restlessness I'd been unable to identify or share. An abrupt shift of perspective coincident with guzzling half a gallon of wine in my friend's basement somehow made me feel sure that both life and I were going to be all right. Just as light is revealed by darkness, and joy by sorrow, alcohol provided powerful subconscious recognition of my desperate strivings for self-acceptance and existential purpose and my inability to negotiate a complex world of relationships, fears, and hopes. At the same time, it seemed to deliver, on a satin pillow, the key to all my blooming angst. Abruptly relieved from an existence both harsh and lackluster, I had finally discovered ease.[9]

Grisel hits a common note in memoirs by people with alcohol addiction: Alcohol provides security, safety, and relief from anxiety so pervasive that it didn't even register until it was, with that first sip, dissolved.[10] But different drugs serve different functions. Opioids are bliss, and relieve pain and suffering. Amphetamines are thrilling, and boost cognitive ability. Alcohol and benzodiazepines—as well as relieving anxiety—are relaxing and loosening of inhibitions. MDMA brings a glow that heightens social connectedness. Psychedelics blow our minds, producing experiences people describe as some of the most meaningful of their lives.[11]

Unsurprisingly, given this panoply of different functions, different people use different drugs in different circumstances and for different purposes. A study by the addiction scientist David Epstein and his colleagues provides a striking illustration of this point.[12] People with polydrug addictions differentially crave and use cocaine and heroin. Cocaine is linked to good mood and good news, while heroin is linked to sadness, anger, and bad news. Why? Because cocaine is thrilling—a party drug—and opioids are comforting—a panacea for negative emotions, pain, and suffering. Indeed, even rats select different drugs in different environments, preferring heroin in their home cage (where they can relax) and cocaine outside of it (where they need to be alert).[13] But, nuances of drug choice aside, the key point is that drugs have tremendous value because of what they do for us. Using drugs is a means to satisfying many ordinary but powerful desires.

Hence from a basic, psychological perspective, we know all too well why people use drugs. They have good reasons to use, namely the benefits drugs bring. Of course, there are also the costs. We know this, too. Too much coffee can make you jittery. Opioids can make you constipated. Cannabis can make you paranoid. You can have a bad trip with psychedelics. Cocaine can make you reckless. Alcohol can lead to hangovers as well as pub brawls—although it is far from clear whether this latter is due to the neurophysiological effects of alcohol or the fact that certain cultures associate alcohol with violence, thereby creating expectations, permissions, and excuses.[14] No matter. Whether the explanation is neurobiological, cultural, or a bit of both, we can certainly find ourselves doing stupid, bad, and dangerous things when we use drugs, putting ourselves and others at risk. And then there is the risk of addiction. Nonetheless, in a great many ordinary cases of drug use, the benefits easily balance the costs that are risked let alone incurred.[15]

By contrast, addiction occurs precisely when it looks like the reasons to use have run out. From the same basic, psychological perspective, we can no longer straightforwardly understand why a person is using drugs. Why not? Because of the apparent tip in the balance of costs and benefits. There comes a point when the benefits no longer easily balance the costs that are risked let alone incurred—quite the contrary.

This happens gradually, over time. No one becomes addicted the first time they use drugs. And there is no one, precise moment—no sip of alcohol, snort of cocaine, injection of heroin—when ordinary drug use tips into addiction. Here is the journalist and writer Caroline Knapp making this point in her memoir *Drinking: A Love Story*:

> Alcohol is everywhere in your life, omnipresent, and you're both aware and unaware of it almost all the time; all you know is you'd die without it, and there is no simple reason why this happens, no single moment, no physiological event that pushes a heavy drinker across a concrete line into alcoholism. It's a slow, gradual, insidious, elusive *becoming*.[16]

And here is the writer William S. Burroughs, bemoaning the many myths perpetuated about heroin and heroin use in his memoir *Junky*:

> The question is frequently asked: Why does a man become a drug addict?
> The answer is that he usually does not intend to become an addict. You don't wake up one morning and decide to be a drug addict. It takes at least three months' shooting twice a day to get any habit at all. And you don't really know what junk sickness is until you have had several habits. It took me almost six months to get my first habit, and then the withdrawal symptoms were mild. I think it no exaggeration to say it takes about a year and several hundred injections to make an addict.[17]

Nonetheless, however slow, however hard to pinpoint, there is a transition. A pattern of drug use that was perfectly ordinary shifts. Whatever the benefits of drug use, they no longer easily balance the costs. These costs include the loss of jobs, housing, educational opportunities, standing in one's community, and, in jurisdictions that criminalize drug possession, basic freedom. The loss of people and relationships—colleagues, friends, family, parents, children. The loss of health—both physical and mental. Feelings of shame, grief, despair, self-loathing. The distress of self-opacity—of not being able to make sense of one's behavior to oneself (see chapters 14 and 15). Sometimes even the ultimate loss—of life itself. I asked why people ordinarily use drugs and the answer was straightforward. People use drugs because they have tremendous value. But now suppose we ask: Why do people use drugs, despite costs such as these? Whatever benefits of drug use remain in addiction, these costs are so evident and so severe that using seems in no way worth it—and yet, people with addiction persist.

This is what I will call *the puzzle of addiction*. From the basic, psychological perspective that we use to understand ourselves and others, drug use in addiction is no longer easily intelligible because the costs appear to have become so evident and severe that, whatever the benefits, the balance seems to have tipped. Drug use looks to be destroying a person's life—it looks to be starkly counter to their own good. It thereby appears to violate a basic, psychological assumption we make when explaining behavior, namely an assumption of *self-concern*. We ordinarily take people to be guided by *a concern for their own good*, where this is broadly construed to include not only what is good for them, considered in complete isolation, but also what is good for the people and things they care about, that is, the people and things their own good is woven together with and hence dependent upon. Drug use in addiction appears to flout this assumption of self-concern. How then to understand what a person is doing? How to explain why a person is persisting in using drugs when doing so seems so counter to their own good—in no way worth it?

I am not the first to articulate something like this puzzle. In particular, addiction researchers inspired by behavioral economics often see addiction in somewhat similar terms, namely as a puzzle of irrationality.[18] This is because drug use in addiction appears to violate the classic economic assumption that we act rationally insofar as we maximize expected utility. Despite the apparent tip in the balance from benefits to costs, people with addiction keep using drugs. How could this be rational? How to explain it if it's not? This way of articulating the puzzle is similar to the articulation I have offered in the following respect: In both cases, the puzzle derives from the fact that drug use in addiction appears deeply self-destructive. However, the articulations are not identical.

I am suggesting we see the puzzle as arising because drug use in addiction is not easily intelligible from the perspective of ordinary psychology—because it appears so deeply inconsistent with what is good for a person. This is not the same as seeing it as arising because it is irrational from the perspective of classic economic theory—because it appears to fail so spectacularly to maximize expected utility. Classic economic theory is a formal idealization that may helpfully model aspects of ordinary psychology, but ordinary psychology is both broader and, quite simply, different. On the one hand, psychological explanation can confer intelligibility on a great deal of behavior that either does not seem to maximize utility or does not lend itself to the question of whether utility is maximized at all. Consider, for example, explanations of behavior by recourse to habits, whims, perversions, conformity, willful ignorance, negligence, recklessness, laziness, stubbornness, randomness, boredom, weakness of will, wishful thinking, and, perhaps most importantly of all, emotion and desire—fear, anxiety, sadness, grief, disgust, anger, rage, vengeance, hatred, contempt, shame, guilt, greed, love, lust. Behavior thus explained is perfectly intelligible to us, whether it is rational or not. On the other hand, sometimes behavior succeeds in maximizing expected utility while yet being deeply inconsistent with what is good for a person: It is the best of a bad set of options. I will return to this latter point shortly. For now, what is important is that psychological intelligibility is a different thing from the rationality of classic economics; and behavior that maximizes expected utility is a different thing from behavior that is good for a person. This is the theoretical reason why I believe it is important to resist an unthinking translation from the language of psychology to that of economics. But this refusal also has the consequence of avoiding a characterization of drug use in addiction as irrational. This is welcome, since charges of irrationality are often levied at people as critical attacks, while expressions of puzzlement—of struggling to understand another—more naturally invite, even if they far from guarantee, conversation and compassion.

The puzzle of addiction, as I have articulated it, is both anchored in ordinary psychology—it is a question we can all of us find ourselves asking when we encounter people who use drugs—and the foundation of the paradigm shift I am proposing. It is the foundation because of the work it can do. The puzzle can be used to construct an explication of addiction that can advance a shared understanding of what addiction is, and, in so doing, identify one of the questions driving research on addiction and which many models of addiction aspire to answer.

Explication is a term of art developed by the philosopher Rudolf Carnap.[19] Carnap argued that science proceeds in part through the clarification of inexact, ordinary language concepts, such that they become fit for the purpose of formulating scientific questions. He called this process explication. The concept that results from an explication should be as exact as possible while yet being both simple and fruitful. It also needs to be sufficiently similar to the original ordinary language concept to count as a refinement or regimentation, as opposed to a change of subject. But the resulting concept will obviously deviate from the original—in particular, it does not need to capture everything ordinary users mean by the concept or all cases and contexts where they would (or wouldn't) apply it. This is because an explication is not an analysis of a concept to be measured by its fit with ordinary language intuitions, but an engineering of a concept to be measured by its fitness for scientific purpose.

The puzzle of addiction can be used to explicate a concept of addiction fit for scientific purpose by demarcating it from ordinary drug use. We begin with the idea that addiction occurs precisely when drug use is, prima facie, psychologically unintelligible to us, by contrast with ordinary drug use. We can express our puzzlement by means of a why-question: Why is this person continuing to use drugs, when the costs appear so evident and severe, so profoundly counter to their own good? Notice that, in developing the puzzle and formulating this question, I have used terms like "looks," "seems," and "appears." The puzzle arises because of how things appear to observers. "Observers" can include the person with addiction themself, insofar as they adopt an outside perspective on their actions—stepping back from a more immersive agency and reflecting on what they are doing and why, just the way that another person might. But the puzzle is a puzzle of appearances: It arises when we, observers, can't make sense of a person's drug use because of the lack of self-concern it appears to evince—when we, observers, don't understand why a person is using. There is therefore a subjectivity inherent in the puzzle. But we can nonetheless use it to provide a working explication of addiction, by contrast with ordinary drug use, by dropping the reference to appearances thereby leaving a more objective formulation:

Working explication. Addiction is a pattern of drug use that persists despite evident and severe costs such that it counts profoundly against a person's own good.

I now present seven points to clarify the working explication. Note that, for ease of exposition as the book progresses, I will sometimes describe addiction as drug use "despite evident and severe costs" or "that counts against a person's own good" or simply say that it is "a puzzling pattern of drug use"—rather than write out the whole of the working explication.

First clarification. Although the puzzle arises because of how things appear, appearances can deceive. Addiction itself does not depend on how things appear but on how they are. It is a pattern of drug use that *actually* persists despite evident and severe costs such that it counts profoundly against a person's own good—not a pattern of drug use that merely appears to. It is therefore possible that what appears to an observer to be a case of addiction is not, in fact, a case of addiction. Most straightforwardly, we observers may be wrong about what is and is not in a person's own good. Chapter 4 takes up this point in detail.

Second clarification. What counts as a "pattern of drug use" requires judgment to determine, but there are three points that help narrow down what this means. First, a "pattern of drug use" requires *regular* use. This need not mean daily or continuous use, but it must mean use that occurs often enough to be a significant and central feature of a person's ordinary life and routines.

Second, a "pattern of drug use" requires drugs to be *used*, raising the question of when exactly a pattern of drug use comes to an end because drugs are no longer used in such a way as to constitute it. Just as the transition from ordinary drug use to addiction is a process, so too is the transition out of addiction and toward abstinence or moderation—which may involve single lapses and longer relapses, thereby complicating judgments of how much time needs to pass since the last occasion of use for the pattern to be broken. But there comes a point when it is broken. Although some people in recovery from addiction may have—and may feel like they have—a *disposition* to addiction that recommends caution in relation to drugs, once the pattern of drug use has ended they are no longer addicted. I return to this point briefly in chapters 2 and 5.

Third, "a pattern of drug use" involves drug-taking *behavior* as that term is commonly understood: a form of agency originating with the subject. The pattern is not, for example, a pattern of forcible drug delivery by another— even if there may be cases where forcible drug delivery by another creates physical dependence (see chapter 4) and is part of *the history* of a person's addiction. Part II (especially chapters 6 and 7) takes up the question of what kind of behavior drug taking in addiction is; part III turns to what explains it.

Third clarification. For costs of drug use to be "evident" is for them to be knowable by ordinary people in ordinary conditions—not fundamentally hidden from view. But costs that are knowable by ordinary people in ordinary conditions can, of course, be unknown in practice. In particular, costs of drug use may be unknown in practice by people with addiction themselves, because they are in denial or prey to various forms of cognitive difficulties; this is the topic of chapter 13.

Fourth clarification. There is a spectrum of costs that are "severe" even if some costs are too trivial to make it onto the spectrum at all. An occasional mild hangover in the morning is a cost, to be sure, but it is not a severe one. Genuinely risking or actually losing a job or a friend or a marriage to drugs—or your sense of self and self-worth—will typically count as severe even if these are not as severe as, for example, dying from addiction. Note that, as these examples illustrate, severe costs can include *the risk* of severe costs when this risk is high (as well of course as evident).

Fifth clarification. "Profoundly" signals that the inconsistency between the pattern of drug use and the person's own good is not minor but substantial. Where exactly this threshold lies will again require judgment to determine. But just as the occasional hangover, despite being a cost, is not a severe one, so too some costs that typically count as severe—losing a job or a friend or a marriage to drugs—may not *on balance* count against a particular person's own good sufficiently for the pattern of drug use to be a case of addiction. It will depend on what is (and is not) in that person's own good. Relatedly, the phrase "such that" indicates that the pattern of drug use counts profoundly against a person's own good *because* of its evident and severe costs, thereby yoking these together.

Sixth clarification. The working explication employs the phrase "a person's own good" as opposed to the simpler phrase "a person's good." What is gained by the addition of the word "own"? The answer, as I have just intimated in the fifth clarification, is that it serves to flag that we are interested in a substantive question about a particular individual—what, specifically, is good *for them*, or what *their* good consists in. This is a different question from what makes a life good or what the good life is, *in general*. Philosophical theories about the good life are varied. Some measure it by appeal to happiness. Some by the satisfaction of desires. Some by a set of species-specific objective goods such as (for humans) security, prosperity, health, friends, family, and intellectual, cultural, and personal activities and riches. Some by a combination of the above.[20] These theories will constrain answers to the substantive question of what is good for a particular individual. If the good life is to be measured by appeal to happiness or the satisfaction of desires, then what is good for a particular person is whatever makes them happy or whatever they desire; if the good life is to be measured by a set of species-specific objective goods, then what is good for a particular person is for their life to contain at least some of these goods.

But these abstract schemas do not tell us what, concretely, is good for a particular person, given the specific individual they are. What makes *them* happy? What do *they* desire? How do *they* think about the value and balance of this set of supposedly objective goods? Which friendships, forms of family life, or activities and cultural riches are good for *them*? Which risks to security, prosperity, or health might be worth incurring for the sake of some of the other goods that matter to *them*? The substantive question of what is good for a particular person or what their good consists in is, at bottom, a deeply personal one. Chapter 4 discusses the idea of "a person's own good" in detail, where I will propose one, but only one, general constraint on how to understand it.[21]

Seventh clarification. As I have developed the puzzle of addiction, it arises when it looks as if the costs of drugs have come to outweigh the benefits. So why not objectively formulate the working explication of addiction simply as a pattern of drug use whereby costs exceed benefits? Why drop the reference to benefits while introducing this more complicated formulation of a pattern of drug use that persists despite evident and severe costs such that it counts profoundly against a person's own good—a mouthful, to be sure?

Part of the answer is to be found in the previous clarifications: We need to think about what's evident, what's severe, and what is or isn't in a person's own good in order to identify which costs matter and how much. But part of the answer lies in an implication that the phrase "costs exceed benefits" is naturally taken to have, namely that if the costs of an option exceed the benefits, then it is irrational to take it. After all, if the costs of an option exceed the benefits, it can seem as if it must at least be better *to abstain from taking it*—in other words, to do nothing. But for many prototypical cases of addiction, the costs of drug use may be evident and severe, such that drug use counts profoundly against a person's own good, even though it is, in fact, the best of the options genuinely available to the person. That is, even though taking drugs is bad, *not taking drugs is worse.*

Consider again Bozarth and Wise's rats, alone in their cages with nothing but cocaine. Arguably, the choice to take a lot of cocaine is the best of the options available to these rats. Why? Think of the caged rats as having two options only: abstinence or cocaine. Abstinence avoids the costs of cocaine, that is, exhaustion, starvation, dehydration to the point of death. But this is at the expense of securing cocaine's benefits, that is, relief from what it is like to live permanently in that empty cage *without* cocaine—to live for weeks on end without any respite from the boredom, the loneliness, the misery and the suffering. Let us now stipulate that, notwithstanding the costs, taking cocaine is better for the rats than not taking it. Are these rats therefore not addicted to cocaine, because it is the best of the options available to them? No. Their cocaine use carries evident and severe costs—it kills them. It is surely not consonant with their own good (however we should ultimately understand the idea of a rat's own good) even if it is the best that life in the cage has to offer.

As with rats, so with humans. In certain circumstances—especially those faced by some of the most vulnerable people with addiction, who come from backgrounds of severe adversity and limited socioeconomic opportunities and may suffer from mental health problems in addition to addiction—drug use may be the best realistically available option *despite* the evident and severe costs. Chapter 6 returns to this point briefly, and chapters 10, 11, and 12 take it up in more detail. But the fact that an option is the best of those realistically available does not eradicate or render insignificant its costs; nor does it make it false to say that, in circumstances such as these, drug use carries costs such that it counts profoundly against a person's own good. A person's life can be made terrible *by* drugs even if it would be even more terrible *without* them. This is the misery of a life where addiction is the best thing on offer.

An explication of addiction objectively formulated simply as a pattern of drug use whereby costs exceed benefits risks obscuring the existence and the significance of these cases. Abstinence may not be better (because it is at the expense of securing the benefits of drugs). Drug use may not be irrational (because it is the best of the realistically available options despite the costs). Yet a person may be addicted: What matters is that they are persisting in using drugs despite evident and severe costs and against their own good. Indeed, to think otherwise is to make a mockery of treatment. Were it true that a pattern of drug use constituted addiction only if abstinence was better and drug use was irrational, then we could in theory cure addiction by intervening to make it the case that abstinence was worse and drug use was rational. That is, we could cure addiction by holding the pattern of drug use and its costs fixed but *punishing* a person for *not* taking drugs.

With these seven clarifications in hand, suppose we provisionally accept the working explication of addiction as generated by the why-question that puzzles us. Addiction is a pattern of drug use that persists despite evident and severe costs such that it counts profoundly against a person's own good. Many models of addiction can then be understood to embody hypotheses that aim to answer the why-question, thereby conferring the understanding that we lack. In other words, these hypotheses are answers to the question of why a person is continuing to use drugs despite such evident and severe costs and counter to their own good.

This suggestion resonates with a traditional way of thinking about the nature of science and scientific explanation, namely as fundamentally question driven. Scientific inquiry begins when there is something that perplexes us, something about which we are curious, something we do not understand. In other words, it begins with a question, typically a why-question or a how-question. Once the question is asked, we can then look for answers. When we light on a possible answer, we test it. For empirical validity, of course—but we also test our answers for explanatory adequacy, that is, for their ability to resolve our puzzlement and confer understanding. Science aims, at least in part, not just at descriptions that are accurate but at explanations that bring understanding. Indeed, as the philosopher Jaegwon Kim emphasizes, we often want to explain things because we want to understand them. Understanding is part of the point of explanation.[22]

There are three important upshots of this way of explicating addiction and understanding the relevant areas of addiction science:

First upshot. We have a way of diagnosing why, from a theoretical perspective, there is so much disagreement in addiction research.

Second upshot. We have a way of moving beyond the impasse in addiction research by appeal to heterogeneity, thereby also aligning addiction science with good clinical care.

Third upshot. We must recognize that the line between ordinary drug use and drug use in addiction cannot be drawn independently of values. Crucially, these values must give consideration to a person's conception of their own good.

The following three chapters are devoted to each of these three upshots, taken roughly in order. The fifth and final chapter in this part compares the working explication I have proposed to the *Diagnostic and Statistical Manual of Mental Disorders* (DSM-5) construct of substance use disorder (SUD) and considers objections.[23]

2

Diagnosing Disagreement

THINK BACK to the start of the previous chapter and the proliferation of models and definitions of addiction. Why so much disagreement? No doubt, the need to compete for research funding and academic status can drive division in any area. But from a more theoretical perspective, explicating addiction by appeal to the puzzle of addiction and treating models of addiction as embodying hypotheses that aim to answer it suggests a way of diagnosing—and ultimately moving beyond—the disagreement.

The diagnosis is that the disagreement stems from eliding the distinction between the *explanans* (that which does the explaining) and the *explanandum* (that which is to be explained) such that the explanandum is redefined by reference to the explanans. Applying this to addiction: The disagreement stems from eliding the distinction between that which is hypothesized to explain addiction, and addiction itself, such that addiction is then redefined by reference to a particular model's proposed explanation of it. In other words, addiction researchers deploy their answer to the why-question embodied in the puzzle of addiction to redefine what addiction is. This creates disagreement about the nature of addiction that need not otherwise exist and limits the range of possible explanations.

Suppose we are considering two explanatory hypotheses: the hypothesis that addiction is explained by some factor **X** and the hypothesis that addiction is explained by some distinct factor **Y**. Although it is certainly true that not all explanations are compatible with each other, many are. The claim that something is explained by **X** (or by **Y**) is not naturally taken to imply that it is the only explanation—just as the claim that something is caused by **X** (or by **Y**) is not naturally taken to imply that it is the only cause. We are used to a multiplicity of explanations (see chapter 3 and part III) and a diversity of causes (see chapter 9) of the same phenomenon. Schematically, therefore, these hypotheses need not compete: It is theoretically possible that *both* **X** and **Y** factor in the explanation of addiction. But now suppose that the addiction researchers studying factor **X** and the addiction researchers studying factor **Y** redefine addiction—whether implicitly or explicitly—in terms of **X** and **Y** respectively. Instead of saying addiction is *explained by* **X**, the researchers studying factor **X** say that it *is* **X**. Instead of saying addiction is *explained by* **Y**, the researchers studying factor **Y** say that it *is* **Y**. The claim that addiction *is* **X** is naturally taken to imply that there is addiction if and only if there is **X**. The claim that addiction *is* **Y** is naturally taken to imply that there is addiction if and only if there is **Y**. These claims are incompatible with each other and compete. Given that **X** and **Y** are distinct: If there is addiction if and only if there is **X**—**X** is necessary and sufficient for addiction—then **Y** is neither necessary nor sufficient for addiction. If there is addiction if and only if there is **Y**—**Y** is necessary and sufficient for addiction—then **X** is neither necessary nor sufficient for addiction. Disagreement is thereby created and, relatedly, the range of possible explanations is limited. For example, suppose that factor **X** is brain pathology and factor **Y** is circumstances that—by analogy with being alone in a cage with nothing but cocaine—mean that drug use despite the costs is the best of a bad set of options (as described briefly in chapter 1 and discussed further in chapters 6, 10, 11, and 12). Then it is far from obvious that explaining some cases of addiction by appeal to **Y** is compatible with its redefinition in terms of **X**. For, to put it crudely, drug use that is explained by **Y** looks rational, not pathological: How could **Y** possibly be an explanation of *addiction*, when addiction is *a brain disease*? Perhaps we can even begin to hear the rumblings of contempt for other addiction researchers and their models: Once you've redefined addiction in terms of your own model, it is as if they don't even understand what addiction *is*.

Explicating addiction by appeal to the puzzle of addiction and treating models of addiction as embodying hypotheses that aim to answer it is diagnostic of this disagreement—for it insists on the distinction between explanans and explanandum—as well as corrective. To avoid any possibility of misconception, let me hasten to add: It is not corrective because it is neutral about what addiction is—far from it. According to the working explication I have proposed, addiction *is* a pattern of drug use that persists despite evident and severe costs such that it counts profoundly against a person's own good. That is, addiction is a very specific kind of behavior. What is corrective is that the working explication is neutral about what *explains* the kind of behavior that addiction is. Because it is constructed via the puzzle of addiction, no particular model or hypothesized explanation of addiction is built in. In consequence, and by contrast with any redefinition of addiction cast in terms of a particular model's proposed explanation, the working explication holds the door open to a multiplicity of explanations of addiction (see chapter 3 and part III) and a diversity of causes (see chapter 9). It offers a shared understanding of the object of study, grounding a paradigm with more collaborative and conciliatory theoretical potential and which better aligns with clinical care (see chapter 3).

The tendency of addiction researchers to redefine addiction in terms conducive to their own model spans the brain-disease divide—even if, of course, there are individual researchers on both sides who never succumb to it. But its consequences on our thinking about addiction are particularly pronounced in relation to the brain disease model. This is not only because the brain disease model is the dominant model, so that what it says goes, so to speak. It is also because the concept of disease at its core is committed to there being an underlying essence to addiction: namely brain pathology. The brain disease model therefore does more than redefine addiction in such a way as to create disagreement and limit the range of possible explanations. It also relocates it—removing addiction from the realm of behavior and lodging it within the brain.

The concept of disease can mean different things in different contexts of use. Within medical science, the brain disease model of addiction is what is known as a *strong* or *hard* disease model. As the philosopher Dominic Murphy and the psychiatrist Kenneth Kendler have argued, the strong disease model emerged over the course of the nineteenth century as an alternative to a *minimal* or *soft* disease model. The simplest way to understand the strong disease model is therefore by contrast with it.[1]

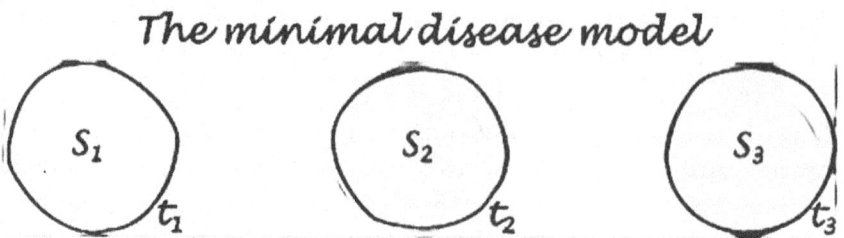

The minimal disease model

S1–S3 are signs and symptoms unfolding over a period of time t_1–t_3.
Note that there are no arrows representing causation.

The minimal model dates to the seventeenth century and treats diseases as *syndromes*: collections of signs and symptoms that co-occur and unfold over time in a characteristic way. It makes no claims about any causes of these signs and symptoms; nor does it posit any causal connections between the signs and symptoms themselves. Diseases just are syndromes according to this model: collections of signs and symptoms that co-occur and unfold over time in a characteristic way.

By contrast, the strong disease model treats diseases as pathological states and/or processes in the body that cause the collection of signs and symptoms constitutive of syndromes. This causal hypothesis is the crucial difference between the strong and minimal models. Paradigmatic examples of diseases that fit the strong model include genetic deficits and infectious diseases, where there is a single, clear pathological state or process that causes a collection of signs and symptoms: a gene whose function is disrupted, or an invading organism. Over the course of the twentieth century, the strong model has become firmly embedded in our ordinary thinking about disease. Arguably, our default conception of disease is that of an underlying pathology that causes signs and symptoms. It is not those signs and symptoms themselves.

In the nineteenth century, the psychiatrist Emil Kraepelin famously applied the minimal disease model to differentiate and diagnose psychiatric conditions.[2] This remains how mental disorders are differentiated and diagnosed to

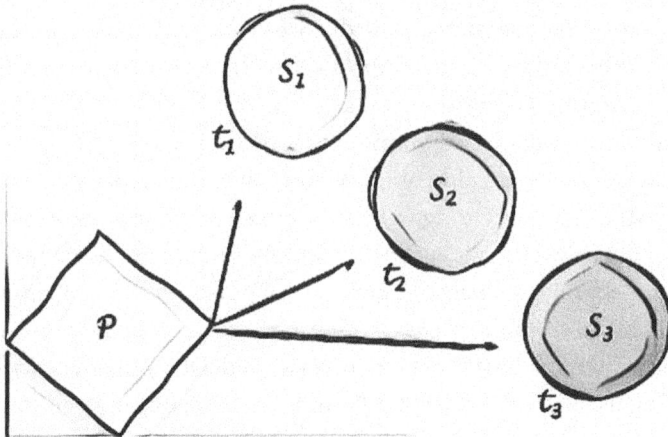

The strong disease model

$S_1 - S_3$ are signs and symptoms caused by underlying pathology **P** over a period of time $t_1 - t_3$. Arrows represent causation.

this day. Although the fifth edition of the *Diagnostic and Statistical Manual of Mental Disorders* (DSM-5) formally defines mental disorders as clinically significant syndromes that "reflect a dysfunction in the psychological, biological, or developmental processes underlying mental functioning," underlying dysfunction in fact plays no role in their differentiation and diagnosis.[3] This is done solely on the basis of a collection of *personal-level* criteria. "Personal level" is something of a term of art (further described in chapter 8), but we are all familiar with this level in virtue of being persons and living our lives as self-conscious, self-reflective subjects who experience a shared world. Personal-level criteria include signs that can be observed in ordinary interpersonal interactions by clinicians or others (for example, patterns of behavior) and symptoms that can be experienced and reported by patients (for example, patterns of psychological states). Note that these criteria are how the group of DSM-5 mental disorders that maps onto the ordinary concept of drug addiction, namely substance use disorders, are diagnosed. Although DSM-5 states that "an underlying change in brain circuits" is an important characteristic of substance use disorders, the "essential feature" of these disorders is "a cluster of cognitive, behavioral, and physiological symptoms indicating that the individual continues using the substance despite significant substance-related problems."[4] I return to the DSM-5 criteria for substance use disorders to compare them to the working explication in the final chapter of this part. The point for now is that, notwithstanding its stated theoretical commitment to the presence of underlying dysfunction, DSM-5 embodies the minimal disease model in practice.

By contrast with DSM-5, the brain disease model embodies a strong disease model. To help explain what this means, I shall make a simplifying assumption. The assumption is that, rather than a collection, there is one and only one kind of personal-level sign or symptom of addiction: a pattern of drug use that has characteristic **A** (for Addiction). According to the brain disease model, **A** is compulsiveness. According to the working explication I have proposed: **A** is persistence despite evident and severe costs such that the pattern of drug use counts profoundly against a person's own good. But the nature of **A** does not matter for present purposes—for now, we can be neutral between these views. What matters is that the brain disease model hypothesizes that the pattern of drug use with characteristic **A**—the sole kind of personal-level sign or symptom of addiction—is caused by some form of underlying brain pathology **BP** (for Brain Pathology). On the strong disease model, the underlying pathology *is* the disease: **BP** is what addiction *is*. The claim that addiction is a

The strong brain disease model

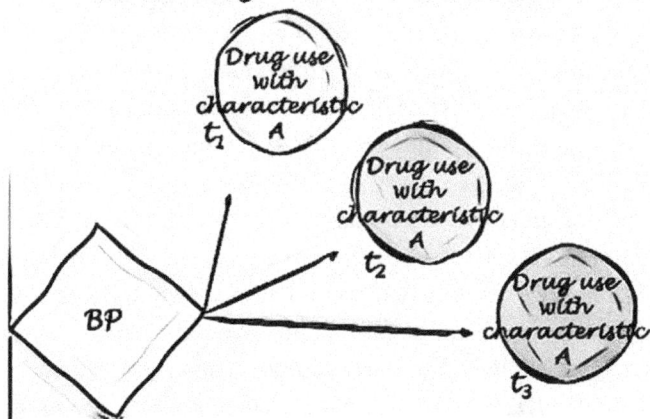

The signs and symptoms are a pattern of drug use with
characteristic **A** over a period of time **t₁–t₃**. **BP** is brain pathology.
Arrows represent causation.

brain disease is the claim that it is *not* a syndrome. That is, it is not a kind of
personal-level sign or symptom; it is not a pattern of drug use with characteristic **A**. The pattern of drug use with characteristic **A** is simply the effect of the
underlying brain pathology—the effect of the brain disease that is identified
as addiction—and therefore distinct from it.

The claim that addiction is a brain disease therefore has two profound
consequences for our thinking about addiction. The first consequence is to
open up the possibility of asymptomatic addiction. Think of an infectious
disease, for example, COVID-19. You can have COVID-19 but have no signs
and symptoms. You are asymptomatic. How is this possible? The answer is that
the signs and symptoms are the effects of the disease, and so distinct from it.
The virus that has invaded your body is the disease itself. Just so, if addiction
is a brain disease, you can have the disease but not show any of the signs or
symptoms: not exhibit any drug use with characteristic **A**. You are asymptomatic. How is this possible? The answer is the same. The signs and symptoms—a
pattern of drug use with characteristic **A**—are the effects of the disease. The
pathological brain states and/or processes are the disease itself. This is indeed
akin to how addiction is often conceived, particularly by some treatment and
recovery services, such as Alcoholics Anonymous (AA) and Narcotics Anonymous (NA). According to these organizations, you can be abstinent for
decades—without using drugs at all and, therefore, without using drugs in a

way that exhibits **A**—yet remain "an addict." "Once an addict, always an addict," as the saying goes. By contrast, on the working explication we are considering, decades of abstinence cannot but mean that the pattern of drug use characteristic of addiction has come to an end. A person who has not used in decades is not addicted, even if they may nonetheless have—and feel like they have—a *disposition* to addiction that recommends caution in relation to drugs.

The second consequence of the claim that addiction is a brain disease is to close down the possibility of addiction in the absence of pathological brain states and/or processes. Everyone with addiction must in fact have a brain disease, on pain of not being addicted at all. In particular, a pattern of drug use with characteristic **A**—whether **A** is compulsiveness or **A** is persistence despite evident and severe costs such that it counts profoundly against a person's good or indeed something else entirely—does not make you addicted. No matter how much your drug use is out of control, destructive of your life, or inconsonant with your own good, you count as addicted to drugs if and only if you have a brain disease.

My aim in this chapter has been relatively modest: to diagnose the disagreement plaguing addiction research, explain how the working explication grounds a paradigm with more collaborative and conciliatory theoretical potential, and describe some of the consequences of the brain disease model for our thinking about addiction. These consequences derive from the tendency to redefine addiction as a brain disease in conjunction with a conception of disease as underlying pathology. But to avoid the possibility of any misconception: My aim in this chapter has not been to argue that addiction—understood as a puzzling pattern of drug use in accord with the working explication—is never explained by brain pathology. Indeed, part II concludes that we should be open to the possibility that brain pathology is the cause of drug use in some (although by no means all) cases of addiction.

Our words matter. The tendency to implicitly or explicitly redefine addiction in the terms of specific explanatory hypotheses together with the dominance of the brain disease model has propelled us toward a way of thinking about addiction that is homogeneous as well as committed to the idea that its essence lies in a broken brain. The working explication helps to diagnose and correct this tendency through its explanatory neutrality. In so doing, it refocuses our gaze on the idea of addiction as a pattern of drug *use*, anchoring it within the realm of behavior.

3

Heterogeneity

ADDICTION IS A PUZZLING pattern of drug use: a kind of behavior. Keeping this fact squarely in focus helps to ground a more collaborative and conciliatory paradigm that recognizes the heterogeneity of addiction. Recall the why-question embedded in the puzzle of addiction: Why is this person continuing to use drugs, when the costs appear so evident and severe, so profoundly counter to their own good? Now ask yourself: Why would we ever think there would be only one answer to this question? From the perspective of ordinary psychology as well as clinical diagnosis, we are used to there being multiple explanations of what, on the surface, is the same phenomenon.

As illustration, let us begin with a clinical example. Diagnosis in medicine is a complicated art because the same collection of signs and symptoms can be explained by different kinds of disease—or by conditions that are not diseases at all. Suppose a patient presents with three symptoms: headache, fatigue, and a very sore throat. What is wrong?

Here are three different explanations:

1. The patient has COVID-19.
2. The patient has Strep throat.
3. The patient spent every night this week up late drinking with friends in a noisy bar where they had to shout to be heard.

The same collection of symptoms can be explained by either of two diseases or by one condition that has nothing to do with disease.

Understanding ourselves and others is a complicated art for exactly the same reason. The same kind of behavior admits of different psychological explanations—or explanations that lie beyond ordinary psychology. Suppose three people are deliberately not eating, thereby risking death. Why?

Here are three different explanations:

1. The first person is a political prisoner, acting in protest.
2. The second person is a parent living in conditions of extreme poverty who is giving all the food they have to their child.
3. The third person has late-stage cancer and therefore neither appetite nor will to live.

Same kind of behavior—deliberately not eating, thereby risking death. Three different explanations. Two combine ordinary psychology and life circumstances: political belief and commitment in conditions of confinement; a parent's love for their child in conditions of scarcity. The final explanation appeals to disease and its physical and psychological toll.

The working explication of addiction I have proposed locates the unity of addiction at the personal level—in the same way that syndromes are defined by the minimal disease model and mental disorders are differentiated and diagnosed by DSM-5. What all cases of addiction have in common is that they consist in a pattern of drug use that persists despite evident and severe costs such that it counts profoundly against the person's own good. But, beneath this surface unity, addiction fractures. There can be different explanations for why different people are using drugs in this way. Which explanation is correct depends on the individual case. There is no reason to expect a one-size-fits-all explanation or theory of addiction.

Many of the chapters that follow explore hypothesized answers to the why-question. As noted previously, the explanations canvased include the possibility of brain pathology (chapters 8 and 9), but also self-medication and a person's social, cultural, and economic circumstances (chapter 10); the development of a security-based attachment to drugs (chapter 10); self-harm and a desire to die (chapter 11); an "addict" identity (chapter 12); denial and cognitive difficulties (chapter 13); problems of control (chapter 14); and cravings for drugs (chapter 15). Despite the abundance of this list, it is nonetheless selective. There is more that could be added and no doubt more to be learned. Part of the value of heterogeneity is that it makes it easy to accommodate all of what we learn. This is because, rather than proceeding with a competitive "winner takes all" approach—to borrow a phrase from the addiction scientist David Epstein[1]—different models of addiction can become allied by adopting a strategy of divide and conquer. What this means is simply that some explanations will apply to some people with addiction, while other explanations will apply to others; and sometimes more than one explanation will apply to one and the same person—potentially interacting in complicated ways—even though some are mutually incompatible. For example, as we shall see in part III, the explanation of why a particular person is using drugs in a way that counts as addicted could involve both the use of drugs as a form of self-medication and their embrace of an "addict" identity; but no one who is in deep denial can embrace an "addict" identity, because to do so would mean that they were not in deep denial.

Key to the possibility of a divide-and-conquer alliance is to guard against the tendency to redefine addiction in terms conducive to any one particular model. This is what the explanatory neutrality of the working explication delivers (see chapter 2). But we might nonetheless wonder: For how long must we be on our guard? Imagine that at some point in the future there is collective agreement within addiction research about the heterogeneity of explanations of addiction. Could we at that point safely deploy each different kind of explanation of addiction to define a different kind of addiction, thereby embracing a heterogeneity not only of explanations of addiction but of addiction kinds? The answer is that nominally we could, but there would be nothing to be gained and something potentially to be lost. Theoretically, we would come no closer to carving the world of addiction at its joints (as the saying goes), for the different kinds of explanations overlap and interact. This is the nature of psychological explanation. It is complicated, holistic, and individually specific.[2] There are some discernible patterns, but there are no fault lines dividing the heterogeneity of explanations of addiction into tidy kinds. Meanwhile, practically, we would risk creating silos of addiction research—again fostering division, even if not fomenting disagreement.

Heterogeneity also promises to better align addiction research with good clinical practice.[3] In many jurisdictions, addiction treatment is shockingly unregulated, allowing individuals and corporations to charge extraordinary sums for treatment that is lacking in both theoretical foundations and an empirical evidence-base.[4] Nonetheless, there are many addiction specialists—counselors, therapists, psychologists, psychiatrists, experts by experience—with knowledge, wisdom, and experience, who treat and help a great many people. It is a basic and uncontroversial truth that good clinical care across all domains of medicine is individually tailored, putting the patient and their experience and needs at the center of any treatment plan. This is so even when the condition being treated is a disease with a standard and reliable treatment protocol. For example, consider insulin therapy for Type I diabetes. Insulin therapy typically involves a demanding regimen of self-injections. Treatment can therefore fail because of the practical and emotional burden it places on patients. Failing to attend to the individual patient's experience and needs heightens the risk that they do not successfully implement the regimen. But, if individually tailored care is essential with respect to diseases like Type I diabetes, it is surely all the more essential if the condition being treated is heterogeneous and there is no one standard and reliable treatment.

Individually tailored care is in fact routinely delivered by many addiction specialists: The heterogeneity of explanations of addiction is reflected in the heterogeneity of care. How you treat a person who keeps using opioids because they are terrified of withdrawal is different from how you treat a person who craves escape from the miseries of life, and a moment, however fleeting, of euphoria. How you treat a person in denial that they have a drinking problem is different from how you treat a person who identifies as an alcoholic—as many successful musicians, writers, and artists do. And how you treat a person who is wealthy is different from how you treat a person who is homeless. To put it as plainly as possible, the chance of any treatment, no matter how effective it would otherwise be, helping a person who is homeless to deal with their addiction is next to nil. The first step is to help the person gain access to housing.[5]

Nothing I am saying here is new. As I have already emphasized, it is what many good clinicians know and do. Indeed, the philosopher Herbert Fingarette emphasized the heterogeneity of alcohol addiction and the consequent necessity of attending to the individual to effectively help them in his book *Heavy Drinking*, published in 1988.[6] What you aim to do, when working clinically with people with addiction, is to understand why they are using drugs. The answer to this question is key to understanding what their drug use depends on. It therefore provides a handle to try to grab and turn—to leverage in treatment. Hence, although the new paradigm proposed in this book is generated out of an explication of addiction that aims to be fit for scientific purpose, it has the additional virtue of better aligning addiction research with good clinical practice, which already recognizes and embodies heterogeneity.

As noted in the introduction to this book, the brain disease model of addiction lacks translational results. This is despite decades of research and large sums of money spent on addiction neuroscience. To take just one example, at the end of 2024 the two leading addiction research funding bodies in the US, the National Institute on Drug Abuse (NIDA) and the National Institute on Alcohol Abuse and Alcoholism (NIAAA), had a combined budget of over two billion dollars per year and a strong commitment to the brain disease model and its funding.[7] In response to the failed promise of translation, a group of pioneering neuroscientists led by Marco Venniro have called for a new method they label "reverse translation." In essence, their idea is to start with what we already know works clinically; we then work backward, from the clinic to the scientific bench, studying how and why preexisting effective treatments actually work. These scientists hope this procedure will lead to the discovery of new neural circuits and medications for addiction—and perhaps it will. But their call for reverse translation—for starting with what we know works clinically, presuming that is broadly conceived as opposed to restricted to pharmacological treatments from the outset—is far more revolutionary than this hope suggests. For, if we genuinely start with what works, much of it is unlikely to lend itself to the methods and techniques of neuroscience or to the discovery of neural circuits and medications, but to point instead toward a more multidisciplinary and expansive approach to addiction research, involving cognitive, behavioral, and social sciences—as well, crucially, as the testimony of people with addiction themselves. For example, it is now well established that the provision of alternative rewards or "reinforcers" as they are called—that is, the availability of valuable, meaningful goods other than drugs, or, relatedly, what is sometimes described as "a stake in conventional life"[8]—is protective against addiction and a crucial component of recovery in a great many cases (see chapters 9 and 10).[9] Interventions that aim to change social, cultural, and economic circumstances, such as addressing homelessness and providing education, employment, community, relationships, and a sense of meaning and belonging fall into this category. So too do therapeutic workplaces, the form of contingency management treatment mentioned in the introduction to this book.[10] But what, exactly, do we expect to find in the brain, in connection with many of these interventions? And, supposing we did somehow find a neural circuit associated with any or all of them and that we could try to target through medication, how could it possibly be right to do so—at least as anything other than as a very last resort? Should we not rather be putting our efforts and money into helping people find homes, jobs, relationships, and communities?

I shall return to this issue repeatedly over the course of this book: the ethical importance of broadening our thinking about how to understand and relate to people with addiction, as well as how to help. The point for now is simply that the working explication can provide something we need. This is a paradigm with ample room for a multiplicity of explanations and a diversity of causes—a paradigm that, in its heterogeneity, helps us move beyond the impasse.

4

Values and a Person's Own Good

KEITH RICHARDS, lead guitarist for the Rolling Stones and sex, drugs, and rock 'n' roll icon, famously said that he never had a problem with drugs, he only had a problem with the police. Richards did have a problem with the police. His notoriety as a Rolling Stone and as a drug user meant he was targeted and harassed both at home and on the road, leading to multiple drug-related charges during the 1960s and 1970s and one prison sentence. But Richards was also devoted to drugs. He was a daily polydrug user and physically dependent on heroin at various stages of his life. In his memoir, *Life*, he is clear that, although drugs sometimes took a toll on his work and his relationships, they also greatly enhanced both.[1] For Richards, drugs are connected to his creativity and his intensity, to living in a way that squeezes the most out of life. He is also honest about the fact that his wealth protected him from costs that other drug users face. Richards was able to use only the purest and highest quality drugs and to get excellent medical care whenever he needed. By saying that he never had a problem with drugs, I take Richards to mean that whatever the costs of his drug habit—which at times in his life were surely severe—they were in his view worth it. His drug use, despite its costs, accorded with his own set of values—his conception of the good life, for him. His problem was that his values did not accord with those embodied by the law—witness his problem with the police.

What counts as a cost and what counts as a benefit and how much weight to attach to either presupposes a set of values by which they are measured, that is, a conception of the good. One person loves to feel wild and chaotic and out of control—to escape from the rigid confines of their ordinary life and self. This is part of the good life, for them. Another person hates it. Their good life is one of calm routine. Their drug of choice is a nice cup of tea. What for the first is a benefit of alcohol or amphetamines or psychedelics is a cost for the second. But how much does the first person love that feeling of wild abandon—enough to risk their job, their relationship, their health? It depends. How much do they value their job and their relationship and their health? The working explication of addiction as a pattern of drug use that counts profoundly against a person's own good presses these questions. Which values? Whose conception of the good? And how can we know? Suppose we ask these questions about Richards. We might wonder: Was he right that he never had a problem with drugs or was he in denial?

To answer this question, we must begin by noting a standard but underappreciated distinction between addiction and physical dependence. Opioids, alcohol, and nicotine are classes of drugs that, if taken regularly and at sufficient doses, produce physical dependence: a physiological condition defined by the occurrence of a physical withdrawal syndrome upon sudden abstinence or dose reduction. Richards was certainly, at times, physically dependent on heroin. Withdrawal from heroin typically lasts up to one week, and, similarly to withdrawal from any opioid, can include fever, nausea, diarrhea, aches, cramps, runny nose, watery eyes, insomnia, formication, and more. Opioid withdrawal is not life-threatening. But as this list attests, it is awful to experience. It can be alleviated through medication, including methadone and buprenorphine (themselves opioids), clonidine (a psychiatric medication used to treat pain and hypertension) and over-the-counter medications for symptom relief.

Physical dependence is highly relevant to weighing costs and benefits of drug use. Although the nature and severity of withdrawal symptoms varies with drug class, experiencing withdrawal is a significant cost of not using, and avoiding it a significant benefit of using. Indeed, with respect to severe alcohol addiction, withdrawal can be life-threatening. But physical dependence is neither necessary nor sufficient for addiction. Although there are inevitably psychological effects of sudden abstinence or dose reduction if a person is addicted,[2] various drugs to which people become addicted do not have a physical withdrawal syndrome, for example, cannabis and cocaine.[3] This is why physical dependence is not necessary for addiction. But equally, it is not sufficient, because people can be physically dependent on drugs when we would never consider them to be addicted.

Many psychiatric medications, such as antidepressants, have a physical withdrawal syndrome. Antidepressants are psychoactive. They affect cognition, emotion, mood. Sudden abstinence or dose reduction will cause people to go into withdrawal, which typically lasts between one and three weeks and has symptoms that are similar to opioid withdrawal. Yet we do not consider people to be addicted to antidepressants. Similarly, people who suffer from debilitating pain may be on standing opioid prescriptions. This is a routine part of palliative care but can also be appropriate for some chronic, long-term pain patients.[4] These patients will be physically dependent. In the wake of the US opioid epidemic and widespread recognition that—in large part due to relentless propaganda, manipulation, and incentivization by pharmaceutical companies—doctors had been overprescribing opioids, many pain patients had their prescriptions suddenly discontinued.[5] Overprescription was a terrible problem, but this was an equally terrible response. Sudden discontinuation precipitates withdrawal—as well as the return of debilitating pain—pushing people toward sourcing opioids on the streets to relieve both. It also fails to recognize that a patient who is physically dependent on opioids is not thereby addicted. In the context of debilitating pain, a stable opioid prescription can make it possible to function—to work, to sleep, to have the capacity to be present and engaged in relationships with others, to live a fulfilling life. So too can taking the very same opioid at the very same dose if it is sourced not from a pharmacy but from the streets. With respect to psychiatric medications, we do not consider people addicted simply because they are physically dependent. Similarly, with respect to opioids, we should not consider people addicted simply because they are physically dependent—no matter where the drugs are sourced. This is because, in both cases, drugs can make life significantly better, not worse.

I have attempted to make the distinction between physical dependence and addiction compelling by means of examples. But it is in fact codified in the history of the *Diagnostic and Statistical Manual of Mental Disorders* (DSM). To sketch the history crudely: DSM-I, published in 1952, conceptualized drug addiction, with the exception of alcohol, as a symptom of personality disorder, which was considered the primary diagnosis.[6] The recognition of addiction itself as a possible primary diagnosis emerged over the course of DSM-II, published in 1968, and DSM-III, published in 1980. DSM-III introduced two diagnostic categories: substance abuse and substance dependence.[7] Substance abuse was conceptualized as drug use with costs of the sort I described when introducing the puzzle of addiction in chapter 1, but with a particular emphasis on criminality. Substance dependence was conceptualized as physical dependence. This conceptualization was immediately subjected to criticism, out of recognition that physical dependence was neither sufficient for addiction nor indicative of any disorder. By 1987, with the publication of DSM-III-R, a diagnosis of substance dependence required not only physical dependence but also for there to be costs to drug use—just as required for a diagnosis of sub-stance abuse.[8] DSM-IV, published in 1994, explicitly states that physical dependence is neither necessary nor sufficient for a diagnosis of substance dependence.[9] Needless to say, calling a condition "substance dependence" which need not involve physical dependence on substances is not semantically ideal, and may have contributed to the ongoing tendency to confuse addiction with physical dependence. DSM-5, published in 2013, combines substance abuse and substance dependence into a single category of substance use dis-orders, which can be diagnosed with or without physical dependence. It also explicitly states that physical dependence is not necessary for diagnosis of a substance use disorder, and warns that it is a mistake to diagnose patients who are on prescriptions for opioids, sedatives, and stimulants based on physical dependence alone (for further discussion, see chapter 5).[10] The bottom line is that physical dependence is neither necessary nor sufficient for addiction—no matter how addiction is defined.

Back now to the working explication and the role of values within it. Rich-ards was certainly physically dependent on heroin at various stages in his life. But that is neither necessary nor sufficient for addiction. Was he addicted, or was he right to say that he didn't have a problem with drugs—apart that is from his problems with the police? Reading his memoir, it is hard not to feel that he was right. Richards knows perfectly well that the good life, for him, involves taking a lot of drugs. He is honest about the costs, and reflective about the value of drugs to him notwithstanding. But now consider the writer Cheryl Strayed's depiction of her ex-boyfriend Joe in her memoir *Heroin/e*. At this stage in Strayed's story, Joe is still using while she is trying to quit:

> I saw Joe two more times. I'd kept in touch with him; calling him late at night from Minneapolis, against the advice of my friends. When we talked I could hear the heroin in his voice, making it soft and open. Within a month he was at my door, looking weak and pale. He sat on my couch and shot up and then lurched into my kitchen and bent to vomit into the sink. He wiped his face and smiled. "It's worth it," he said, "getting sick. Because you feel so good through it all." We spent a week in my apartment using the supply of heroin he'd brought with him. I knew I had to end this, and finally I did. He left when I asked him to.[11]

Contra the impression Richards gives in his memoir, as Strayed presents Joe, it is hard not to feel that he is in denial. His protestations notwithstanding, his heroin use is not, by his own lights, "worth it."

Suppose you want to know whether a person's drug use is or is not good for them. How do you go about determining this? The answer is that you start by asking them. You have a conversation, and you listen to what they say. Humans are self-conscious and self-reflective beings who have their own conception of what is and is not good for them. By this I mean: of how they want to live and how they want not to live; of what they care about, and what they don't; of what gives life purpose and meaning, making it worth living, and what bleeds it dry. Each person's conception serves as an ideal for them, a set of values by which to guide and measure their lives and their actions. Here then is the general constraint on the substantive idea of a person's own good that I promised in chapter 1 when initially clarifying the working explication: No account of what is good for a self-conscious and self-reflective being can ignore their conception of their good.

My focus in the rest of this chapter is on the significance of this general constraint to the working explication of addiction. To this end, I will discuss a series of cases, including Richards and Joe. But to briefly clarify what the general constraint means and orient to what is to come: The conclusion of this chapter is that serious and caring conversations with people about their drug use and their values is essential to diagnosis—that is, to the delineation of addiction from ordinary drug use—especially in complicated cases. This is because the general constraint has *epistemic* consequences for how we can know what is good for a person. (As alluded to above: We must start by asking them.) Such conversations can also be important to sustaining personal relationships with people with addiction; the discussion in this chapter therefore prefigures the ethical framework to be developed in part IV. But the general constraint itself is not epistemic but what we might call *constitutive* or *metaphysical*. By saying that no account of what is good for a self-conscious and self-reflective being can ignore their conception of their good, I mean that their conception of their good is *in part* determinative of what *is* good for them.

Intuitively, the reason for this is simple. Think of your own life, and how you want to live it. Irrespective of the details of your conception of your good, it is good for you both to act from your conception and to live in accord with it—to act and live in a way that reflects how you aspire to conduct your life and what you experience as giving it purpose and meaning. Philosophically, we can ground this intuition in the idea that, for self-conscious and self-reflective beings like us, *self-determination*—being the conductor, as it were, of your own life—is a basic good. But to recognize that there is good for you in both acting from and living in accord with your conception of your good, is not to claim that this is the only thing that is good for you. As we shall see, a person's life might sometimes be better if they failed to act from and live in accord with their conception of their good. Why would this be? The answer is that their conception may be deeply flawed. The general constraint states only that for a self-conscious and self-reflective being, an account of what is good for them must give some place to their conception of it—it cannot ignore it. It does not fetishize or oversize the good of self-determination.

We sometimes fail to live in accord with our conception of our good for reasons that are external to us. We can live in conditions of oppression or coercion or control by another. We can just be unlucky. But sometimes we fail to live in accord with our conception of our good because we fail to act from it—we fail to conduct our lives according to its score. This can be one of the most painful aspects of living with addiction: knowing that you, yourself, are acting in ways that are destroying what you most value. Consider, in this light, how the philosopher Owen Flanagan describes his addiction in his book *What Is It like to Be an Addict?*:

> I was—all the empirical evidence suggested—in a pathetic losing battle with the economy of my desires run amok, sometimes fighting off overwhelming craving for my drug, other times knowing, in some sense of "know," that my relationships with genuinely good people, my work, my life could, indeed, would be lost if I chose to use. And I'd still choose to use. Well, I'd use. That much was clear.[12]

Suppose we ask: Was Flanagan's drug use good for him or not? The answer is straightforward. It was not. He tells us this plainly, and there is no reason to question what he says. Most cases of addiction are like Flanagan's. Drug use is not good for the person, and this is what they plainly say. But some cases are more complicated, for two kinds of reason. The first is the possibility of denial—as I have already intimated in reflecting on the examples of Richards and Joe. The second is that a person's values are inevitably shaped by their history and life circumstances—including a life of addiction.

To begin with denial. People can be in denial about different kinds of things. Perhaps the most familiar object of denial is that drug use is the cause of severe costs at all. This is the kind of denial I will discuss in chapter 13. But consider again Joe, Cheryl Strayed's ex-boyfriend. In so far as he is in denial, this is not its object. Joe, like Richards, does not deny the costs of his use: its toll on relationships, work, health. He is vomiting in the sink, after all, in front of his ex-girlfriend who left him because that was the only way to escape from her own addiction and whom he appears still to want—possibly to love. Rather, Joe claims that these various costs are "worth it"—that his drug use, notwithstanding the costs, is on balance consistent with what he values. If Joe is in denial, the object of that denial is his *true* values, that is, his *true* conception of his good. We are supposing that he is not being insincere in saying he values the euphoria of heroin over his health and relationship with Strayed, for example. He genuinely believes what he says while he stands there vomiting at the sink. But *deep down*, as we often put this kind of point, he values his health and his relationship over heroin. Were he not in denial, this is what he would say. Denial of values may be less familiar than denial that drug use is the cause of severe costs, but it is no less real. And it reveals a gap: between what a person sincerely professes about their conception of their good, and what this conception truly is.

Consider now the effect of history and life circumstances on a person's values. If any of our lives had been radically different, then, in all likelihood, so too would be our values. I was raised an atheist, became a professor of philosophy, and am a mother. My conception of my good would be different if I had been raised religious, become a banker, and never had children. But my values are no less my own for depending on the details of my history and circumstances—for being shaped by a life of atheism, the pursuit of philosophy, and motherhood. Yet the same would be true of my imagined counterpart. Her values would be no less her own for depending on the details of her history and circumstances—for being shaped by a life of religion, the pursuit of wealth, and childlessness.

The fact that a person's conception of their good is shaped by the life they have led does not mean it is not their true conception. But it introduces the possibility of a new kind of question. Is their conception of their good what is *truly* good for them? Are the values comprising their conception of their good the values they *ought* to have? When I consider the values possessed by my imagined counterpart, I find it hard not to see them as mistaken and diminished—shaped by the false gods of religion and capitalism, and lacking in what, for me, has given my life some of its deepest meaning and joy, namely being a mother to my daughters and the life of the mind. But no doubt, were my imagined counterpart to consider the values I possess, they would appear just as misshapen to her—my life utterly bereft of the power and thrill of money, the freedom to fashion a self apart from gender-based roles and duties, the grace of her god. Who is right? Which values ought I to have? How could we know? I will return to these questions in due course. The point for now is that the fact that we can coherently raise them at all shows that there is an additional potential gap: between a person's values and what they ought to value, or between a person's conception of their good and what is truly good for them.

Like any life, a life of addiction can shape a person's values and conception of their good. If you ask someone who has lived with addiction for years or indeed decades whether their drug use is or is not good for them, their answer may reflect values that are truly theirs, given where they are now in their life, but which would not be the values they would have had, had they not lived with addiction all this time. This is the general problem of "adaptive preferences," as applied to addiction.[13] To borrow a vivid metaphor from the philosopher Jeanette Kennett, addiction can be like a series of grenades exploding in one's path. It destroys the landscape, blocking off many ways of going forward, narrowing what is both realistically and imaginatively possible.[14] Meanwhile, people typically find what good they can in what is familiar and available to them. As the philosopher and economist Amartya Sen puts the point, we survive by making "compromises with a harsh reality."[15] We get used to things; we find ways of making do with the hand we are dealt—of making it our own. At the extreme, a person may identify as an "addict," and that identity may, for them, be both a source of value and an imaginative constraint on their sense of who they are and what a good life, for them, could ever be. I take up the topic of an "addict" identity in detail in chapter 12; but, as an initial illustration, consider the addiction specialist Gabor Maté's report of a conversation with his patient Jake in his book *In the Realm of Hungry Ghosts*. Jake is on methadone to treat his heroin addiction, but he remains a heavy user of cocaine, which he injects. Maté asks Jake about his cocaine habit, and Jake replies:

> Yeah, the coke's my life. . . . I care more about the dope than my loved ones or anything else. For the past fifteen years . . . it's part of me now. It's part of my every day. . . . I don't know who to be without it. I don't know how to live everyday without it. You take it away, I don't know what I'm going to do. . . . If you were to change me and put in a regular-style life, I wouldn't know how to retain it. I was there once in my life, but it feels like I don't know how to go back. I don't have the . . . It's not the will I don't have; I just don't know how.[16]

Maté then asks Jake if he even wants a regular-style life. Jake sadly replies no, not really. He has been using for so long that the life of addiction has become normal to him. What he cares most about is cocaine, which he calls his "old lady" and "partner."

Notice the contrast here between Jake's testimony and Flanagan's. Jake does not say that his desires for drugs have run amok, undermining what he values. Rather, he says that what gives value and structure to his life is cocaine. As Flanagan notes at a different moment in his reflections on his own addiction, "it can seem to be a choice between being two different versions of myself—me with addiction and me without addiction—both of which have their attractions."[17] The point is that, whether by choice or lack thereof, Jake seems to have become the version of himself with addiction. Maté puts it thus: "Jake is so identified with his addiction that he doesn't dare imagine himself sober."[18]

To determine what is good for a person, we must start with what they say. This is as true of a person in the grip of addiction as of anyone. But simply to leave it there without further thought is perverse. This is not only because of the possibility of denial. It is because we cannot simply equate what is good for a person with their conception of their good, even if this conception is as truly their own as any of our conceptions ever is. Let us suppose that, now, given where he is in his life, Jake truly values cocaine as much as he says. Without it, his life would be shattered. He is not in denial about this. Perhaps the note of sadness in his voice reveals the possibility that, at some level, Jake himself recognizes that what he values is not what he ought to value—or perhaps not. Either way, Maté is clearly of the view that, notwithstanding the fact that Jake truly values cocaine and cannot imagine a good life, for himself, without it, cocaine is not in fact what he ought to value. Cocaine is not good for him.

Hence there are two potential gaps. One is between what a person sincerely professes their values or their conception of their good to be, and what these truly are. The second is between a person's values and what they ought to value—between a person's conception of their good and what is truly good for them. Together these gaps reveal that, if we want to know whether a person's drug use is or is not good for them, there are four variables to consider:

1. The pattern of drug use, with its consequences.
2. The person's *sincerely professed* values and conception of their good.
3. The person's *true* values and conception of their good.
4. What the person *ought* to value or what is *truly* good for them, apart from the values and conception of their good they either sincerely profess to have or truly have.

Note that I have italicized "*true*" in 3 and "*truly*" in 4 in order to help emphasize the differences; but I will on the whole drop these adjectives in what follows.

In a great many cases of addiction, 2, 3 and 4 are in accord. The pattern of drug use counts against what is good for a person, which is reflected both in their conception of their good and in what they sincerely profess. This is so with Flanagan. But there are two more complicated kinds of case.

In cases of denial of values, such as we are supposing Joe's to be, 2 and 3 are not in accord, while 3 and 4 are. To help see this, imagine that, like Strayed herself, you are a person who cares for Joe. You might decide to talk to him about your concern that he is in denial. You might push back against his claim that heroin is "worth it," by questioning whether it is true that he really cares more about heroin than he cares about his health and relationship with Strayed.

In cases where a person's conception of their good has been shaped by a life of addiction, 2 and 3 may be in accord with each other, but not with 4. What the person sincerely professes to value is indeed what they value. They are not self-deceived. But it is not what they ought to value. To help see this, imagine that a person you care about has lived with addiction for many years. Their sense of self-worth is fragile and eroded. But at this point, like Jake, their addiction is woven into their life and identity. They can envisage no other. And they value what they have. As Chris, another of Maté's patients, says: "I don't want to give up being an addict. I know this sounds pretty fucked up, but I like who I am."[19] You might, out of care, try to help someone like Jake or Chris break free from this conception and envisage a life and identity in accord with a set of values that they do not, now, possess, but that you sincerely believe that, *for their own good*, they ought to. This, indeed, is what Maté tries to help Jake to do: To imagine himself "sober."

The working explication of addiction we have been considering is a pattern of drug use that persists despite evident and severe costs such that it counts profoundly against a person's own good. We are now in a position to clarify the nature of this good. "A person's own good" means what is truly good for them—what they ought to value. But here's the rub: This cannot ignore their conception of their good. Why not? Because their conception of their good is in part determinative of what is truly good for them. Self-determination matters to self-conscious and self-reflective beings. It is good for us to be the conductors of our lives—to act from and live in accord with our conception of our good. There is truth in this even when our conception of our good is flawed and, for our own good, we ought to have a different conception—we ought to have different values.

For example, suppose that Maté is right about Jake, as suggested by the note of sadness in Jake's voice. Even taking into account everything cocaine means to him, Jake's habit is not in accord with what is good for him. Indeed, let us go further, and suppose that, on balance, his cocaine use counts profoundly against his own good—notwithstanding the fact that it is *a* good for him, as it is for any of us, to act from and live in accord with his conception of his good. Then Jake is addicted to cocaine, according to the working explication.

Alternatively, suppose that Maté is in fact wrong about Jake, despite the note of sadness in Jake's voice. Given everything cocaine means to him, Jake's cocaine habit *is* in accord with what is good for him—at this point in his life—notwithstanding its costs. Then Jake is not addicted to cocaine—just as Richards may not have had a problem with drugs but only with the police. This is because we are now supposing that the values by which Jake's cocaine habit is to be measured accord with it. His drug use, on balance, given who he is and where he is in his life, is good for him.

Summing up: To use the working explication to demarcate addiction from ordinary drug use, we must determine what is good for a person. What is good for a person cannot be equated with their conception of their good. Nonetheless, their conception of their good is, in part, determinative of their good: This is why it cannot be ignored. But throughout this chapter, I have worked with suppositions and hypotheticals to present this view: I imagined that Richards was not in denial, while Joe was; I explored what to think if Maté was right about Jake, and what to think if he was wrong. You might object that this is a philosopher's charade. In complicated real-world cases of addiction, we cannot just work with suppositions and hypotheticals. We need to know. How can we ever really determine what is truly good for a person? This kind of epistemological quandary lies at the heart of the clash of values I previously imagined between me and my counterpart, when I asked which of us is right about the values that I ought to have—me or her?

The answer is that we cannot answer this question—that is, the question of what is truly good for a person—apart from having a serious conversation with them about their conception of it. There are two intersecting reasons why, one metaphysical and one epistemological. The metaphysical reason is embodied in the general constraint: Their conception of their good is in part determinative of their good. It must be part of the answer to what is truly good for them—even if it is not all of it. The epistemological reason is that we cannot know what their conception of their good is—and so, in the real world, we will not be able to include it in any answer to the question of what is truly good for them—without having a serious conservation with them about it. This, then, is where we must start—with what they say—even if it is not always where we end.

To make this more concrete: Although my counterpart and I cannot have a serious conversation except in my imagination, we can have serious conversations with the people in our lives whose drug use raises a puzzle for us— where the pattern of use has evident and severe costs such that it appears *to us* to count profoundly against their own good. Recall how in illustrating the gaps between 2 and 3 as well as 3 and 4, I invited you to imagine having a conversation with someone you cared for—a person whom you feared was in denial about their values in relation to their drug use, or a person whose values had been shaped by a life of addiction. Assuming they are taking the conversation seriously, you must take seriously what they say. This is part of what it is to care for someone and to respect them.[20] But the fact that you must take seriously what they say doesn't mean that you can't question it. You can notice inconsistencies: between what they say at one time and what they say at another time, or between what they say and what they seem to feel or to do. You can say when something strikes you as just outright impossible to fathom. You can wonder if they are being honest with themself. You can let them know that, as someone who cares about them, what they are saying doesn't sit right. You can help them try to imagine a different way of living, a different relationship to drugs. You can commit to being there for them if they decide to try it out. In other words, in your conversation with them, you put the possibility of there being gaps—between what they sincerely say they value and what they truly value, between their conception of their good and what is truly good for them—to practical use in order to try to come to know what their conception of their good truly is, thereby taking a crucial step to determining what their good truly is.

In having this conversation, you may also be hoping to change their conception—if you are convinced it is flawed and does not reflect what is truly good for them. Sometimes you may succeed. Conversations can have this effect—of putting our values and conception of our own good into flux, changing them one way or another. The general constraint entails that, if a person's conception of their good changes in a significant enough way, so too will their good. In consequence, the answer to the question of what is truly good for a person is never immutably fixed. For it is in part determined by their conception of their good, which is itself never immutably fixed.

The kind of conversation I have described in this chapter is perfectly common in clinical and treatment settings as well as between friends and family. I return to it in chapters 5, 16, and 19. But it is not easy to have, let alone to conduct well. It takes time and trust, and likely requires not just one conversation but many. And despite caring for the person who is using drugs, any of us involved in such a conversation may flounder and fail, behaving obtusely, hurtfully, coercively—as may they. But there is just no alternative—no other way, in the real world, to determine what is good for a person given the general constraint. For consider: Although you must start with what they say, you cannot simply end there, if you have any reason to think that their sincerely professed values may not accord either with the values they truly have or ought to have. But nor can you simply jump to what you, yourself, believe about what they truly value or ought to value, because it is their conception of their good—not yours, not anyone else's—that is in part determinative of their good. You can't ignore it, and you are best placed to learn about it and come to understand it if you listen to their sincerely professed values—in other words, if you listen to what they say. In complicated cases, there is just no way forward apart from this kind of conversation.

In the ideal world, the conclusion of such a conversation is genuine agreement between the two of you about whether their drug use is or is not good for them. Perhaps you are convinced by them. Perhaps they are convinced by you. But in practice, the conversation may not end in agreement. And, at some point, you may just have to stop talking, agreeing to disagree.

When there appears no genuine possibility of agreement about whether a person's drug use is or is not good for them and yet the conversation must come to an end, we may decide to leave open whether or not the person is addicted. Clearly, in cases like these, there are serious questions about the nature of their drug use and to what extent it is a problem. Perhaps establishing this is enough. But if practical considerations force a decision one way or another, then the presumption should be that the person who gets to decide is the person themself.

This is not a hard rule. Presumptions can be overruled: Perhaps your conversation has revealed so much inconsistency and unclarity in what they say about their values in relation to drugs—or such an obvious failure to recognize and retain basic empirical facts about the consequences of their drug use—that the evidence that they are in denial or not thinking straight about their conception of their good is unequivocal (for further discussion, see chapters 11, 13, 14, and 19). But in absence of such evidence, if you cannot agree about their conception of their good or what is truly good for them, you must still agree that it is *a* good for them to act from and live in accord with their sincerely professed conception of their good—the conception of their good that, as a self-conscious and self-reflective being, they honestly claim reflects how they aspire to conduct their life and what they experience as giving it purpose and meaning. This is why—after serious and sustained conversations conducted out of care and with respect—the presumption should be that they get to decide. It's their life, after all. But it is also part of why the working explication is the foundation for a paradigm that is humanistic. It foregrounds each person's understanding and evaluation of their own drug use, placing their voice at the heart of their diagnosis.

5

Comparisons and Objections

READERS OF A MORE clinical bent may wonder how the working explication and the paradigm it founds compare to the *Diagnostic and Statistical Manual of Mental Disorders* (DSM-5) construct of substance use disorder; those who are more philosophically minded may have objections. This chapter wraps up part I by offering a brief comparison between the working explication and substance use disorder before considering five objections.

I begin with a reminder of the working explication and a recap of its upshots:

Working explication. Addiction is a pattern of drug use that persists despite evident and severe costs such that it counts profoundly against a person's own good.

First upshot. We have a way of diagnosing why, from a theoretical perspective, there is so much disagreement in addiction research. The diagnosis is a tendency to implicitly or explicitly redefine addiction in the terms of specific explanatory hypotheses, thereby creating disagreement about the nature of addiction and limiting the range of possible explanations (see chapter 2).

Second upshot. We have a way of moving beyond the impasse in addiction research by appeal to heterogeneity, thereby also aligning addiction science with good clinical care. The key is a paradigm with ample room for a multiplicity of explanations and a diversity of causes. There is no one-size-fits-all explanation or theory of addiction (see chapter 3).

Third upshot. We must recognize that the line between ordinary drug use and addiction cannot be drawn independently of values. Values are the measure of what counts as a cost or a benefit and how heavily these weigh in the balance. Addiction occurs when a pattern of drug use counts profoundly against a person's own good—where this means what is truly good for them. But what is truly good for them cannot ignore their conception of their good even if it cannot be equated with it either. Ultimately it can only be determined through conversations with people who use drugs that are conducted out of care and with respect (see chapter 4).

The DSM-5 chapter on substance use disorders begins thus: "The essential feature of a substance use disorder is a cluster of cognitive, behavioral, and physiological symptoms indicating that the individual continues using the substance despite significant substance-related problems."[1] As noted in chapter 2, changes in underlying brain circuits are recognized as an important characteristic of substance use disorders, especially in relation to relapse and craving in the presence of drug-related cues. But differentiation and diagnosis is made solely on the basis of a complex set of personal-level criteria—a syndrome. Substance use disorders are a "pattern of behavior related to use of the substance."[2] The DSM-5 construct is therefore similar to the working explication and dissimilar to the brain disease model in locating addiction in the realm of behavior—not in the brain. Diagnosis is made on the basis of eleven criteria organized into four groupings:

Impaired Control

1. Substance taken in larger amounts or over a longer period than was intended.
2. There is a persistent desire or unsuccessful efforts to cut down or control use.
3. A great deal of time is spent in activities necessary to obtain or use the substance, or recover from its effects.
4. Craving, or a strong desire or urge to use the substance.

Social Impairment

5. Recurrent substance use results in failure to fulfill major role obligations at work, school, or home.
6. Continued substance use despite having persistent or recurrent social or interpersonal problems caused or exacerbated by the effects of use.
7. Important social, occupational, or recreational activities are given up or reduced because of substance use.

Risky Use

8. Recurrent substance use in situations in which is it physically hazardous.
9. Substance use is continued despite knowledge of having a persistent or recurrent physical or psychological problem that is likely to have been caused or exacerbated by substance use.

Pharmacological Criteria

10. Tolerance, as defined by either of the following (NB: must be measured relative to individual baseline):
    a. A need for markedly increased amounts of the substance to achieve intoxication or desired effect.
    b. A markedly diminished effect with continued use of the same amount of the substance.
11. Withdrawal upon cessation of substance use or continued substance use to avoid withdrawal (NB: withdrawal symptoms vary greatly across class of drug).

Substance use disorders come in degrees. Severity is indicated by the number of criteria that are met. Two criteria are the minimum for diagnosis; meeting two to three criteria only is considered a mild case of the disorder, four to five is moderate, and six or more is severe. The pharmacological criteria 10 (tolerance) and 11 (physical dependence) do not need to be met at all. However, in relation to prescribed medications, if the only two criteria met are 10 and 11, this is insufficient for diagnosis according to DSM-5.[3]

Despite the complexity of the DSM-5 diagnostic criteria for substance use disorders as compared with the working explication, there is much affinity between them:

1. As noted already and by contrast with the brain disease model, both focus on a "pattern of behavior" with certain characteristics.
2. Criteria 1 and 2 are met when individuals report using more than they intend or want to use, or when they report trying to use less and failing. This indicates there are problems of control. Problems of control are not themselves part of the working explication, but they can be viewed as a hypothesis explaining the puzzle of addiction: an explanation of why, in a particular person's case, use persists despite evident and severe costs. I return to this point in chapters 7 and 14. Here, I want

simply to note that criteria 1 and 2 do more than indicate such problems. They also serve as evidence that a person's drug use counts against their own good—*as they themself conceive of that good*. This is an obvious reason why a person would intend to use less, want to use less, or try to use less.

3. Criterion 3 specifies that a great deal of time is spent on drug use and related activities. This is similar to the working explication's focus on the idea of "a pattern" that is *regular*: a significant and central feature of a person's ordinary life and routines.

4. Criterion 4, craving, was introduced in 2013 with the publication of DSM-5, and so is relatively new in the DSM's history. Cravings are experienced by many, although not all, people with addiction, and have been productively studied by addiction neuroscience—hence the DSM-5's reference to underlying brain circuits in relation to craving and relapse. The nature and explanation of cravings and their role in addiction is discussed in chapters 6, 7, and 15; but, as with problems of control, cravings can be viewed as part of the explanation of why use persists despite evident and severe costs, rather than as essential to addiction itself. That said, the presence of drug *desires* in addiction is at least gestured at by the working explication. The reason is that, although the working explication leaves the kind of behavior constituting the pattern of drug use open, there is evidence that, like much human behavior, it is in fact flexible and goal directed (see chapter 6). That is, the pattern of behavior in question is voluntary action explained by beliefs and desires. Cravings are a kind of desire (see chapter 15).

5. Criteria 5, 6, 7, 8, and 9 specify typical kinds of negative consequences of substance use and knowledge thereof. This is parallel to the working explication's emphasis on evident and severe costs.

6. Neither DSM-5 nor the working explication require the presence of criteria 10 and 11, tolerance and withdrawal. In relation to prescriptions of opioids, sedatives, and stimulants, these two criteria alone are insufficient for diagnosis according to DSM-5. But there is no good reason to limit this restriction to prescriptions of opioids, sedatives, and stimulants only. On this point, we should part ways with DSM-5: Criteria 10 and 11 should not be sufficient for diagnosis no matter the status or origin of the drug. This is because physical dependence is neither necessary nor sufficient for addiction (see chapter 4). The same point holds for tolerance.

7. The application to an individual of some of the terms used to formulate the DSM-5 diagnostic criteria will require judgment, for example, what counts as "a great deal of time," or "major obligations," or "social or interpersonal problems," or "important activities." This is similar to the need for judgment in the interpretation of some of the terms of the working explication, for example, "pattern of drug use," "evident," "severe," and "profoundly."

8. Both the DSM-5 construct of substance use disorder and the working explication admit a great deal of individual variation. Indeed, given the fact that there are eleven criteria and only two are needed to receive the diagnosis, there are technically $2^{11}-12$ (that is, 2,036) possible combinations of symptoms or patient profiles (or 2,035—if we refuse to countenance a diagnosis if the only two criteria met are 10 and 11, no matter the origins and status of the drug). The same kind of variation will be present in the working explication given the obvious range of patterns of use, costs of use, and conceptions of the good.

9. Lastly, both the DSM-5 construct of substance use disorder and the working explication theorize addiction as on a continuum with ordinary drug use and hence as coming in degrees. There are easy-to-classify cases at either extreme. But there is also a gray zone of complicated, difficult-to-classify cases in between. It may sometimes not be possible to determine whether a person meets the criteria for diagnosis with a substance use disorder (this is in fact true of all mental disorders, as DSM-5 recognizes).[4] Similarly, and as we saw in the previous chapter, it may sometimes not be possible to determine whether a person is addicted according to the working explication. Of course, practical considerations may sometimes force a decision.

Like every edition of the DSM, DSM-5 is a work in progress with room for improvement. But it is nonetheless the repository of decades of clinical wisdom. Alongside its emphasis on heterogeneity, the working explication's affinity with the DSM-5 construct of substance use disorder reflects its alignment with clinical practice. Note, however, the dissimilarity of both to the brain disease model, which delineates ordinary drug use from addiction by the absence or presence of underlying brain pathology (see chapter 2).

I turn now to five natural objections that may have been mounting over the preceding chapters—many of which stem from the brain disease model's grip on our thinking (no doubt in combination with a philosophical propensity to look for counterexamples). I address these objections here in the hope of beginning to loosen the grip. Part II treats the brain disease model in detail.

Objection 1. Surely the brain disease model is at least correct that compulsion is part of addiction. Yet the working explication ignores it. Whatever compulsion means, and whether or not addiction is a brain disease, this must be an oversight?

Reply 1. It is not an oversight. The meaning of compulsion and whether it is an explanation of the puzzle of addiction are the topics of chapters 6 and 7. But compulsion should not be built into the working explication. To do so would be to redefine addiction in the terms of a specific explanatory hypothesis, namely the hypothesis that people with addiction use drugs *because they are compelled to.*

Objection 2. Given that neither compulsion, nor craving, nor problems of control are part of the working explication, then a person could be addicted to drugs even though drugs had no real power over them. This flouts our intuitions about what addiction is. Here are two examples by way of illustration. The first is more realistic: Imagine a teenager who uses drugs for no other reason than to enrage their parents, but whose use comes to carry costs both evident and severe. Yet, they persist in using—not because they have any intrinsic desire for drugs, but because they continue to want to enrage their parents. Surely this teenager is not addicted? The second example is more fantastical, part of a philosophical lineage of appealing to hypothetical demons to make a point: Imagine a demon who offers to bring peace to the world if you become addicted to drugs—if you undertake and persist in a pattern of drug use that counts profoundly against your own good. You accept the demon's offer, but at no point do you have any intrinsic desire for drugs. All you want is to save the world. Surely you are not addicted?

These counterexamples press the idea that an intrinsic desire for drugs—the idea that a person wants, needs, yearns for drugs for their own sake, the idea that drugs have a kind of direct, unmediated power over a person—is necessary for addiction. This idea is ignored by the working explication.

Reply 2. The minimal reply to this objection is that an explication is not a set of necessary and sufficient conditions. It is to be measured not by its fit with every one of our ordinary intuitions, but by its fitness for scientific purpose.

There will therefore be counterexamples: cases where the working explication flouts our intuitions.

However, there is a more robust reply. This is that many cases of addiction that fit ordinary language intuitions perfectly well do not contain an intrinsic desire for drugs—a desire for drugs for their own sake, as it were, unmediated by anything else—but rather a desire for drugs because of what drugs do for a person or because of what they mean to them. As we will see in chapters 10, 11, and 12—where I discuss self-medication, a security-based attachment to drugs, self-harm and a desire to die, and an "addict" identity—this is where the power of drugs often lies, and I see no reason to rule out of hand why the value or meaning of drugs could not include a teenager's desire to enrage their parents or your desire, as imagined by the objection, for world peace. To think otherwise is to be in the grip of the brain disease model as opposed to recognizing the psychological nature of addiction. This point is extremely important: I will return to it again in chapter 15 where I consider the nature and role of cravings for drugs in addiction—some but not all of which count as intrinsic desires for drugs—after the necessary groundwork to develop it fully has been laid over the course of the book.

Objection 3. The working explication of addiction is an *actual* pattern of drug use with certain characteristics. But now imagine a person who is addicted to drugs but who suddenly finds themself living in a context where no drugs are available. Surely, they do not cease to be addicted in a case like this? For, if they could persist in using—that is, if drugs were available—then they would. Hence the working explication needs to be *dispositional.* Addiction is a disposition to a kind of pattern of drug use, not the pattern itself.

Reply 3. I have already acknowledged that any transition out of addiction toward abstinence or moderation is complicated by the need for judgment with respect to how much time must pass since the last occasion of use for the pattern to be broken. The objection is therefore correct that a person is no longer addicted merely because there is *some* period of time in which they do not use, no matter the reason. But, once this is conceded, a dispositional account complicates more than it clarifies, thereby undermining its success as an explication.

Dispositions only manifest in certain conditions. Which ones are relevant to an explication of addiction? Following on from the objection, you might be inclined to say: drug availability, obviously. But now consider other, equally obvious factors, such as wealth and trauma. As discussed in the previous chapter, Keith Richards's wealth protects him from many costs of use. Suppose that, were Richards to be stripped of his wealth, he would nonetheless keep using, incurring a different order of costs such that his drug use would no longer be in accord with his own good. Does this mean he is addicted now, while still living a life of privilege and wealth, and despite never facing these costs—never using in a way that fails to accord with his own good? Consistency with the intuition driving the objection pushes us to answer "yes," unless a principled distinction can be drawn between drug availability and loss of wealth as conditions enabling the manifestation of addiction. Perhaps this can be done. But now consider: What if at least part of the reason why Richards would keep using despite evident and severe costs were his wealth to be stripped from him is that living in poverty is traumatic? Is trauma like drug availability, or like loss of wealth? Should we say Richards is addicted now, because he would keep using drugs in a way that incurred a different order of costs if he was miserable and suffering, no matter if he was rich or poor? Well, what would you do alone in a cage with nothing but cocaine? Let us suppose the answer is: Just like Bozarth and Wise's rats, you would take a lot of cocaine. Does this mean you are addicted now, because you have a disposition to use drugs in a way characteristic of addiction, which, luckily for you, is not manifest, since you are not currently in the condition of being alone in a cage with nothing but cocaine?

A dispositional account of addiction is a rabbit hole. Our intuitions become harder to discern let alone elegantly systematize as we go down it. It is in consequence a poor explication, unfit for scientific purpose. Meanwhile, the working explication straightforwardly handles these cases. The fact that a person would use drugs in a way characteristic of addiction in different conditions—if they had access to drugs, if they had their wealth stripped from them, if they experienced the trauma of poverty, if they were alone in a cage with nothing but cocaine—does not mean they are addicted in the conditions they are actually in. For they are not currently using drugs in a way characteristic of addiction—if indeed they are using drugs at all. But, of course, if they end up in these or other conditions, and they start to use drugs in a way characteristic of addiction, then, at that point in their lives, they are indeed addicted to drugs. Even if we cannot be precise about when exactly it begins or fades, addiction should still be defined as an actual pattern of behavior. Addiction is not a disposition to such a pattern any more than a disposition to addiction is addiction (see chapters 1 and 2). Note that this point is entirely consistent with the fact that identification of risk factors for addiction can be important to prevention and hence a valuable object of scientific study; and that caution in relation to drug use is recommended for anyone at risk of addiction no matter the reason—whether that is because they used to be addicted but are now recovered, or because addiction runs in their family, or because they are in a psychological state of mind and/or living in socioeconomic conditions associated with addiction.

Objection 4. Perhaps a dispositional account of addiction is a rabbit hole, but it remains the case that the role accorded to context by the working explication flouts additional intuitions. Context can create and diminish costs. For example, consider the criminalization of drug possession. This is a contingent feature of a society. Which drugs are criminalized in a particular jurisdiction notoriously changes with the times; and some jurisdictions do not criminalize drugs at all. But criminalization creates severe costs that people would not face in its absence; meanwhile, wealth protects against costs they otherwise would. Richards exemplifies both these points. Putting so much emphasis on costs means that a change in context can in effect cure or cause addiction. Transport a drug user from a jurisdiction where drugs are legal to one where they are criminalized, and the costs of their use ratchet up. Give a drug user who is living in poverty on the streets access to housing, a reliable and safe drug supply, and healthcare, and the costs of their use dial down. According to the working explication, two people could be identical with respect to their drug use—they could use exactly the same kinds of drugs in exactly the same amounts, with exactly the same psychoactive and functional effects on their minds and their behavior respectively—yet one is addicted and the other isn't simply because they happen to live in different contexts.

Reply 4. Contexts can indeed create and diminish costs. It is correct that there could be two people whose drug use was identical in these respects, one of whom is addicted and the other of whom is not; alternatively, this could be true of one and the same person, at different times in their life. This is precisely *because* there is a difference, as we are imagining these cases, in the costs of use due to context. What the objection overlooks is that the working explication does not merely emphasize the existence of drug costs, but that drug use must persist despite them. The transportation of a drug user from a jurisdiction where drugs are legal to one where they are criminalized will not mean they count as addicted; it is only if, in this new context, their pattern of drug use persists despite a ratcheting of costs both evident and severe such that it comes to count profoundly against their own good that they will be addicted. And if, over time, the provision of housing, a reliable and safe drug supply, and health care, really does significantly diminish the costs of a pattern of drug use that remains stable in other respects, then I see no reason why this diminishment of costs should not, over time, affect diagnosis. This is in fact how many diagnoses with a substance use disorder are made—and removed. Suppose these changes in context come to mean that it is no longer the case that criteria 5–9 (social impairment and risky use) are met; then, because criteria 5–9 are not met, criteria 1–4 (impaired control) come to abate, since, in absence of criteria 5–9, the person no longer has the same reasons to try not to use, nor, with a reliable and safe supply to hand, urges to use; what remains (let us suppose) are criteria 10–11 (pharmacological). Then the person has shifted from active addiction to a state where they experience tolerance and/or physical dependence. The trigger for this shift is a change in context—housing, a reliable and safe drug supply, health care—but the shift itself is a process, involving a great deal more than change in context.

Objection 5. Perhaps the role accorded to context by the working explication is indeed reasonable, but the role accorded to values is not. Addiction is a medical condition, in which values should play no part on pain of making a mockery of diagnosis and treatment. If addiction is demarcated from ordinary drug use partly in relation to what is good for a person, and what is good for them cannot ignore their conception of their good, then we could in theory cure or cause addiction by changing a person's conception of their good. Holding his pattern of drug use constant, transform Keith Richards from a sex, drugs, and rock 'n' roll icon into a deeply religious person who believes all drug use is morally wrong and he would become not simply physically dependent on heroin but addicted. Transform a deeply religious person who believes all drug use is morally wrong but who has nonetheless ended up addicted to opioids into a sex, drugs, and rock 'n' roll icon—like Keith Richards—and they are no longer addicted but only physically dependent.

Reply 5. The reply to this objection has a similar structure as the previous reply: concession, but an insistence on nuance and realism. Changes in a person's conception of their good can indeed affect diagnosis. This is an upshot of the working explication. But values are an important part of treatment apart from it.

In chapter 4, I asked you to imagine a kind of conversation that is perfectly common in clinical and treatment settings as well as between friends and family. When there is reason to be concerned that people who use drugs are in denial about their true values—or alternatively that their values have been shaped by a life of addiction—we do not typically begin to engage them in treatment by directly targeting their behavior, for example, by providing resources to help them to quit. We begin to engage them in treatment by talking about values: by having conversations with them in the hope of helping them recognize their true values or what they ought to value, thereby encouraging them to want to quit and hence to make use of whatever resources we are able to provide to help them quit. We need to get better at having these conversations. To do so, we need to be real about what we are doing and why we are doing it. I will return to this point in part IV, when I discuss relationships with people with addiction.

The kind of conversation I asked you to imagine in chapter 4 aims at shifting a person's professed or real values *away* from drugs. But the objection also presents a different possibility: shifting a person's values *toward* drugs, thereby transforming the person from addicted to physically dependent according to the working explication. The objection takes this possibility to be devastating to the working explication. But, shocking as it may initially sound, this kind of conversation is also not uncommon, perhaps especially when working clinically with deeply religious people who struggle with addiction. Religious moralism about drugs is no guarantee that a person does not use them and end up addicted. But, once addicted, people who are religious and moralistic about drugs may refuse to consider medication-assisted therapy, such as methadone or buprenorphine for opioid addiction. These are themselves opioids, which have psychoactive effects and will produce physical dependence. They are also highly effective treatments for opioid addiction, without which people often end up in a perpetual cycle of quitting and relapsing. Suppose a religious person is stuck in this cycle, but doesn't want to consider medication-assisted therapy, seeing it as a form of out of the frying pan into the fire, as the saying goes. Perhaps they believe they ought to overcome their addiction—which they think of as a sin—by strength of will alone. If you are a clinician or friend or family member trying to help them, you might well hope to have a conversation with them about their values—their religious moralism about drugs—which are stopping them from considering an effective treatment and so are not, in your view, reflective of what is truly good for them. You do try to shift them just that little bit in the direction of Keith Richards—even if it probably wouldn't be wise to put it like this. Note that there should be no question that methadone and buprenorphine, as well as being medications, are also drugs. This is why they have street value and can be used recreationally. The problem is not that this person is mistaken in believing these medications are drugs. The problem is that, notwithstanding their opioid addiction, they do not want to take any drugs because of a belief that doing so is morally wrong, and so they are refusing to take a drug that would, in fact, do them good.

Values and what is good for a person matter—to demarcating addiction from ordinary drug use and physical dependence, and to what we routinely need to talk about in treatment and in our relationships with people with addiction (see parts III and IV). This however is not uniquely true of addiction. The literature on the role of values in the nature, diagnosis, and treatment of mental disorders is vast, and we do not make a mockery of psychiatry—which treats minds, not just brains—by acknowledging this.[5]

For the rest of the book, I shall take what I have been calling the working explication of addiction to provide a shared understanding of what addiction is, namely a pattern of drug use that persists despite evident and severe costs such that it counts profoundly against a person's own good.

Shifting the Paradigm

Introduction to Part II

TO BEGIN with a reminder of what the puzzle of addiction is and the work it can do: We start with the observation that, from the basic, psychological perspective that we use to understand ourselves and others, we can easily explain why people use drugs, apart from addiction. The explanation is that people use drugs because they have tremendous value. Using drugs is a means to satisfying many ordinary but powerful desires; there may of course be costs, but they appear more than balanced by the benefits. By contrast, from this same, basic, psychological perspective, we cannot so easily explain why people use drugs once addicted. Why not? Because the balance between costs and benefits appears to have tipped. Whatever benefits remain, the costs have become so evident and so severe that using seems in no way worth it. Drug use in addiction therefore appears to flout an assumption we make when explaining behavior, namely an assumption of *self-concern*. This generates a puzzle, which we can express by means of a why-question: Why is a person continuing to use drugs, when the costs appear so evident and severe, so profoundly counter to their own good? This is the puzzle of addiction. It is a question any of us can find ourselves asking; it can be used to explicate addiction, delineating it from ordinary drug use; and it can be used to identify one of the questions driving addiction research. Many models of addiction embody hypotheses that aim to answer this why-question: to explain why people persist in using drugs *despite* costs that are self-destructive, rather than desist out of self-concern *because* of these costs. Models of addiction aim, in other words, to solve the puzzle and confer understanding on behavior that is otherwise prima facie unintelligible to us.

The brain disease model of addiction embodies a hypothesis that offers a powerful solution to the puzzle. The hypothesis is that people with addiction persist in using drugs despite evident and severe costs because they have a brain disease that strips them of the kind of freedom of will that we normally take for granted: Their drug use is compulsive. The reasoning behind this solution is beautifully simple. If people with addiction could stop using, then of course they would. We all act, in so far as we can, out of concern for ourselves and the people and things we care about. But note the caveat: *in so far as we can*. According to the brain disease model, people with addiction can't stop using, which is why they don't. They have no choice for they are compelled. *Compulsion* therefore explains the flouting of self-concern and the descent into self-destruction; it explains why a person persists in using drugs despite evident and severe costs and against their own good. But what in turn explains compulsion? *Brain disease.* After prolonged drug use, "a metaphorical switch in the brain" is flicked and the brain is "hijacked" by drugs.[1] Ordinary, voluntary drug use such as downing a drink, swallowing a pill, injecting, inhaling or snorting a substance—or, if you are a rat, pressing a lever—is transformed into a passive, involuntary symptom of a brain disease. Drug use is merely an effect of whatever is wrong with a person's brain—analogous, perhaps, to how signs and symptoms of Parkinson's disease, such as tremor and slow movement, are caused by brain degeneration.

The primary aim of this part of the book is to evaluate both explanatory components of the brain disease model: *compulsion* and *brain disease*.

Chapters 6 and 7 are about compulsion. As the psychologist Nick Heather has documented, "compulsion" has become a catchall concept in addiction science, often used in ways that are inconsistent, vague, or at best loosely descriptive rather than explanatory.[2] Nonetheless, there is a long-standing way of understanding it that is both intuitive and explanatory of the puzzle: Compulsion derives from the extreme nature of *cravings for drugs* in addiction, understood as desires of unimaginable and irresistible force, driving people to use no matter the costs. Note that this is not how craving is characterized in the fifth edition of the *Diagnostic and Statistical Manual of Mental Disorders* (DSM-5). Craving is there described simply as a strong desire or urge—not as an unimaginably or irresistibly strong desire or urge. But, as we shall see, the more extreme image has been part of addiction discourse at least since the nineteenth century, and is central to the picture of addiction that Alan Leshner, former director of the US National Institute on Drug Abuse (NIDA), paints in his classic statement of the brain disease model: "continued repetition of voluntary drug taking begins to change into involuntary drug taking, ultimately to the point that the behavior is driven by a compulsive craving for the drug."[3]

Chapter 6 returns to the opening gambit of this book—the rat in a cage, pressing a lever. Using a learning theory framework, I tell the history of animal models of addiction in conjunction with relevant human studies to analyze and ultimately reject as empirically discredited the idea of compulsion as deriving from a desire for drugs of unimaginable and irresistible force. In offering this analysis, I also consider and reject an alternative idea of compulsion based on the idea of "automaticity." To preview the conclusion of this chapter: Drug use in addiction is not compelled by irresistible desires but is flexible and goal directed—voluntary in an ordinary sense. Therefore, since drug use in addiction is not compulsive, compulsion cannot solve the puzzle of addiction.

Two immediate clarifications to avoid any misunderstanding from the outset. First, the fact that drug use in addiction is voluntary in an ordinary sense does not mean that everything about it is ordinary. Contra the moral model of addiction (described in the introduction to this book), there can be real and significant differences between ordinary drug use and drug use in addiction despite the fact that *both* are voluntary. Put otherwise, it is hardly as if voluntariness is the only possible way to distinguish them. Parts III and IV discuss the many differences between ordinary drug use and drug use in addiction—including differences that are relevant to attributions of responsibility (see chapter 19). Second, the fact that drug use in addiction is voluntary in an ordinary sense does not mean that cravings for drugs have no role to play in explaining addiction. Of course they do. But we shall only be in a position to see what their role is when the idea of irresistibility is put to rest and other solutions to the puzzle have been developed. In consequence, I offer a more positive proposal about how to understand cravings only at the end of part III, in chapter 15.

Chapter 7 is more philosophical in orientation. I use the learning theory framework presented in chapter 6 in conjunction with a hypothetical experiment—that is, a philosophical thought experiment about an experiment—to draw a theoretical lesson: Given their role in action explanation, we should be skeptical of the idea that desires *could* be irresistible. I then raise a natural objection to this lesson; I start a discussion of the nature of loss of control in addiction which I continue in part III, chapter 14; and I conclude with some reflections of a more ethical bent about why the need to jettison the idea of irresistible desire is nothing to lament.

Taken together, chapters 6 and 7 put the final nail in the coffin of compulsion. Insofar as addiction can be considered a brain disease at all, it must be one whose signs and symptoms consist in voluntary behavior—a brain disease of *choice*, as this idea is often put by its advocates.[4]

Chapters 8 and 9 are about brain disease. As we saw in chapter 2, the brain disease model hypothesizes that underlying brain pathology is the cause of the personal-level observable signs and experienced symptoms characteristic of addiction. Assessing the truth of this causal hypothesis has a theoretical and an empirical component. Theoretically, we need to clarify what brain pathology is and what counts as establishing causation; empirically, we need to determine whether brain pathology is present in people with addiction and, if it is, whether it causes them to use drugs.

Chapter 8 focuses on brain pathology; chapter 9 focuses on causation. Both chapters do little more than make a start on what are extremely complicated questions. To briefly preview the discussion of brain pathology: Addiction is correlated with brain changes and brain differences. But to assess whether these count as brain pathology, we need something we do not currently have, namely a serious account of the nature of normal—not just typical—brain function, by which to measure brain dysfunction. Chapter 8 considers some of the challenges to developing such an account. I also introduce a model of disorder that contrasts with both the minimal and strong disease models, and which may illuminate some aspects of at least some cases of addiction: *the mismatch model.*

Despite the reservations of chapter 8, chapter 9 proceeds on the assumption that there are at least two standout candidates for brain pathology in people with addiction: reductions in volume of white and gray matter associated with atypical brain activity; and neuroadaptations in the mesocorticolimbic dopamine system. The question it asks is how we could establish that these (or other forms of brain pathology) are not merely present in people with addiction, but are the cause of their drug use. To answer this question, I sketch the standard interventionist method used in experimental science and suggest a series of hypothetical experiments that in theory could test the causal significance of brain pathology as compared with one possible competing cause of drug use in addiction, namely a lack of alternative reinforcers. I conclude that we should be open to the possibility that brain pathology is the cause of drug use in some cases, but certainly not in all cases.

This, then, is the take-home lesson of part II: Despite its explanatory promise, the brain disease model cannot on its own solve the puzzle of addiction, for drug use in addiction is not compelled, and brain pathology as the cause of drug use in addiction is not sufficiently let alone universally established. This is part of why we need a new paradigm that jettisons what is wrong with the brain disease model but retains what is right. Once again, it is time to recognize and respect the heterogeneity of addiction.

6

Compulsion in Rats and Humans

DO YOU EVER CRAVE company, solitude, sex, food, or drugs of any kind—a coffee, a smoke, an oxy, a glass of wine? For many of us, for at least some of these things, the answer is obvious. *Yes.* For all who answered yes, let me ask another question. When you have such a craving, is it irresistible? Before you answer, a qualification. The word "irresistible" can mean different things in different contexts of use. So, let me be more specific: When you have a craving, and assuming that you are not addicted to the thing you are craving, do you consider your craving to be irresistible in the way you take cravings for drugs in addiction to be? Thus specified, for many of us, the answer seems just as obvious. *No.* Of course you may really, really want whatever you crave. You might want it so much that you act rashly—perhaps breaking a past resolution or knowingly risking future regret. But however strong your craving is, you would probably be inclined to distinguish it from the irresistibility commonly supposed to characterize cravings for drugs in addiction. Your desire for companionship or solitude does not compel you to act in the way that drugs are routinely portrayed as compelling people with addiction to act. Nor are you forced to eat the food, have the sex, or take the drugs that you crave.

The image of craving in addiction as different in kind from ordinary craving—different in kind precisely because irresistible in the sense of compelling action—has long shaped scientific, philosophical, and popular imagination. Consider the famous nineteenth-century ode to craving penned by the medical theorist Benjamin Rush, repeated by the philosopher and psychologist Williams James, and liberally quoted ever since:

The craving for drink in real dipsomaniacs, or for opium or chloral in those subjugated, is of a strength of which normal persons can form no conception. "Were a keg of rum in one corner of a room and were a cannon constantly discharging balls between me and it, I could not refrain from passing before that cannon in order to get the rum"; "If a bottle of brandy stood at one hand and the pit of hell yawned at the other, and I were convinced that I should be pushed in as sure as I took one glass, I could not refrain": such statements abound in dipsomaniacs' mouths.[1]

Craving is here portrayed as a desire of a strength unimaginable to "normal persons"—a desire so strong it is impossible to resist, no matter the consequences of acting on it, including cannonballs and hell. This, of course, is literary license. Although people with addiction face a wide range of severe costs because of their drug use, these do not typically include the inferno. But the rhetorical flourish does not matter to the fundamental point. Thus portrayed, craving elegantly solves the puzzle of addiction—explaining the apparent lack of self-concern in risking death and eternal damnation for a keg of rum or bottle of brandy by removing the possibility of choosing life and salvation over drugs. By contrast with more ordinary cravings, cravings for drugs in addiction are supposed to be impossible to resist, compelling action that satisfies them—no matter the costs. In the language of the philosopher Harry Frankfurt, people with addiction are "helplessly violated" by their own desires that "invariably conquer" them and are "too powerful to withstand."[2]

What would it be for a desire to be irresistible? The idea of a force so strong as to be impossible to resist invites interpretation through physical metaphors. The philosopher Jay Wallace describes this conception of desire as hydraulic, likening it to water bursting through a dam; the philosopher Gary Watson compares it to bladders and lungs that are full to the point of exploding; we might alternatively think of a train with no brakes barreling down a track.[3] But metaphors are just that: metaphors. Can they be made good?

Watson considers the following analysis.[4] Just as if you try your hardest to move a slab of stone, giving it your absolute all, but fail, then you can't move the stone, so too if you try your hardest to resist a desire, giving it your absolute all, but fail, then you can't resist the desire. However, Watson then argues, in contrast to moving a stone, you can't give your absolute all to resisting your own desire. The reason is that part of you—your desire—is resisting your resistance. You are psychologically conflicted, not wholeheartedly of one mind. Hence the antecedent of the conditional cannot be met, leading Watson to skepticism about the very possibility of irresistible desires.

In the next chapter, I will argue that we should agree with Watson's skepticism. But I do not think we can yet draw this conclusion. Here is why: Watson's conditional analysis attempts to provide an operationalization—a test or measure, capable of yielding a clear answer—of the construct of irresistibility. We observe whether someone is trying their hardest to resist a desire. Then we observe whether they act. If they act, the desire counts as irresistible. If they don't, it doesn't. The problem is not only that, as Watson points out, it is unclear what "trying your hardest" could mean in a context where your desires conflict. The problem is that it is natural to interpret this operationalization as presupposing a subject susceptible to a certain kind of psychological conflict: a self-conscious, self-reflective subject who is capable of taking what are called "metacognitive attitudes" toward their mental states, such as deciding to resist their own desire. Yet, name notwithstanding, nothing in the idea of an irresistible desire—metaphorically depicted as a physical force of such strength as to be unstoppable by various objects it encounters, such as dams, bladders, lungs, an obstacle on the tracks—should block its ascription to animals incapable of metacognitive attitudes. Crucially, this includes one of the animals at the very heart of addiction science, namely the rat. What we should expect, if drug desires are "irresistible" in rats whose behavior mirrors, so far as possible, human addiction, is not that *attempts to resist drug desires fail*—since rats make no such attempts—but that *drug desires always win out*. How then to make good this new metaphor of winning out? To do so, the idea of irresistibility must be operationalized along two dimensions. On the one hand, drug use must evince *behavioral inflexibility*—use persists, no matter what. On the other hand, this behavioral inflexibility must be explained by *desire*.

Early experiments attempting to model addiction in rats indicated behavioral inflexibility. A classic experimental chamber contains a lever that, if pressed, delivers reward: water, food, social access to a peer, an intravenous drug dose—typically a psychostimulant or an opioid. Rats are curious animals. The first time they are placed in the chamber, they explore. In textbook experiments, a light goes on. The light functions as a stimulus, signaling reward availability. At some point, the rat happens to press the lever. The reward is delivered. The delivery of the reward is then signaled by a second stimulus, like a second light or a sound. These cues, signaling reward availability and delivery, help the rat learn to instrumentally press the lever to receive the reward; but, once this is learned, their presence has minimal effect on self-administration. In this way, rats learn how to self-administer rewards, including drugs.

This book opened by reflecting on the animal experimentalists Michael Bozarth and Roy Wise's seminal 1985 studies: Rats placed in an experimental chamber containing only food, water, and a lever for cocaine pressed the lever repeatedly, forsaking food and water. Ninety percent of them died within a month.[5] What would make any animal ignore rewards essential to survival? The instinctive answer is: the power of drugs to compel use. This image of the rat pressing the lever again and again—abandoning itself to cocaine at the expense of food and water—is the animal model of risking death and eternal damnation for a keg of rum or bottle of brandy. The first dimension of the operationalization appears to be met. Use persists, no matter what. The question then is: Is this behavioral inflexibility explained by desire?

Learning theory. To answer this question, I shall introduce a basic, learning theory framework, distinguishing two kinds of behavioral response, habitual and goal directed. *Habitual* or stimulus-response (S-R) behavior is controlled by a stimulus, for example, a cue (such as the light previously described) that the animal has learned to associate with a reward. By contrast, *goal-directed* behavior is controlled by a representation of the outcome—an expected reward—that the animal has learned can be achieved by a behavioral response. In other words, goal-directed behavior requires the animal to represent the response-outcome (R-O) relationship or "contingency," as it is called.

Because of this requirement, goal-directed behavior is naturally explained by belief-desire psychology. Why does the animal press the lever? Because it believes doing so will deliver the reward and it desires the reward. There is therefore a striking parallel between learning theory and the philosophy of action. The orthodox view in the philosophy of action is that what makes a piece of behavior an action is that it is explained by the agent's reason for acting, understood as a belief-desire pair, where the agent believes that the means to satisfying a current desire is to act as they do: Action is goal directed.[6] Unlike goal-directed behavior, habitual behavior is *autonomous* from the outcome, in the sense that the behavior is directly controlled *by* the stimulus rather than directed *at* a goal. There is no mediation by an R-O representation and hence no explanation of the behavior by a belief-desire pair.

The operationalization of the distinction between habitual and goal-directed behavior is differential sensitivity to the manipulation of belief or desire. Belief can be manipulated by degrading the learned R-O contingency, a procedure known as "contingency degradation." Although this sounds technical, the idea is simple: Make it the case that the animal no longer believes the behavior is an effective means to achieving the desired outcome. For example, after the animal has learned that pressing a lever reliably delivers a reward, the reward-delivery schedule is altered to be independent of lever-pressing. When the reliable pairing between behavior and outcome is disrupted, the animal's belief in this contingency changes. Desire can be manipulated by devaluing the outcome of the behavioral response, a procedure known as "outcome devaluation." Again, the idea is simple: Make it the case that the animal no longer desires the reward it expects to get by acting. Devaluation is typically achieved in either of two ways: reward-specific satiety or aversion conditioning. Reward-specific satiety works by satisfying the desire prior to the animal entering the experimental chamber. For example, having learned that lever-pressing delivers food, an animal is allowed to eat its fill before testing. Aversion conditioning pairs the reward with an aversive experience prior to testing (for example, an injection of lithium chloride to induce nausea), aiming to create a lasting association between the reward and the aversive experience.[7] But no matter the procedure, once the contingency is degraded or the outcome devalued, then either the animal no longer believes that lever-pressing will deliver the reward, or it no longer wants the reward that it believes lever-pressing delivers. It is then returned to the experimental chamber and tested under a condition called "extinction." No reward is available should it press the lever, so its behavior cannot be influenced by present reward but must be based on past learning. Its behavior is observed and compared to a group that has not undergone contingency degradation or outcome devaluation. Does the animal press the lever at a different rate from the animals in the control group? If its rate of lever-pressing is decreased relative to the control group, then its behavior is goal directed. The manipulation of belief or desire has had an effect. If no difference is observed relative to the control group, then its behavior is not goal directed. The manipulation of belief or desire has had no effect. Hence the animal's lever-pressing is not explained by a belief-desire pair. It is responding habitually. Its behavior is directly controlled by a stimulus, unmediated by a belief-desire pair. Note that S-R behavior is here defined as absence of evidence for goal-directed behavior. It is not independently operationalized. More on this to follow, when we turn to human drug use.

Rat experiments using food reward demonstrate that lever-pressing is initially goal directed.[8] But, over time and with training, it becomes habitual: impervious to contingency degradation or outcome devaluation under extinction. It is important to recognize that there is yet some degree of behavioral flexibility: No animal will lever-press *ceaselessly* under extinction conditions; equally, if an animal is *not* under extinction conditions but allowed to sample a devalued outcome, it will typically cease lever-pressing. Nonetheless, the finding that, over time and with training, behavior that is initially goal directed becomes habitual looks poised to explain why the rats in Bozarth and Wise's experiments given unlimited access to cocaine pressed the lever repeatedly— even if not ceaselessly—forsaking food and water, and risking death. The explanation is that, as with food, so too with drugs. Behavior that was goal directed and hence sensitive to expected reward outcome becomes habitual: a direct response to a stimulus that is outcome-autonomous, unmediated by a belief-desire pair.

Habit theory. Drawing on this S-R framework, the neuroscientists Barry J. Everitt, Trevor W. Robbins, and Christian Lüscher have proposed a habit theory of addiction.[9] Habit theory explains the puzzle of addiction by appeal to behavior that is outcome-autonomous and in this sense "automatic." I shall review the evidence for and against habit theory in both humans and rats shortly. But first a general and crucial remark: Habit theory does not vindicate, but rather denies, the power of craving in explaining drug use.[10] As the philosopher Peter Railton puts it, desire is "a beckoning idea that draws us forward, rather than a blank drive that pushes us from behind."[11] If habit theory is true, then the behavioral inflexibility revealed in Bozarth and Wise's experiments is precisely not to be explained by desire. Drugs do not beckon. Use is not goal directed. Drug use is, rather, a blank drive: a kind of repetitive mindlessness. This is how S-R behavior is operationalized and defined. To be sure, it is explained by psychological processes—namely control of behavior, such as drug use, by stimuli. But it is not explained by psychological states like beliefs and desires. Hence according to habit theory, craving, understood as an irresistible desire *for* an object, has nothing to do with why anyone—rat or person—continues to use drugs despite evident and severe costs. What explains this apparent behavioral inflexibility is that it is stimulus-controlled and so outcome-autonomous.

I shall discuss the evidence for habit theory in rats shortly. But habit theory is unlikely to be the correct explanation of human addiction. There is some general evidence of habit in humans. In an ingenious field experiment, the psychologists David T. Neal, David Kurlander, and their colleagues demonstrated that people who routinely eat popcorn at the movies show less sensitivity to outcome devaluation than controls who don't. So long as they are eating in a typical context and with their usual hand, it makes little difference if the popcorn is stale or fresh.[12] Strictly speaking, the delivery of stale popcorn means that this experiment did not test the subjects under extinction conditions, which would have required *no* popcorn. Nonetheless, stale pop-corn is surely less valuable than fresh popcorn, so this experiment offers at least some general evidence of habit in these popcorn-eaters. It also accords with common sense. Consider how, with a drink or a pack of cigarettes in front of you, anyone who drinks or smokes—addicted or not—can find themself mindlessly reaching for it—sated or not.

But getting and taking drugs (especially illegal drugs) is typically a complex affair, requiring problem solving, planning, and flexibility—unequivocal hall-marks of goal-directed behavior. This point is supported by outcome devalu-ation and contingency degradation human laboratory experiments. In these experiments, human subjects typically learn that two responses, R1 and R2, earn two distinct rewarding outcomes, O1 and O2. One reward is then devalued by reward-specific satiety, adulteration, pharmacotherapy, or health warnings; or the R-O contingency is degraded by verbal instruction that the reward is no longer available. Choice of response is then tested in extinction. Habit theory predicts that addiction will be associated with habitual respond-ing for drug rewards. People with addiction should be less sensitive to out-come devaluation and contingency degradation than controls who are not addicted to drugs. But, as the psychologist Lee Hogarth has demonstrated, the majority of studies do not show this effect. Meanwhile, in rare cases where it has been found, it cannot safely be attributed to habit, because the subjects additionally displayed impaired knowledge of a host of contingencies (includ-ing R-O contingencies), probably arising from task disengagement or cogni-tive impairment. Moreover, in studies where knowledge of contingencies is matched, addicted and nonaddicted subjects show comparable goal-directed control over their behavior.[13] This points to a fundamental problem operation-alizing S-R behavior as absence of evidence for goal-directed behavior. There are alternative hypotheses for insensitivity to outcome devaluation or contin-gency degradation, namely impairment in the psychological processes ex-plaining goal-directed behavior, as opposed to control of the behavior by S-R processes.[14] Notwithstanding the popcorn field experiments, and in striking contrast with rats, it has proven extremely difficult to train humans to behave habitually in the laboratory,[15] raising a concern that the methods used to test habitual versus goal-directed behavior in animals may have limited transla-tional validity in general[16]—never mind that humans are rarely in real-world extinction conditions.

Nonetheless, something about the idea of a "drug habit" is surely compel-ling. As the cognitive neuroscientist Fiery Cushman and his colleagues have demonstrated in humans, and the animal experimentalists Serge H. Ahmed and Youna Vandaele have demonstrated in rats, there is evidence that habitual and goal-directed behavior can work in tandem, with habits controlling the selection of goals that can then be implemented through flexible planning.[17] Drawing on this idea, the computational neuroscientist Nathaniel Daw has intriguingly suggested that what is habitual in addiction may not be behavior itself, but goal selection: which expected reward outcome is selected for action out of all those that are possible—or, we might say, which desire, out of all possible desires, is acted on.[18] The actions typically required to find and take drugs are complex and instrumental: explained by belief-desire psychology, not S-R processes. But perhaps drug goals themselves, in addiction, are selected for action over other goals mindlessly—people with addiction act on drug desires *by force of habit*.[19]

Could this suggestion explain the apparently unstoppable force of drug desires? Drug desires always win out because people with addiction mindlessly pursue drug goals. Remember the rat, pressing the lever again and again for cocaine, forsaking any desire it might also have for food or for water. Perhaps its behavior is not blind—drugs beckon it forward. But, the suggestion would be, it mindlessly follows its desire for drugs at the expense of all other possible goals. Drug use is therefore hypothesized to satisfy both dimensions of the construct of irresistibility. The behavior is inflexible because drug desires are inflexibly selected for action. As the bioethicist Carl Elliott evocatively puts something like this idea in relation to people with addiction, they "must go where the addiction leads, because the addiction holds the leash."[20]

Forced-choice studies. In theory, the suggestion has explanatory promise. In practice, it turns out that neither rats nor people mindlessly follow their desires for drugs in addiction. Notwithstanding early animal drug self-administration experiments, drug use is not in fact inflexible.

To begin, let us return once again to rats. Inspired by the experimental psychologist Sidney Spragg's seminal work with monkeys,[21] the animal experimentalist Serge H. Ahmed pioneered a forced-choice paradigm demonstrating that rats escalate drug intake in an addiction-like manner only when no alternative rewards are available.[22] As briefly described in the introduction to this book, the forced-choice experimental chamber has not one lever, but two. Each lever is retractable and paired with a separate light cue. One lever delivers a drug dose and the other an alternative reward, such as saccharin water.

Self-administration training is conducted in a manner that ensures the rats do not default to either lever simply out of familiarity. Once training is complete, the rats are introduced to the forced-choice procedure. Both lights come on and both levers are extended. If either lever is pressed, the associated reward is delivered, and both levers are retracted. Over a series of studies, Ahmed found that 90 percent of rats—none of whom were water or food deprived—chose saccharin water over drug reward. This was so even under the following three conditions: (i) the drug dose was high; (ii) the cost to the rats of getting the saccharin water was significantly higher than the cost of getting the drug reward, as measured by number of lever-presses required to get either; and (iii) the individual animal had a long history of self-administration and escalation and showed signs of withdrawal and sensitization, a behavioral measure involving locomotor hyperactivity when the drug is delivered and associated with neural changes.[23] More recently, Marco Venniro, Yavin Shaham, and their colleagues adapted Ahmed's forced-choice study paradigm to social reward.[24] They found that almost 100 percent of rats—who were socially housed, so in no way socially deprived—chose social over drug reward, irrespective of training conditions, drug class, dose size, length of abstinence since last dose, and "addiction score" based on a *Diagnostic and Statistical Manual of Mental Disorders* (DSM) style of model adapted to rats.[25] Rats chose drug reward only if choice of social reward was punished by moderate to high foot shock, or delivery of social reward was significantly delayed. However, neither of these measures correlated with addiction score. It was not the case that, the higher a rat's score, the faster they switched to drugs when social reward was punished or delayed.

What do these studies show? Even when rats have a history of drug self-administration designed by experimentalists to mirror addiction, they choose alternative rewards to drugs in many circumstances. Note that, although it is natural to interpret these findings as indicating goal-directed behavior in rats, this cannot be concluded. Habits, operationalized as stimulus-controlled behavior, are not guided by a desire for an outcome, but they are nonetheless sensitive to level of reward achieved by the behavior over the animal's learning history. When habits compete with each other, the habit associated with greater past reward will dominate. Therefore, in the forced-choice study procedure, it is at least in theory possible that rats press the lever associated with the nondrug alternative out of habit because that response has been more rewarding in the past than the alternative; in other words, *not* because they are guided by a representation of the outcome of doing so.[26] Nonetheless, whether the allocation of the rats' behavior to the nondrug alternative is controlled by habitual or by goal-directed processes, it is simply false that drugs always win out. *When alternatives are available,* either other habits are elicited, or other goals are pursued instead. Hence, what explains why rats in Bozarth and Wise's experiments self-administered cocaine until death is not the overwhelming power of drugs in forming either habits or desires. It is the lack of anything better as they lived alone, for weeks on end, in barren, experimental chambers.

Strikingly similar findings hold for humans. As noted already, by contrast with rats, there is strong evidence that drug use in human addiction is not habitual but goal directed. But, similarly to rats, there is a robust, inverse relationship between drug use and the availability of alternative reinforcers in humans,[27] with choice of reward in both species influenced by a range of factors such as relative reward size, delay, cost, and, of course, the consequences associated with the options (for example, punishment).[28] This may explain a discovery much emphasized by the behavioral economist Gene Heyman: Large-scale epidemiological data reveal that a great many people who meet criteria for a substance use disorder (probably a majority, although precise rates are difficult to establish), including those who are physically dependent, recover without clinical intervention by their late twenties or early thirties as the responsibilities and opportunities of life change—a process known as "maturing out."[29] Arguably, the most important illustration of this general finding, in relation to humans, derives from contingency management treatment, briefly described in the introduction to this book. Contingency management is a highly effective therapeutic modality that in effect structures a person's environment to mirror forced-choice animal studies. Alternative rewards, such as small prizes, vouchers, money—or, as in the behavioral psychologist Kenneth Silverman's inspired innovation of a *therapeutic workplace*, skills training and employment—are available on condition of abstinence.[30] Contingency management likely works through two mechanisms. Some of the alternative rewards offered are large, for example, the skills training and employment associated with therapeutic workplaces. These may straightforwardly outweigh drug rewards. But other alternative rewards are relatively small, for example, small prizes and vouchers. These may not outweigh drug rewards. Rather, the treatment may work by explicitly engaging goal-directed deliberation,[31] thereby countering any habitual influence on goal selection and enabling longer-term, global considerations to weigh more heavily in the balance.[32] But, whatever the mechanism, the bottom line is that contingency management works. As the addiction psychiatrist Eric C. Strain notes with despair: It is an outrage that it is so rarely available to treat addiction, for what one can only presume are ideological reasons to the tune that no one should be "rewarded" for not using drugs.[33]

Drawing this discussion together: The cumulative evidence indicates that responsiveness to alternative reinforcers is retained in human addiction. In other words, as with rats, so too with people. Whether explained by habit (as appears at least possible in rats) or belief-desire psychology (as appears to be the case with people), drug behavior is not inflexible after all. In many circumstances, drugs do not win out, but are cast to the side when better rewards are available.

Hence human drug desires are not of unimaginable and unstoppable force. Other desires are frequently acted on instead. Indeed, if we replace the literary license taken by Rush and James with qualitative studies of people with addiction, this point is borne out. Both retrospective self-report and ecological momentary assessment (EMA) studies—which prompt subjects to electronically report real-time fluctuations in psychological state, behavior, and daily circumstances, and hence have high validity compared with retrospective studies—suggest cravings are no stronger than many ordinary desires.[34] In addition, laboratory studies find that when asked how pleasant or desirable it would be to eat food, have sex, or take drugs, cocaine-addicted subjects rate food and sex over drugs "in general."[35] Neuroimaging studies by Leonie Koban, Tor Wager, and Hedy Kober complement these findings.[36] Using functional magnetic resonance imaging (fMRI) and machine learning, a Neurobiological Craving Signature (NCS) was discovered that predicts self-reported strength of cue-induced drug and food cravings. NCS response to drug cues can discriminate heavy smokers as well as alcohol-addicted and cocaine-addicted subjects from subjects who do not use these drugs. However, the response to drug cues in the drug-addicted subjects as compared to the response to food cues in the nonusing subjects was not dissociable at the fMRI level. In other words, the difference between addicted subjects and subjects who do not use drugs resides in *which cues cause* the NCS response, not in the nature of the response itself.

People with addiction may really, really want to use drugs. Their desires for drugs may in consequence be hard to resist. But a desire that is "hard to resist" as opposed to "impossible to resist" cannot by itself solve the puzzle of addiction. Given the evident and severe nature of the costs of drug use in addiction—loss of jobs, housing, educational opportunities, standing in one's community, relationships with the people one loves, physical and mental health, and even life itself—appealing merely to the difficulty of not using is insufficient to explain why people would keep using *when they don't have to*. Despite its explanatory promise, compulsion is a myth. But without compulsion, desires on their own are unexplanatory.

7

The Idea of Irresistible Desire

THE PUZZLE OF ADDICTION cannot be solved simply by appeal to compulsion, understood as irresistible desire. As we saw in the previous chapter, the evidence from animal models and human studies demonstrates that drug desires do not always win out. But I believe there is a stronger and more philosophical lesson to be drawn from the learning theory framework presented in chapter 6: We should be skeptical of the idea that desires *could* be irresistible—of the very possibility of irresistible desire, not just its actuality. The reason is that there is a tension between the two dimensions used to operationalize the construct of irresistible desire: *behavioral inflexibility*, on the one hand; and *behavior that is explained by desire*—and of course belief—on the other. This chapter makes this argument and considers an objection to it. In so doing, I draw attention to an underappreciated distinction between the irresistibility of desire and loss of control.

Recall one of the contingency degradation assays used in human subjects to determine whether their behavior is habitual or goal directed: Subjects are told that a reward that they have learned to get by behaving a certain way is no longer available—meaning that behaving that way is no longer a means to satisfying any desire for the reward they may have. Consider now a hypothetical contingency degradation experiment rather than an actual one—in other words, a philosophical thought experiment about an experiment. Imagine that a person with addiction is presented with the drug to which they are addicted. Suppose they are at a bar, sitting in front of what they take to be an ordinary glass of vodka and on the verge of drinking. It is their first drink of the day, and their craving is very strong—palpably so. But they suddenly get convincing evidence—for example, authoritative testimony from a person they trust, like the bartender or a friend—of one of the following: (i) the glass does not contain vodka, but poison; (ii) there is a 9:1 chance that the glass contains vodka or poison; (iii) the glass contains a 9:1 solution of vodka to poison, enough to make you sick, but not enough to kill you.[1] Let us stipulate that they change their belief accordingly, but that their craving for vodka persists despite this change in belief. Note that it is of course possible that, in some cases, getting this information could serve to extinguish the craving altogether, or fail to result in a change of belief. Neither possibility impugns the hypothetical contingency degradation experiment, which is designed to probe a different kind of case: How a person addicted to alcohol might act when they continue to experience the craving while changing their belief. So, with this clarified, here is the question: Do they drink?

Although this is ultimately an empirical question that could only be answered with absolute certainty case by case, we can nonetheless make a series of plausible predictions based on what we know of human decision-making in general, and addicted decision-making in particular. On the assumption that they do not have an independent desire to die from drinking poison (but see chapter 11 for discussion of suicidality and addiction), no one, however severely addicted to alcohol, drinks in (i). After all, they no longer believe the glass contains *any* alcohol; drinking will not satisfy their craving. But it is likely that some (not all) people addicted to alcohol will drink in (ii); and it is likely that some (not all, and not necessarily the same) people will drink in (iii). In (ii), there is a 9:1 chance that a person's craving can be satisfied by drinking. In (iii), their craving will be satisfied by drinking, but they will also get sick. Drinking in (ii) will depend in part on a person's tolerance of risk. Drinking in (iii) will depend in part on a person's tolerance of costs that are certain. Meanwhile, increasing or decreasing the 9:1 ratio in either (ii) or (iii) will of course affect what we should predict. Make the risk or quantity of poison low enough, and everyone will drink. Make the risk or quantity of poison high enough, and no one will. Different people with addiction will have different tolerance thresholds, creating significant individual variability in the cutoff point for drinking.

What this hypothetical contingency degradation experiment suggests is simply that, *holding craving in addiction constant*, changes in belief relating to the object of a craving and hence to response-outcome (R-O) contingencies affect whether or not a person uses. In other words, holding craving constant, use is not inflexible, precisely because goal-directed behavior is sensitive not only to desire but to belief. Of course, people who are addicted to alcohol are likely to have higher tolerance thresholds for alcohol-related risks and costs than people who are not addicted. But it cannot be that, in addiction, use persists when a person is palpably gripped by craving, *no matter what.* To think otherwise is to ignore the fact that if drug use is explained by desire, then it is also explained by belief.

The tension in the operationalization of irresistibility such that it can be modeled in animals—and studied experimentally in rats and humans alike—derives from the fact that if the behavior under investigation really is to be explained by belief and desire, then it is not inflexible. The basis for attributions of beliefs and desires to explain behavior—as opposed to explaining it by appeal to habit or S-R responding—*is* behavioral flexibility consequent on interventions to manipulate either psychological state. If changes in desire for an object, or in belief relating to the desired object, could not affect a subject's behavior, then we should be skeptical that the behavior should be explained by belief and desire at all. Hence, given their role in action explanation, we should be skeptical that desires could be irresistible. No doubt, desires can be more or less strong. They can therefore weigh more or less in decision-making and be more or less hard to resist for subjects, like humans, capable of deciding to do so. But we should be skeptical of the idea that they could be forces of unstoppable strength—driving behavior forward like a train barreling down a track.

The argument that I just presented naturally invites the following objection. Wouldn't this person simply get up and find another bar? The answer is: Yes, likely they would. The objection may then continue: Doesn't this mean that their craving is indeed irresistible, if we take a diachronic rather than a synchronic view of irresistibility? In other words, the person may not use *now*, at this very moment, but, assuming that their craving persists, and no matter how much they try to abstain, they will in all likelihood use *eventually.* That is the nature of craving for drugs in addiction. It persists if unfulfilled and recurs if fulfilled. This means that, over time, use becomes, practically speaking, close to inevitable. We should see craving as *diachronically* irresistible.

It is important to recognize that drug use is not, strictly speaking, inevitable. The majority of people who meet diagnostic criteria for substance use disorder eventually come to see themselves as recovered.[2] But that said, I do not claim that we can make no sense of an idea of the "irresistibility" of desire as the likely "inevitability" of acting on it over time;[3] nor do I deny the possibility that anyone who is addicted, no matter how much they are trying to abstain, may use again. Recovery is hard and far from guaranteed, with a high probability of lapses and relapses along the way. Hence the objection can be interpreted as raising a real and important question: Granting that cravings are not irresistible at a time, why do drug desires trend toward winning out over time?

In evoking the idea of diachronic irresistibility, the objection invites us to answer this question by returning to an image of craving as a force so strong as to be impossible to resist—as if cravings for drugs that are initially resistible build to a breaking point with time. We might again be tempted to invoke a physical metaphor: Think of water slowly amassing behind a dam before it bursts, or bladders and lungs slowly filling up before exploding. Not immediately, but eventually, the force is just too much to be contained. But this image is precisely what must be exorcised from our thinking. If it is indeed incorrect that drug use persists, no matter what, when a person is palpably gripped by craving, then the answer to the question of why a person eventually uses cannot be that they are palpably gripped by craving up to and including the time when they use. For, at that time, when they use, their use is no more inflexible than it is at any other time. Although time increases the likelihood of use, this cannot be because time transforms cravings that were once resistible into cravings that are now irresistible. The question therefore remains: Why do drug desires trend toward winning out over time?

The philosopher and psychiatrist Chandra Sripada has offered an explanation of loss of control that elegantly answers this question.[4] Let us loosely define loss of control in addiction as using drugs despite either one's better judgment or a sincere intention to abstain (or as using more than one sincerely intended)—that is, as more or less in keeping with the fifth edition of the *Diagnostic and Statistical Manual of Mental Disorders* (DSM-5) criteria (1) and (2) for substance use disorders (see chapter 5). Sripada argues that loss of control is due not to the *irresistibility* of desire, but to the *fallibility* of the cognitive systems necessary for behavioral control. He begins by noting that cravings for drugs occur with high frequency during addiction and in the early months of recovery. Abstaining from use therefore requires repeatedly exercising control over one's actions in the face of cravings. But exercising control is a multistage metacognitive process with a "complex choreography," as he puts it, involving a cyclical procedure of monitoring, attending, reasoning, and revising. These processes are all susceptible to brute error due to noise, indeterminacy, elements of randomness, and the limitations on resources that plague any cognitive system. Hence Sripada's explanation of loss of control answers the question raised by the objection but without invoking anything like diachronic irresistibility. Drug desires may trend toward winning out over time because the cognitive systems necessary for behavioral control are fallible. The more time, the more they must be exercised. The more they must be exercised, the more errors.

The fallibility of the cognitive systems necessary for behavioral control offers a simple explanation of this diachronic trend—but there are alternative (if more complicated) explanations. Consider this quotation from the writer Augusten Burroughs's memoir of alcohol addiction, *This Is How: Surviving What You Think You Can't*:

> What has worked for me is to find something I wanted more than I wanted to drink, which was a fuck of a lot.
>
> This is less a decision than a discovery. And it's for this reason that not everybody will get sober.
>
> My view that the way to stop drinking is to stop drinking is laughably simplistic on the surface. It's "Just say no."
>
> It's also true. The way to stop drinking is to want sobriety more. And then when you feel a craving, feel the craving until it passes. But don't act on it—any more than you wouldn't kill somebody you feel like killing when they cut you off in traffic.
>
> Just because you want something doesn't mean you have to have it.
>
> I know how infuriating that is to hear.
>
> Relapse is the temper tantrum you allow yourself to have when you forbid yourself from drinking.
>
> To stop drinking, you stop drinking. You pour it out right now.
>
> Everything else—all the books, therapies, and programs—are merely hand-holding. They all strive to accomplish the same thing: to talk you into not drinking.
>
> I'm saying, if you want to stop, you will. But most do not want to stop enough to actually stop. And until there's a medical fix, alcoholics will die as drunks.
>
> To be successful at not drinking, a person needs to occupy the space in life drinking once filled with something more rewarding than the comfort and escape of alcohol. This is the thing you have to find.
>
> You might not. Most alcoholics won't.
>
> The truth is that people who cannot stop drinking are people who, however guilty they may feel and however dire the consequences, have become so addicted to the drug and the experience that they prefer it to the remainder of their lives. While they may truly want to be sober, they want to drink more.

The thought that precedes a relapse—certainly in my case and I bet in others as well—is, "screw it." Screw it is an idiom that means, "I no longer care."[5]

I quote Burroughs at length rather than cherry-pick his remarks about craving and relapse both for veracity and for the unusual frankness and starkness of this passage. Note the resonance between what Burroughs says about needing to find something more rewarding than drinking to occupy the space in life it fills, and two recurring themes of this book: the value of drugs and the robust, inverse relationship between drug use and the availability of alternative reinforcers (see chapters 6, 9, 10, 11, and 12). Burroughs does not see cravings as irresistible. Indeed, he counsels to simply let them pass, as you would other wayward pulls or urges. He also does not see relapse as caused by cravings. Rather it is a "temper tantrum" you permit yourself in defiance of a self-imposed prohibition on alcohol. Wanting to drink but not drinking leads to frustration, bitterness, resentment—all emotions that can affect behavioral control by demanding an answer to the question of what exactly the point is of exercising it, thereby chipping away at both the intention and the motivation to do so. You relapse out of anger—in a fury at it all—because you just don't care anymore. *Screw it.*

Loss of control in addiction—loosely defined as using drugs despite either one's better judgment or a sincere intention to abstain (or as using more than one sincerely intended)—is only possible for subjects susceptible to a certain kind of psychological conflict. That is, self-conscious, self-reflective subjects capable of taking metacognitive attitudes toward their mental states: of reflecting on their conception of the good life or the best course of action, all things considered; of forming judgments and intentions in line with this conception; of deciding to resist the pull of desires and urges and whims and emotions that they reject as out of line with it. Although the idea of the will can obscure as much as it clarifies, we might nonetheless put this point by saying that loss of control is only possible for subjects who have a kind of will that they could end up acting against: subjects like us, not like rats. As the philosopher Gary Watson notes: "Since nonhuman animals lack a capacity for critical evaluation, they are not even prima facie candidates for either motivational compulsion or weakness. Addictions may move them contrary to their own good but not contrary to their own conceptions of the good."[6] But, for subjects like us, *explaining why* loss of control occurs—why we act despite our better judgments or sincere intentions—can contribute to solving the puzzle of addiction. We have already considered two ways of explaining loss of control apart from irresistibility of desire: the simple fallibility of the cognitive systems necessary for behavioral control, and the complex attrition of the intention and motivation to exercise behavioral control due to the frustration, bitterness, and resentment that can come from denying oneself what one wants when there is no end in sight and nothing better on the horizon. But there are many more. I shall label these and all other possible explanations of how a person ends up acting against their better judgment or sincere intention *problems of control*. These problems are the topic of chapter 14.

But for now, there are two important points. First, not all cases of human addiction (and no cases of addiction in rats) involve loss of control, thus defined. DSM-5 criteria (1) and (2) may not be met: The drug may not be taken in larger amounts or over a longer period than was intended; there may be no persistent desire or unsuccessful efforts to cut down or control use. Moreover, as we shall see in chapters 10, 11, 12, 13, and 15, many solutions to the puzzle of addiction have nothing to do with loss of control. Second, skepticism about irresistible desires in no way threatens the reality of loss of control in those cases of human addiction where it is indeed present. This is because the supposed irresistibility of desire is only one of a host of possible explanations for why a person might act against their better judgment or sincere intention, as we have already seen in this chapter and as will be seen further in chapter 14.

Compulsion—understood as a desire for drugs of unimaginable and irresistible force—is a myth that must be relinquished. But the myth has tremendous pull. If compulsion was a credible and coherent explanation of drug use in addiction, then in one fell swoop it could solve the puzzle of addiction in both rats and humans, explain loss of control in humans and, in addition, mitigate responsibility for any wrongs associated with drug use in virtue of offering a simple, blanket excuse—people with addiction couldn't help but use drugs. It can be hard not to feel misgivings about the demise of an idea so simple yet so powerful—perhaps especially when the alternative solutions to the puzzle and ways of thinking about responsibility that are articulated in parts III and IV have yet to be presented. What I will say now by way of consolation is simply that, whatever the theoretical elegance of compulsion, I do not believe its demise is anything to lament in reality. Addiction is complicated. People are complicated. Responsibility is complicated. As theoretically appealing as it may be, we should be suspicious of any attempt to do so much with so little—to explain so much of addiction and answer so many serious questions of agency, responsibility, and ethics by appeal to something so simplistic.

The bottom line is that the image of craving as a force of unstoppable strength of which so-called "normal persons"—to again quote Rush and James—can form no conception is dehumanizing. It invites us to see people with addiction—and for them to see themselves—as different, as other, as possessed by an alien force they are incapable of resisting and hence as needing to be controlled. I will return to this theme at the end of part III, especially chapter 15, as well as in part IV. But in the meantime, consider that the complications of agency, responsibility, and ethics are not only burdens on us. They are also part of what binds us together and allows us to relate to one another, as humans.

8

Brain Pathology

IN 1822, *general paresis of the insane* was identified as a distinct disease by the French doctor Antoine Bayle, then working as an intern in a mental asylum.[1] Its symptoms included paranoid, grandiose, and melancholic delusions, as well as disinhibition and confusion—classic psychiatric symptoms. Although originally attributed to bad character, by the early twentieth century its cause was identified: Years or even decades after the original infection, the syphilis bacterium *T. pallidum* can enter the brain. *Neurosyphilis* is diagnosed by extracting and testing cerebrospinal fluid, and it is cured by penicillin. To this day, patients suffering from neurosyphilis can be misdiagnosed with schizophrenia—as many surely were in the past.[2] This is the Holy Grail of biological psychiatry: the discovery of a distinct brain pathology that is the cause of a cluster of personal-level observable signs and experienced symptoms—originally attributed to bad character, no less—and that has a pharmacological cure. The question is: Is anything remotely like this true of addiction?

Before beginning to answer this question, some reminders drawn from the introduction to this book and the preceding chapters.

First, a brain disease label is not an antidote to addiction stigma but at best a "mixed blessing" with a host of complicated effects on public attitudes, research and policy, friends and family, and people with addiction themselves.

Second, these effects—whether good or bad—are entirely irrelevant to the question at hand, which is one of model validity.

Third, the question of whether addiction is a brain disease must be distinguished from the question of whether neuroscience and cognitive science can contribute to an understanding of—or even fully explain, without remainder—the pattern of drug use characteristic of addiction. It should hardly need saying that these sciences illuminate aspects of mind and behavior that are perfectly ordinary. Hence, the promise of a neuroscience or cognitive science of addiction in no way requires addiction to be a brain disease.

Fourth, since drug use in addiction is not well characterized by compulsion, it cannot be a brain disease of compulsion. Insofar as addiction can be considered a brain disease at all, it must be one whose signs and symptoms consist in voluntary behavior. The neuroscientist Kent Berridge puts the point thus: "I also believe this neural and psychological 'disease' remains entirely compatible with the person's own free will and ability to make choices. . . . Addiction doesn't replace choice, it distorts choice." The neuroscientist Markus Heilig and his colleagues argue for a "revised" brain disease model of addiction: "There is a freedom of choice, yet there is a shift of prevailing choices that nevertheless can kill. . . . Addiction is a brain disease in which a person's choice faculties become profoundly compromised."[3] I prefer on the whole to use the word "voluntary" instead of "choice" since I believe the latter risks suggesting a process of principled, conscious deliberation (when no such deliberation need have occurred) and inviting moral condemnation of the choice made (given the existence of addiction stigma). But choice of terminology aside, I take these neuroscientists to be endorsing a nonorthodox version of the brain disease model that rejects compulsion and so is consonant in this respect with the arguments of the previous two chapters.

Fifth, in asking whether anything remotely like neurosyphilis is true of addiction, our question is not whether addiction *is* a brain disease in line with a strong disease model (see chapter 2). The burden of part I was to argue for an explication of addiction as a puzzling pattern of drug *use*—a kind of behavior. This is what addiction *is*. Our question, therefore, is whether there is evidence that the causal hypothesis embodied in the brain disease model is correct. Is addiction—that is, a puzzling pattern of drug use—caused by brain pathology in some or all cases? Any serious attempt to answer this question will have both theoretical and empirical components. Theoretically, we need to clarify what brain pathology is and what counts as establishing causation; empirically, we need to determine whether brain pathology is present in people with addiction and, if it is, whether it causes them to use drugs. This chapter focuses on brain pathology; the next chapter focuses on causation.

Let us begin with a point that is crucial but often unrecognized. Brain-imaging technologies—such as functional magnetic resonance imaging (fMRI) and positron emission tomography (PET) scans—have revealed the existence of brain changes correlated with the development of addiction and brain differences between people who are and people who are not addicted to drugs.[4] But neither brain changes nor brain differences, on their own, are sufficient to justify the claim that there is *pathology* in the brains of people with addiction.

With respect to brain changes: As the neuroscientist Marc Lewis and the journalist Maia Szalavitz—both of whom are recovered from addiction—have emphasized, *all* forms of learning produce brain changes. For example, learning to read or to ride a bicycle changes the brain—as does acquiring knowledge of any response-outcome (R-O) contingency (see chapter 6). So too, we might add, does medication prescribed *to treat* mental disorders, including medication prescribed to treat addiction. But we would never consider any of these brain changes to be pathological. Brain changes do not suffice to establish brain pathology. Hence, the fact that brain changes are correlated with addiction does not show that there is brain pathology in people with addiction.[5]

With respect to brain differences: As Heilig and his colleagues note, the differences that have been observed between people with and without addiction are on the whole nonspecific. In particular, they do not distinguish addiction from other possible mental disorders, and so cannot be used to differentiate or diagnose it.[6] But even if there were brain differences specific to addiction, difference is not the same as disease. This point is now a truism within philosophy of medicine—accepted by orthodox theorists of medicine who argue for biological accounts of disease,[7] as well as by more radical and critical theorists who see it as foundational to theories of disability or disorder as forms of diversity.[8]

Here is the argument for the point. To say **X** is different from **Y** is not yet to say which if either is pathological. To establish this, we need an independent measure of *normality* against which they can each be compared. A standard suggestion is that the measure of normality is species-typicality.[9] What is normal is what is average for the species—accounting for factors considered to be of biological significance, like sex and age. Difference is pathological when it represents deviation from the normal understood as the typical. The problem is that this suggestion falls prey to a vast array of counterexamples. Atypicality is neither necessary nor sufficient for pathology. It is not necessary because some forms of pathology can be close to universal—and so perfectly species-typical—relative to populations or times. For example, consider atherosclerosis or tooth decay in modern societies, infectious diseases during pandemics, or prostate cancer cells in older males. It is not sufficient because many forms of atypicality are not pathological. For example, consider athletic prowess, hyperosmia, left-handedness, type O blood, low resting pulse rate, or low levels of D2 neuronal receptor binding—alongside a great many kinds of physical and neurological diversity. Note that atypicality is insufficient for pathology even if, as with resting pulse rate in relation to psychopathy[10] (or D2 receptor binding in relation to addiction[11]), it is associated with increased risk of a condition that is (or is taken to be) a disease. Risk of disease is not the same as disease—just as being associated with a condition is not the same as being it.[12] The question to ask, when we find either brain changes or differences in a person or a population and wonder if they constitute a brain disease, is whether these changes or differences amount to brain *dysfunction*. Is something *wrong* with the brain? And, to answer this question, we need an account of normal—not just typical—brain function.

We do not currently have an account of normal brain function. The theoretical and empirical challenges to developing one are not insurmountable, but they are nonetheless substantial. Three forms of challenge deserve mention here.

The first challenge is to provide an analysis of the concept of function as it applies to biology and related sciences—as opposed to artifacts which have a function by human design. Within philosophy, there are two classic analyses. The first is due to Larry Wright, who defines functions as effects that explain *why* something exists.[13] Although this definition is highly general, it can be given an evolutionary interpretation: The function of a part, mechanism, or trait is whatever effect explains its existence by contributing through natural selection to the survival and reproduction of the species over its evolutionary history.[14] The second analysis is due to Robert Cummins, who defines functions as effects that explain *how* something contributes to specific capacities of the system containing it.[15] As the philosopher Peter Godfrey-Smith has argued, both analyses do scientific service, albeit with respect to different types of scientific explanation.[16] To see this, consider the claim that the function of the myelin sheaths surrounding nerve cells is to conduct signals efficiently. This may be an explanation of why the myelin is there. Or it may be an explanation of how the brain performs this task. Although the alignment with ordinary uses of *why* and *how* is not precise, I shall nonetheless label these *why-explanations* and *how-explanations*, respectively. Functions understood by appeal to why-explanations are a standard part of evolutionary biology and evolutionary psychology. Functions understood by appeal to how-explanations are a standard part of neurobiology and cognitive science. However, these analyses can diverge: The function of a part, trait, or mechanism that explains why it exists may not be identical to its function within a system. For example, the explanation of why the visual cortex exists is, plausibly, to enable sight. But, as the cognitive neuroscientist Marina Bedny has shown, it is repurposed in congenitally blind people to serve higher-cognitive functions, including language and mathematical reasoning.[17] Is this dysfunctional? Yes, and no. Dysfunction depends on the analysis of function.

The second challenge is epistemological—but also ethical. With respect to either analysis of function, how do we avoid telling what are often called "just-so stories"[18] (that is, hypotheses that may strike us as "making sense" but are wildly under-evidenced if not outright unfalsifiable) in attempting to scientifically establish what something's normal function is? Just as pathological function is not simply atypicality, so too normal function is not simply typicality. We need a substantive and scientifically objective way of identifying what counts—or doesn't—as normal biological function.

This challenge is pressing given that biology is often commandeered in the service of conservative social and political ends. As the philosopher Jonathan Glover has documented in his book *Alien Landscapes,* psychiatry in particular has a long and terrible global history of being deployed as a tool of oppression.[19] To take but one example, consider in this respect the classification of homosexuality as a mental disorder over the history of the *Diagnostic and Statistical Manual of Mental Disorders* (DSM).[20] First published in 1952, the DSM did not waver from this classification until gay rights activists demanded its removal in the 1970s. In response, DSM-III, published in 1980, classified only "ego-dystonic homosexuality" as a mental disorder—a classification that was not fully removed until the publication of DSM-5 in 2013. Ego-dystonic homosexuality is diagnosed by distress at experiencing homosexual desires and/or not experiencing heterosexual desires. In other words, it is diagnosed by distress that homophobic societies create in people who are gay, and which would not exist in the absence of homophobia. Meanwhile, diagnosis with a mental disorder is not only stigmatizing. It also serves to legitimate and facilitate coercive treatment. "Just-so stories" are all too easily made up about what supposedly is and isn't "natural" or "normal" and—once made up—are all too readily used as medical tools to control people who are perceived as transgressive. This is why the need for a substantive and scientifically objective account of normal biological function is ethically pressing.

The third challenge is specific to providing an account of normal function with respect to the mind and the brain. We can study these from at least three perspectives or levels of explanation (as they are often called): the personal, the cognitive, and the neurobiological. These levels are obviously related, but distinct. They typically ask different questions and draw on different disciplines and methods to answer them.

We are all familiar with *the personal level* in virtue of being persons and living our lives as self-conscious, self-reflective subjects who experience a shared world. The personal level is rooted in this collective perspective and the focus of much (although by no means all) of this book. We take our minds to be made of—and much of our behavior to be explained by—psychological states such as thoughts and feelings, beliefs and desires, pleasures and pains, hopes and fears, plans and intentions. And we take ourselves to know our own minds and to understand why we do what we do—not perfectly to be sure, but substantially, nonetheless. As emphasized already (and to be returned to in part III): Attributions of psychological states and their power to explain behavior are specific to individuals and must be contextualized within life circumstances. But these explanations are nonetheless guided by generalizations, expectations, and assumptions that capture common psychological and behavioral patterns—for example, the assumption of self-concern that appears to be flouted in addiction and makes it so puzzling (see chapter 1). Note that the diagnostic criteria for many DSM-5 mental disorders represent violations of these generalizations, expectations, and assumptions. These disorders are personal-level *syndromes*, that is, particular collections of signs (including patterns of behavior) and symptoms (including patterns of psychological states) that are observed in ordinary interpersonal interactions by clinicians or others, and experienced and reported by patients themselves (see chapter 2).

The cognitive level is studied by cognitive and behavioral science, broadly construed. It seeks to explain our minds and behavior by appeal to mental representations and the procedures that operate on them. Many, if not all, of these representations and procedures lie outside of consciousness and so are not part of our lived perspective as self-conscious, self-reflective subjects. The vision scientist David Marr famously distinguished between two kinds of question we can ask at the cognitive level—and one kind of question we can ask at the neurobiological level.[21] The first kind of question is computational. What problem is a given cognitive system solving or what task is it performing? That is, what is it doing—what is it for? The second kind of question is algorithmic. How is the problem solved or the task performed? That is, how is the system doing whatever it is doing or achieving whatever it is for? To use the computing metaphor that has dominated our understanding of minds and brains for decades: The cognitive level is about the software. Mental representations are analogous to data structures; the procedures that operate on them are analogous to algorithms; and the system is designed to solve a specific problem or achieve a specified task. By contrast, and in keeping with this metaphor, *the neurobiological level* is about the hardware. Marr's third kind of question focuses on the workings of the physical system or machine—that is, the brain—that runs or implements the software. The neurobiological level trades in explanations that are more mechanistic. How is the brain physically constructed? What are its constituent parts, what are they made of, and how do they work together to realize both cognitive-level mental representations and operations, and personal-level psychological states?

This characterization of the levels is minimal and crude. It ignores many complexities and controversies. But it is nonetheless sufficient to make the point of relevance here, which is that it is possible that everything is functioning normally at one level but not another. Once again, the levels are related but distinct. On the one hand, neurobiological dysfunction may not manifest at the cognitive level; and neurobiological and cognitive dysfunction may not manifest at the personal level. On the other hand, although the nature of psychological dysfunction is far from clear, there is no question that people can experience psychological and behavioral problems that are distressing and impair their capacity to live well in the absence of any neurobiological or cognitive dysfunction at all. This means that, contra the biological psychiatrist Nancy C. Andreasen and many other advocates of broken brain models of mental disorder, we cannot slide between levels and infer that, because there is something wrong at one level, there is also something wrong at another level.[22]

The sociologist and interdisciplinary scholar of mental disorder Jerome Wakefield has offered a parable to illustrate this general point.[23] Imagine a gosling that has the misfortune of imprinting on a fox rather than its mother. The gosling follows the fox everywhere and is distressed at its absence— species-typical behavior, *given* that it has imprinted on the fox—until it is, all too predictably, eaten. Absolutely nothing is wrong with the gosling's brain at the neurobiological level. It is functioning just as it should. But arguably something has gone wrong at the "personal level" for geese. A gosling who is chasing after a fox is not doing what "normal" goslings do.

Has something gone wrong at the cognitive level—is there dysfunction? Wakefield's own view is that there is. This is because he takes the function of the imprinting system to be the storage of a representation of the gosling's mother, which has failed to occur. But Wakefield does not distinguish the computational and algorithmic dimensions of the cognitive level, nor the idea of function understood by appeal to why-explanations and the idea of function understood by appeal to how-explanations. What happens when we do?

Consider first *why* the imprinting system exists—the effect for which it was naturally selected over goose evolution. There is a well-known problem of indeterminacy in specifying functions thus understood.[24] Wakefield assumes that the why-explanation function of the imprinting system is to store a representation *of* the gosling's mother *because* the effect for which it has been naturally selected is a mother-directed pattern of behavior. But why specify this pattern in relation to the mother, as opposed, for example, to a nurturing object? After all, it is only *because* mother geese are reliably nurturing that it would have been fitness-enhancing over goose evolution for goslings to imprint on them. This matters, because how the why-explanation function is specified affects what counts as dysfunction. If the function of the imprinting system is to store a representation of *the mother goose*, then there is dysfunction when the gosling stores a representation of the fox—or a goose that is not its mother. If the function of the imprinting system is to store a representation of *a nurturing object*, then there is dysfunction when it stores a representation of any animal—fox or goose—that is nonnurturing, but not when it stores a representation of an animal that is nurturing, no matter the species.

Consider next *how* the imprinting system works. The system has some inbuilt parameters. It is not merely that the object imprinted upon is the first object perceived. There must be some low-level specification, however minimal, of the sort of object that can serve as input—for example, constraints on object shape, size, and capacity for movement, say. Let us assume that foxes fall within these parameters. This is why the gosling imprinted on the fox. Hence, just as the gosling's brain is functioning as it should at the neurobiological level, so too it may be functioning as it should, considered in its algorithmic capacity, at the cognitive level. The imprinting system received input about an object that fell within its parameters and which it processed correctly leading to successful storage of a representation of the object—which just happened to be a nonnurturing fox. This is bad luck, not cognitive dysfunction.

Summing up: Whether or not Wakefield's gosling is dysfunctional at the cognitive level depends on how we understand normal cognitive function. If we understand it by appeal to why-explanations, we must solve the problem of indeterminacy in a way that is scientifically credible, not based on "just-so stories." If we understand it by appeal to how-explanations, then it does not seem likely that the gosling's imprinting system is dysfunctional at all. To be sure, the gosling is not behaving as most goslings do—it does not appear "normal." Nor is its behavior conducive to its survival and reproduction. But this may be true and yet nothing is wrong with its brain—either at the neurobiological level or at the cognitive level.

The moral of Wakefield's parable applied to addiction is *the mismatch model*.[25] The mismatch model explains addiction as a mismatch between the ancestral and current environment. The possibility of normal function at one level of explanation but dysfunction at another arises in part because natural selection occurs not in a vacuum but in a specific ancestral environment. To continue with Wakefield's parable: We assume geese to have evolved in an environment where their mothers are reliably nurturing and visible upon hatching. Otherwise, the imprinting system would not exist in the form it does. But it takes some luck in any environment for the system to have the effect it was selected for in the ancestral environment—the conditions are not guaranteed.

Turning now to addiction: As we saw in chapter 1, drug use not only has many benefits but is pervasive across human civilization, dating back millennia. Partly in light of these facts, the evolutionary anthropologists Edward Hagen and Roger Sullivan have argued for what they call *the neurotoxin regulation hypothesis*.[26] Hagen and Sullivan note that many drugs are found in plants. Despite their potential toxicity, these drugs have biological benefits, including medicinal properties, such as defending against pathogens and parasites, and social properties, such as facilitating mating and bonding. They are therefore potentially fitness-enhancing natural rewards, akin to food and sex. Notwithstanding their toxicity, herbivores ingest such plants. Hagen and Sullivan hypothesize that we are like herbivores. They argue that we have evolved biological systems to reap the benefits of drugs while protecting against their costs by careful regulation of intake—particularly during critical periods of fetal and individual brain development. To put this point crudely, they argue that we have evolved to take drugs.

Suppose for the sake of argument that Hagen and Sullivan's hypothesis is correct: We have indeed evolved to take drugs. Nonetheless, we have never before lived in an environment where drugs are so readily available, potent, and able to overcome natural toxin defenses, for example, through hypodermic injections or pills that are swallowed whole—both of which sidestep an evolved aversion to bitter taste, and the former of which also increases speed of delivery to the brain compared to oral ingestion. Even if nothing is wrong with the brains of people with addiction at either the neurobiological level or the cognitive level, something at least appears to be wrong with them at the personal level. This is why there is a puzzle of addiction: People with addiction appear to flout one of the basic, psychological assumptions we make when explaining behavior, namely of *self-concern*, broadly construed (see chapter 1). The mismatch model's explanation for this is simply that, although we may have evolved to take drugs, we have not evolved to deal with the drug availability, potency, and methods of delivery found in our current environment. Hence, according to the mismatch model, the pattern of drug use characteristic of addiction can be explained without recourse to pathology—that is, dysfunction—at either the neurobiological or the cognitive level. The problem is explained by an unfortunate mismatch between a normal, well-functioning brain and the current environment.

A virtue of this model is its capacity to unify drug and behavioral addictions, which display a similar syndrome at the personal level despite the fact that behavioral addictions do not involve ingestion of substances that could directly affect the brain thereby potentially causing brain pathology. The philosopher Don Ross has argued that gambling addiction is the result of a mismatch between our ancestral and current environment. Slot machines have been engineered to exploit normal learning mechanisms to make money for the industry—both literally and metaphorically at the gambler's expense. For example, they exploit the fact that variable reinforcement schedules produce high rates of responding in humans and other animals alike. When a kind of behavior is unpredictably rather than reliably rewarded, subjects tend to persevere. This learning mechanism may have been beneficial in our ancestral environment—but we did not evolve in the company of slot machines.[27]

To draw the discussion of this chapter together: Advocates of the brain disease model tend to locate pathology at the neurobiological level. If there is neurobiological dysfunction in individuals with addiction, then addiction is correlated with brain pathology. But there is no reason to rule out the cognitive level from what is meant by "the brain." There can be bugs in software, just as there can be breakdowns in hardware.[28] If there is cognitive dysfunction in individuals with addiction, then addiction is correlated with brain pathology. I consider cognitive-style solutions to the puzzle of addiction in chapters 13 and 14 where I discuss cognitive differences and problems of control—although I take no view on whether any of these differences and problems count as pathological. In the next chapter, I focus on how we might establish that brain pathology—assuming it is present—is the cause of drug use in addiction. But the conclusion of this chapter is simple if minimal: Establishing that addiction is correlated with brain pathology is a significant undertaking. It may be, but to know that it is we need something we do not currently have. This is a serious account of the nature of normal—not just typical—brain function by which to measure whether brain changes and differences count as brain dysfunction.

9

The Cause

THE QUESTION we are currently considering is whether there is evidence that the causal hypothesis embodied in the brain disease model is correct. Is addiction—that is, a puzzling pattern of drug use—caused by brain pathology in some or all cases? To answer this question, we must therefore do more than establish whether brain pathology is present in people with addiction. We must establish whether it is *the cause* of their drug use.

Despite the reservations of the previous chapter, I assume that there are at least two standout candidates for brain pathology in people with addiction:

1. Reductions in volume of white and gray matter associated with atypical brain activity and found across many classes of drug addiction, and especially advanced alcohol addiction.[1]
2. Neuroadaptations in the mesocorticolimbic dopamine system caused by the direct effect of drugs on extracellular dopamine levels, for example, excessive neural sensitization or hyper-reactivity to drug reward cues,[2] potentially in combination with blunted striatal activations or hypo-reactivity to nondrug reward cues.[3]

With respect to reductions in volume of white and gray matter: Although associated with atypical brain activity, strictly speaking reductions in volume constitute changes and differences in brain structure, not brain function. But, with this nuance noted, I will ignore it in what follows, and simply speak as if reductions in volume of white and gray matter associated with atypical brain activity are dysfunctional and pathological alike.

With respect to neuroadaptations: The crucial questions are how hyper-reactive and hypo-reactive the response to drug and nondrug reward cues respectively is, and whether there is reason to view either response as dysfunctional. Strong neural activation to reward cues is found across drug and behavioral addictions.[4] There are functional magnetic resonance imaging (fMRI) studies comparing response to cocaine, sexual, neutral, and aversive backward-masked cues in cocaine-addicted subjects;[5] choice of images of drugs, food, and neutral objects in active and currently abstinent but previously cocaine-addicted subjects and nonusers;[6] alcohol and neutral images in light and heavy drinkers;[7] alcohol, food, neutral, and aversive images in light and heavy drinkers;[8] alcohol images and anticipated monetary reward in healthy controls and currently abstinent but previously alcohol-addicted subjects;[9] drug and food images in heavy smokers, alcohol-addicted subjects, cocaine-addicted subjects, and nonusers[10]—and no doubt more. There are also positron emission tomography (PET) studies comparing dopamine response to cocaine-cue and neutral videos in cocaine-addicted subjects;[11] choice of images of drugs and pleasant, unpleasant, and aversive objects in methamphetamine-addicted subjects and nonusers[12]—and no doubt more. But there are not yet, to my knowledge, studies either directly comparing dopamine response to drug cues versus dopamine response to meaningful nondrug reward cues in individuals with drug addiction, or directly comparing dopamine response to drug cues in individuals with drug addiction to dopamine response to meaningful nondrug reward cues in nonusers. Drugs can be extremely personally meaningful to people with addiction—as we saw in chapter 4 and shall see again in part III. To establish the extent of hyperreactivity to drug cues and hypo-reactivity to nondrug reward cues, we would need to compare response to drug cues to response to cues that are matched so far as possible in personal meaning—not merely to cues that are aversive, neutral, generic, or minimally rewarding. Meanwhile, to establish whether the extent of hyper-reactivity or hypo-reactivity is in fact dysfunctional, we would need an account of what response is normal, not just typical. Nonetheless, I will proceed on the assumption that, like reductions in volume in white and gray matter, neuroadaptations are dysfunctional and pathological. The question, then, is whether either reductions in volume and/or neuroadaptations are the cause of drug use in some or all cases of addiction.

The answer depends in part on what we mean by and how we operationalize "the cause." Although there are competing analyses and many unresolved issues concerning causation,[13] within experimental science there is nonetheless a relatively standard method used to establish it: intervention. Causes are difference-makers. Suppose we know that there is a correlation between two variables, and we hypothesize that one is the cause of the other. To test this hypothesis, we can design an experiment that, holding all else equal, manipulates the variable hypothesized to be the cause; we then observe whether this manipulation has an effect on the other variable. If so, that is prima facie evidence for the causal hypothesis. If not, that is prima facie evidence against it. Effect size can be taken as an indication of causal significance. Note that talk of "*the* cause" is therefore a misnomer. As causes can be diverse, the phrase must be taken loosely, indicating a cause that is either very significant and/or more significant compared to other variables that are tested—more on which to follow. Interventionist models of causation use this operationalization to provide a nonreductive analysis of what causation is.[14] Given that a range of background conditions are met—the two variables are independent, there is no common cause of both, the intervention does not influence the variable hypothesized as effect otherwise than by influencing the variable hypothesized as cause—something is the cause of an effect if and only if there is a possible intervention on it that changes the effect. But whether or not we adopt an interventionist analysis of causation, we can recognize the importance of intervention as one of the core scientific methods for establishing it.

Imaging studies are typically cross-sectional. They do not establish causation, only correlation. How then would we establish whether reductions in volume and/or neuroadaptations are not merely correlated with addiction but the cause of drug use in addiction? In theory, the simplest test of this hypothesis would be to take two sample groups of individuals with addiction matched for brain pathology, and, holding all else equal, intervene to fix the brains of one group while leaving the other unchanged, while observing the effect on drug use.

In practice, we cannot run this experiment for many reasons, including that we cannot just "fix" the brain. However, we can nonetheless test whether other variables are causes of drug use—and compare effect size. The psychiatrist Kenneth Kendler has argued that alcohol addiction does not fit a strong disease model because of the plurality of causes that occur across many levels of explanation (including but not restricted to the personal, cognitive, and neurobiological levels discussed in the previous chapter), none of which is privileged.[15] According to Kendler, this plurality includes genetic risk, molecular genetic variants, executive deficits, personality traits, childhood sexual abuse, peer substance use, cultural norms, personal expectations surrounding drinking and reasons for drinking, as well as alcohol availability and cost. To this list we might add further specific factors, including those to be explored in part III—self-medication, security-based attachment, self-harm and the desire to die, self-identity, denial and cognitive differences, problems of control, cravings—as well as the factor previously discussed in relation to addiction in both rats and humans in chapter 6, namely the lack of alternative reinforcers to compete with drugs.

Recall that there is a robust, inverse relationship between drug use and the availability of alternative reinforcers,[16] with choice of reward in both species influenced by a range of factors such as relative reward size, delay, cost, and, of course, the consequences associated with the options (for example, punishment).[17] If we manipulate the environment so that it straightforwardly supports a richer array of goods—as therapeutic workplaces do for people, and forced-choice studies do for rats—people and rats will forgo drugs. This includes rats who show behavioral sensitization, a measure involving locomotor hyperactivity when the drug is delivered, and associated with neural changes.[18] Meanwhile, as previously noted, a great many people with addiction (probably a majority, although precise rates are difficult to establish), including those who are physically dependent, "mature out" without clinical intervention as the responsibilities and opportunities of life change (see chapter 6).[19] Kirsten Smith is an addiction scientist who was once addicted to heroin; she twice robbed a bank to fund her habit, ending up in federal prison where she had no access to drugs. She overcame her addiction but, since leaving prison, has used opioids from time to time. Here is Smith, describing her recovery:

> The factors associated with my maintaining control over opioids on the few occasions that I used them since being addicted are too many to count. However, they can be roughly divided into environmental and person-level factors. Environmental factors include living in a home and neighborhood where drugs are neither pervasively used nor readily available: without being surrounded by people who use drugs or try to sell them to me, I would have to invest time and effort to acquire them. I live in a city where they are accessible, but purchasing them from strangers is not simple, safe, or convenient. Such an errand does not fit into my routine. Relatedly, and more importantly, I now have too many things that I *prefer* to give my time and attention to, other than acquiring and using opioids. Since my release, I have had an ever-increasing availability of nondrug choices and ever-increasing opportunity costs associated with use. I am extremely fortunate in this respect. The longer I have been in remission, the more rewarding opportunities (e.g., school, fulfilling career, athletics) have emerged. The more I engaged with these opportunities, the less desirable becoming

addicted again seemed. Life became not only bearable, but good and imbued with meaning. This accrual of access to nondrug rewards is a commonly cited mechanism for a sustained transition away from addiction. However, from discussions with addicted or formerly addicted people, I know that seemingly insurmountable barriers can exist between drug abstinence and access to nondrug rewards. For those people, the barriers can cause anger, hopelessness, resentment, and a return to addiction. My deep gratitude for the opportunities available to me has been another individual-level factor associated with my maintaining control over drug use. I desire to be the version of myself that I always imagined that I could be. I want to make my family proud and myself proud. Not every addicted person is given those kinds of opportunities.[20]

Note the parallels between Smith's testimony and the writer Augusten Burroughs's reflections on relapse, first quoted in chapter 7: "To be successful at not drinking, a person needs to occupy the space in life drinking once filled with something more rewarding than the comfort and escape of alcohol. This is the thing you have to find."[21] Might lack of alternative reinforcers—not brain pathology—be the most significant cause of addiction, at least in some cases, some of the time?

A possible response to this challenge on behalf of the brain disease model is to note that, although the effect of alternative reinforcers on addiction is large, it is not without exception. Even if almost 100 percent of rats choose social reward over drugs—including those who show behavioral sensitization—and even if a great many people "mature out," nonetheless, some don't.[22] Meanwhile, contingency management treatment doesn't work for everyone. A natural suggestion, then, is that it is the presence of brain pathology that makes the difference. Some people do not forgo drugs for alternative reinforcers in contexts where many others do because they—by contrast with the others—suffer from a brain disease.[23]

In theory, we could experimentally test this hypothesis, pitting alternative reinforcers and brain pathology against each other as possible causes. Take two sample groups of individuals with addiction matched in that brain pathology is significantly present and alternative reinforcers are significantly absent, and one control group. Fix the brains of one sample group while leaving their environment unchanged. Fix the environment of the other sample group while leaving their brains unchanged. Compare to the baseline provided by the control group and observe which intervention has the greater effect on drug use.

This, of course, is a simplified example of the kind of complicated experiment routinely designed by scientists to determine causation under real-world constraints.

What would we find if we could do this experiment? It's hard to know. On the one hand, in cases where individuals suffer from brain pathology and impoverished environments, *both* are likely to be causally significant to their addiction. This is Kendler's point about causal pluralism—and why he is inclined to reject a strong disease model of alcohol addiction. Suppose that, in the short term, we found a larger effect in the sample group whose brains were fixed than in the sample groups whose environment was fixed, relative to baseline. Do we really think this difference would last in the long term, without also fixing the environment? People need things to live for—things that make life good and imbue it with meaning, as Smith puts it—to compete with the value of drugs. (Recall again the rats, alone in their barren cages with nothing but cocaine.) On the other hand, the supposition that, at least in the short term, fixing the brain would have a larger effect than fixing the environment is surely not unreasonable—we should be open to it. Suppose this is indeed what we find. Would it vindicate the causal hypothesis embodied in the brain disease model, namely that drug use in addiction is caused by brain pathology? Well, on the assumption that reductions in volume and/or neuroadaptations constitute pathology, and with the understanding that "the cause" does not mean "the only cause" but either a very significant cause or the most significant cause compared to the other variable(s) tested via controlled experiments, and given the proviso that we are talking about a short-term effect, the answer is: Yes it would, *but only in these cases.*

This caveat is crucial. The experiment is only able to pit alternative reinforcers and brain pathology against each other in theory by selecting a subject pool matched in that brain pathology is significantly present and alternative reinforcers are significantly absent in all subjects. Individuals with addiction who do not lack alternative reinforcers or who do not have brain pathology have been excluded from the sample. Indeed, the hypothetical experiment is a response to the challenge to the brain disease model posed by the fact that a great many people with addiction—and let us remember, virtually all rats, including those who show behavioral sensitization—respond to alternative reinforcers, suggesting the problem lies less with their brains than with their environments. In other words, the experiment is designed to test the hypothesis that brain pathology is present only in those people with addiction who do not respond to alternative reinforcers, precisely because, if it is present at all in the great many who do, then it does not appear to be causally significant. Yet the great many people with addiction who respond to alternative reinforcers cannot be discounted—as if they are not *really* addicted—because the cause of their drug use does not appear to be brain pathology. To do so would be *to stipulate* that addiction is a brain disease—to rule out all other hypotheses and models by definition (see chapter 2)—rather than *to vindicate* the causal hypothesis embodied in the brain disease model.

A theory of addiction—never mind an ethics of addiction—must care about determining the relative size of the effects of all possible causes for all people who struggle with it. As the addiction scientist David Epstein rightly remarks in his long-standing advocacy for the heterogeneity of addiction, "the questions are *when, for whom,* and *to what extent*."[24] This is part of why we need a new paradigm. Not because we know that drug use in addiction is never caused by brain pathology—we do not know this. But because, once we have taken seriously that the hypothesis embodied in the brain disease model requires both the presence and the causal significance of brain pathology, we know enough to say that this is highly unlikely to be true in every case of addiction and that there is more work to be done—of both a theoretical and empirical bent—before we could be confident that it is true in any case of addiction. We should be open to the possibility that brain pathology is the cause of drug use in some cases, but we should be clear that the evidence points against it in many others.

A final, cautionary note: To say the brain pathology is the cause of drug use in some cases is not to say that, in these cases, we have thereby solved the puzzle of addiction without remainder. The identification of a cause is not the same as the conferral of understanding: We can discern causes even when we have no idea how or why they are creating an effect. The vision scientist David Marr made this point many decades ago, arguing that neuroscience needs to work in concert with cognitive and behavioral science if it is to deliver results that increase our understanding of how the visual system works.[25] More recent champions of the importance of understanding in science include a group of distinguished neuroscientists led by John Krakauer who complain: "Understanding something is not the same as just describing it or knowing how to intervene to change it. To most it is not news that description is not understanding, but too often in neuroscience causal efficacy is taken as equal to understanding."[26] Applying this general point to addiction: The identification of brain pathology as the cause of a person's drug use is not in itself an explanation of why they are persisting in using drugs despite evident and severe costs and against their own good—it is not yet a solution to the puzzle of addiction.

The orthodox version of the brain disease model provided this explanation by appeal to *compulsion*. Compulsion was what brain pathology was hypothesized to explain: In its crudest form, drugs were supposed to "hijack" the brain, rendering desires for drugs irresistible and eliminating the capacity for voluntary action. But, as we saw in chapters 6 and 7, desires for drugs are not irresistible and drug use remains voluntary in an ordinary sense. It is therefore not possible for the brain disease model to trade on the explanatory power of compulsion. To solve the puzzle of addiction by appeal to brain pathology, the model would need to explain how and why, in the relevant subset of cases, reductions in volume and/or neuroadaptations (for example) cause the flexible, goal-directed pattern of drug use characteristic of addiction. This will require working across levels of explanation, integrating neuroscience with cognitive and behavioral science as well as with first-person reports—a reorientation that the neuroscientist Yael Niv argues for powerfully in her unflinching critique of "neuroscience chauvinism."[27] But the crucial point is that, no matter the level of explanation where a cause is found—neurobiological, cognitive, personal and/or the social, cultural, and economic circumstances in which each person finds themselves and within which they fashion a life—finding a cause does not in itself constitute a theory of addiction, important as it may be in pointing to where we might try to intervene to help a person recover. For we want our theories to do more than serve as pointers. We want them to help us understand.

Where does this leave us? The orthodox version of the brain disease model treats addiction as a brain disease causing compulsive drug use. It is currently the dominant paradigm. This part of the book has argued that:

1. Drug use in addiction is not compulsive.
2. We do not yet have a serious account of normal brain function by which to measure whether the brain changes and differences correlated with addiction are dysfunctional.
3. Granting that some of the brain changes and differences correlated with addiction are dysfunctional and hence that brain pathology can be present in people with addiction, we have strong evidence that, in many cases, either brain pathology is not present, or, if it is present, it is not significant compared with other causes, such as alternative reinforcers.

It is time to shift the paradigm: to recognize and respect the heterogeneity of addiction and to ensure that disciplines and perspectives other than neuroscience—in particular cognitive, behavioral, and social sciences, along-side the first-person perspective of people with addiction themselves—get their due.

I conclude this part with a lingering question. After all this, you might yet be wondering whether addiction is a *disease*. Perhaps I have convinced you that it is not a *brain* disease in line with a strong disease model. But are there no other conceptions of disease that could make for a better fit with the heterogeneity of addiction?

The answer is: *Yes*, there are. In addition to the minimal model introduced in chapter 2, some theorists analyze the concept of disease by appeal to values, as any mental or physical condition that adversely affects well-being;[28] others locate it in relation to medical practice, as any mental or physical condition treated by doctors and allied healthcare professionals;[29] still others argue that it belongs to epidemiology, collecting together conditions that undermine public health and so warrant public health interventions.[30] These analyses all diverge to some extent from ordinary usage. They make no commitment to the pathological status or causal origins of disease. And, between them, they entail that conditions as diverse as aging, hunger, pregnancy, and normal, ordinary suffering—to name but a few processes and states that affect well-being and are of relevance to medicine and/or public health—all count as disease. But ordinary usage need not be the final word. If we think that we have reason to want addiction to be labeled a "disease," then we could so label it. We could explicate a concept of disease to fit this purpose—just as I explicated a concept of addiction in part I to fit a scientific purpose. For example, pulling these various analyses together, we might define "disease" as a mental or physical condition that negatively impacts well-being and is within the remit of medicine and/or public health, broadly construed. Then addiction is a disease—obviously.

The question is whether we have reason to want this—to want addiction to remain a "disease" across a paradigm shift even if it is recognized not to be a brain disease in line with a strong disease model. Do we? Cards on the table: I don't know. As noted in the introduction to this book, labeling addiction a brain disease has been at best a mixed blessing.[31] There have been serious costs to doing so, including the perception of dangerousness and difference that the label creates alongside its negative effects on problem recognition as well as self-efficacy, self-identity, and recovery. I also worry that calling addiction a "disease" may train our gaze on the individual—because if they have a disease, then it is hard to avoid the implication that something is *wrong with them*—thereby deflecting attention from the environmental conditions and life circumstances in which addiction flourishes (see chapters 10, 11, and 12). As the cultural anthropologist Natasha Schüll has documented in her book *Addiction by Design*, the gambling industry has actively used a disease label to deflect attention away from the fact that it deliberately creates machines that hook people in to make money for itself—and to focus attention instead on the personalities and vulnerabilities of the minority of people who have severe problems with gambling.[32] On the other hand, of course, we should remember that the label increases public support for research and treatment for addiction and can have a positive impact on relationships between people with addiction and families, friends, and colleagues (but see chapter 16 for a fuller picture).[33]

How should we balance these pros and cons? And is there any reason to think the answer could ever be stable and universal, as opposed to changing and local? This last question is pressing. I cannot see how to strike a balance apart from considerations such as these:

1. The nature of the problem of addiction that a society is facing at a time—which drugs, which people, how are they getting them, what kinds of interventions might work.
2. The reliability of a society's political and economic commitment to medical care for its members as well as public health and socioeconomic interventions that promote their well-being.
3. Moral attitudes toward drugs and drug users.
4. Social attitudes toward disease and the sick.
5. The extent of the economic interests and political power and influence of a host of industries that potentially stand to profit from casting addiction as a "disease"—for example, the alcohol, tobacco, cannabis, and pharmaceutical industries, and even, alas, some areas of addiction research and treatment—similarly to the gambling industry.

Doubtless there are further considerations. The bottom line is that whether the pros of calling addiction a "disease" outweigh the cons is likely to depend on the ever-changing situation on the ground. You will know the situation where you are better than I. You must decide whether you think that, as part of a paradigm shift, it would be wise to explicate a concept of disease to ensure that addiction is one.

Solving the Puzzle

Introduction to Part III

THE PUZZLE OF ADDICTION is to understand why a person is continuing to use drugs when the costs appear so evident and severe—so profoundly counter to their own good. Had drug use in addiction proved to be compulsive, the puzzle would be solved. But drug use in addiction is not compulsive, so the puzzle is even harder to solve. For the puzzle is now explicitly a puzzle about actions that are, in an ordinary sense, voluntary. Why would anyone keep using drugs in the face of such costs, *when they don't have to*? Whatever value drugs may have had looks to be lost. So why persist—why not just quit?

Voluntary actions are flexible and goal directed. They are guided by representations of their expected outcome—that is, by the value the agent takes them to have—and explained by beliefs and desires. Meanwhile, the puzzle of addiction is a puzzle of appearances. It arises when we, as observers, can't make sense of a person's drug use because of the lack of value that—given the costs to them—we take their drug use to have. We can therefore think of the puzzle as embodying a clash of appearances: a clash between how drug use appears to the agent and how it appears to observers. Thus understood, there are two schematic approaches to solving the puzzle.

The first schematic approach focuses on how the benefits of drug use are hidden while the costs are salient *from the perspective of observers*—particularly those observers who may have limited familiarity with the life circumstances in which addiction flourishes and the psychological mindset that some people with addiction have. This form of solution involves coming to understand *the value* of drugs for people with addiction—a value that may be hidden from us, as observers.

The second schematic approach focuses on how the costs of drug use may be hidden while the benefits are salient *from the perspective of people with addiction themselves*. This form of solution involves coming to understand what a person struggling with addiction is failing to see—and why they are failing to see it—despite its obviousness to us, as observers. Why do people with addiction appear so blind to costs—almost as if they are deliberately squinting their eyes when they look at the role of drugs in their lives?

Chapters 10, 11, and 12 offer examples of the first schematic approach; chapters 13 and 14 offer examples of the second.

Chapter 10 is about the self-medication hypothesis. At its core, this is the idea that people with addiction use drugs to "medicate" negative psychological states—that is, to help them cope with them. Although anyone can use drugs to self-medicate, the self-medication hypothesis is a particularly powerful explanation of the puzzle of addiction for people who come from backgrounds of severe adversity and limited socioeconomic opportunities and suffer from mental health problems in addition to addiction. This is because of the extraordinary power of drugs to relieve misery and suffering when no alternative means are available and there is little hope. In such cases, despite using drugs in ways that are profoundly counter to their own good, people may not be failing to act out of self-concern *given the options*. Chapter 10 also explores how self-medication can create a form of security-based attachment to drugs, making it all the more painful and unmooring to quit.

Chapter 11 is about deliberate self-harm and the desire to die, as well as the gray zone between them. Self-harm is a diagnostic criterion for borderline personality disorder (BPD). I distinguish two possible motives: self-medication versus a desire to self-harm as an end in itself. I then explore the possible origins of such a desire by reflecting on another diagnostic criterion for borderline personality disorder—a sense of the self as empty, bad, and worthless—as well as the human propensity to reenact past trauma, first theorized by the father of psychoanalysis, Sigmund Freud. The chapter then applies this framework to addiction to argue that, in some cases, people with addiction have a self-harming mindset or may be using their addiction as a way to die. As this brief description indicates, the chapter is about a part of human psychology that is hard to look in the eye and talk honestly about. It is not easy reading.

Chapter 12 is about the power of an "addict" identity to solve the puzzle. *Addict* is a social kind that embodies group-specific norms prescribing what "addicts" are supposed to be like. When we identify as a member of a social kind, we tend to self-regulate to abide by its group-specific norms—especially if this identity is a source of value for us. Think, for example, of identifying as a father, a fashionista, a feminist. After presenting this theoretical framework, chapter 12 explores five reasons why an "addict" identity can be a source of value, thereby motivating people to abide by its norms. These include:

1. Social reward, belonging to a community and meaningful relationships.
2. Social cachet, or "coolness."
3. Daily structure and purpose, a way of filling time.
4. Grounds for self-worth.
5. An anchor for a sense of self when otherwise there would be only emptiness within.

I argue that for some people, without an "addict" identity they would not know *who they would be*. This imaginative obstacle means that quitting represents an existential threat, rendering utterly comprehensible why a person might choose to continue to be an addict rather than face it. Chapter 12 concludes by considering how people can be helped (and hindered) to overcome this obstacle and imagine and enact a new identity.

Chapter 13 switches to the second schematic approach. It is about denial, a notorious part of addiction lore. Given that people can be in denial that their drug use is the cause of severe costs, denial solves the puzzle of addiction straightforwardly by producing a state akin to ignorance. If you don't know your drug use is a problem, you have no reason to quit. I describe the nature of denial as a psychological defense mechanism, consider the various kinds of strategies that people with addiction may use to deny they have a drug problem, and explore some potential means and models of denial, ranging from epistemically nonideal and motivated belief formation processes, to outright self-deception. The chapter concludes with a brief discussion of findings that suggest that, rather than being prone to denial, some people with addiction may have cognitive difficulties that impede the acquisition of knowledge of the outcomes of their actions (that is, response-outcome [R-O] contingencies, if you hark back to chapter 6).

Chapter 14 is about what explains loss of control in addiction, loosely defined as using drugs despite either one's better judgment or a sincere intention to abstain (or as using more than one sincerely intended). Not all people with addiction experience a loss of control, and no cases of loss of control are explained by irresistible desire. But there is nonetheless a sweeping catalog of explanations of loss of control that I label *problems of control*. The catalog includes:

1. The fallibility of the cognitive systems necessary for behavioral control and the emotional attrition of the intention and motivation to exercise it (see also chapter 7).
2. Shifts in judgments and intentions.
3. Induction and low self-efficacy.
4. Local versus global bookkeeping.
5. Mechanisms by which lapses end up as relapses.
6. Difficulties forming judgments and intentions in a manner that is standing and sincere rather than fleeting and fickle—or indeed forming them at all.
7. Ambivalence.

Chapter 14 is a whirlwind tour of decades of research in cognitive science and behavioral economics about human decision-making in general—and as applicable to addiction in particular—simplified and synthesized to reveal how the mind can be tricked into weighing costs and benefits such that drugs always seem to come up trumps.

Chapter 15 exemplifies neither schematic approach. Rather, with the necessary groundwork laid, it makes good on the promise in chapter 5 to address the nature and role of cravings for drugs in addiction. The chapter starts by mapping the landscape of desire, to identify which desires are cravings. To preview, *cravings for drugs* are occurrent, present-directed, appetitive desires to use drugs. It then proceeds to delineate three varieties of craving that I call cue induced, goal focused, and attachment based, each of which corresponds to an answer to the question of *why* people crave drugs. Like solutions to the puzzle, cravings are themselves heterogeneous. I conclude by considering how we might expand our strategies to help people manage their cravings—strategies that, as things stand, are all too often ineffective and controlling.

Both schematic approaches to solving the puzzle require that we take up the perspective of the person with addiction—to listen to what they say and imagine what it would be like to live as they live, see what they see, think as they think. Some of the solutions I canvas are compatible with each other. For example, a person may use drugs to self-medicate sometimes, to self-harm other times, and as part of an "addict" identity. But some are incompatible. For example, no one who is in deep denial that they have a drug problem can embrace an "addict" identity, on pain of not being in deep denial after all. When solutions are compatible, drug cravings may embody multiple dimensions of a person's addiction.

Despite the breadth of the solutions I consider in this part, it is curated. Just as many of the solutions are not exclusive of each other, so too they are not exhaustive of all possible solutions. I have also omitted an ocean of further considerations that could have been included. This is particularly true of the wealth of information about brain regions, states, and circuits that neuroimaging has demonstrated to be associated with some of the psychological states and processes relevant to the solutions that I do consider; and of the details of computational models that have been proposed to fit relevant behavioral data. Integration of findings from neuroscience and cognitive and behavioral science with psychology and a more first-person perspective is necessary for a full picture of the mind and how it works—whether that mind is addicted or not—a point already made, albeit briefly, both in the introduction to the book and at the end of chapter 9. But what I believe to be currently missing from our understanding of addiction is a solid grasp of the myriad ways it can be straightforwardly psychologically explained—whatever brain regions, states, and circuits ultimately prove to underlie the psychological states and process that are doing the explaining, and whatever computational models best fit whatever behavioral data we collect. This is what I hope to achieve in this part. *Psychology first.*

10

Self-Medication

OVER A SERIES of publications in the 1980s and 1990s, the psychoanalytic psychiatrist Edward Khantzian formulated a general theory of addiction called *the self-medication hypothesis.*[1] As with any specific theory, the details of Khantzian's can be criticized.[2] But the theory is based on a fact that is incontrovertible—and familiar to many of us from our own experience. You do not need to be addicted to know that drugs provide relief from negative psychological states, such as pain, exhaustion, stress, insomnia, boredom, loneliness, and intense negative emotions—really all forms of misery and suffering. Details aside, the core of the self-medication hypothesis is the idea that people with addiction use drugs to "medicate" negative psychological states— that is, to cope with them.

Over twenty-five hundred years ago, Homer wrote of opium that it serves "to lull all pain and anger and bring forgetfulness of every sorrow."[3] In her memoir, the journalist and writer Caroline Knapp writes of "booze: the liquid security blanket; the substance that muffles emptiness and anger like a cold snow."[4] Knapp proceeds to describe her active addiction thus: *"Fill it up, fill it up, fill it up. Fill up the emptiness; fill up what feels like a pit of loneliness and terror and rage; please, just take it away, now."*[5] Meanwhile here is how she describes her recovery: "Anxiety looms and you think: *This is why I drank.* Sadness and shame wash up. *This is why I drank.* Feelings of rage surface. *This is why I drank.*"[6] After her mother's early death, the writer Cheryl Strayed says of heroin: "Heroin was different. I loved it. It was the first thing that worked. It took away every scrap of hurt that I had inside of me."[7] Finally, consider how the novelist Barbara Kingsolver puts words in the mouth of her protagonist, Demon Copperhead—a young man living in poverty in Appalachia, who never knew his father, loses his mother to an overdose, and then becomes addicted to opioids himself after an accident destroys his ability to play football and with it his chance to escape from his life circumstances. Though a fictional character, Demon speaks to the point eloquently:

> If you've not known the dragon we were chasing, words may not help. People talk of getting high, this blast you get, not so much what you feel as what you don't; the sadness and dread in your gut, all the people that judged you useless. The pain of an exploded leg. This tether that's meant to attach you to something all your life, be it home or parents or safety, has been flailing around unfastened all this time, tearing at your brain's roots, whipping around so hard it might take out an eye. All at once, that tether goes still on the floor, and you're at rest.[8]

Can self-medication explain why people persist in using drugs despite costs that make it profoundly counter to their own good? *Yes*, it can, at least in some cases and some circumstances.

Recall the core of the epidemiological finding previously discussed in chapters 6 and 9: A great many people who meet criteria for a substance use disorder "mature out," that is, they recover without clinical intervention, by their late twenties or early thirties as the responsibilities and opportunities of life change.[9] This raises an important question: Who doesn't? In the broadest possible terms, the answer is: People like Kingsolver's protagonist, Demon Copperhead, who come from backgrounds of severe adversity and limited socioeconomic opportunities[10] and suffer from mental health problems in addition to addiction[11]—for example, problems with anxiety, depression, paranoia, flashbacks, intrusive thoughts. This raises a further important question: Why are these life circumstances associated with addiction chronicity and severity? The answer is unsurprising: self-medication. As the psychologist Lee Hogarth has demonstrated, the association between these life circumstances and addiction is mediated by use of drugs as a coping strategy as measured by self-report.[12] For vulnerable groups of people, the more they say they use drugs to cope, the more likely their addiction is severe.

What does this mean, if we try to make concrete its academic-sounding labels, translating from abstract language into plainer, more ordinary terms?

A background of severe adversity. The anxiety of poverty. The threat and reality of hunger and homelessness. How are you going to eat? Where will you sleep? Do you have a place to live? The threat and reality of violence—when might it come? Where are you safe? Stress. Exhaustion. The shame of having to ask for help and not getting it. The anger and humiliation of discrimination based on your class, race, age, sex, sexual orientation, gender identification, religion, ethnicity, national background. The disrespect. The sense of being shunned—the ostracization and isolation. Loneliness. Trauma as an adult. Trauma from childhood. Memories that are like raw wounds. Emotional abuse. Emotional and physical neglect. Physical abuse. Sexual abuse. Rape. Parents who struggle with mental health problems. Parents who struggle with addiction. Domestic violence. Broken families. Family deaths. Disease. Being taken into care. Bullying. Migration. War.

Limited socioeconomic opportunities. Schools that are failing their students. Students who are dropping out of failing schools. Barriers to returning to education and employment: no diploma, a criminal record, no money for college or skills training. No meaningful work to be found. No work at all to be found. Boredom. Purposelessness. More humiliation. Once again, discrimination based on your class, race, age, sex, sexual orientation, gender identification, religion, ethnicity, national background. More disrespect. Insufficient and unreliable government aid at best. Sometimes no government aid at all. Powerlessness. All of which means: No realistic hope for changing your circumstances—for forging a better life.

Suffering from mental health problems. Anxiety, fear, and paranoia. Depression and despair. Desperation. Rage at the world. Rage at yourself. Flashbacks. Intrusive, self-critical thoughts. Feelings of self-hate. Feelings of chaos. Feelings of shame. Desires to self-harm. Desires to die. Treatment? Probably not, if you are living in conditions of severe adversity and limited socioeconomic opportunities.[13]

Perhaps you have some experience of what it is like to live in such circumstances. If not, try to imagine what it would be like if you did. Imagine that you come from a background of severe adversity and limited socioeconomic opportunities and that your mental health is poor. You see no realistic hope that anything in your life will change, that anyone will help, that you will get any treatment. But drugs you can get. And they will take away the misery and the suffering—they will give you some comfort, some ease, perhaps even a moment, however brief, of joy. This is the human analog of being alone in a cage with nothing but cocaine. I ask again: What would you do?

Self-medication can explain the puzzle of addiction because, in life circumstances such as these, it is possible that life is better with drugs than without. This may be so no matter that addiction creates its own misery and suffering, and that a life of addiction is a bad life—profoundly counter to what is good for a person. As noted in chapter 1, sometimes the best option is a truly terrible option. If this is so, then a person who takes the best but truly terrible option—who persists in using drugs despite costs both evident and severe—is not failing to be guided by a concern for their own good in so persisting. There is no puzzle about why they are failing to act out of self-concern, for, *given the options*, they are not. Rather, understanding why they are using drugs requires that we recognize what it is it like to live in such circumstances—something that observers with limited familiarity with such circumstances may not immediately see.

This solution to the puzzle rests on three elements.

First, the degree of misery and suffering that people can live with for months, years, decades—its intensity, its complexity, the way it is rooted in socioeconomic conditions but branches out into a person's psychology, shaping their worldview, their values, their sense of self. This is a theme I first touched on in chapter 4 and have returned to repeatedly; the following two chapters continue it.

Second, the hopelessness. What makes it the case that, despite the costs, life is better with drugs than without? Suppose that you are a person who is addicted to drugs and uses them to self-medicate—and you are contemplating whether to quit. If you quit, then to be sure, you avoid the costs of drug use. But you also no longer get its benefits: the relief from misery and suffering. Suppose that the costs of drug use, *in the here and now*, do not outweigh the value of relief. Nonetheless, it could still be that, on balance, you have reason to quit. This would be so if there were benefits available to you *in the future* if you quit—that is, benefits that come over time, from abstinence. For many people who do not live in life circumstances such as those we are considering, this is indeed the case. But if your socioeconomic opportunities are limited, then it is quite possible that this is not the case. Quitting may make no material difference to your prospects in life. Education, employment, social standing, state aid and treatment for additional mental health problems will not suddenly materialize if you give up drugs. Nor—as is the case with everyone who uses drugs, irrespective of socioeconomic status—will relationships lost to drugs necessarily heal. In consequence, if you quit, and go through the pain of living without the relief you get from drugs, there may be few if any countervailing benefits on the horizon. Limited socioeconomic opportunities translate into limited reasons to quit, given the value of drugs as a way of coping with severe adversity compounded by poor mental health. To put it plainly: It is only worth suffering in the present if there is a genuine chance of payoff sometime in the future.

To be clear, the point I am making is not that *time discounting* can help explain the puzzle of addiction. Time discounting is well documented in humans and other animals. Its relevance to addiction has been widely studied; I discuss it further in chapter 14. But the basic idea is simple and intuitive. When selecting between rewards, we tend to value rewards that are delivered immediately compared to rewards that are delayed, holding all else equal.[14] Consider being presented with either of two sets of options:

Set A	Set B
Option 1: $100 now	Option 3: $100 in 30 days
Option 2: $110 tomorrow	Option 4: $110 in 31 days

Most people choose Option 1 if presented with Set A and Option 4 if presented with Set B. Yet in both sets, only one day's wait would make for a $10 increase in reward. What then is the difference between them? Only in Set A is a reward available immediately. Immediacy functions like a bonus, tempting us to choose what, apart from their immediacy, are *smaller, sooner* (SS) rewards over *larger, later* (LL) rewards.

Time discounting can help explain the puzzle of addiction. Consider how most drug rewards are immediate while drug costs are delayed. Meanwhile, abstinence brings immediate costs—at a minimum, the loss of the rewards of taking drugs—while its rewards are typically delayed. Let us stipulate that, without regard to time, the reward of using drugs now is V and the reward of abstinence in the future is $2 \times V$. Then the choice to use drugs rather than reap the reward of abstinence is a choice of an SS reward over an LL reward. Why would anyone make this choice? One explanation is the bonus of immediacy. But any appeal to time discounting to explain the puzzle assumes that abstinence comes with a payoff that—were immediacy not a bonus—could at least compete with, and possibly plainly outweigh, the reward of drugs. That is precisely the assumption I am suggesting may not hold in at least some cases of people with addiction who come from backgrounds of severe adversity and limited socioeconomic opportunity and whose predicament is compounded by poor mental health. To put this as bluntly as possible, if these are your life circumstances, there may be no real chance of a payoff from quitting, *ever*. Quitting is a net loss, not a net gain, no matter how far into the future you look. By way of illustration, consider the following first-person report from a subject interviewed by the philosopher and qualitative researcher Anke Snoek: "I'm totally unemployable. I'm over the hill, got no references, no appreciable skills, patchy work history at best, . . . I mean [participating in treatment] is not the answer to all my problems. Recovery is not going to make my problems go away."[15]

The third and final element on which self-medication as a solution to the puzzle rests is the extraordinary power of drugs to relieve misery and suffering.

In her telling of Demon Copperhead's story, Kingsolver writes of the tether that attaches us to something—be it home, parents, safety—flailing unfastened, whipping you. The dragon stills it, all at once, and you're finally at rest. Here is a story of my own. I have two daughters. When they were little, I used to cycle them to nursery school on the back of my bicycle. One morning a car drove straight into us. My shoulder was shattered. My bike was destroyed. By some miracle, both girls escaped from the crash uninjured. But as I fell from my bike to the ground, I did not yet know that against all odds, they were in fact safe. During that fall, time slowed down. It seemed to take an eternity to hit the pavement, and in that eternity a crack opened in my life. I felt the overwhelming terror and grief of the world where they were dead. Half an hour later, I was alone in an ambulance. Even though I knew my daughters were safe, the world where they were dead would not stop pressing down on my mind. Then I was given a large injection of morphine for the pain of my shoulder. I have been given morphine in medical contexts on other occasions for physical pain; and I have had a drink or two too many at home, when life was hard and I felt utterly overwhelmed. But on no other occasion has my experience of any drug been anything like it was in that ambulance. The morphine took away all my terror and grief. The possibility of the world where my daughters were dead was gone from my mind, like a mistake, a mirage—its disappearance was bliss. The experience also taught me something that—despite my clinical work and study of addiction—I did not know: just how powerful drugs can be when you truly need them. And it forced me to ask myself a variant of the question that I have repeatedly asked you about being alone in a cage with cocaine: What would I do, if I was living in the world where my daughters had died in the accident? In that world, what would my relationship with drugs be?

The philosopher Monique Wonderly has used attachment theory to illuminate the relationship that people with addiction can have to drugs.[16] Attachment theory emphasizes how the special bond that children have with their primary caregivers provides them with a sense of security.[17] This *security-based attachment*, as Wonderly calls it, is crucial to healthy child development. In its essence, the idea is that children rely on their relationships with primary caregivers for a sense of safety. They need them to be physically and emotionally present, connected, and available, in order to feel at ease; the absence of primary caregivers can therefore create deep emotional distress. Importantly, the objects of security-based attachment are not substitutable.[18] Of course, in their distress, children can sometimes be soothed (or alternatively just distracted from their feelings) by other people or things. But the bond to primary caregivers who are the objects of security-based attachment is special because it is experienced as unique. This creates a need for the attachment objects *themselves*—a dependence on *them*, over and above the need for the function they perform to be fulfilled in some way or other. There is no substitution without significant loss. Attachment theory has been productively extended from classic caregiving to other kinds of relationships, especially romantic.[19] Wonderly argues that security-based attachment also characterizes some of our relationships to ideas and objects—and in particular, for some people with addiction, their relationship to drugs. Note that the fundamental reason why this is possible is that drugs have the ability to provide a sense of safety—to soothe, to still, to make things better—in the face of deep emotional distress. Over time, this function translates into a security-based attachment relationship, where drugs themselves are experienced as unique and therefore as uniquely needed.

Wonderly's analysis is true to how some people with addiction describe their relationship with drugs. Knapp titles her memoir *Drinking: A Love Story* and opens it thus: "It happened this way: I fell in love and then, because the love was ruining everything I cared about, I had to fall out."[20] She continues: "By the end it was the single most important relationship in my life."[21] After explaining how her love of heroin stems from its ability to take away every scrap of hurt, Strayed comments: "When I think of heroin now, it is like remembering a person I met and loved intensely. A person I know I must live without."[22] In her book *Unbroken Brain*, the journalist Maia Szalavitz writes that quitting drugs makes her feel "utterly stripped of safety and love" and that "what tormented me most as I shook through August of 1988 wasn't the nausea and the chills but the recurring fear that I'd never have lasting comfort or joy again."[23] Such testimony speaks to a kind of dependence on drugs that is emotional and relational—going far beyond mere physical dependence.[24] People with addiction can feel that drugs are irreplaceable—like a person you love—and so absolutely necessary in order to feel secure in themselves and in the world.

Although Knapp, Strayed, and Szalavitz all suffered deeply at various points in their lives, they do not come from backgrounds of severe adversity. Nor do they face limited socioeconomic opportunities. Indeed, they are all accomplished writers. All too evidently, self-medication and any attachment to drugs that results are not confined to people facing the life circumstances we have been considering in this chapter. For people who do not face these life circumstances, self-medication and attachment typically explain why a person is persisting in using drugs in combination with other factors. In Strayed's case, an additional factor may be her desire to self-harm; this is the topic of the next chapter. In Knapp's case, an additional factor is most certainly denial; this is the topic of chapter 13. In Szalavitz's case, an additional factor may be problems of self-control; this is the topic of chapter 14. I shall return repeatedly to the importance of self-medication, security-based attachment, and emotions throughout the chapters constituting this part. In the meantime, however, note that all three of Knapp, Strayed, and Szalavitz *recovered* despite using drugs to self-medicate and, by their own accounts, developing a strong attachment to them.

Just as the absence of alternative reinforcers creates and entrenches addiction, the presence of alternative reinforcers—for example, the possibility of a successful career as a writer—enables and sustains recovery. Recall the writer Augusten Burroughs's and the addiction scientist Kirsten Smith's testimony to this point, quoted in chapters 7 and 9 respectively. People need "a stake in conventional life": education, employment, housing, health, family, friends, lovers, community, belonging, respect, purpose, hope, self-worth, a sense of life's promise and possibility—the things that give life meaning and weigh heavily in the balance as a counter to the value of drugs. Yet all too often, these ordinary, crucial needs are not what we talk about what we talk about addiction.

11

Self-Harm

THE PROTOTYPE OF SELF-HARM is self-directed violence. Common examples include cutting, scratching, or burning one's skin; smashing parts of one's body with weapons or banging them against walls; swallowing blades or sharp glass, or inserting these under the skin or in orifices; ingesting poisons or overdosing on drugs or prescribed medications; tying ligatures around one's neck; hanging oneself; shooting oneself; throwing one's body under trains, into oncoming traffic, or off bridges and buildings. As these examples reveal, self-harm bleeds into suicide. These can be distinguished in principle via intent: to harm oneself, or to die. In reality, however, people can be ambivalent or unsure what they intend, indifferent to outcome, and reckless in method, so that self-harm knowingly risks and possibly even welcomes death, even if it does not directly aim at it.

Before I started working clinically with people with personality disorder and complex needs in 2007, to my knowledge no one I knew well self-harmed, and I had no understanding of why anyone would. Since then, the prevalence of self-harm has increased, especially among young people, and there is greater public awareness.[1] But it is painfully hard to think about, and we still do not talk about the psychology of self-harm—or suicide—often or seriously enough. Self-harm is an ordinary aspect of human psychology. That is, a common and wholly intelligible response to what it can mean to live in some of the circumstances described in the previous chapter—to live really with any form of misery and suffering. This chapter aims to start us talking. I hope to render the desire to self-harm—and the willingness to risk or welcome death—psychologically intelligible and to show how it can be a part of addiction and a solution to the puzzle.

Many people desire to self-harm who are not diagnosed with personality disorder. But "self-mutilating" behavior is one of the most common of the nine

Diagnostic and Statistical Manual of Mental Disorders (DSM-5) criteria for borderline personality disorder (BPD). Borderline personality disorder is characterized as "a pervasive pattern of instability of interpersonal relationships,
self-image, and affects, and marked impulsivity."[2] Here are the criteria, at least
five of which must be present to meet the threshold for diagnosis:

1. Frantic efforts to avoid real or imagined abandonment.
2. A pattern of unstable and intense interpersonal relationships characterized
   by alternating between extremes of idealization and devaluation.
3. Identity disturbance: markedly and persistently unstable self-image or
   sense of self.
4. Impulsivity in at least two areas that are potentially self-damaging (e.g.,
   spending, sex, substance abuse, reckless driving, binge eating).
5. Recurrent suicidal behavior, gestures, or threats, or self-mutilating
   behavior.
6. Affective instability due to a marked reactivity of mood (e.g., intense
   episodic dysphoria, irritability, or anxiety usually lasting a few hours and
   only rarely more than a few days).
7. Chronic feelings of emptiness.
8. Inappropriate, intense anger or difficulty controlling anger (e.g., fre-
   quent displays of temper, constant anger, recurrent physical fights).
9. Transient, stress-related paranoid ideation or severe dissociative
   symptoms.

DSM-5 lists the criteria used to diagnose a mental disorder as if they are
independent of each other. But as anyone familiar with any disorder will know,
they are inevitably interconnected, forming clusters of symptoms that cohere.
For example, recall how in chapter 5 I described a process by which the
provision of housing, a reliable and safe drug supply, and health care to a person with a substance use disorder could come to mean that they no longer met
criteria 5–9 (social impairment and risky use); but then, because criteria 5–9
were not met, criteria 1–4 (impaired control) might come to abate, since in
absence of criteria 5–9, the person no longer has the same reasons to try not
to use, nor, with a reliable and safe supply, urges to use. For borderline personality disorder, a salient, cohering cluster of symptoms is the use of self-
damaging and self-mutilating behavior as a way of coping with the negative
psychological states embodied in other criteria, such as fear of abandonment,
intense dysphoria, anxiety, anger, paranoia, dissociative states, and more. In

this light, consider this anonymous description of what it is like to live with borderline personality disorder:

> Being a borderline feels like eternal hell. Nothing less. Pain, anger, confusion, hurt, never knowing how I'm gonna feel from one minute to the next. Hurting because I hurt those who I love. Feeling misunderstood. Analyzing everything. Nothing gives me pleasure. Once in a great while I will be "too happy" and then anxious because of that. Then I self-medicate with alcohol. Then I physically hurt myself. Then I feel guilty because of that. Shame. Wanting to die but not being able to kill myself because I'd feel too much guilt for those I'd hurt, and then feeling angry about that so I cut myself or O.D. to make all the feelings go away. Stress![3]

Note the self-reported use of both alcohol and cutting or overdosing to self-medicate the cascade of negative psychological states—as well as the creation of a self-perpetuating cycle. On the one hand, like drugs, self-harm can be a coping strategy. Self-harm offers immediate relief from misery and suffering by distracting from emotional pain and replacing it with physical pain—thereby also releasing endorphins, an endogenous chemical potentially providing relief over and above mere distraction. It also offers respite from the dysphoric emotional numbness of dissociative states by making people feel *something*.[4] On the other hand, and again like drugs, self-harm can create a self-perpetuating cycle. People may use drugs or self-harm to cope in the short term with negative psychological states; but drugs and self-harm themselves cause negative psychological states in the long term—such as guilt, shame, and the experience of drug-associated or self-harm-associated costs—leading to further drug use or self-harm to cope with these further negative psychological states.

When self-harm is used as self-medication, it is a means to ends that are perfectly intelligible—relief from misery and suffering—and can be consistent with a concern for one's own good. How? Recall from the previous chapter how drug use may be truly terrible for a person—yet the best option realistically available under the circumstances. This can be equally true of self-harm. Although more mundane examples can make the point, here is one that cannot but make it vivid: Imagine that a person with borderline personality disorder is put in prison—they are in effect alone in a cage—thereby intensifying the onslaught of negative psychological states while removing all other possible means of coping with them, leaving only self-harm. In a case like this, a person may deliberately self-harm *despite* the costs of doing so—namely the damage to the body and the psyche—just the way people may use drugs despite the costs when facing life circumstances of severe adversity, limited socioeconomic opportunities, and poor mental health. This is because self-harm may be the only means of getting any emotional relief for a person with borderline personality disorder who is in prison—just as drugs may be when facing these life circumstances. It is the best of the realistically available options: self-harm or suffer without any relief. If so, then there is no puzzle about why such a person is failing to act out of self-concern. For, despite the fact that they are deliberately self-harming, *given the options*, they aren't.

But people can also self-harm *because* of the costs. That is, what is driving them is not a desire for relief from misery and suffering, but, broadly speaking, a desire to self-inflict it. In which case, self-harm is not a means to ends that are consistent with a concern for one's own good. Its point is precisely to undermine one's own good—to harm oneself, to incur the basic cost of self-directed violence, namely damage to the body and psyche, perhaps even risking or welcoming death.

Suppose a person with addiction occupies what I shall call a *self-harming mindset*. The evident and severe costs of drug use function, in effect, like benefits. They willingly embrace them. In a case like this, there is a simple explanation for why this person is persisting in using drugs despite costs and against their own good. The explanation is that this is what they mean to be doing. They are deliberately *not* acting out of self-concern, but in opposition to it. They want to harm themself—to undermine their own good—and drug use is a means to that end. The deeper question, then, is why a person would occupy this mindset. Why would anyone want to harm themself, as an end in itself?

For many people, the answer begins with their sense of self. The diagnostic criteria for borderline personality disorder include identity disturbance as well as chronic feelings of inner emptiness. These are established in a clinical interview by asking whether a person's sense of who they are and where they are headed has ever suddenly changed and if they often feel empty inside. In my experience, these criteria are nearly always met. The people I worked with who had borderline personality disorder almost all felt like this—as if they were flailing, untethered, desperately trying to construct a sense of self when all there was inside of them was a dark and terrible void. As this language suggests, the emptiness is not neutral, a mere absence. According to DSM-5, it involves feeling as if one is at core *bad*, or even worse, *evil*.[5] The writer Tracy Barker begins her memoir *A Sad and Sorry State of Disorder: A Journey into Borderline Personality Disorder (and Out the Other Side)* by stating her core belief: *"who I am is wrong."*[6] Here is a selection of her poetry and prose, describing the emptiness:

MIRROR, MIRROR

My eyes are not deceived
Truly, this is what I see.

> A monster;
> Seething, clutching
> At chances long expired.
> A beast;
> Heaving, drooling,
> Insatiable and wild.
> An animal,
> Untethered.
> Wiley, swift and sly.
> An alien;
> Abnormal, strange,
> Come to bleed you dry.

My eyes are not deceived.
This is truly what I see—
Every time I face the mirror
This wretch stares back at me.[7]

My default belief was that I was, essentially, a worthless person.[8]

Chronic emptiness is a hard state to describe. I was tempted to use the word "hunger," but that implies that there is something to fill, and that for me was not the case. I was an empty shell, empty yes—but I did not need filling because what would be the point of filling me? Life had no meaning. I had no purpose.

I wanted to believe there was meaning to life, but that felt too incongruous to me as I was certain there was no meaning to *me*. How could life mean something when *my* life doesn't mean anything, when *I* don't mean anything?[9]

Chronic emptiness is a black hole within our very fabric—an endless cavern of nothing. I tried to compensate for it in all sorts of ways, but nothing I tried was match enough for the profound emptiness I felt.[10]

BARREN LAND

You will find so signs
of life on my land.
Signs that you trespass,
that you are not welcome,
but no signs to suggest
there is life here.
There will be no fruit
for you to harvest,
and no fruit will come
from what you sow.
My land is barren
but for the shell that is me.[11]

The concept of a *sense of self* is extremely difficult to theorize—let alone to operationalize. As the philosopher David Hume famously remarked, "For my part, when I enter most intimately into what I call *myself*, I always stumble on some particular perception or other, of heat or cold, light or shade, love or hatred, pain or pleasure. I never can catch *myself* at any time without a perception, and never can observe anything but the perception."[12] However we come to have a sense of self, it is nothing like how we come to know about a material object that we discover and observe. Rather, as the social psychologist R. H. Turner puts it, it is more of "a vague but vitally felt idea of what I am like in my best moments"[13]—a description whose aptness itself relies on its vagueness. But philosophical quandaries aside, we can nonetheless recognize the value of a positive, stable, strong sense of self—of *not* feeling as if one has a black hole inside, as Barker so painfully describes. It is, for example, what we want for our children—and what we hope our love will gift. We want them to know, in their bones, that they have worth, that they are good. We want them to feel, deep down, at peace with who they are—that the last thing they are is wrong or bad or evil. And we want them to feel safe and secure—capable of dealing with whatever the world throws their way.

Why would anyone—any child—*not* feel this way? Perhaps for some, the explanation is that they were born feeling like something was wrong inside—it's in their makeup. Or perhaps we all carry a window to this feeling within, but luckily for many of us, we manage to keep it firmly shut (see the discussion of Freud, below). But for plenty of people, at least part of the answer is environmental. They come from backgrounds of severe adversity. Risk factors for personality disorder include complicated family circumstances, where there is breakdown, death, institutional care, and parental psychopathology; childhood trauma, with high levels of sexual, emotional, and physical abuse, emotional and physical neglect, as well as social isolation and bullying; and social stressors, such as war, poverty, and migration.[14] These factors do not all need to be present. One can be enough to create vulnerability, insecurity, hurt and terror—the very opposite of the safety, security, and love that supports the development of a strong, positive, stable sense of self. Hence the genesis of a sense of self as worthless can be as simple (and painful) as this: The person feels treated as worthless. But there can also be a doubling down on this self-conception. Sometimes the best way to make sense of severe adversity is to believe that something *is* wrong with you—that you are worthless or bad or evil—and so you deserve it. What else could explain it? Randomness? Bad luck? Or that your parents or peers or the world at large are bad? Better that the problem lies in you. At least then you have some power over it.

If you are lucky enough to have a positive, stable, strong sense of self, try to imagine for a moment that you don't. Imagine that you don't feel that, deep down, you are good. Imagine you look within and sense a dark and terrible void. Self-harm can be a way of expressing the horror of what you have found and punishing yourself for it. Possibly, in punishing yourself, you also find a way of momentarily expiating the bad or purging the evil inside of you.[15] Here is an anonymous patient with borderline personality disorder, describing this function of self-harm:

> I needed to kill something in me, this awful feeling like worms tunneling along my nerves. So when I discovered the razor blade, cutting, if you'll believe me, was my gesture of hope. All the chaos, the sound and fury, the confusion and uncertainty and despair—all of it evaporated in an instant and I was for that minute grounded, coherent, whole. Here is the irreducible self. I drew the line in the sand, marked my body as mine, its flesh and its blood under my command.[16]

One answer to the question of why a person might want to harm themself is the note struck at the beginning of this self-report: to kill the bad in them—creating, if only for a moment, a better self. But another answer is the note struck at the end. Self-harm is a way of seizing ownership and control of one's body and one's fate.

Sigmund Freud, father of psychoanalysis, was the first to seriously theorize what he called *the compulsion to repeat*: the tendency to actively seek to relive past experiences of trauma. This tendency appears to contradict the principle that Freud otherwise took to govern our most basic behavior—the germ of which remains foundational to contemporary cognitive theories of learning, notwithstanding their many differences from Freudian psychoanalysis. This is the search for pleasure (reward) and the recoil from unpleasure (punishment). In *Beyond the Pleasure Principle*, Freud explains what we might think of as re-traumatization *by one's own hand* as arising from an instinct for mastery.[17] We are typically passive victims of original trauma: under the power of others who may hurt us in countless ways, from failing to satisfy our basic needs to violently violating our bodies, leaving a permanent injury to our self-worth and undermining our sense of security. In actively seeking to relive it ourselves, we metamorphosize from victim to perpetrator, from powerless to powerful.

Self-harm can be a repeat of past trauma arising from the instinct for mastery. By taking the threat of violence into our own hands, we are able to seize ownership and control of it. The thought lying behind an act of self-harm can be: If anyone is going to harm this body, it is *me*, right here, right now. By way of illustration, consider the following testimony from Maria, a woman with a history of sexual abuse by men and who occupies a self-harming mindset in relation to sex, as reported by the cultural anthropologist Natasha Schüll in her book *Addiction by Design*: "Rather than take the chance of living with the fear of when they would do it to me, I would rather start from a place where I knew they were going to do it and by God, I was going to pick *who* was going to do it and *when* it was going to happen. I would gravitate to risky people, almost like *I* was causing my own losses, not them—I was the one controlling it, like with the gambling."[18] Maria understands the instinct for mastery arising from her experience of trauma as the driving force of her sex life—and also her addiction to gambling. Schüll takes this up, arguing that, however paradoxical it may seem from the outside, the instinct for mastery is one part of why people with backgrounds of severe adversity latch onto slot machines and lose everything.

Here is another of Schüll's subjects, Sharon, explaining this thinking:

Most people define gambling as pure chance, where you don't know the outcome. But at the machines, I do know: either I'm going to *win*, or I'm going to *lose* . . . I don't care if it *takes* coins, or *pays* coins: the contract is that when I put a new coin in, get five new cards, and press those buttons, I am allowed to *continue*. So it isn't really a gamble at all—in fact, it's one of the few places I'm certain about anything. If I had ever believed that it was about chance, about variables that could make anything go in a given way at any time, then I would've been scared to death to gamble. *If you can't rely on the machine, you might as well be in the human world where you have no predictability either.*[19]

Sharon then describes her panic when a machine malfunctions. Although there are countless other machines, she doesn't just move to another. She is explicit that she no longer feels "safe"—notice her use of the language of attachment—because the one thing she could rely on has betrayed her and she is confronted by the fact: "YOU ARE NOT IN CONTROL."[20] She weeps, because rather than give her what she needs, the machine has let her down—like everyone else: *"How stupid this is, to be sitting in front of a machine crying, like the machine really cares."*[21]

Summing up: People certainly self-harm as a means of self-medication—to gain relief from misery and suffering. But, in what I have called a self-harming mindset, people also self-harm as an end in itself—to express, punish, and momentarily expiate or purge the bad self within, to seize ownership and control over their bodies and fates. As with self-medication, this further explanation is commonly if not necessarily rooted in backgrounds of severe adversity, which can make people feel both worthless and vulnerable. Hence, in so far as the persistent use of drugs despite evident and severe costs that is characteristic of addiction is driven by a self-harming mindset, the puzzle of addiction is explained by a desire to self-harm as an end in itself. The question that remains is simply: Is there reason to think people with addiction sometimes occupy a self-harming mindset?

Do we really need to ask?

From a purely empirical perspective, the presumption is surely reasonable, given the association between addiction, severe adversity, and problems with mental health, including personality disorder. Of course, not everyone with addiction who has a self-harming mindset has borderline personality disorder—any more than everyone with addiction has a self-harming mindset. But the mindset is present in memoir after memoir—palpably so. Here is one of the subjects from the philosopher and qualitative researcher Anke Snoek's studies, expressing it clearly: "Part of my use was to punish myself and when I did use I would punish myself more by . . . because I would be regretful and thinking 'oh why did I do that?' and then it would become a prolonged punishment and 'oh well you don't deserve any better.'"[22] Here is the journalist and writer Caroline Knapp once again, riffing off the eighteenth-century writer Samuel Johnson: "Drinking alone is what you do when you can't stand the feeling of living in your own skin. Boswell describes this in his *Life of Johnson*: 'I drink alone,' Johnson explains, 'to get rid of myself, to send myself away. Wine makes a man better pleased with himself.'"[23] And here is the writer Cheryl Strayed, describing her addiction to heroin in the context of her relationship with Joe, one of the men discussed in chapter 4: "What I loved about Joe is that he didn't love me, or himself. I loved that he would not only let me but help me destroy myself. I'd never shared that with another person. The dark glory of our united self-destruction had the force of something like love. *I get to do this*, I thought. *I get to waste my life.* I felt a terrible power within me. The power of controlling the uncontrollable. *Oh*, I thought, *I get to be junk.*"[24]

Until we start taking the psychology of self-harm seriously, we will be in no position to understand why some people with addiction are using drugs—or to help them recover. For what needs understanding—and transforming—is nothing less than a sense of self as wrong, bad, evil. This can be the source of the desire to self-harm—a desire that drug use in addiction can satisfy because of its evident and severe costs to the body and the psyche.

At the start of this chapter, I distinguished self-harm from suicide in principle via intent—to harm oneself, or to die—while acknowledging that in reality the line between them is not sharp. I have argued for the importance of self-harm to addiction; but we might also wonder whether some people with addiction are instead suicidal, wanting not merely to harm themselves but to die. In *Beyond the Pleasure Principle*, Freud follows his discussion of the instinct for mastery with an exploration of the possibility of *a death drive*, where this is to be understood not as a drive toward biological death but an instinct toward quiescence: a respite from the tension produced by the drive toward pleasure and the recoil from unpleasure—together with respite from that part of the self that is doing the driving.[25] However, given that biological death guarantees the end of the self and its drives, it is hard not to take up the invitation in Freud's choice to call this instinct "a death drive" and see it as precisely that: an instinct toward death, because of the escape death offers from *all* aspects of life. For many, this is, of course, precisely the value of suicide—the ultimate escape from life.

Clancy Martin is a philosopher with a history of alcohol addiction and suicide attempts. In his philosophical memoir *How Not to Kill Yourself*, he suggests that, for him, both were driven by a desire to escape not only from life but from himself: *"Please, somehow, get me away from me."*[26] He expands: "The modest thesis I'm developing here is that thinking about killing oneself and addictive thinking have a lot more in common than is normally recognized. They may even be different variations of the same fundamental kind of thinking. With this model—which, granted, may only characterize one kind of suicidal inclination—wanting to kill yourself is like an extreme version of the relief you find after drinking a few glasses of wine, and the pungent smell of yourself seems to drift into the breeze."[27]

The upshot of seeing some cases of suicide and some cases of addiction as stemming from a common cause—the desire for escape from life and the self—is that addiction, in these cases, comes into view as a form of suicide. As Martin notes, many of the most effective means of killing oneself are extremely violent: hanging oneself, shooting oneself, throwing one's body under a train, into oncoming traffic, off a bridge or building. Martin has attempted to kill himself using some of these methods. But he has an aversion to violence, which he finds difficult to overcome no matter how much he wants, in that moment, to die. Might some cases of addiction be a form of suicide, driven by a desire to die that is modulated by aversion to dying by a single act of extreme violence? Here is Martin, developing this idea in relation to Amy Winehouse—a singer and songwriter known for her struggle with addiction and mental health, who died of alcohol poisoning and whose hit song "Rehab" begins, "They tried to make me go to rehab but I said no, no, no":

> Though I've certainly tried to drink myself to death in the past, in some sense I *want* to say no, these acts are not akin to more obvious attempts at suicide. Death by alcohol poisoning is not the same as lying down in a nice warm bath with a bellyful of whiskey, several hundred milligrams of Valium, and a sharp razor (another of my failed attempts). But then, thinking about it more, does it really make sense to say that Amy Winehouse *didn't* commit suicide? Like so many other members of the so-called 27 Club[28]—Robert Johnson, Brian Jones, Jimi Hendrix, Jim Morrison, Janis Joplin, Basquiat, Kurt Cobain, it's a long list—she lived with self-destruction as the guiding principle and herself anticipated she wouldn't live past twenty-seven. She was alive, but she was trying to die. So while I might argue that Amy Winehouse didn't commit suicide per se, she did deliberately kill herself. The tools were different, but

the mission was the same. This is why, when considering suicide and related behaviors, people talk about categories like "deaths of despair":[29] it doesn't matter much whether it took a person three years of worsening heroin addiction or three days of ferocious drinking or three terrible minutes with a handgun to end his or her life. The goal is death.[30]

People who use addiction to self-harm can be ambivalent or reckless about dying—knowingly playing with death. Perhaps death is sometimes even the goal, as Martin suggests. But, whether or not Freud is right that all of us harbor a death drive within, a self-harming and, possibly, suicidal mindset drives many cases of addiction, straightforwardly explaining why a person would persist in using drugs in a way that counts profoundly against their own good. They use drugs in this way because they want to harm themself or even to die. Yet this mindset is rarely given voice or recognition in relation to addiction. As I noted at the opening of this chapter, I hope not only to have made a start on the task of rendering the desire to self-harm—and the willingness to risk or welcome death—psychologically intelligible, but also simply to have started us talking. We do need to talk about this, if for no other reason than that one very simple but powerful way to help people who struggle with these desires can be to make space for them to bring them into the open and voice them— without fear of being morally shamed or met with horror and incomprehension. Anne Sexton is a poet who herself died by suicide. I give this chapter's last word to the speaker of her poem "Wanting to Die."[31]

> Since you ask, most days I cannot remember.
> I walk in my clothing, unmarked by that voyage.
> Then the almost unnameable lust returns.
>
> Even then I have nothing against life.
> I know well the grass blades you mention,
> the furniture you have placed under the sun.
>
> But suicides have a special language.
> Like carpenters they want to know *which tools*.
> They never ask *why build*.
>
> Twice I have so simply declared myself,
> have possessed the enemy, eaten the enemy,
> have taken on his craft, his magic.

In this way, heavy and thoughtful,
warmer than oil or water,
I have rested, drooling at the mouth-hole.

I did not think of my body at needle point.
Even the cornea and the leftover urine were gone.
Suicides have already betrayed the body.

Still-born, they don't always die,
but dazzled, they can't forget a drug so sweet
that even children would look on and smile.

To thrust all that life under your tongue!—
that, all by itself, becomes a passion.
Death's a sad bone; bruised, you'd say,

and yet she waits for me, year after year,
to so delicately undo an old wound,
to empty my breath from its bad prison.

Balanced there, suicides sometimes meet,
raging at the fruit a pumped-up moon,
leaving the bread they mistook for a kiss,

leaving the page of the book carelessly open,
something unsaid, the phone off the hook
and the love whatever it was, an infection.

12

Self-Identity

READER, I do not know who you are. In particular, I do not know whether you use drugs, whether you are addicted to drugs, or whether, in addition to being addicted to drugs, you identify as an addict. If you do identify as an addict, I hope this chapter will speak to some of what that identity means to you, albeit in general, not personal, terms. If you don't, I ask you to begin by trying to imagine that you do.

Choose whatever drug makes this imaginative endeavor easiest. Alcohol, benzodiazepines, cannabis, cocaine, crack, heroin, ketamine, kratom, MDMA, oxycontin, Quaaludes, speed. Or imagine being a polydrug user: You take just about anything. Choose whatever context makes this imaginative endeavor easiest. Picture yourself using in restaurants, pubs, clubs, festivals, parties, your home, your friend's home, the beach, the streets. Draw on whatever experience you may have, with drugs or with people who are addicted to drugs, to get an image of yourself as a person who lives as an addict and identifies as such clearly in mind. Got it? You must imagine how drug use structures your life. Your daily routines will revolve around getting and using drugs. Probably many if not most of the people you spend time with use drugs. Perhaps you live in a community of people who use drugs together. Outside of that community, you may have to work to hide your drug use—whether from family, friends, colleagues, or even the police. Indeed, to sustain your identity, you may even hide some aspects of your drug use from yourself—some of what it has cost you. But, to really imagine what it would be like to identify as an addict, you must imagine that drug use is one of the defining features of your life and a significant part of what defines *you*. That is what it is *to identify as an addict*.

This chapter explores how an addict identity can solve the puzzle of addiction. This is the final chapter exemplifying the first schematic approach to the puzzle that I described in the introduction to this part, which focuses on how some benefits of drug use can be hidden *from the perspective of observers*— particularly those observers who may have limited familiarity with addiction. Be honest, if you are not a reader who already identifies as an addict, did you struggle to imagine what it would really and truly be like to do so? The aim of this chapter is to illustrate how, for people who do identify as addicts, the opposite may be the case. They may struggle to imagine what it would really and truly be like for them not to so identify. This imaginative obstacle has practical bite. If you can't see *yourself* on the other side of the road from addiction to recovery, then crossing over to a life that is free of addiction represents an existential threat. If you're not an addict, then who would you be?

A note about language before proceeding any further: As you may have noticed, this is the first chapter where I use the term "addict" as opposed to speaking of people with addiction. Many people view the term as stigmatizing and essentializing, and no doubt it is often used in a derogatory fashion. But, for better or for worse, it is the term used by many addicts about themselves, and the effect of this self-identification is precisely the theme that this chapter explores. I therefore use it freely in this chapter, as part of the project of entering this first-person psychological perspective, but I ask you to read it as it is intended: to capture a self-identification, not to stigmatize or moralize. I will return to this issue briefly at the end of the chapter, to discuss how the shift to person-centered language may offer one small step toward helping addicts embrace alternative identities.

How then does an addict identity explain why a person would persist in using drugs despite evident and severe costs and against their own good? The way to approach this question is backward: by looking first at the role that an *ex*-addict identity plays in recovery.

In his classic book *Theory of Addiction*, the psychologist Robert West—an expert on smoking and smoking cessation—tells of an informal study that he conducted.[1] West asked a group of chronic smokers who had quit that very week whether they identified as smokers or as ex-smokers. Half said they identified as ex-smokers. This is extremely optimistic, to put it mildly. As West notes, smoking cessation rates are notoriously poor: Relapse rates are approximately 75 percent within a year. In addition, the subjects themselves, as individuals, had smoked for years if not decades. Induction therefore strongly predicts that, in their own case, they will continue to do so. But at a six-month follow-up, West found that half of the people who had identified as ex-smokers in that first week were not smoking: 50 percent were abstinent. By comparison, every single person who had identified as a smoker in that first week was smoking again: 0 percent were abstinent. Unless the individuals who had identified as ex-smokers somehow "knew" they would remain abstinent—against the odds and induction alike, and by contrast with the individuals who identified as smokers—the intriguing hypothesis to emerge from this study is that *the act of identification* as an ex-addict dramatically increases the chance of successfully becoming one.

Subsequent large-scale studies by West and his colleagues support this idea. Nonaddict identities are associated with ongoing abstinence.[2] They also decrease the tendency to substitute alternative unhealthy behaviors and they increase a sense of self-efficacy.[3] Alongside these results, new theories have emerged that posit an ex-addict identity as a crucial mechanism for the transition from active use to stable abstinence, such as the Social Identity Model of Cessation Maintenance (SIMCM) and the Social Identity Model of Recovery (SIMOR).[4] Although these interwoven research projects are preliminary, the instinct behind West's informal study appears to be sound: An ex-addict identity promotes cessation and abstinence alike. But why?

A plausible answer to this question draws on the combination of Self-Categorization Theory (SCT) and Social Identity Theory (SIT)—a theoretical framework developed by the social psychologists Henri Tajfel and John Turner.[5] Think of social kinds as ways of categorizing individuals according to socially meaningful properties, such as sex, gender, race, religion, nationality, family role, profession, political affiliation, recreational interest—and more. Although the reality of some social kinds is debated, and the exact criteria for membership of some social kinds is contested, what matters for Self-Categorization Theory and Social Identity Theory is that social kinds in general are associated with specific sets of beliefs, desires, emotions, values, and ways of behaving, to which members are expected to conform simply in virtue of their membership. These expectations embody what we can think of as *group-specific norms*. To provide just a few examples: Boys don't cry. Muslims pray five times a day. Mothers love their children. Doctors care for their patients. Conservatives don't believe in big government. Sports enthusiasts spend a lot of time following sports.

Group-specific norms may or may not be part of the criteria for membership of a social kind. They can change over time and are rarely (if ever) written in stone. They admit of exceptions. And they often embody stereotypes and warrant social critique. Nonetheless, they are highly informative. When we identify an individual as a member of a social kind, for better or for worse, we expect them to conform to its group-specific norms: to share the beliefs, desires, emotions and values of the group and to behave like members of the group do. As the philosopher Sarah-Jane Leslie has argued, these expectations are not merely descriptive. They are not based simply on what the majority of group members are in fact like. Rather, they embody normative standards. Group-specific norms *prescribe* what group members *are supposed to be like.*[6] For this reason, if a person identifies as a member of a social kind, they are likely to both explicitly and implicitly self-regulate to ensure their beliefs, desires, emotions, values and ways of behaving conform to the norms of the group.[7] Conformity functions to ensure individuals are viewed as good (enough) members of the social kind, thereby protecting them from the possibility of failing to be identified by third parties as members of the group or being rejected by the group. Crucially, fear of failed social identification and group rejection will be especially strong if group membership is an important source of value for the individual.

Self-Categorization Theory and Social Identity Theory therefore offer an elegant framework for understanding why an ex-addict identity promotes cessation and abstinence. The group-specific norms associated with these identities involve beliefs, desires, emotions, values, and ways of behaving that coalesce around a commitment to not using drugs. In so far as these identities are an important source of value, individuals will be fearful of identity loss and group rejection, and so motivated to abide by the norms of the group. If you value an ex-addict identity, you want to maintain it. If you want to maintain it, you must not use drugs.

The success of Self-Categorization Theory and Social Identity Theory in explaining the power of an ex-addict identity to recovery has a flip side: Might an addict identity possess a comparable explanatory power in relation to addiction? In other words, perhaps addicts persist in using drugs in ways that count profoundly against their own good because they identify as addicts and these identities are an important source of value, thereby motivating them to abide by the norms of drug use associated with addiction. For, after all, this is precisely what addicts *are supposed to do*. They are supposed to use drugs, self-destructively.

The success of this explanation depends crucially on the assumption that there is value in identifying as an addict, making it the case that a person might fear identity loss or group rejection. Why might that be? The answer is no different from the value of any kind of identity. An addict identity can provide:

1. Social reward, belonging to a community and meaningful relationships.
2. Social cachet, or "coolness."
3. Daily structure and purpose, a way of filling time.
4. Grounds for self-worth.
5. An anchor for a sense of self when otherwise there would be only emptiness within.

Let us take these in turn.

Social reward. Social reward is a potent source of value for many species. Recall how, in the forced-choice studies conducted by the animal experimentalists Marco Venniro, Yavin Shaham, and their colleagues, almost 100 percent of rats chose social reward over drugs.[8] But, importantly, these were forced-choice studies. Social reward was offered as an *alternative* to drugs. Notwithstanding the fact that addiction can destroy relationships with family, friends, and colleagues, social reward is often an *accompaniment* to drug consumption for human addicts—not an alternative. Think, for example, of how adolescents can be initiated into peer groups through a willingness to use drugs; how smokers enjoy the in-group camaraderie of huddling outside together for a cigarette; or how alcoholics can find not only alcohol but company and solace at the pub. But it is even more pronounced for addicts who are members of some of the most vulnerable and marginalized drug user communities, such as long-term homeless polydrug heroin users.

The anthropologist Philippe Bourgois and the photojournalist Jeffrey Schonberg spent over a decade following two dozen addicts living in a homeless encampment in Edgewater, San Francisco. Their resulting book *Righteous Dopefiend* documents in intimate detail the nature of life and relationships in the encampment. Although Bourgois and Schonberg do not shy away from depicting the conflicts and betrayals between group members, these exist alongside many long-standing, deep, and meaningful relationships, structured in part by what they call "a moral economy of sharing."[9] The community loves, protects, and cares for each other, while they face their collective daily need for drugs in a context of poverty, disease, disability, and perpetual police harassment and violence. Their shared identity as addicts is what binds them together. Quitting drugs would mean quitting the community and losing these relationships. Meanwhile, many of these addicts have few if indeed any remaining relationships outside of the community; and, given the stigma surrounding this form of addiction—never mind the lack of treatment, housing, and employment opportunities—there is very little possibility of forming replacement relationships of comparable commitment and depth were they to quit drugs. In this light, consider the following stark depiction of addiction stigma from a subject in the philosopher and qualitative researcher Anke Snoek's studies of similarly vulnerable and marginalized addicts in Australia: "You're a drug addict person. People look to you . . . a different way . . . they judge you, they're scared of you, lots of things. Different from . . . normal people . . . You're really low, you're just like nobody."[10] Addiction can be a way of belonging to a group and maintaining social connections and meaningful individual relationships when people would otherwise face the prospect of severe social isolation and loneliness. Identifying as an addict can therefore have value because it functions as a ticket to a community of people who are similar and who care. As another of Snoek's subjects puts it: "The only time I feel comfortable is around other drug addicts and other people who are on substance because they accept [me] no matter what and I'm a pretty hard person to tolerate at times."[11]

By way of contrast, consider this testimonial from an anonymous philosophy professor, whose life has never revolved around a user community, even in the depths of their addiction:

> When I was an undergraduate, for about two years, I was a very serious user of narcotics, and was, by the time I was done, completely strung out and fairly lucky to be alive and not in prison. I worked in a hospital pharmacy. This gave me easy access to drugs, and I took that access. I can say that I never did anything that harmed a patient, but otherwise I did a bunch of stuff that was, shall we say, less than legal. I started out with oral codeine, but before long I was injecting narcotics—usually fentanyl, but also morphine and other things, basically nonstop. Fentanyl is short acting, so I'd fix up every few hours, every day, waking up in the middle of the night to do so. It was terrible for me—I was constantly sick, cold, lost a ton of weight. There were several times when I was seriously worried that I might die. It wasn't unusual for me to have a felony amount of drugs on me, so I was just lucky I never got stopped by the police. Unsurprisingly, it also wasn't great for my studies. Eventually, I was found out. I was told that I'd be fired but that if I'd go to outpatient "rehab" for a few months, they'd not do anything else. The rehab was incredibly stupid, I hated every minute of it, except that the alternative was possibly prison. For me, though, quitting—after the initial bit of feeling very sick, something I was already familiar with—was

no big deal, because it wasn't my life anymore. None of my friends did drugs. They all were really against it and were very worried about me. I had no way of getting them outside of the hospital—especially as I no longer had a job and so had, at the time, literally no money. I wasn't around people who were doing drugs. So, I felt bad for a bit, felt highly anxious for a bit longer. One thing that was difficult at the time was that when I was on narcotics, the day was broken down into lots of little bits—just the time between fixing up again. When I stopped, that bit became infinitely long. That took a lot of getting used to for a few weeks. But because narcotics were related to "my job" and not "my life," once that job was gone, that part of things was also gone. My impression is that this is very different from people whose drug use is connected with their friends and lives more deeply. People usually say that quitting narcotics is hard, but I say no, it's easy, what's hard is if you have to leave all of your friends and old connections behind.[12]

Social cachet. In his classic book *Outsiders*, the sociologist Howard Becker documents how "deviant" subcultures hold allure for people who find themselves at odds with—and their values and lifestyles thus pigeonholed by—conventional society.[13] This is certainly the case for some members of the Edgewater homeless community, as documented by Bourgois and Schonberg. As they put the point: "Being willfully and oppositionally self-destructive feels like an empowering alternative to conceiving of oneself as a sick failure who lacks self-control."[14] It is also a trope of many addiction memoirs. As the writer and critic Maggie Nelson notes, we have a tendency to celebrate various forms of transgression, including addiction, as forms of freedom.[15] But it is not just on the margins that drugs hold allure. In reflecting on his own addiction, the philosopher Owen Flanagan argues that drug consumption—including heavy consumption—is an important part of many conventional celebrations, rituals, and rites of passage.[16] Flanagan is himself Irish. To illustrate this idea, he considers the writer and journalist Pete Hamill's description of growing up Irish in New York: "And so the pattern had begun, the template was cut. There was a celebration and you got drunk. There was a victory and you got drunk. It didn't matter if other people saw you; they were doing the same thing. So if you were a man, there was nothing to hide. Part of being a man was to drink."[17] As for many men, drinking for Hamill is both a core part of a masculine identity and ubiquitous within his community: Boys don't cry, and Irishmen drink.

Drugs are also reliably sexualized and glamorized in the media and across artistic genres, especially in memoirs, films, and photography.[18] This depiction has an effect on us all—perhaps most obviously in relation to our attitudes toward alcohol. We routinely boast about what we drink (whether it is high-end champagne or bottom-shelf whiskey) and how much we drink (or how drunk we got). Consider the following quip about drinking from the writer Augusten Burroughs: "*A Ketel One martini please, very dry with olives*, I want to say. "Um just a selzer with lime," I say instead. I might as well have ordered warm tap water with dirt. I feel that uncool."[19] And here is Caroline Knapp, striking a similar note: "Sometimes I still can't believe I'm sitting in church basements after work instead of elegant bars, sipping coffee from a foam cup instead of wine from a lovely glass. The act seems so contrary to the image I cultivated for so long, ridiculous almost: Me?"[20]

Drug use, even to the point of addiction itself, is romanticized within our culture as part of a life that is *worth wanting*. Let me hasten to add: I am not condoning this depiction of addiction. Its accuracy ought to be in serious dispute for the vast majority of real-life cases. But we should not fail to recognize what is a basic fact about the depiction of drugs and addiction in our society—and part of the allure of drugs themselves—out of fear or condemnatory haste. Drugs can be sexy, problems with drugs can be cool. We could speculate about why this association is seared into so many of us, but the important thing is to look it in the eye. As routinely if not invariably depicted, drugs and addiction possess a kind of *social cachet*—a desirability. This may contribute to the value an individual derives from an addict identity—whether they live on the margins of society or maintain a more conventional lifestyle. The writer and self-proclaimed "junkie" William S. Burroughs muses on this theme in his memoir, *Junky*: "'Heroin was our badge,' said Rodney King, onetime partner of Charlie Parker, the great bebop junkie. 'It was the thing that said, "we know. You don't know". It was the thing that gave us membership in a unique club, and for this membership we gave up everything else in the world.'[21] . . . I have learned the junk equation. Junk is not, like alcohol or weed, a means to increased enjoyment of life. Junk it not a kick. It is a way of life."[22]

Daily structure and purpose. In addition to the provision of social reward and social cachet, addiction can create structure and a sense of purpose in daily life. For many addicts, their daily routine is defined by their addiction. Life revolves around securing and using drugs. Securing drugs may either follow a set pattern or require creativity and cunning; using may be valuable not only because of the psychoactive effect of the drug but, as the psychiatrist Norman Zinberg documents in his classic book *Drug, Set, and Setting,* because of the pleasure in enacting the rituals surrounding use.[23] As with membership of other social kinds defined by, for example, family role, profession, or recreational interest, being an addict can shape a person's daily life.

This point emerges forcefully in Snoek's interviews with her subjects, a group of vulnerable and marginalized addicts in Australia:

> Waking up in the morning . . . I feel . . . my body feels . . . I got to get drugs. How am I going to get it, who am I going to rob, who am I going to rort [scam], where am I going to get money.[24]

> Your whole life revolves around amphetamines and speed. You have it when you get up and you have it . . . before you go to bed, and spend weeks or whatever not eating, you stay in your clothes all day every day. . . . after a while it becomes just a part of life, just a way of life. You use it like you clean your teeth every day.[25]

Drugs define what addicts think about, plan to do, and actually do with their day. Indeed, the loss of this structure and purpose can be part of what is so difficult about quitting: "It's hard, you know. You've just got to replace it and get in another routine sort of thing . . . it's a way of life since I was . . . you know, before I was a teenager so if you're doing something all your life and then suddenly you got to change everything about it, it's really hard."[26] In this connection, recall the anonymous philosophy professor's comment about how "fixing up" regularly marked time—structuring the day into parts— which then felt like an infinite expanse when they quit. Like many identities, an addict identity gives structure and purpose to the day.

Self-worth. The provision of structure and purpose in daily life is connected to the final sources of value in identifying as an addict: *self-worth and a sense of self.* I will consider these in order, but I want to introduce both by reference to the following first-person report by an addict in recovery named Kate, which provides a striking illustration of these themes and which I therefore quote at length:

> Just as a person can feel loss of identity when they lose a long-standing job, or their children have grown and left home, it is also very common, I believe, to feel loss of identity when recovering from a drug-addicted

lifestyle. I used drugs and lived a fairly loose lifestyle from about age 16–22, and that stage is quite formative in a young person's identity. I had established myself as a druggie. My friends and family knew me as such, and in a way I was proud of my varied life experiences and my street-smarts. . . . I took pride in the fact that I knew more about drug taking than most my own age, by virtue of hanging out with older and more experienced drug users. At age 18 I already knew how to cook and filter different drugs for IV use, and how to prepare poppies to extract the opium, I knew dosages and strengths for illicit use of prescription meds, I knew all sorts about scoring and smoking dope and lots of quirky little tricks for increasing your buzz. I was proud of that knowledge base. . . . Seeing as I'd not done much else with myself over those formative years of early adulthood, I didn't have a heck of a lot else going on with my sense of identity. . . . I began to leave my drug identity behind, but felt like I didn't have much else to equate myself with, there was a real void. . . . I felt not so much like I missed the druggie lifestyle, but that I was starting to lose my grip on who I was, and was finding it hard to function. I was tempted to return to old habits for it was all I knew. I felt like I was a sell-out and was disloyal to my past. . . . Around my 24th birthday I had a big poppy design tattooed on my thigh. It's my way of remembering and respecting what I went through. My parents were half expecting me to die at times, I got that thin and sickly. When you've lived all that to such an intensity, it's hard, and feels quite disloyal to move on and forget it. You fear forgetting it, in all its realness and richness. I worked really hard for a few years in racking up a few qualifications, and also began to invest myself more into being a mother. Over the years I found I didn't forget the druggie life as I had feared. My role is now more about being an "ex-user," and I'm comfortable with that. I also made some progress on professionalizing my past deviances, by using my experience with drugs to help others—recently becoming a board member at an organization that provides needle exchange services and also studying trauma, loss and grief. This has further cemented my new identity and filled the void I felt. I think a lot of the time when a person is trying to quit drugs and keeps relapsing, the personality/identity side of it is overlooked, I think that's just as difficult to gain control over as the physical drug usage. . . . I would encourage anyone who's dissatisfied with a drug-chasing lifestyle to change it. But you've got to want it. And you've got to work at becoming someone and something else, otherwise you're still empty, and your inner self is still left craving and wanting.[27]

With respect to self-worth: Kate is explicit that she took pride in her knowledge of drug pharmacology and her skill in drug delivery. She knows more and is better at this than her peers. Importantly, drug *know-how* is not the only possible source of pride for addicts in relation to their addiction. Mothers who are addicts can take pride in managing their drug use such that it interferes minimally with parenting;[28] analogous pride is in principle available to any addict who manages to use in a way that interferes minimally with other important roles and activities. In contrast, as Flanagan notes, some addicts may take pride precisely in pushing their body to its limits—there can be a kind of machismo in adopting a reckless "devil may care" attitude toward drug use.[29] To be clear, I do not claim that addicts like Kate who take pride in their addict identity embrace it wholeheartedly and are devoid of all feelings of regret and shame. Ambivalence is not only possible in addiction but likely common (for further discussion, see chapter 14). The point is that it is possible to find a sense of self-worth in the fact that, if you are an addict, *then at least you are a good one.* This is a straightforward consequence of the fact that *addict* is a social kind and so subject to group-specific norms that set standards by which people can then measure themselves and others. Of course, what exactly the standards are for being a good addict (or a bad one) may be up for debate. Kate focuses on drug know-how. Other addicts may focus on drug management or drug machismo. But this disagreement does not tell against the fact that there can be standards to which addicts may aspire *qua* addicts, and which can therefore be a source of self-worth (or its opposite, self-denigration) in relation to their addict identity.

A sense of self. The further theme strikingly illustrated by Kate's testimonial is that being an addict provides her with a sense of *who she is*: "I had established myself as a druggie" and "didn't have a heck of a lot else going on with my sense of identity." We often think of addiction as involving *identity loss*—as "spoiling" the self, according to the sociologist Erving Goffman, and destroying all that is meaningful in a person's life.[30] Correspondingly, we may think of recovery as reclaiming this past self and life. One problem with this image is that it is too black-and-white. It fails to recognize that many addicts maintain other meaningful elements of their identities and lives despite their addiction. But another is that it fails to recognize that, as in Kate's testimonial, addiction can be experienced as an *identity gain.*[31] There is little for Kate to identify herself with apart from her addiction: "I didn't have much else to equate myself with." Her addict identity is therefore of value because it provides a sense of who she is when otherwise she would have none. As one of Snoek's subjects puts the point: "I feel myself when I'm using and it's when I don't use . . . I don't feel myself. . . . But I'm trying to . . . find myself without using, it's hard."[32]

Why would an addict have no alternative identities? There are at least three possible explanations. The first is that their addiction started early in childhood or adolescence—too early for the person to have had the chance to develop alternative identities through taking up a range of roles and activities. Recall what another of Snoek's subjects says: "It's a way of life since I was . . . you know, before I was a teenager." In this kind of case, there may simply be no adult past identity to be reclaimed. The second is that the social scaffolding required to support a past identity no longer exists. Consider in this respect the plight of many people who were part of the coal mining communities in Appalachia, as documented by the journalist Beth Macy in her book *Dopesick*.[33] Suppose that, prior to addiction, the crux of a person's identity was as a coal miner. But now the mines are closed and there is little if any possibility of finding another kind of work. In a case like this, there may be no possibility of reclaiming a past identity in the here and now—to return to being a coal miner—and no alternative work identity to be found even if the person quits drugs. The third is that years if not decades of living as an addict have created a psychological barrier between the person and their past identity. That identity used to be theirs. By contrast with the coal miner, let us suppose, there are no insurmountable external barriers to reclaiming it. But there is an internal barrier. The psychological gap between the person *then* and *now* is too great to be traversed. As illustration, recall how Gabor Maté's patient, Jake, describes his relationship to cocaine, first quoted in chapter 4: "I don't know who to be without it. I don't know how to live everyday without it. You take it away, I don't know what I'm going to do . . . If you were to change me and put in a regular-style life, I wouldn't know how to retain it. I was there once in my life, but it feels like I don't know how to go back. I don't have the . . . It's not the will I don't have; I just don't know how."[34]

Although these various explanations are different, the upshot is the same. There is no alternative identity ready and waiting to be reclaimed in recovery. A nonaddict identity must instead be actively imagined and created if the person is to have any alternative identity at all. As Kate says, "you've got to work at becoming someone and something else"—otherwise there is an emptiness, *a void*, where that sense of self should be. Note the similarity between Kate's testimony and the testimonials quoted in the previous chapter. For people who do not have a positive, stable, strong sense of self, an addict identity may function not only to provide them with a sense of who they are, but equally as a psychological defense mechanism—a barrier protecting against the experience of looking inward and finding only a dark and empty space.

To summarize the argument presented thus far: Although easy to miss from the outside, an addict identity can be a source of genuine value. It binds communities of drug users together, acting as a foundation for meaningful relationships, when otherwise people would face social isolation and loneliness. It creates structure and purpose in daily life. It offers grounds for self-worth and can anchor a person's sense of self when otherwise there would be emptiness within. People embrace addict identities because of their value. But, once embraced, addict identities explain persistent drug use despite evident and severe costs such that it counts profoundly against a person's good. The explanation is that this is what it is to be an addict—this is what addicts are like, what they do. If you identify as an addict—if you embrace this identity—then this is what *you* are supposed to be like, what *you* are supposed to do. Hence, to quit using drugs, you need in effect to quit your addict identity.

Let us return to West's informal study. The subjects who identified as ex-smokers were more likely to become ex-smokers. How was this new identity forged? Not through rational consideration of the evidence, for the evidence was not in its favor. Rather, as the philosopher Berislav Marušić has argued in relation to broadly comparable cases, the act of identification must be seen as expressive of *a commitment to be an ex-smoker*.[35] Although it is of course no guarantee of success, identifying as an ex-smoker increases the likelihood of becoming one, insofar as it sincerely expresses this commitment (and no doubt especially if it is announced to others who will be monitoring your commitment, as was the case for West's subjects). How then is it possible to sincerely make such a commitment—to commit to being something you currently aren't as a way of becoming it?

Identifying as a smoker is an unusual kind of addict identity. In contrast with other drug-specific identities—such as being an alcoholic or a cocaine or heroin addict—being a smoker is less likely to conflict with and thereby erode nondrug identities, which can in consequence anchor a sense of self if indeed the smoker identity is abandoned. For this reason, the identification as an *ex*-smoker may not be based on rational consideration of the evidence, but it is nonetheless straightforwardly *imaginable*. What would life really and truly be like to *not* be a smoker? Well, probably quite a lot like it is now, except that you don't smoke. Who would you be if you're an *ex*-smoker? Well, pretty much who you are now, minus your identity as a smoker. As the philosopher

David Velleman has argued, with this image of yourself as an ex-smoker clearly in mind, a commitment to being an ex-smoker can be understood as a decision to act in accord with this image. Given that ex-smokers don't smoke, this means that you no longer smoke.[36]

In contrast, for people whose identity as an addict provides their main if not only source of relationships, community, daily structure and purpose, self-worth, and sense of self, the act of imagining their life and identity in absence of their addiction is far from straightforward. Which people and relationships will replace the people they live among and care for? What activities will fill the day? And most of all, *who would they be?* This is why abandoning their identity as an addict represents an existential threat: There may be no alternative identities—nor an underlying positive, stable, strong sense of self—to fall back on. If so, then for addicts whose addiction is constitutive of their identity, quitting is in effect a *transformative experience* of the sort elucidated by the philosopher L. A. Paul.[37] If it is not possible to imagine *yourself* without imagining being an addict, then you lack not only a rational but also an imaginative basis for a commitment to being an ex-addict. If you make this commitment, it is as if you jump blind, with no certainty that you will survive the fall. This is terrifying—and renders utterly comprehensible why a person might choose to continue to be an addict rather than face this existential threat.

Yet people who identify as addicts do sometimes quit drugs and recover from addiction—even people, like Kate, who report no meaningful identity apart from their addiction. Perhaps some people do this by jumping blind. But if not, the only alternative is to find a way to imagine, however minimally and tentatively, a life and self that is truly their own but without addiction. I therefore conclude this chapter by considering three ways this can be possible.

The first way is obvious, but very limited. Person-centered language can offer a small, first step. "Person with addiction" serves to name drug use as a problem without making it an essential part of the person, by grammatical design. I will myself return to using person-centered language in the next chapter. But although words matter, they are not all that matters. From a first-person perspective, thinking of yourself as *a person with addiction* as opposed to as *an addict* offers nothing more than a skeleton upon which to hang a possible alternative identity. It provides no indication of what this identity might be.

Somewhat paradoxically, the second way to imagine a life and self that is truly *yours* but without addiction is drug derived. Psilocybin-assisted therapy

is a new treatment for various kinds of drug addiction currently in development.[38] Psilocybin is a naturally occurring classic serotonin 2A receptor agonist hallucinogen (otherwise known as a "psychedelic") found in many species
of "magic" mushrooms. The treatment typically occurs over twelve to fifteen
weeks. It begins with counseling sessions designed to build motivation, develop rapport between subject and therapist, and prepare the subject for the
psilocybin sessions. The first of these is a moderate dose delivered under
the supervision of a therapist after approximately one month of counseling. It
is followed by fairly intensive debriefing in the hours or days after the session,
so that the subject can explore and consolidate the experience. A maximum
of two further psilocybin sessions are offered during treatment, with the possibility of taking a higher dose if desired. Follow-up counseling as well as debriefing post-session are continued for the duration of the therapy.

Standard trials are, for understandable reasons, open label. This means that
both the researchers and the participants in the study know that the treatment
is being delivered. Efficacy is therefore complicated to measure, because outcomes may be influenced by any number of additional factors, for example,
the individual relationship between them, their expectations, and placebo
effects. Nonetheless, cessation rates are high and substantially exceed those
for other addiction treatments. Qualitative analysis of debriefing and follow-
up sessions reveal that subjects themselves find the psilocybin sessions extraordinarily meaningful and believe they have a profound effect on their recovery. One recurring theme is a change in identity:[39]

> For a few seconds, it was just like "I'm me, and there are no defining char-
> acteristics!" . . . that made me realise that I'm not a "smoker".[40]

> It felt like I'd died as a smoker and was resurrected as a non-smoker. Because
> it's my perception of myself, and that's how I felt. So I jumped up and I said
> "I'm not a smoker anymore, it's all done."[41]

> The self-defeating talk is gone, the extremely negative talk is gone, the de-
> pression [and] the anxiety is gone, the sleeplessness is gone . . . I learned to
> be me. And that it's ok to be me.[42]

For these subjects, psilocybin-assisted therapy seems to have created on the
one hand an experience of shedding a previous identity as an addict, and on
the other an experience of a positive, stable, strong sense of self. As a result,
they do not have to imagine themselves, however minimally or tentatively,
apart from their addiction. That work is done for them. As these patients tell

their story, psilocybin-assisted therapy is *actually* transformative of their identity and sense of self. They emerge from it with a sense of who they are which is free of their past addiction. What they must now do is live in a way that is true to this new self.

The third way to imagine a life and self that is truly your own but without addiction is to do the work of imagining it for yourself—despite the fact that, from your current position, you cannot make the imaginative leap. How is this possible? As the philosopher Agnes Callard has emphasized, the answer must be that, in cases such as these, it is not an act but a process.[43] You work toward a new identity, feeling your way slowly but surely. It takes time and effort, and it requires hope and creativity. This is no easy task, for any of us. To borrow a phrase from the philosophers and qualitative researchers Doug McConnell and Anke Snoek, it demands *narrative work*.[44] You must actively tell a new story about yourself that breaks free from your past, in effect surprising yourself with what might be possible for you in future.[45] But despite the break from the past, your story must be credible if it is to successfully create a new identity.

The life circumstances of many people with addiction—together of course with what it is to live with addiction itself—constitute a major obstacle to successfully accomplishing this narrative work. What makes the difference between a fantasy and an imagined but realistically possible alternative identity often rests, in part, on being able to try it out not just in imagination but in reality. If you imagine yourself participating in nondrug-using relationships for the first time in decades, the credibility of that imaginative act may require that, if you make overtures, however small, to people outside of your drug community, there is uptake. If you imagine yourself in a new job after decades of unemployment, the credibility of that imaginative act may require that there really is some prospect of getting one. If you imagine making a home for yourself, it is hard to feel the person you imagine is really you if you see no chance of ever making it off the streets. In consequence, the process of imagining an alternative life and self may be stymied in addiction not just by a failure of imagination—something we can all struggle with—but by a failure of material resources. That is, the failure of our society to provide the socioeconomic support that people with addiction need to live purposeful and meaningful drug-free lives. Put otherwise, people can be stuck within an addict identity due to social injustice. Arguably, this is yet another reason why recovery rates for addiction are particularly poor for people who come from backgrounds of severe adversity and limited socioeconomic opportunities and suffer from

mental health problems in addition to addiction. The lack of alternative reinforcers translates into a lack of genuinely possible alternative *identities*.

Self-medication and security-based attachment. Self-harm and the desire to
die. Self-identity. These explanations are examples of the first schematic approach to solving the puzzle of addiction identified in the introduction to this
part of the book. They reveal how there can be benefits to drugs and rationales
for using that are hidden to outside observers, despite being salient to people
who use. But they only come into view if we take seriously a first-person psychological perspective on addiction. The next chapter turns to the second
schematic approach, to show how taking seriously a first-person psychological
perspective can also reveal the opposite. There can be costs of drugs and rationales for not using that are salient to outside observers, despite being hidden
from people who use themselves.

13

Denial

IN THE 1940s and 1950s—thanks to a substantive and collective research effort involving extensive longitudinal comparisons of smoking versus non-smoking populations and confirmatory evidence from animal models—scientists established that smoking cigarettes causes cancer. Prior to this, no one knew for certain that smoking carried this cost—even if some people suspected that it did. Indeed, some people may have believed the opposite—that smoking was actually good for you—due to a prolonged and misleading advertising campaign (alongside government lobbying) by the tobacco industry.[1] Now we all know that smoking is bad for you. But imagine what it was like to smoke before the finding was established and disseminated. Everyone smoked. It was enjoyable, cheap, and without any social cost. People were in fact dying from it, to be sure, but no one knew. Now ask the why-question constituting the puzzle of addiction. Why were all these people persisting in smoking despite the evident and severe costs of doing so, namely the risk of cancer? The answer is all too obvious. Even though the costs are evident *to us*, they were not evident *to them*. The fact that smoking cigarettes causes cancer had not yet been established. Although many smokers were no doubt physically dependent on nicotine (see chapter 4), the costs of smoking were not knowable by ordinary people in ordinary circumstances during this period—the costs were not "evident" (see chapter 1). In consequence, these smokers were not addicted according to the explication proposed in this book. They did not persist despite evident and severe costs. Nor did they evince any lack of self-concern by smoking. What they lacked was knowledge—they were ignorant, not self-destructive.

Ignorance solves the puzzle of addiction. Suppose you are a person who uses a lot of drugs, and your use carries costs and is against your own good. If you don't know this, then there is an obvious explanation for why you persist.

You have no reason that you know of to quit. If this is your situation, how then can you learn that your drug use carries costs? Just as the scientific community had to discover that smoking causes cancer, so too you must discover that your drug use carries costs. It is not knowable through introspection or intuition alone. You must acquire *causal knowledge* of the outcomes of your actions. That is, you must learn what effects, good or bad, drugs are having on your life.

Broadly speaking, there are two kinds of causal knowledge relevant to addiction, typically acquired by two kinds of route. On the one hand, there is knowledge of large-scale generalizations, such as the finding that smoking cigarettes causes cancer. Crucially, as individuals, we do not typically have the ability to acquire knowledge of large-scale generalizations on our own. We are dependent on scientists to discover them, and on the state, corporate agencies, and the media to disseminate these discoveries to us, the general public. But, once disseminated, this knowledge is available to individuals to use to guide actions. If you know the large-scale generalization that smoking causes cancer, then you can infer that if you smoke, you put yourself at risk of cancer. Hence, to reduce your risk of cancer, you shouldn't smoke.

On the other hand, there is knowledge of small-scale individual associations, connecting our own actions to their more local and idiosyncratic outcomes—that is, knowledge of the response-outcome (R-O) contingencies or beliefs that interact with desires to explain goal-directed action in animals, including us (see chapter 6). By contrast with large-scale generalizations, we are often able to acquire such knowledge based on individual experience alone. If we observe an association between an action of ours and some possible outcome, we can test the possibility of a causal relation, by intervening and manipulating the hypothesized cause (our action) while monitoring the effect of doing so (the outcome) (see chapter 9). For example, although we cannot on our own typically discover a generalization like smoking causes cancer, we can potentially discover that, in our own case, smoking gives us a headache, say. We can do this by first noticing an association between smoking a cigarette and getting a headache, and then testing the causal hypothesis by manipulating our actions. Smoke a cigarette, then observe what follows. Don't smoke (and don't make any other changes), then observe what follows. Once this causal knowledge is acquired, it can be used to guide actions. So, armed with the knowledge that, in your own case, smoking gives you a headache, you can choose not to smoke, if you want to avoid getting a headache.

Just as drug-related, large-scale generalizations are difficult to discover, so too drug-related, small-scale individual associations are difficult to confirm. Given that causal networks are invariably complicated and that drugs are inevitably one of many contributory causes to outcomes, interventions may not yield knowledge. Suppose, for example, that a person with addiction opts not to use drugs on some occasion. They refrain from use. That is unlikely to mean that their problems—including those that may have been initially caused or exacerbated by drugs—just disappear. For instance, the damage to their body will not immediately reverse itself; the damage to their relationships will not immediately heal. Indeed, things may get worse before they get better as, at least in the short to medium term, life without drugs may be more of a struggle and contain more misery and suffering than life with them. As one of the subjects in the philosopher and qualitative researcher Anke Snoek's studies puts it: "I've tried, there's been very short times where I've been without drugs and I've been even more unhappy and miserable than when I'm on drugs."[2] Hence an intervention (forgoing drugs now or in the short to medium term) may not produce the effect (the disappearance of drug costs) that would support the acquisition of knowledge of a causal connection between drug use and drug costs. To take a classic kind of example: If a person's drinking is part of what is ruining their relationship, but they are drinking in part because they are unhappy in their relationship, then abstaining from drinking will neither immediately fix the relationship nor correspondingly offer clear evidence that their drinking is part of the problem.

Acquiring causal knowledge of the costs of drug use—whether large-scale generalizations or small-scale individual associations—must therefore be seen as *an achievement*. It can be hard to come by, and the evidence supporting it may be equivocal or open to reasonable doubt. Perhaps it is no surprise, then, if such causal knowledge is particularly subject to *denial*.

Denial is a notorious part of addiction lore. Yet it has received limited attention within addiction research. The remainder of this chapter shows how, similarly to ignorance, denial solves the puzzle of addiction. To preview what follows: I start by explaining what denial is. I then turn to how and why people with addiction can be in its grip. And I conclude by briefly describing some scientific findings and philosophical ideas that can help illuminate how denial in addiction is possible, before turning back, albeit briefly, to ignorance.

The nature of denial. Denial is a defense mechanism: a psychological process whose function, broadly speaking, is to protect us from psychological pain. In addition to denial, defense mechanisms include repression, suppression, avoidance, distraction, dissociation, projection, introjection, regression, reaction formation, compartmentalization, displacement, sublimation, intellectualization, rationalization, and cognitive dissonance. As this list attests, they are many, varied, and overlapping; and they can be either conscious or unconscious, or active or passive. Although historically integral to psychoanalytic theory as developed by Sigmund Freud and Anna Freud,[3] many kinds of defense mechanism are now a familiar part of our ordinary psychological understanding of ourselves—routinely invoked to explain behavior as well as productively studied by cognitive science.[4]

Denial is a species of motivated belief or self-deception that protects us against psychological pain by "denying" the reality that would otherwise provoke it. To bring a bit more precision to this gloss: Denial is a failure to straightforwardly believe a proposition despite evidence that would ordinarily suffice to make you straightforwardly believe it, because of the psychological pain doing so would involve. "Straightforwardly" is necessary because some cases are complicated: Perhaps you know *at some level* the very belief you deny (see below). "Ordinarily" can be understood in different ways: as what an average impartial observer would believe, or what you yourself would believe were it not for the pain of believing it.[5] "Failing to straightforwardly believe a proposition" admits of many varieties: from outright belief that it is not true, to withholding judgment as to whether it is true, to forgetting that it is true or avoiding considering it altogether. Despite the difference in genesis, denial results in a state that is akin to ignorance. It creates a lacuna in the mind where there could have been knowledge. Hence, like ignorance, it can straightforwardly solve the puzzle of addiction. If you are in denial that your drug use has severe costs, then there is a simple explanation for why you persist in using. Even if the costs are evident *to others*, they are not recognized by you. From your perspective, you have no reason to quit and every reason to persist. Hence you do not evince a lack of self-concern by using, *given that you are in denial.*

Strategies of denial in addiction. Suppose a person with addiction is considering whether their drug use has become a problem (as it's often put). In some cases, they might fully acknowledge that their use comes with severe costs but deny that these costs give them reason to quit. This is the kind of denial evinced by Joe: denial of values (see chapter 4). Recall that, as Joe is presented by the writer Cheryl Strayed, he does not deny the reality of the costs of his heroin habit to his health and relationships. What he denies is that these costs mean that using isn't "worth it." But there is another and more familiar kind of denial. In some cases, people deny that their drug use is really so much of a problem—that is, they deny that it is the cause of costs that are severe. This more familiar kind of denial can take different forms. People may acknowledge that their drug use is having some unfortunate effects on their lives, but deny their severity. Or they may acknowledge that they are having some serious problems in their lives, but deny that using drugs is the cause. Or both.

Caroline Knapp suggests that "denial *is* the disease of alcoholism."[6] Certainly in her case, denial is one of the core factors that kept her drinking. It took both forms. One way Knapp denied that her drinking had severe costs was to cling to the fact that she continued to be responsible and successful as a journalist. No matter what happened the night before, Knapp always made it to the office and worked hard all day, not drinking until work was over. Another was by comparing herself to other people whose problems with alcohol were *worse*. Yes, perhaps she had a small car accident, but she never totaled the car or killed anyone. Yes, she might have thrown up at the end of the night when alone in her apartment, but never in public or on strangers.[7] Knapp also downplayed the role of alcohol as a cause of her problems by focusing on other potentially relevant causal factors—exploiting the complexity of causal networks to minimize alcohol's role. Her car got broken into because of the increasing problem of urban crime, *not* because she was so drunk she abandoned it in a dangerous part of the city. She blacked out and woke up in a stranger's bed not because she *drank* too much, but because she hadn't *eaten* enough so couldn't hold her drink that particular night.[8] In other words, although she acknowledges she is having problems that are connected to her drinking, she finds strategies to avoid the conclusion that her drinking is the real cause. In its most general form, she describes this form of denial thus: "'You'd drink, too, if you had my problems.' That's the thinking. 'I'm not unhappy because I drink; I drink *because I am unhappy.*' That is the logic, and every alcoholic on the planet uses it."[9]

Knapp's strategies are familiar. She took them to the extreme, but many of us will have used similar tactics at some point to deny a truth we would rather not face. But some cases of denial seem less familiar, perhaps even verging on delusional. Indeed, Alcoholics Anonymous judges some cases of denial in alcoholism to be a kind of "insanity."[10] By way of illustration, consider the following anonymous testimonial, reported by the philosopher Gabriel Segal: "[I] drank 2 1/2 weeks after an esophageal hemorrhage. Couldn't bring that into my mind with sufficient force because I had already convinced myself that scar tissue is stronger than normal tissue (they cauterized the wound). Even brought photos home they took with the endoscope to remind myself. I now had a super esophagus and was good to go, so to speak."[11] This person's doctor had told them plainly that if they continued to drink, they would die. Obviously, in their desperation to drink, they convinced themself they were "good to go." But how could they actually believe this? I shall return to this question briefly in what follows.

Finally, there are also cases where people seem to conveniently forget—rather than actively deny—that their drug use comes with severe costs. Alcoholics Anonymous calls this a "mental blank":

> *As I crossed the threshold of the dining room, the thought came to my mind that it would be nice to have a couple of cocktails with dinner. That was all. Nothing more.* I ordered a cocktail and my meal. Then I ordered another cocktail. . . . As soon as I regained my ability to think, I went carefully over that evening. . . . *Not only had I been off my guard, I had made no fight whatever against the first drink. This time I had not thought of the consequences at all.* I had commenced to drink as carelessly as though the cocktails were ginger ale.[12]

Whether active or passive, conscious or unconscious, deluded or careless, the upshot of these various examples is similar: a motivated lacuna in the mind, making the knowledge that drug use has severe costs unavailable.

The pain of knowing. People with addiction are often in denial; and denial protects against psychological pain by "denying" the reality that would otherwise provoke it. This raises an important question: Why is the knowledge that drug use has severe costs so painful to people with addiction?

One all too obvious reason is that the costs are devastating in and of themselves, constituting as they do terrible losses—of people and relationships, physical and mental health, jobs, housing, social standing. But, in addition, there is the fact that these costs have not come about through accident or chance, but by the person's own actions. People with addiction are the agents of their own destruction. This can be shameful enough as it stands, but now consider that the costs of addiction are typically borne not only by the person with addiction themself but also by other people (for further discussion, see chapters 16 and 19). People with addiction often hurt the people they love, sometimes destroying not only their own lives but the lives of others. The philosopher Owen Flanagan has written poignantly about the shame of being such an agent:

> My morning fix did temporarily suppress the self-loathing that was my constant companion if I was awake and semi-sober. It mitigated briefly, maybe for thirty seconds or a minute, the inglorious shame of being the pathetic being I was, that I had become. And although it may seem hard to believe, I loved that half-minute, that minute, in which I was briefly, ever so briefly, saved from my self-loathing. Then I would enter into numbness—until the next morning when the cycle would repeat itself.
>
> I was a wretched, worsening train wreck of a person—a whirling dervish, contaminating, possibly ruining, the lives of my loved ones. What if they weren't strong enough to escape the harm? This was always my worst thought. And it was my constant tortuous companion if I was awake and not using, which by the end was not often. This was self-caused torture and self-degradation but possibly also the ruination of those I loved the most—my own private waterboarding.[13]

Lastly, consider the simple fact that acknowledging that your drug use is a problem *is* acknowledging that you have reason to quit. But, as I have hoped to convey over the previous chapters in this part, drugs can have tremendous value to people with addiction. Living without them can be terrifying to contemplate. How will you cope? What will you do? Who will you be? The knowledge that your drug use has severe costs is therefore painful because it confronts you with the demand that you quit what you desperately feel you need—even love.

Addiction is defined by drug use with evident and severe costs. These are psychologically painful to acknowledge: for what they are in themselves, for what they say about a person, for the demand they place on a person to quit. Denial protects against all this pain. But it also solves the puzzle of addiction in the simplest possible terms. Just as, if you are ignorant that smoking causes cancer, then the fact that it does cannot weigh with you as a reason not to smoke, so too if you are in denial that your drug use carries severe costs, then the fact that it does cannot weigh with you as a reason to quit. Denial relieves you of this weight, leaving you free to carry on using.

Mechanisms and models of denial. Denial and ignorance alike solve the puzzle of addiction. Denial is a species of motivated belief or self-deception; ignorance need not be motivated at all. I conclude by considering some cognitive

mechanisms and philosophical ideas that can help illuminate how denial—
and ignorance—in addiction is possible.

Let us begin with what is now a truism: Human cognition is far from rational. Our processes of belief formation and evaluation differ markedly from the
epistemic ideal.[14] We struggle to reason probabilistically and assess risk. We
are prone to an astonishing slew of cognitive biases, such as attentional, con-
firmation, and conservatism biases, as well as the availability heuristic, the
representativeness heuristic, the anchoring effect, and the "better-than-
average" effect—that is, the tendency to view oneself, as the name suggests, as
better along any number of dimensions than the average person. Our processes of belief formation are also influenced by our desires and emotions.[15]
We are more likely to adopt a skeptical mindset and question the validity and
quality of preference-inconsistent than preference-consistent evidence; our
evidential standards for forming, retaining, and abandoning beliefs shift in
relation to what we want to believe (or not to believe) and what beliefs would
make us feel better (or worse). Irrational and motivated belief is therefore a
perfectly ordinary feature of human cognition. Meanwhile, as previously
noted, acquiring causal knowledge of the outcomes of drug use—both large-
scale generalizations and small-scale individual associations—is an achievement. It can be hard to come by, and the evidence supporting it may be
equivocal or open to reasonable doubt. There are in consequence ample opportunities for cognitive biases and motivational influences to prevail: enabling us to minimize what in truth are significant risks, see ourselves as exceptions to the rule, squint and skew the evidence, and shape beliefs to our liking.
Human cognition is prone to denial, and the ground of addiction is ripe for it.

Over and above the passive influence of cognitive biases, desires, and emotions on belief formation processes, humans are also prone to active self-
deception. Traditional philosophical accounts of self-deception model it on
interpersonal deception. In prototypical instances of interpersonal deception,
the deceiver intends to make the deceived believe a proposition that the deceiver knows to be false. By analogy, traditional accounts of self-deception
claim that, in prototypical instances of self-deception, the self-deceiver intends
to make themself believe a proposition that they know to be false and so don't
believe.[16] The possibility of paradox therefore lurks within this traditional account. How can it be coherent to intend to make yourself believe a proposition
that you know to be false and so don't believe? And—should such an intention
somehow manage to be effective—how could there be two contradictory beliefs existing at the same time in the same mind?[17] But we should not deny the

reality of self-deception for fear of paradox. Put the traditional account to one side, and simply notice that there are cases of denial in addiction that have *the feel* of self-deception: cases where the person seems *in some sense* active in their denial and as if they know *at some level* the very belief they deny.

Consider, for example, the testimonial from the person with alcohol addiction who drinks after an esophageal hemorrhage (previously quoted). This person reports that they bring photos from the endoscopy home in order to be able to remind themself that they have a "super esophagus" and are "good to go." Bringing the photos home is an action. Why do it? Presumably, because of nagging if murky thoughts that their belief that they are "good to go" is in fact ludicrous. Remember, their doctor told them in no uncertain terms that they will die if they continue to drink. Here is Caroline Knapp, describing how knowledge occasionally breaks through the darkness of denial:

> A light bulb goes on and then—click!—just like that, it goes off again and you're back in the dark, unable to see.
> Click: *Fuck. Something is very wrong. I am in trouble.*
> Click: *I'm okay. Fine. Not to worry.*[18]

An account of self-deception that does justice to the phenomenon but avoids paradox therefore has two parts. First, an explanation of what it is to be "in some sense active" in deceiving oneself without imputing a conscious intention to self-deceive. Taking a cue from the philosopher Mark Johnston, this explanation may begin simply by noting that some of what we do serves a purpose without it being true that we do it intentionally for that purpose.[19] This is precisely what is evidenced by the example of the person who drinks after an esophageal hemorrhage. Bringing photos from the endoscopy home serves the purpose of seeing off doubts that they aren't in fact "good to go," but they do not bring the photos home with the intention of seeing off doubts that they aren't in fact "good to go." Second, an explanation of how a proposition can be known "at some level" but not another. There are different possible ways to theorize this metaphor. One suggestion is that a belief might be available to guide thought and action in one context or for one purpose, but not for another context or purpose. Another is that a belief might lurk at the edges of conscious awareness only—capable of casting a shadow that influences thought and action, but always shrinking from the spotlight and so never itself becoming the object of conscious attention or active reflection. Another is what Knapp describes: A belief is momentarily the object of conscious attention or active reflection, but then a switch is flicked, and it's out of the spotlight entirely. These suggestions do no more than gesture toward a general account of self-deception. Hard questions remain about each of them, and it is also possible that, when properly developed, some would be apt for some cases, but none would be apt for all.[20]

Lastly, let us return to where we began, namely ignorance. Ignorance, like denial, solves the puzzle of addiction. But, unlike denial, it need not be motivated by avoidance of pain. We can be ignorant simply because we have not managed to discover the truth—as we were all ignorant of the truth that smoking causes cancer prior to its scientific discovery and dissemination. Once again, the acquisition of knowledge of response-outcome (R-O) contingencies—that is, beliefs about the outcomes of one's actions, including drug use—should be seen as an achievement. Might people with addiction be prone to cognitive difficulties affecting their capacity to acquire this knowledge, making it especially hard for them to achieve?

The cognitive scientists Philip Jean-Richard-Dit-Bressel, Gavin McNally, and their colleagues have shown that, in laboratory experiments, there is significant individual variation within the general population with respect to the acquisition of knowledge of the causal connection between actions and outcomes that are punishing—especially when the action type results in a punishing outcome only infrequently as opposed to reliably (as is surely the case with some of the costs caused by drug use).[21] They hypothesize that some people with addiction might fall within the subgroup of the general population whose performance in these experiments is relatively poor, and therefore might struggle to learn the causal connections between drug use and its costs. This is an intriguing suggestion, which arguably finds support across a series of addiction studies conducted by the neuroscientists Rita Goldstein, Scott Moeller, and their colleagues.[22] These studies demonstrate that, as compared with control groups, on average people with addiction show reduced sensitivity to error-monitoring, high-risk decision-making, and actual losses across a range of laboratory tasks as measured by decreased activation across select brain regions, including the rostral anterior cingulate cortex (rACC)—an area involved in the processing of personally relevant information. On the plausible assumption that the brain needs to treat errors, risks, and losses as personally relevant in order to use them to learn R-O contingencies and guide future actions, this suggests that some people with addiction may indeed have difficulties acquiring knowledge of the costs of their drug use.

This chapter has aimed to explain how ignorance and denial solve the puzzle of addiction. These explanations are examples of the second schematic approach to the puzzle, showing how the costs of drug use may be hidden from the perspective of people with addiction themselves, while all too obvious to observers. But the corollary of this solution is that recovery can require people with addiction to overcome ignorance or denial and gain knowledge—not just at some level but front and center—of the effect of drugs on their lives. The effectiveness of techniques of motivational interviewing and cognitive behavioral therapy that target ignorance and denial—by nonjudgmentally pointing out and thereby bringing to awareness the consequences of use—testifies to the importance of knowledge to recovery.[23] So too does the experience of "hitting rock bottom." Knapp begins her memoir by stating that, if she has to pinpoint when her relationship with alcohol started to fall apart and she began the process of quitting, it was the night she nearly killed her oldest friend's two young daughters while drunk. She just couldn't delude herself anymore after that.[24] But important as knowledge is, sometimes it is not enough. Even when a person with addiction knows what drugs are doing to their life and has resolved to quit, they may yet continue to use. This is the phenomenon of "loss of control," first defined in chapter 7 and to which the next chapter returns.

14

Problems of Control

THE IDEA OF "loss of control" has had a long and complicated history, making its meaning unclear. In his classic book *The Disease Concept of Alcoholism* published in 1960, the alcohol researcher E. Morton Jellinek famously distinguished an "inability to abstain" from a "loss of control," sowing confusion from the outset.[1] According to Jellinek, some people were unable, quite generally, not to drink. He labeled this problem an "inability to abstain." By contrast, some people were able to abstain as he defined it—they were able, quite generally, not to drink—but if and when they started, they couldn't stop. Jellinek labeled this problem a "loss of control."[2] Jellinek's distinction between kinds of problems that people can have with alcohol is valuable, but his terminology was unfortunate. On the one hand, the terms "inability to abstain" and "loss of control" are semantic bedfellows. It is natural to think that, if a person has an "inability to abstain" from drinking then they have "lost control" over drinking, and vice versa. On the other hand, both of these terms imply that alcohol addiction is characterized by the impossibility either of remaining abstinent or of controlling drinking—evoking an idea of compulsion either way. Yet, as the alcohol researchers Griffiths Edwards and Milton Gross note in their seminal 1976 article commenting on Jellinek, "Alcohol Dependence: Provisional Description of a Clinical Syndrome": "It is unclear . . . whether the experience is truly one of losing control rather than one of deciding not to exercise control. Control is probably best seen as variably and intermittently impaired rather than 'lost.'"[3]

Edwards and Gross therefore replaced Jellinek's talk of "inability to abstain" and "loss of control" and the supposed distinction between them with a single idea of "impaired control." This is how they describe the idea: "The desire for a further drink is seen as irrational, the desire is resisted, but the further drink it taken."[4] Far from evoking an idea of compulsion, "impaired control" as described by Edwards and Gross is nothing more than a simple series of events unfolding over time. There is an occurrence of a desire to drink, which is followed by a judgment that drinking is irrational, which is followed by an attempt to resist drinking, which is followed by drinking. In theory, this series can occur at any point in time: prior to starting to drink, or after drinking has started. Meanwhile, no explanation is offered of *why* the drink, despite being seen as irrational and (initially, at least) resisted, is taken anyway—no idea of compulsion is evoked, no alternative explanation is offered in its place.

In the decades since Edwards and Gross published their seminal article, the meaning of "impaired control" has metamorphosized. As the philosopher and psychiatrist Chandra Sripada complains, it is now a "murky" placeholder for whatever ultimately *explains* something like the pattern Edwards and Gross initially used it to describe. In keeping with the image of craving that has long shaped scientific, philosophical, and popular imagination (see chapter 6), "impaired control" is usually taken to mean that a person is wrestling with very strong—if not irresistible—desires, or overwhelming urges or impulses.

Given this complicated semantic history, I want to be very clear about what I mean by the various terms in this chapter. By "loss of control," I mean the fact that people with addiction use drugs despite either their better judgment or a sincere intention to abstain (or they use more than they sincerely intended—a caveat that is important to note but that I shall drop for brevity in what follows). This is how I loosely defined "loss of control" in chapter 7. It is in keeping with the *Diagnostic and Statistical Manual of Mental Disorders* (DSM-5) criteria 1 and 2 for substance use disorders. It is also similar, but not identical, to the idea of "impaired control" as described by Edwards and Gross. Both "loss of control" as I have defined it and "impaired control" as defined by Edwards and Gross refer simply to a series consisting of one or more psychological states—a judgment or intention in my case, or a desire, then a judgment, then a trying in their case—followed by a behavior, namely drug use. By contrast, I shall label the range of possible *explanations* of why people with addiction can end up acting against their better judgment or sincere intention "problems of control." So, as I use the terms, problems of control are whatever *explains* loss of control, as I have defined it. I will not use the term "impaired control."

This chapter is a catalog of problems of control: the problems people with addiction can face acting in accord with their better judgments or sincere intentions—as well as some of the problems that can beset their attempts to form such judgments or intentions in the first place. Many of these problems are in no way unique to addiction. They nonetheless help explain why some people with addiction fail to follow the path that they decided upon for their own good—or fail to make such a decision at all. The chapter therefore has some relevance to the traditional philosophical issue of whether weakness of the will—understood in line with my (admittedly loose) definition of loss of control—is even possible.[5] This is because the problems that I catalog to explain loss of control in addiction aim to make the phenomenon psychologically intelligible—thereby suggesting how it could be possible. This does not by itself resolve the traditional philosophical issue, but it does help soften its bite.

I begin with a reminder of three relevant lessons from part II and the previous chapters in this part:

First lesson. Not all people with addiction will experience a loss of control, as defined. This is because it may be false that they are using despite their better judgment or a sincere intention to abstain. DSM-5 criteria 1 and 2 may not be met. Their best judgment may be that, given the difficulty of their life circumstances, they should use (see chapter 10). Or they may have no intention to abstain, whether that is because they desire to self-harm or to die (see chapter 11), they embrace an addict identity (see chapter 12), or they are in profound denial (see chapter 13). This means that addiction cannot be defined as or identified with a loss of control over drug use.[6] Similarly, problems of control are only one of the many possible solutions to the puzzle of addiction.

Second lesson. Although cravings for drugs may be strong, desires for drugs are not irresistible. They do not overwhelm attempts at resistance the way water bursts through a dam or a train with no brakes barrels down a track (see chapters 6 and 7). Hence, whatever explains loss of control in addiction, it is not the irresistibility of desire.

Third lesson. Loss of control, as defined, cannot itself be modeled in animals who are the standard subjects of experimentation. It is a possible phenomenon only for subjects susceptible to a certain kind of psychological conflict. That is, self-conscious, self-reflective subjects capable of taking metacognitive attitudes toward their mental states: of reflecting on their conception of the good life or the best course of action, all things considered; of forming judgments and intentions in line with this conception; of deciding to resist the pull of desires and urges and whims and emotions that they reject as out of line with it. It characterizes (some cases of) human addiction—and no cases of rat addiction (see chapters 6 and 7). However, some of the factors that contribute to its *explanation* in humans can be studied using animal models: for example, the strength (albeit not irresistibility) of some forms of cravings (see chapter 15) and the importance of time discounting (see chapter 9 and below).

Here then is a catalog of problems people with addiction may face acting in accord with their better judgment or sincere intention to abstain:

The fallibility of the cognitive systems necessary for behavioral control. As we saw in chapter 7, Sripada argues that loss of control can be due to the *fallibility* of the cognitive systems necessary for behavioral control.[7] Cravings for drugs occur with high frequency during addiction and in the early months of recovery; abstaining therefore requires repeatedly exercising control over one's actions in the face of cravings. But exercising control is a multistage metacognitive process involving a cyclical procedure of monitoring, attending, reasoning, and revising. These processes are all susceptible to brute error due to noise, indeterminacy, elements of randomness, and the limitations on resources that plague any cognitive system. When errors occur, actions may be more impulsive, guided by cravings for drugs (see chapter 15) or, alternatively, performed out of habit—which, for people with addiction, may involve mindlessly selecting drug use over alternative goals (see chapter 6) thereby exhibiting a kind of "mental blank" and ending up finding themselves using almost without realizing that they are (see chapter 13).

The emotional attrition of the intention and motivation to exercise behavioral control. Chapter 7 also contained a further explanation of loss of control, based on the writer Augusten Burroughs's reflections on craving and relapse in his memoir of alcohol addiction, *This Is How: Surviving What You Think You Can't.*[8] Burroughs sees relapse as a "temper tantrum," whereby people permit themselves to use drugs *in defiance* of their better judgment or sincere intention. Wanting to drink but not drinking can lead to frustration, bitterness, resentment—all emotions that can affect behavioral control by demanding an answer to the question of what exactly the point of exercising it is, thereby chipping away at both the intention and the motivation to do so. Relapse can be a decision to use when someone just doesn't care enough anymore. As Burroughs expresses this thinking: *Screw it.* Note that this cannot be interpreted as a reconsideration and corresponding shift in judgment as to what is best without distortion. To do so would be to ignore the anger and defiance in the decision. Frustrated and fed up, a person decides to act *against* their better judgment and their (at least hitherto) sincere intention.

Shifting judgments and intentions. It is also possible that a person with addiction does reconsider, shifting their judgment as to what is best and relinquishing their (at least hitherto) sincere intention to abstain, rather than deciding to act against them. An ordinary way to explain this appeals to weariness and hope-lessness. Exhausted and worn down (as opposed to frustrated and fed up), perhaps a person no longer believes that life without drugs is best. But there are alternatives to this simple emotional explanation. The psychologist Roy Baumeister and his colleagues have shown that subjects who exert self-control on one task perform less well as compared with control groups on additional self-control tasks.[9] They hypothesize that self-control requires willpower, which they picture metaphorically as a muscle: a limited resource, easily de-pleted by exercise.[10] This picture has had its critics;[11] however, there are less metaphorical ways of explaining the finding.

One is that abstinence no longer looks like the best way forward when you are sitting with the temptation to use. The philosopher Gary Watson sees crav-ings for drugs as clamoring for attention—crowding out all other consider-ations in the moment and seducing people into thinking that drug use is for the best, after all.[12] As psychologists such as Reinout Wiers and Kent Berridge (see chapter 15) have described in detail, drug cues can be highly salient in addiction, capturing attention and biasing in-the-moment decision-making toward drugs.[13]

Another explanation is time discounting (but see below for discussion of *hyperbolic* time discounting). Recall from chapter 10 that, when selecting be-tween rewards, immediacy functions like a bonus, tempting us to choose *smaller, sooner* (SS) rewards over *larger, later* (LL) rewards. Suppose drugs are available *now*. Any reward from abstinence will only come much *later*. If a person sitting with temptation is deciding whether or not to use drugs now— suppose, for example, the drink is on the table, right there within reach—the mere fact that drugs are available now is a bonus, potentially causing use to edge out abstinence in current cost-benefit calculations, thereby creating a momentary judgment shift. With the bonus of immediacy, using is best; ab-stinence is best only when the drug use option to which it is being compared lacks this bonus.

A final explanation is a kind of cognitive dissonance. The philosopher Richard Holton suggests that if people are concerned or convinced that they will in fact use, then they might judge it best to use after all. This shift in judgment will allow them to tell a story that casts them in a better light—as a person who does what they judge to be right, rather than as a person who fails to.[14] Why then might people be concerned or convinced that they will in fact use? Well, induction, perhaps in combination with low self-efficacy.

Induction and low self-efficacy. In general, we do not try to do what we know we can't. What's the point? The psychologist Albert Bandura is famous for applying this general idea to addiction: If people with addiction believe they aren't capable of abstaining, then there's little point in trying.[15] Why then would they believe this? One answer is the cultural dominance of the orthodox version of the brain disease model. If addiction is a brain disease of compulsion that renders a person incapable of resisting cravings for drugs, then they are powerless to abstain.[16] This is the flip side of why, as noted in the introduction of this book and as will be picked up again in part IV, agency and, with it, responsibility, are important tools of effective treatment. But another answer is simple induction. Addiction is a pattern of drug use that is regular if not indeed daily. Meanwhile, attempts to abstain in the past may have been of limited success for any of the various reasons cataloged in this chapter. Induction predicts that a person with addiction will continue to use today, tomorrow, into the future—just as they used yesterday and in days past. To believe otherwise may not be impossible or irrational—after all, there are sometimes reasons to think the future will be different and this time you'll quit—but it is to believe counter to the evidential weight of the past.

Induction and low self-efficacy can function to undermine intentions to abstain while leaving judgments about what is best intact: No matter what you judge best in theory, why bother to try to achieve abstinence if you have strong reason to believe you will fail? Alternatively, as Holton suggests, these undermined intentions may in turn undermine judgments about what is best: If you have every reason to believe you will fail to abstain, better to shift your judgment about what is best so you can appear to yourself to be doing what you should—rather than appear to yourself powerless to resist doing what you know you shouldn't. This is a more pleasing self-story.

Local versus global bookkeeping. Where you are in your self-story also matters. The behavioral economist Gene Heyman argues that addiction is maintained and relapse enabled by local as opposed to global bookkeeping.[17] Suppose a person wakes up every morning to face a choice: Should I use drugs today or should I abstain? *Local bookkeeping* evaluates today's choice just in relation to today, independently from any future choices; *global bookkeeping* aggregates choices, bundling today's choice together with future choices and evaluating them collectively. If you evaluate the costs and benefits of using drugs versus abstaining today (and only today), using may well be better than abstaining. If you evaluate the costs and benefits of using drugs versus abstaining every day (including today) for a year, abstaining may well be better than using. Suppose now that, from this global perspective, a person has indeed judged a year of abstinence better than a year of using and correspondingly formed a sincere intention to abstain. *But when should they quit?* It is often worth it to use one last time today, assuming you will indeed turn over a new leaf tomorrow. But that will, alas, also be true tomorrow. This thinking is part of why people with addiction may act against their better judgment or sincere intention to abstain: *Just one last hurrah for old time's sake, and then tomorrow I'll quit!* But by the time tomorrow comes, it is today—again a good time for a last hurrah. It is also part of why abstinence can be aided by the imposition of certain and immediate costs which make using *today* not worth it *today*; for example, a daily urine test that, if positive, will result in an immediate cost, such as the loss of a job or a license.

Lapses versus relapses. Daily local bookkeeping creates daily lapses adding up to a daily pattern of use—a relapse, understood not as a one-off occasion of use but as a return to a pattern of drug use that counts as addiction. But other of the problems considered thus far—such as fallibility—are one-off and so by themselves explain only a single lapse, not a relapse. But lapses can easily turn into relapses through a number of mechanisms. One is their contribution to induction and low self-efficacy. More evidence that you always use and so more evidence that, try as you might, you fail in your attempts not to use. Another is what is called the *abstinence violation effect*: a way of thinking about lapses that all too easily turns them into relapses. Having lapsed, it is easy to see yourself as back to square one—not only frustrated but also with all the more inductive evidence that you don't succeed in quitting, and in consequence all the more reason to think that you can't succeed in quitting. In which case, you might as well go all out. *In for a penny, in for a pound*—as the saying goes.

Denial, memory sampling, and hyperbolic time discounting. The explanations cataloged thus far address why a person might use drugs despite their better judgment or a sincere intention to abstain—thereby presuming they have successfully made such a judgment or formed such an intention. But people with addiction may also face problems making such a judgment or forming an intention in a way that is standing and sincere rather than fleeting or fickle—or indeed at all. One obvious explanation is denial (or ignorance). Recall the writer Caroline Knapp's metaphor of the light bulb briefly clicking on but then turning off again, keeping her in the dark about the severity of her drinking (see chapter 13). Denial (or ignorance) of the costs of your drug use means you will see no reason to judge it best or to form an intention to quit. But other explanations flow from the effects of time on judgment and decisions: the allure of the distant past, and the hyperbolic discounting of the ever-nearing future.

To begin with the past. Like denial, *chasing the first high* is a notorious part of addiction lore. Early experiences with drugs can be extraordinary in their wonder, their intensity, their bliss—even if, over time, the pleasure of use typically lessens while the costs propagate. Suppose a person with addiction is reflecting on their history with drugs, considering whether to use now. Looking back over their entire history, the view is one of diminishing returns: They are addicted, after all, so their drug use now carries evident and severe costs. But looking back only to those early days of use, the view is seductive. There were no costs then—only bliss. How then do our memories of our past influence our present decisions? In a series of studies, the cognitive neuroscientists Aaron Bornstein, Nathaniel Daw, Kenneth Norman, and their colleagues have shown that we do not always aggregate and average all of our relevant past experiences to come to a view as to what to do.[18] Rather, we sometimes "sample" particular episodic memories that are both salient in themselves but also easy to retrieve in contexts where the present bears some similarity to the past and so brings them to mind. The salience of early drug experiences combined with ordinary memory sampling when considering whether to use—that is, when in a drug-associated context, similar at least in this minimal respect with the drug-associated contexts of the past—may therefore bias deliberation about whether to use toward drugs, inclining people to ignore much of their drug history while chasing after the first high. Memory sampling may therefore decrease the likelihood that people with addiction come to a stable judgment that it would be best to quit or form a sincere intention at all. Like some of the other problems cataloged, this mechanism boosts the salience of drug benefits, ignoring or minimizing the costs.[19]

Now turn to the future. In discussing time discounting, we have already seen how the immediacy of a reward can act as a bonus, increasing its value compared to what it would otherwise be. But our love of immediate gratification and tendency to write off the future is more complicated. The behavioral economist and psychiatrist George Ainslie has argued that—in rats, pigeons, and humans alike—the behavioral data is not best explained either by a one-off bonus merely for immediacy or by an exponential time discounting function; rather, the discounting function that best fits the behavioral data is *hyperbolic*.[20] This means that the difference that time makes to reward value is not the same across all periods of time. As a reward nears in time, the rate at which its value increases itself increases, creating preference reversals over time.

To see the difference between exponential and hyperbolic discounting, imagine that at time t_1 you are considering two future rewards, a smaller reward R_S that you could get at t_5 and a larger reward R_L that you could get at t_{10}. At t_1 you prefer R_L to R_S (after all, it is larger). Suppose now that the discounting function is exponential. For each interval of time between t_1 and t_5 (that is, from t_1 to t_2, from t_2 to t_3, from t_3 to t_4, from t_4 to t_5) the value of R_S increases at the same rate. So, at t_4 the value of R_S is that much larger than it was at t_1. But it still doesn't trump the value of R_L. This is because, for each interval of time between t_1 and t_5, the value of R_L is also increasing at the same rate. At any time—including at t_4 when R_S is about to be available—R_L is always proportionally larger and therefore preferable to R_S. Your preference for R_L over R_S is stable over time.

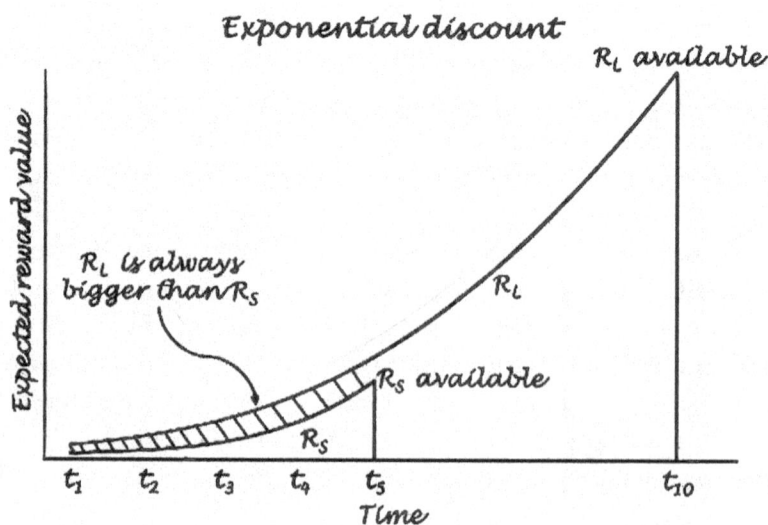

Exponential discount

But now suppose that the discounting function is hyperbolic. Then it is not the case that, for each interval of time between t_1 and t_5, the value of R_S is increasing at the same rate. As t_5 and the availability of R_S approaches, the rate at which its value increases itself increases. So, between t_1 and t_5, the value of R_S increases at a different, higher rate than the value of R_L. This is because R_S is available at t_5 while R_L is not available until t_{10}—it is just that much further away. So, at t_4, when R_S is available imminently at t_5, and R_L is not available until the much more distant time of t_{10}, the value of R_S trumps the value of R_L. Hence, although you prefer R_L to R_S at t_1, t_2, and t_3, this is not the case at t_4. At t_4, you prefer R_S to R_L. Your order of preference is suddenly reversed. It is not stable over time, but fickle.

Apply this to addiction: Imagine that R_S is the opportunity to use drugs at t_5 and that R_L is a reward that accrues from a period of abstinence between t_1 and t_{10}—that is, a reward that comes from *not* using drugs at t_5. Further imagine that the discount function is hyperbolic. Then your preference order between drug use and abstinence is fickle. In the sober light of the morning, say, as you get ready for work, a day of abstinence is preferable to a day where you use drugs. You know you will wake up tomorrow feeling better in your body and about yourself than you are feeling right now. That reward appears bigger than the reward of using drugs later today. But, as the workday is winding up, and with it the possibility of a five o'clock drink nears, that order is reversed, and drug use is now preferable to abstinence. The reward of drinking

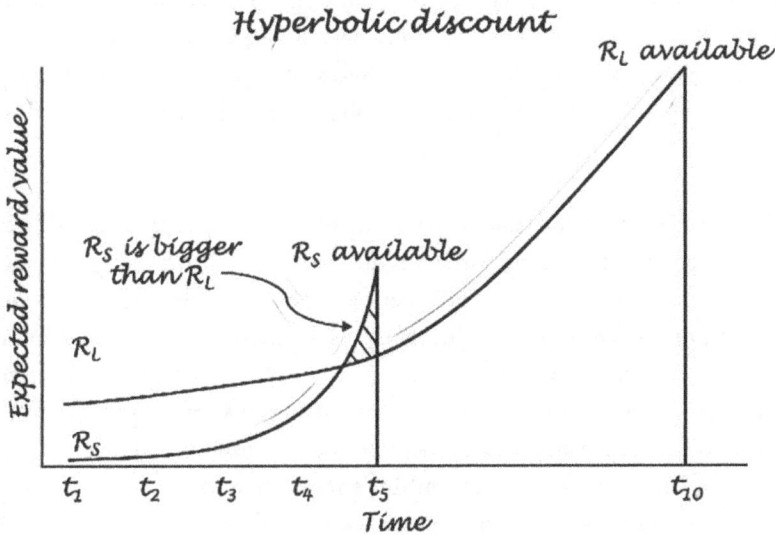

Hyperbolic discount

soon appears bigger than the reward of waking up tomorrow morning after an evening of abstinence. Insofar as preferences constitute or at the very least substantially inform judgments and with them intentions, a person in this predicament may have no stable judgment that abstinence is best nor any sincere intention to abstain—assuming that sincerity is measured, at least in part, by some moderate degree of durability. For a pro-abstinence verdict is all too quickly replaced by its opposite: a pro-drug verdict, in the form of a judgment that drug use is best and a sincere intention to use just as soon as you get off work.

In these kinds of cases, control as I have defined it is not literally lost, for a judgment that abstinence is best and a corresponding intention to abstain either isn't made—or, if made, isn't made to last. The problem is less one of losing control than of failing to achieve the state of mind that makes control possible in the first place. For other animals, perhaps this is less of a worry. What exactly is wrong with changing your mind a lot if you're a rat or a pigeon? But for subjects like us, self-conscious and self-reflective beings, the stakes are different in kind. We know if we are always changing our minds. In consequence, we cannot but live with a sense of our own fickleness. When we wake up in the morning, we can't count on ourselves to live the day in accord with what is then our best judgment or sincere intention, for we know ourselves and so know that, by the evening, we will have changed our mind and decided to drink. We can't trust ourselves. The possibility of diachronic agency—making plans, taking on projects, having life goals—is undermined. At the extreme, we won't have a coherent conception of our own good by which to measure and guide our actions, because we know that whatever conception we light on won't last. As the philosopher Jeanette Kennett has emphasized, perhaps we won't even have a coherent conception of our self.[21] Life is chaos.

Ambivalence. Hyperbolic time discounting means that people with addiction may have different preference orders at different times. But people with addiction may also be ambivalent. Ambivalence sometimes causes a person to have different preference orders at different times—thereby appearing similar to hyperbolic time discounting—but it is not the same. For one, the experience of ambivalence often involves being torn between two incompatible options at one and the same time: neither is preferred, because one sees reason to go both ways. But, as this suggests, ambivalence is therefore more than a brute conflict between psychological states—more than a conflict between a judgment as to what's best, say, and a craving or urge to do the opposite. It is rather a conflict where the pull in different directions typically involves actively and reflectively appreciating the value of each, such that one doesn't know which way is best to go. Here is the philosopher Owen Flanagan describing his experience of loss of control, first as a mere conflict but then as a form of ambivalence:

> At one level, **P** and ~**P** describes the contradictory structure of the addict's economy of desire at many moments of choice: I want not to use, I promise myself and loved ones I will not use, I cross my heart and hope to die if I use, and at that very moment I use. Repeatedly. Conceived exclusively in this way, addiction is a form of weakness of the will, what philosophers call *akrasia*. Two desires, the desire to use and the desire not to use, clash. I root for the first, but the second wins. Perhaps I'm not rooting hard enough or perhaps rooting (willing, hoping, praying) can't penetrate the circuitry at this particular choice node. At another level, **P** and ~**P** describes the structure of something deeper than just repeated episodes of weakness of the will. It can seem to be a choice between being two different versions of myself—me with addiction and me without addiction—both of which have their attractions. Addiction often implicates identity in this deep way. Undoing addiction therefore often involves much more than getting over a bad habit or a weak will.[22]

Because it involves the experience of being pulled two ways, ambivalence is easily misclassified as a problem of control. But, at least in many cases of ambivalence, this would be a mistake. Ambivalence can be more than a mere pull in two directions: If you are ambivalent because there really is reason for you to go either of two incompatible ways, then it is an apt response to your predicament. As the philosopher Justin Coates puts this point, ambivalence can be evidence for—indeed a requirement of—*normative competence*: the capacity to recognize and appreciate the plurality of values and goods to be found in the world, many of which, alas, may conflict with each other, both in principle and in practice.[23] When this is so, ambivalence (unlike indecision) cannot be resolved (rather than becoming moot) merely by picking. The fable of Buridan's Ass imagines a donkey facing a choice between two identical bales of hay positioned at an identical distance away from it. Suppose the donkey is hungry, so eventually ambles over to the left bay of hale rather than going to the one on the right. It decides to go left, but for no reason. By contrast, ambivalence—when there really is reason for you to go either of two incompatible ways—is typically resolved through reason: by figuring out what you should do given your values. That is, by a process of reflecting, imagining, thinking things through, trying them out, feeling your way to a view about what is on balance best—even while acknowledging the value of the path not chosen and any lingering misgivings.

Flanagan locates the source of his ambivalence in considerations of identity. Both versions of himself—with or without addiction—have their attractions to him. But Flanagan is lucky—as he himself would be the first to admit—to be able to imagine the version of himself without addiction. As we saw in chapter 12, some people with addiction may not know who else they could be. No matter how bad life with addiction is, this is, by any reckoning, a reason to stick with it, creating the possibility of ambivalence about quitting. Similarly, as we saw in chapter 10, drugs have tremendous power to relieve terrible misery and suffering in circumstances of severe adversity and genuine hopelessness—potentially becoming objects of security-based attachment. And as we saw in chapter 11, addiction can be a way of satisfying a desire to self-harm or indeed to die—a way of expressing, punishing, or momentarily expiating the bad or purging the evil inside of you, or seizing ownership and control over the body and its fate. In other words, chapters 10, 11, and 12 explored the psychological breadth and depth of the value of drug use for many people with addiction. This value is reason to be ambivalent about quitting. Who would you be if not an addict? What would life be like and how would you cope without drugs? Do you actually want a life that is good for you? Do you believe you deserve one? Do you want to live at all? These questions mean you may not know what is best because you see value in and are torn between incompatible ways of going forward—a life with drugs, or a life without.

Many people with addiction are ambivalent, but no doubt equally many experience a straightforward loss of control. They know what is best—a life without drugs—but nonetheless struggle to live it. Explanations of loss of control—what I have here called problems of control—have been extensively studied and exist as much outside of addiction as within it. The catalog of problems presented in this chapter contains many omissions, and there is a vast amount more to say about every explanation that I have discussed. Problems of control explain the puzzle of addiction in many different ways: from fallibility to defiance to defeat to dissonance; to the boosting of benefits, destabilization of intentions, and erosion of the capacity to trust ourselves caused by various forms of time discounting; to the many ways we can trick ourselves into thinking one more hurrah surely won't hurt. But, notwithstanding the explanatory power of these processes and mechanisms, addiction cannot be defined in terms of loss of control. Many people with addiction don't experience it. And problems of control, despite their number, are only one of many heterogeneous solutions to the puzzle. We should not diminish their importance—they matter greatly to a great many people who struggle with drugs, revealing how the mind can be tricked into weighing costs and benefits so that drugs somehow always seem to come up trumps. But, equally, we should not diminish the importance of everything else that matters, risking a return to where we started: with addiction once again explained and excused for one and only one reason—only this time, not compulsion understood as irresistible desire, but something nonetheless akin, namely the "loss" or "impairment" of the ability to control drug use.

15

Craving

THE IMAGE OF CRAVING that has long shaped scientific, philosophical, and popular imagination is an illusion. Cravings are not irresistible desires, and not all people with addiction experience cravings at all.[1] Yet they are predictive of use and relapse,[2] and some people experience cravings years into recovery, when they neither meet the *Diagnostic and Statistical Manual of Mental Disorders* (DSM-5) diagnostic criteria for a substance use disorder nor count as addicted according to our explication.[3] With the necessary groundwork now laid, this chapter addresses the nature and role of cravings for drugs in addiction.

The addiction scientists Cecilia Bergeria, Kelly Dunn, and their colleagues asked thirty-nine people diagnosed with opioid addiction an open-ended question: "What do you mean when you say you are craving opioids?"[4] They identified eight distinct dimensions of meaning in the answers, including (i) anticipation of positive reinforcement (for example, pleasure or getting high); (ii) anticipation of negative reinforcement (for example, relief from suffering); (iii) interfering thoughts; (iv) having a need; (v) physical withdrawal symptoms; (vi) desire to use; (vii) lack of control over use; and (viii) physical pain relief. Although some of these dimensions may overlap to some extent, no single meaning was identified by all subjects. Answers varied with years in treatment, addiction severity, and race. So, to be clear, by "craving" I mean a kind of desire. But just as not all people with addiction experience cravings, not all desires for drugs *are* cravings. I therefore begin with some general remarks about desire, to identify which are cravings.

The landscape of desire is full of cross-cutting distinctions:

1. Desires can be *standing* or *occurrent*. Standing desires are waiting offstage: not currently "playing a role in one's psyche."[5] For example, most

of us have a desire for the people we love to be happy and healthy. But you probably weren't thinking of it before you read the previous sentence: It wasn't occurrent. Occurrent desires are currently playing a role in one's psyche, but this role varies. They may or may not be guiding behavior, just as they may or may not be conscious. You are now thinking of your desire for the people you love to be happy and healthy—it is conscious. But, if you are still reading, it is probably not guiding your behavior. Rather, your desire to read this book is guiding your behavior. But even though your desire to read is guiding your behavior, you probably weren't conscious of it until you read the previous sentence. You were reading—attending to the book, not attending to your desire to read it.

2. We speak about desires both as *for objects* or *to perform actions*. For example, you can desire food, or to eat.

3. It is not obvious that desires, by contrast with wishes, can be straightforwardly directed at the past. But they can certainly be directed at either the present or the future. You can desire to eat *now*, or *later*.

4. Desires can be *intrinsic* or *instrumental*. You can desire an object or to perform an action for its own sake, or because it is a means to an end you independently desire. For example, you can desire to eat for its own sake, that is, just for the sake of eating. Or you can desire to eat because you desire to put on weight, and you know that to do so, you need to eat. Hence, you desire to eat.

5. Some, but not all, desires are appetitive. The philosopher Wayne Davis argues for a distinction between *volitive* and *appetitive* desires, marked (but not defined) by the difference between a subject *desiring* an object or to perform an action, and a subject *having a desire* for an object or to perform an action.[6] For example, consider that you can desire to eat (because you need to put on weight) but not have a desire to eat (because you are not hungry). Equally, you can desire not to eat (because you have put on too much weight) but have a desire to eat (because you are hungry). Volitive desires are typically based on reasons, which can include the fact that you have an appetitive desire, alongside all-things-considered judgments as to what is best. Appetitive desires, by contrast, are not typically based on reasons. Rather, they view their object or the action to be performed with pleasure, in a general, inchoate way. What this means, at a minimum, is that the object or action that is desired *beckons* (see chapter 6). It does not mean that the

object or action will in fact be pleasurable—nor even that the subject believes that it will. For example, you may have a desire to eat but know it will not be pleasurable to eat, because you have a toothache. Nonetheless, eating beckons.

Cravings for drugs are occurrent, present-directed, appetitive desires to use drugs. Although we speak of craving *drugs*, what we mean is that a person craves *to use them* (not, for example, merely to stockpile them to have for later use—although that is of course a perfectly possible desire to have). They occur at a time or over a period of time, and they are directed (more or less) at the time when they occur. Cravings for drugs are to take drugs *now* (or at least *very soon*). But they are now, at the time when they occur, unsatisfied. You can crave what you don't currently have or more of what you do currently have, but you can't crave only what, at the time of craving, you already have. This may help explain their characteristic phenomenology. Because they are occurrent, present-directed, and unsatisfied, they capture attention and have an immediate, felt, urgency.[7]

Cravings for drugs also have varying degrees of specificity. You can crave alcohol or you can crave a perfect Manhattan—not a beer or a glass of red wine. Amphetamines in general—or cocaine in particular. Heroin—but not oxycontin. But a craving, however specific, may be satisfied and not just extinguished by objects other than what it is for. A craving for a Manhattan may be satisfied by a glass of red wine. A craving for amphetamines may be satisfied by heroin. We can individuate the object of a craving by appeal to the outcomes that will satisfy it, and lose the phenomenological specificity of the experience. Or we can individuate the object of a craving by appeal to the phenomenological specificity of the experience, and lose the connection to the outcomes that will satisfy it. This quandary is not unique to cravings for drugs but characteristic of many appetitive desires.

Lastly, cravings for drugs can also be either intrinsic or instrumental. To see this, consider the relationship between craving and withdrawal. As we saw in chapter 4, some but not all addictive drugs produce physical dependence, such that dose reduction or abstinence results in a characteristic set of physical withdrawal symptoms. For example, withdrawal from opioids typically lasts up to a week and can include fever, nausea, diarrhea, aches, cramps, runny nose, watery eyes, insomnia, formication, and more. As this list attests, it is awful to experience. It is also alleviated by taking opioids. It is often assumed that simply being in a state of opioid withdrawal therefore generates a craving for opioids, but it does not. People must learn through experience that taking opioids is a means to alleviating opioid withdrawal (and rats may never be able to learn).[8] Evidence for this comes from the common phenomenon of what is called "hospital flu." Patients who become physically dependent on opioids after taking them for pain relief while in hospital may not know that they are. After discharge, they go into withdrawal, but they believe they have flu. They do not crave opioids. But if you tell such a person that taking opioids—or, indeed, taking any drug, whatever its nature—will alleviate their symptoms, they will typically desire to do so. They may, indeed, feel a kind of desperation to find and take the drug that they now know will bring them relief. This desire is generated by a process of instrumental reasoning. The person desires relief, they come to believe that taking the drug will bring relief, so they therefore desire to take the drug. The sense of desperation to find and take the drug is inherited from the desperation to feel relief. I do not want to claim that we would never call such a desire a "craving"—craving talk is evidently loose. But it is importantly different from what I think we ordinarily mean by cravings for drugs. The reason is that the desire is formed through instrumental reasoning as opposed to direct experience of the reward of taking an opioid when in withdrawal. To see this difference, suppose that, in the throes of withdrawal, the person gets hold of an opioid and takes it. Doing so brings immediate relief. They now know, *from experience and for themself*, what exactly taking an opioid will do for them—the relief that it will bring. Next time they are in withdrawal, they may therefore crave opioids in the ordinary sense of craving.[9]

Desires can be generated by instrumental reasoning or learned through experience, and we ordinarily take cravings for drugs to be learned through experience. But cravings that are learned through experience can be either intrinsic or instrumental. A person can crave drugs for their own sake. They crave drugs, *simpliciter*. But the person who craves opioids when they are in withdrawal because they know for themself the relief opioids will bring does not crave opioids for their own sake, but because they are a means to alleviating the suffering of withdrawal.

Suppose we ask, of a person with addiction gripped by craving and on the verge of using drugs, *why* they are craving drugs. As the philosopher Michael Smith has noted, even if actions are explained by beliefs and desires, the explanation of an action may be incomplete if we cite only the belief and desire.[10] To make sense of the behavior, we may also need to explain why a person desires what they desire or believes what they believe. In other words, explaining drug use in addiction by appeal to cravings—occurrent, present-directed, appetitive desires that capture attention and have an immediate, felt urgency—is only the first step to explaining the behavior. The second is to explain why a person is craving drugs.

In what follows, I suggest three kinds of explanation of cravings for drugs. Each can be understood as corresponding to a variety of craving that I shall call cue induced, goal focused, and attachment based. These varieties are pragmatic, in the sense that they count as kinds in so far as they have value in explanation and, correspondingly, prediction and intervention. They may well not be exhaustive, they are certainly not in all cases mutually exclusive, and there is little reason to hold that they carve the world at its joints (as the saying goes).

Cue-induced craving. Drug cues are stimuli that have become associated with drug use through individual learning. They can be exteroceptive: people, places, paraphernalia, or advertisements. And they can be interoceptive: memories, moods, emotions, or physical states such as, for example, withdrawal or drug priming.[11] It is uncontroversial that drug cues can instigate drug seeking and drug taking in rats and humans alike. The controversial question is why. As we saw in chapter 6, the psychologist Lee Hogarth argues that drug cues do not cause habitual drug responding in humans, but rather signal that a response has a higher probability than it otherwise would of securing drugs, thereby (potentially) initiating goal-directed behavior.[12] Belief that drugs are available may, of course, lead to cravings. Smokers on short and long flights alike report that they develop cravings only at the end of the trip, when they believe it will soon be possible to smoke—notably, given the difference in length of forced abstinence, their cravings are of similar strength.[13] Similarly, the satisfaction of a craving can depend on believing that a drug has been consumed, not just consuming it. After smoking a nicotine cigarette, smokers report that their craving is satisfied only if they also believe the cigarette is not a placebo.[14] By "cue-induced craving" I do not just mean cravings in some way caused by cues. Cues can no doubt cause goal-focused or attachment-based cravings. I mean cravings that are putatively explained by a particular theory of addiction: the incentive salience theory initially advanced by the neuroscientists Terry Robinson and Kent Berridge.[15]

The incentive salience theory claims that cravings for drugs are caused by neuroadaptations to the mesolimbic dopamine system. This system is hypothesized to imbue stimuli and behavior with "incentive salience." This means, quite simply, that they capture attention and become desired. Many classes of drugs enhance dopamine transmission. The incentive salience theory states that long-term immoderate drug use can cause the mesolimbic dopamine system to become hypersensitized to drug-associated stimuli[16] and behavior, transforming ordinary desires into intense cravings when cues are present (or indeed merely imagined). Crucially, this hypersensitization occurs independently of the neural systems mediating positive and negative reinforcement—in other words, independently of any rewarding outcome of drug use, such as pleasure or relief from the suffering of withdrawal. As Robinson and Berridge colloquially put the point, "wanting" drugs can come apart from "liking" them. Hence, the answer provided by incentive salience theory to the question of why an individual craves drugs is that neuroadaptations cause hypersensitization to drug cues leading to craving that is excessive and—this is key—not to be explained instrumentally (by recourse to what drugs do for a person, for example, bringing pleasure or relieving suffering) or expressively (by recourse to what drugs mean to them, more on which below). In other words, the explanation of drug craving is fundamentally not a psychological explanation. It is a neurobiological explanation.

The incentive salience theory therefore shares something important with the habit theory, which I introduced in chapter 6. By contrast with the habit theory, the incentive salience theory explains drug use by appeal to desire. Drugs *beckon*. But there is yet a kind of mindlessness. Cue-induced craving for drugs is, in effect, *psychologically* inexplicable. There may be no purpose in drug use, nothing for which it is done or that it means. Cue-induced craving is, in its purest form, a "bare" desire—a desire to take drugs, for the sake of taking drugs, *nothing more*. As emphasized in the philosopher Richard Holton and Kent Berridge's coauthored work, it is therefore an intrinsic desire.[17] Indeed it is, in a sense, the pinnacle of all intrinsic desires. In theory, there may be no real or anticipated reward in taking drugs at all, apart from the "bare" reward of doing what is desired. Hence, from an ordinary psychological perspective—whether that of an observer or the person whose craving it is—cue-induced craving has no explanation. To explain why an individual craves drugs, we appeal not to their mind but their brain.

In consequence, cue-induced craving is well positioned to explain something important about some people's lived experience of addiction.[18] Namely the experience of not making psychological sense—to oneself. Consider the philosopher Owen Flanagan's description of his addiction as "**P** and **~P**," initially quoted in chapter 14: "I wanted not to use; I expressed to myself, my loved ones, and to mental-health professionals a sincere desire not to use; and I used. Repeatedly, I enacted a contradiction. **P** and ~**P**."[19] In chapter 14, I suggested that Flanagan uses the idea of **P** and ~**P** first as a way of naming a mere conflict within his desires, then as a way of naming a form of ambivalence. But his repeated use of the phrase over the course of his book to try to describe what it is like to be an "addict" suggests something more. In its logical form, the statement "**P** and ~**P**" is *incoherent*. "**P**" stands for any proposition and "~" stands for negation, so, as Flanagan notes, it expresses a contradiction by asserting a proposition and its negation in conjunction. This is not like a mere conflict of desires or a form of ambivalence—neither of which is incoherent at all. Rather, Flanagan seems to be using "**P** and ~**P**" to reflect something about the psychological unintelligibility to *himself*—from within the first-person perspective—of his cravings for drugs. Drugs beckon—but, at least for some periods of his addiction, there is nothing he can say about why they beckon. In this light, consider the following quotation from the writer and poet Tove Ditlevsen's autobiography, which powerfully illustrates her experience of and alienation from her cravings during her recovery from opioid addiction: "Then my attention was suddenly caught by a well-lit pharmacy window. It radiated a muted light from the containers of mercury and beakers filled with crystals. I kept staring there, while the yearning for the small white pills, which were so easy to get, rose inside me like a dark liquid. Horrified, I realized while I stood there that the longing was inside me like rot in a tree, or like an embryo growing all on its own, even though you want nothing to do with it."[20]

It is a virtue of incentive salience theory that it can help explain the experience of self-opacity. But it is not everyone's experience of craving—nor even, as Flanagan and Ditleven make plain at other points their writings, their experience at all times.[21] Flanagan also describes using drugs to feel absolutely, existentially, exquisitely safe and secure in his own skin. Ditlevsen also writes of how opioids allow her to feel at peace with herself, to escape from her inner emptiness and unfulfilled needs. For the writer and journalist Caroline Knapp, in the throes of her addiction there is hardly anything she needs that she thinks alcohol *can't* do. Here are her "mathematics of self-transformation":[22]

Discomfort + Drink = No Discomfort
Fear + Drinking = Bravery
Repression + Drink = Openness
Pain + Drink = Self-obliteration

There is no self-opacity in these testimonials. There is self-knowledge. At least in these regards, these writers use drugs as means to achieve various ends that we might summarily call *psychic transportation*. Put simply, they use drugs to feel better.

Goal-focused craving. Cravings for drugs are goal focused when drugs are craved because they are means to ends, that is, drugs can be used to achieve *goals*. Craving drugs in anticipation or in the throes of physical withdrawal is an important kind of goal-focused craving, central to opioid and alcohol addiction. Its underlying mechanisms have been much studied, notably by the neuroscientist George Koob.[23] As previously described, such cravings are not generated through a process of instrumental reasoning. Rather, they come from the experience of using drugs when in physical withdrawal and thereby learning what drugs do: namely alleviate its symptoms. Nonetheless they are instrumental desires—desires for drugs in order to achieve a goal.

Psychic transportation is a goal. Drugs allow us to experience many kinds of positive psychological states: from deep and varied forms of pleasure and euphoria, to safety, comfort, peace, exhilaration, joy, connectedness to others and the world. They also provide us with relief from negative psychological states: escape from all forms of misery and suffering. Quite often, they do a bit of both. As we saw in chapter 1, these ends are some of the ordinary reasons why people use drugs, outside of addiction. As we saw in chapter 10, drugs continue to serve these ends in addiction. Self-medication can in principle explain the puzzle of addiction without remainder in cases where people come from backgrounds of severe adversity and limited socioeconomic opportunities and suffer from poor mental health. These life circumstances are associated with addiction chronicity and severity—an association that, as demonstrated by Hogarth, is mediated by use of drugs as a coping strategy as measured by self-report.[24] Of course, people with addiction also use drugs to self-medicate even when they do not come from such backgrounds: Self-medication can be part of the explanation of the puzzle even if it is not all of it. But whenever people routinely use drugs to self-medicate, the explanation of why they crave them is simple and straightforward. If they are anticipating or experiencing negative psychological states, they crave drugs for the psychic transportation that they know, from experience and for themselves, drugs bring.

Psychic transportation is a common goal of drug use in addiction. But there is another kind of goal-focused craving that emerges from the previous chapters: cravings for drugs because drugs constitute a person's go-to means to self-harm. The goal here is not psychic transportation. The goal is self-harm: to express, punish, or momentarily expiate the bad self within, or to seize ownership and control over the body and its fate. Perhaps the goal is even to die—or at least to flirt with death. But the shape of the explanation is the same. If a person has a history of using drugs to satisfy desires to self-harm and so knows, from experience and for themselves, the satisfaction that doing so brings, then they may crave drugs to self-harm—just the way another person may crave drugs to feel better.

Attachment-based craving. Cue-induced cravings are intrinsic and well-explained neurobiologically by the effect of long-term immoderate drug use on the mesolimbic dopamine system. Goal-focused cravings are instrumental and well-explained psychologically by learning from experience what drugs can do and using them to do it. Attachment-based cravings are both intrinsic and well-explained psychologically by considering what drugs mean to a person. This intrinsic meaning can be security based or identity based.

In chapter 10, I introduced the philosopher Monique Wonderly's analysis of the relationship that some people have to drugs as a form of *security-based attachment*. Although the fundamental reason why it is possible to form a security-based attachment to drugs is that drugs are able to provide a sense of safety in the face of deep emotional distress—to soothe, to still, to make things better—once an attachment is formed, drugs become irreplaceable. There are no substitute objects possible without significant loss, creating a need for the attachment object, that is, *drugs*, themselves. There is therefore an emotional dependence on *them*, over and above any need for the original end that drugs served—that is, psychic transportation—to be secured in some way or other.

For illustration, consider how Hank, one of the men depicted in the anthropologist Philippe Bourgois and the photojournalist Jeffrey Schonberg's book *Righteous Dopefiend*, describes his relationship to heroin: "You know how when you're walkin' and you look up and across the street and you see someone you think you know? And then you walk closer, and it turns out to be an old friend, someone you used to kick it with as a kid. And you walk up to each other, and you each ask how the other's doing. And you talk for a while. And then you leave, saying to yourself, 'Wow! It was really good to see him.' That's what heroin feels like to me."[25] Bourgois and Schonberg note that the men they speak with are not embarrassed by lack of sexual and romantic relationships, typically cutting short conversation with a common refrain: "My old lady is heroin and I been faithful to her for over twenty years. I've never cheated on her, and I never will."[26]

Cravings can be security based. As these testimonials intimate, people can have a relationship with drugs that is akin to a relationship with a person whom they care about or love. Of course, there are differences. Drugs can't love them back, and even if someone desires drugs intrinsically, that is, for their own sake, no one cares about drugs for their own sake—or desires what's good *for drugs themselves*—in sharp contrast to how we care about other people. But, as Wonderly notes, we need the people to whom we are attached. They provide us with a sense of security and make us feel stable and safe in the world. And this can be true of drugs. Indeed, a person's relationship with drugs may be the most important such relationship they have—drugs may be the one thing that has never let them down. In consequence, the idea let alone the reality of doing without drugs is daunting, disorienting, unmooring—a cause for grief. Quitting is "heartbreak."[27] When this is so, the explanation of why a person craves drugs may be that it is expressive of a need stemming from security-based attachment and its consequence, the fear of loss. Their cravings for drugs are wrapped up with the meaning of this relationship—similar to the cravings we can all feel to be with and keep close the people we love and never want to lose.

Cravings can also be identity based. In chapter 12, I argued that for some people an "addict" identity may provide the main if not the only source of relationships, community, daily structure and purpose, self-worth, and sense of self. If the shape of your life and sense of self depends on being an "addict," then doing without drugs is not only a cause for grief. It also represents an existential threat. Who are you if not an "addict"? What life is yours to inhabit if not the life of an "addict"? This void can be terrifying, and renders utterly comprehensible why a person might be desperate to keep living as an "addict" notwithstanding its costs. In which case, the explanation of why they crave drugs is that drugs are an essential part of the life they know and the person they are—similar to the cravings we can all feel for any of the things that we experience as essential to our lives and identities.

Whether derived from security or identity, attachment-based cravings are the opposite of psychologically inexplicable drug desires. They are at the heart of ordinary human psychology. But they are not instrumental desires. An important feature of goal-focused cravings is that they make drugs *replaceable*—if, that is, another means to satisfying the desire can be found. Suppose this to be the case. Suppose that a person for whom drugs provide relief from misery and suffering finds another way to achieve this. If this person is, in addition, attached to drugs and a life of using—if their relationship with drugs is both security based and identity based and so a deep and meaningful part of their life—then, even if they opt to replace drugs with this alternative means of relief, we would nonetheless expect them to grieve, to yearn, to crave what they have lost, to crave to be who they were once again. As the writer and critic Maggie Nelson reflects: "I consider early sobriety a form of mourning, insofar as it involves letting go of a self or a past or forms of hoping or coping that one previously felt unable to go on without."[28] That is, no matter that they have another means of relief from misery and suffering, we would still expect them to feel some pull toward a life of using. This is because their relationship with drugs is not just based on what drugs instrumentally do for them. It is based on what they intrinsically mean to them. Security or identity attachment-based cravings are intrinsic desires for drugs—like cue-induced cravings. But unlike cue-induced cravings, they can be explained by ordinary human psychology.

To sum up where we have got to: Cravings for drugs are occurrent, present-directed, appetitive desires to use drugs that are unsatisfied at the time at which they occur. They capture attention, and have an immediate, felt, urgency. They come in (at least) three varieties: cue induced, goal focused, and attachment based. They are not irresistible. They contribute to solving the puzzle of addiction because they are salient and strong. They are therefore both more likely to be acted on than less salient, less strong desires, and to make for problems of control (see chapter 14). But why they are salient and strong depends on why a person is craving drugs. In some cases, the explanation is fundamentally neurobiological. In other cases, it is because of what drugs do for a person or mean to a person and hence what it would be for them to live without drugs. This is a far cry from the image of craving debunked in chapter 6: as a desire so strong that it is impossible even to imagine, let alone to resist. I therefore conclude this chapter, and with it this part, by contrasting the strategies to address addiction that emerge from the image of craving as irresistible desire with the strategies suggested by the complexity and variety of cravings I have here presented.

To begin, suppose that cravings for drugs really were of a strength that made them impossible to resist. What then should we do to address addiction? There are two obvious solutions. The first is supply restriction. *Make it the case that there are no drugs to be found.* Then it won't matter if drug desires are impossible to resist. For there won't be any drugs for anyone to use. The prohibition and criminalization of the possession of many classes of drugs attempts just this. It is not a successful strategy. For the sake of argument, let us put to one side the many serious issues of injustice: the criminalization of conduct that in itself does not constitute a severe harm to or violation of the rights of others; the effects on individuals and communities of incarceration—which in our society disproportionately burdens people of color and the poor.[29] Simply from a practical perspective, this strategy has not been successful. People have always found and continue to find ways to use drugs, despite prohibition and criminalization. Meanwhile, drugs that are pharmacologically identical to those prohibited or criminalized for recreational purposes are necessary for medical purposes. Are we going to stop using all drugs? What about for surgeries? To help people cope with pain? To help people sleep? To help people manage mental health problems other than addiction? It is simply not realistic to try to address addiction by banishing drugs from our society. They have always been out there (see chapter 1). They always will be.

The second solution is restriction of freedom. *Make it the case that people with addiction have no access to any drugs that can be found.* Then it won't matter if drugs are out there and drug desires in addiction are irresistible, because people with addiction won't be able to find them and use them. The confinement of people addicted to drugs—whether in prisons or treatment centers— attempts this. This strategy is also unsuccessful. Drugs pervade many prisons and treatment centers. Meanwhile, you cannot—again for practical reasons, putting aside the many serious issues of injustice—confine people indefinitely to stop them from using. Yet despite their evident failures, both strategies remain prevalent.

Notice that both of these strategies are fundamentally *controlling*. They control supply, and they control people. This focus on control also characterizes the translational orientation of addiction science and clinical treatment—not now of supply or people, but of desires. This is evident in the continuous scientific search for new pharmacotherapies to block the generation of cravings,[30] and in a corresponding clinical emphasis not just on the prescription of pharmacotherapies but on the use of cognitive strategies to improve behavioral control such that patients are better placed to deal with any cravings that pharmacotherapies fail to eradicate. In other words, at least in some jurisdictions, a standard treatment plan is to use drugs (the "good" ones) to control the desire for drugs (the "bad" ones). And if (the "good") drugs fail, we try to get people to control their desires for themselves.

Lest I be misunderstood: Pharmacotherapies that help—which many do—should be unconditionally and universally offered. These include, among others, nicotine patches for nicotine addiction, disulfiram for alcohol addiction, naltrexone for alcohol and opioid addiction, and methadone, buprenorphine, and even injectable heroin (in refractory cases) for opioid addiction.[31] Equally, all tips, tricks, and therapeutic techniques that help people develop better control over their drug use should be deployed—whether these involve direct exercise of control over cravings, or methods to guard against fallibility, time discounting, cognitive dissonance, and all the other ways we are able to convince ourselves that one last hurrah surely won't hurt (see chapter 14). My point is not to suggest that we *restrict* interventions that could help, like pharmacotherapies and cognitive strategies to improve behavioral control, *but to expand them.* This is why recognition of the complexity and variety of craving matters.

First, consider cue-induced craving. This variety of craving is most at risk of invoking an image of irresistibility. This is for two reasons. First, and most simply, its label. Phrases like "cue induced" and its cognates such as "cue driven" or "cue reactive" sound deterministic. Second, the mindlessness of this form of craving that I argued was in fact a virtue insofar as it explains the self-opacity that people with addiction sometimes experience. But incentive salience theory has never claimed that cravings are irresistible—only that hypersensitization of the mesolimbic dopamine system is a good explanation for why drug cravings are strong in the face of drug cues.[32] Proper appreciation of the theory therefore invites two kinds of intervention. First, the social regulation of drug cues, through state oversight of advertising, packaging, and control of outlet density.[33] All too often, avoiding cues is left up to people with addiction themselves. For example, consider the injunction "don't go to the pub." Good advice, but hard to take in our drug-obsessed society. Much more could be done to limit cue exposure. Second, the necessity of offering contingency management treatment—especially therapeutic workplaces, as discussed in chapters 1 and 6—as well as ensuring what social justice anyhow demands, namely fair distribution across all strata of society of the opportunity to avail oneself of alternative reinforcers, such as, for example, education, employment, social belonging, or "a stake in conventional life." We can address cue-induced craving by the provision of meaningful and competing alternative rewards.[34] Rather than try to control cravings for drugs, why not intervene to provide socioeconomic opportunities that will create and support *alternative* desires and goals—things that make life good and give it meaning and purpose?

Next, consider goal-focused craving. The basic strategy to address these is straightforward. Figure out what drugs are doing for a person and find something else to do it instead. As the writer and self-proclaimed "junkie" William S. Burroughs is notorious for saying: "Anything that can be accomplished chemically can be accomplished in other ways."[35] Find these ways. Some may in fact be chemical—just different chemicals. If heroin or fentanyl is being used to stave off withdrawal, try methadone or buprenorphine. In more severe cases of alcohol addiction, get people to a detox center so stopping drinking doesn't threaten their lives. But some are far from chemical. If drugs are being used for pleasure, think about how to expand possibilities for and repertoires of other, nonchemical pleasures. If drugs are being used to cope with negative psychological states, try alternative coping strategies, like developing techniques for emotional regulation, talk therapies, forms of self-care, mindfulness, and peer-to-peer or group support. Over time, these strategies may also help diminish the occurrence of the negative psychological states themselves.

Note that this is especially important when considering how to help people who crave drugs because they are a go-to means of self-harm. When working with self-harm in general, strategies that satisfy the desire but harm a person *less* than their go-to method can be an essential step in effective treatment, improving their overall well-being and reducing the level of damage and risk. Consider a person who both cuts and uses drugs to self-harm. As shocking as this may initially sound, in some cases it may be less risky for them to cut in a superficial and safe way at home—where blades can be sterilized and wounds can be cleaned and bandaged—than to impulsively source and use drugs on the streets, where they don't know what or how much they're getting, and are vulnerable to theft as well as sexual and physical assault when they're high. A first step of treatment might therefore be to support such a person to replace risky drug use with superficial and comparatively safe cutting. The second step, of course, would then be to replace such cutting with a coping strategy that does no damage and carries no risk. Just as harm reduction can be a central component of addiction treatment, so too it can be a central component of treatment for self-harm. But for the vast majority of people who self-harm—through drugs or otherwise—the ultimate hope of treatment is for the desire to self-harm itself to abate. The same alternative coping strategies that can replace drugs can be tried for self-harm—techniques for emotional regulation, talk therapies, forms of self-care, mindfulness, and peer-to-peer or group support. Again, over time, these strategies may help diminish the occurrence of the negative psychological states themselves that are driving the desire to self-harm, thereby making it abate.

Finally, consider attachment-based craving. One of the many puzzling features of addiction is that relapse can occur long after abstinence has been achieved. Lasting neuroadaptations to the mesolimbic dopamine system offer one explanation.[36] Attachment-based craving offers another. If a person's relationship with drugs is a deep and meaningful part of their life and identity, then drugs are irreplaceable. That is what it is to be attached. Imagine if you could once again see a person whom you loved and lost years after the rupture. Even if you decided on balance not to reopen that relationship, wouldn't the pull to do so be strong? There are moments in all our lives when relationships and identities we have cast away still call to us—even if on balance we do not want to reinhabit them. Here is Knapp making just this point: "I once heard a woman say that as an alcoholic, a part of her will always be deeply attracted to alcohol, which seemed a very simple way of putting it, and very true. The attraction—the pull, the hunger, the yearning—doesn't die when you say good-bye to the drink, any more than the pull toward a bad lover dies when you finally walk out the door."[37]

As noted in chapter 12, to successfully recover and resist relapse typically requires a kind of *narrative work*.[38] It may not be sufficient to stop using drugs and to create a new life structured around activities, projects, relationships, and identities that do not involve drugs. People with addiction may also need to find a way to tell a life story that makes sense of the depth of this transition, to stabilize their new life and identity and protect them from the pull of the past. But crucially, and as the philosopher Jeanette Kennett has argued, the authenticity and credibility of this narrative will be greatly enhanced if it is embraced and validated by others.[39] There are in consequence three ways to help people who experience attachment-based cravings quit and not relapse. The first is to acknowledge the depth of their relationship with drugs, allowing them to voice the reality of attachment and loss. Support and validation make difficult experiences more bearable for us all. The second is to leverage the intervention I suggested was not only required as a matter of justice but potentially helpful to addressing cue-based cravings and to scaffolding new identities: Construct activities that constitute "a stake in conventional life" and create opportunities to fashion a "nonaddict" self. The third is to offer ourselves for relationships and make our communities places of compassion and welcome. Many people with severe addiction will have lost friends and family and may find themselves socially isolated and deeply ostracized from other people and wider society. Indeed, that may be part of why their relationship with drugs has become so important. To put it in the simplest possible terms, to address addiction and to help people crave drugs *less* we need to stop stigmatizing and blaming them and find ways to reach out.

Ethics and Relationships

Introduction to Part IV

GIVEN THAT DRUG USE in addiction is voluntary, solving the puzzle and explaining why a person would persist when the costs appear so evident and severe requires taking up their perspective—listening to what they say and imagining what it would be like to live as they live, see what they see, think as they think. When we undertake this kind of dialogical and imaginative work, the solutions to the puzzle that come into view schematically divide in two. Some solutions approach the puzzle by focusing on how the benefits of drug use may be hidden while the costs are salient *from the perspective of observers*. Chapters 10, 11 and 12, on self-medication and security-based attachment, self-harm and the desire to die, and an "addict" identity, are examples of this approach. They attempt to illuminate how drugs can have value and meaning to people with addiction that we, observers, may not see. Other solutions approach the puzzle by focusing on how the costs of drug use may be hidden while the benefits are salient *from the perspective of people with addiction themselves*. Chapter 13, on denial and cognitive difficulties, and chapter 14, on problems of control, are examples of this approach. They attempt to illuminate how drugs can carry costs that people with addiction may minimize, rationalize, ignore—or not see at all. Chapter 15 is a solution of neither type. Rather, it makes good on the promise of an account of the nature and role of cravings for drugs in addiction. There are three varieties of craving—cue induced, goal focused, and attachment based—each of which corresponds to an answer to the question of *why* people crave drugs. Strategies and interventions to help people manage their cravings need to reflect what kinds of cravings they have. Once again, there is heterogeneity. But there are also two more general lessons. The first is that the debunked image of craving as a desire so strong that it is impossible even to imagine let alone to resist has driven us toward a range of strategies to address addiction that are ineffective and *controlling*—not just of supply but of people. The second is that, notwithstanding the heterogeneity of solutions to the puzzle of addiction and kinds of craving alike, to address addiction we need to stop stigmatizing and blaming people and find ways to reach out.

Part IV takes up these lessons. Because drug use in addiction is voluntary, strategies to address addiction need to engage with a person's *agency*. Yet recognition of agency can lead to attributions of responsibility and a tendency to stigmatize and blame—especially when drug use not only harms the person themself but in addition wrongs or hurts others. Part IV aims to square this circle. It offers an ethical framework—an interlocking set of ideas and practices—for how to reach out, acknowledging agency without thereby inviting stigma and licensing blame.

Chapter 16 sets the stage. It constitutes a philosophical reflection on my experience working in a UK therapeutic community for people with personality disorder and complex needs, many of whom struggled with drug and behavioral addictions. These conditions involve behavior that harms the person themself and/or others, often leading clinicians and staff teams to get stuck in what I call *the rescue-blame trap*. A rescuing mindset takes the view that people with these conditions can't help behaving as they do. It denies agency, and in consequence sees them as neither responsible nor to blame. A blaming mindset takes the view that people with these conditions can help it. It attributes agency, and in consequence sees them as both responsible and to blame. The brain disease model of addiction invites a rescuing mindset, while the moral model of addiction invites a blaming mindset. Neither mindset is conducive to supporting people to change their relationship to drugs or to repairing and maintaining a relationship that has been damaged by drugs. In a slogan, what is needed is a stance of *responsibility without blame*. I describe some of the clinical practices of answerability and accountability constructed to help people do things differently—to engage their agency in order to support psychological and behavioral change—while also facilitating the relational work required to sustain positive, meaningful relationships with others who have been wronged or hurt. These practices hold responsible, but without blame.

Chapters 17 and 18 are more philosophical in orientation. They articulate the ideas of responsibility and blame that inform the responsibility without blame stance, thereby providing a conceptual foundation for it. To give fair warning: Although I see these ideas as rooted in the clinical practices of answerability and accountability described in chapter 16, chapters 17 and 18 approach them in relatively abstract terms, positioning them within a philosophical landscape.

Chapter 17 is about responsibility. I begin by presenting an idea of responsibility that is standard within moral philosophy and society at large and that functions as a foil to the idea of responsibility found in the clinic: *the juridical image*. According to the juridical image, attributions of responsibility constitute a kind of moral verdict, like criminal findings of fault for wrongdoing. They give us prima facie license to blame and punish in proportion to the wrong done, legitimating hostile attitudes and punitive treatment that would otherwise be morally questionable if not outright impermissible. The juridical image makes an entitlement to blame and punish another person *the point* of determining whether they are responsible. By contrast, according to a responsibility without blame stance, the point of attributing responsibility is to identify where a person has the capacity to do things differently and relationships with them can be expected to take shared work to repair and sustain. Do they have *agency for change*, as it is sometimes called? In keeping with a long tradition of philosophical theorizing about responsibility, the clinical idea of responsibility therefore sees it as flowing from cognitive and volitional capacities. I explain how it can nonetheless sidestep the quagmire of questions—including but not limited to the perennial question of free will and determinism—that plagues this tradition, and I compare it with an alternative way of sidestepping it. This is to approach the idea of responsibility through the lens of our *reactive attitudes*—hostile, negative emotions such as resentment, indignation, anger, outrage, disgust, and contempt.

Chapter 18 is about blame. Blame-talk is loose, so I begin by distinguishing three different things we can mean by saying that another is to blame:

1. They are blameworthy.
2. We should actively blame them.
3. We do actively blame them.

By illustrating how these come apart, I thereby illustrate how what I call *active blame* is in part constituted by our reactive attitudes. These attitudes can be irrational and ripe with a sense of entitlement—a feeling of being in the right in relation to another's wrong—thereby inviting us to inflict them onto others. Active blame is, in effect, guided by the juridical image: It is what the responsibility without blame stance does without. To illustrate these points, I draw on Robert Browning's epic poem *The Ring and the Book*.[1]

Chapter 19 is the final chapter not only of this part but of the book as a whole. It brings the previous nine chapters together, to show how the solutions to the puzzle of addiction considered in part III intersect with the responsibility without blame stance described in the first three chapters of part IV. It thereby presents an alternative to the black-and-white thinking about addiction and ethics alike that both the brain disease model and the moral model have fostered. Although the picture presented in this chapter is complex, the message is simple: The heterogeneity of addiction and of relationships with people with addiction matters to an ethics of addiction.

The chapter begins with some general considerations about relationships, distinguishing wrongs from hurts. Although it is of course true that people with addiction sometimes wrong others by using drugs, we can also be hurt when we can have no expectation or right that they not use. With this distinction in view, I turn first to questions of how to temper a tendency to actively blame people with addiction, and second to questions of whether their responsibility is reduced and, if so, how nonetheless to hold them answerable and to account. With respect to tempering blame: I draw an analogy between addiction and being under duress. The value of drugs for people with addiction emphasized throughout this book—and especially in chapters 10, 11, and 12 in relation to self-medication and security-based attachment, self-harm and a desire to die, and self-identity—means that the pain of not using can be significant and real. This pain must be balanced against wrongs and hurts to others. With respect to reductions in responsibility: Ignorance, denial, and elements of a self-harming or suicidal mindset affect cognitive capacities; cravings and problems of control affect volitional capacities. Responsibility in addiction is therefore often reduced (and very occasionally eliminated). However, in many cases, cognitive and volitional capacities are sufficiently intact for it to be appropriate to hold responsible notwithstanding the reduction—*without active blame.*

In writing about the meaning and practice of responsibility without blame, I have tried in part to model it. But there is no standard script for how to be when we are wronged or hurt by people with addiction—any more than there is a universal solution to help people with addiction stop harming themselves. At the end of the day, there is nothing for it but to put in the work to understand another person in all their specificity, and to figure out how move forward and shape a relationship together. I hope this part will provide some tools to help with that work.

16

The Rescue-Blame Trap

MY FIRST EXPERIENCE working clinically was in a National Health Service (NHS) outpatient therapeutic community for people with personality disorder and complex needs, many of whom struggled with drug and behavioral addictions. As noted in the introduction to this book, UK therapeutic communities are distinctive care environments, different from what often falls under this label in the US as well as more conventional medical contexts. They work by requiring genuine and sustained relationships between group facilitators and group members—relationships that are personal, if also shaped by respective roles—as well as between group members themselves. In more conventional medical contexts, relationships between clinicians and patients are more formal and hierarchical, and there is no therapeutic peer-to-peer engagement. The patient has a problem they can't resolve on their own, which the clinician tries to cure. The clinician's expertise relative to the patient, together with the social norms and practices standardly governing such contexts, creates a divide between them. By contrast, UK therapeutic communities are informal, communal, egalitarian environments that are committed to flattened hierarchies between group facilitators and group members and to shared decision-making and responsibility for treatment. Authenticity and emotional intimacy are central to the relationships between everyone in the group, which are always up for discussion and negotiation. A great deal of time is spent together, not only in therapy but as a community: cooking, eating, playing games, going on outings, running the business of the group. The majority of our groups met for at least one full day every week—some met every day.

Personality disorder is defined in the fifth edition of the *Diagnostic and Statistical Manual of Mental Disorders* (DSM-5) as "an enduring pattern of inner experience and behavior that deviates markedly from the expectations of the individual's culture, is pervasive and inflexible, has an onset in adolescence or early adulthood, is stable over time, and leads to distress or impairment."[1] There are currently ten varieties—paranoid, schizoid, schizotypal, antisocial, borderline, histrionic, narcissistic, avoidant, dependent, and obsessive-compulsive—divided into three clusters formally labeled as A, B, and C, but informally known as *mad*, *bad*, and *sad*. Within psychiatry, patients with personality disorder are notoriously difficult to treat and historically stigmatized relative to other patient groups. Although the past decades have witnessed a concerted effort to address stigma and challenge stereotypes, patients with personality disorder are still widely considered to be "manipulative" and "attention-seeking" and to create division and burnout among staff.[2] Stigmatizing and stereotyping patients is inconsistent with the basic clinical duty of care and so always necessary to guard against. Why then does it occur? With respect to personality disorder, one part of the answer is that staff are reacting to the "culturally deviant" diagnostic behavior, some (but not all) of which does serious harm both to patients themselves and to others. This can include, for example, deliberate self-harm and other forms of self-damaging as well as suicidal behavior, intense anger, threats, cruelty, aggression, and violence toward others.

Although it is common to think of this behavior as dividing neatly into two kinds—harm to self, harm to others—in truth it all typically harms both. To state the obvious: Self-harm, self-damaging, and suicidal behavior can be psychologically devastating for other people, including most obviously friends and family—especially children. It also has a profound impact on clinicians, who often care a great deal about their patients, and may feel as if they have failed them. Depending on the method, this behavior can also have devastating physical or psychological consequences for people in the wider community. Reckless driving—a relatively common kind of self-damaging behavior—puts pedestrians and other drivers at risk. Train drivers are traumatized if they can't stop their train in time when someone throws themself on the tracks. But the reverse is also the case: Behavior that is in the first instance harmful to others almost inevitably rebounds on the person themself. Violence (and its cousins) can of course be reciprocated, as well as resulting in criminal convictions, prison sentences, and the destruction of relationships that perpetrators (notwithstanding their violence) genuinely value—alongside lasting feelings of shame, guilt, and self-hate.

In stark contrast to what it can be like to work in inpatient or forensic psychiatric settings, I witnessed no direct physical violence toward other people in the outpatient therapeutic community where I worked. But there could be violence toward objects—throwing of chairs, punching of walls—as well as outbursts of anger, emotional cruelty, or verbal aggression toward facilitators and other group members. There were also occasions where group members threatened to self-harm, commit suicide, or sever contact with the group—as well as occasions where they did—provoking high levels of anxiety and distress in us all. When people behave in these ways, the deep question in any therapeutic context is *why*. What is the "inner experience"—that is, the thoughts, impulses, and feelings diagnostic of personality disorder—driving the so-called culturally deviant behavior and that, if we could only get a handle on, we could try to alleviate for its own sake and leverage to address the behavior? How has the person's history and life circumstances contributed to them feeling and acting like this? But it is all too easy for the behavior to stop people from asking, let alone answering, such questions. It captures attention, distracting from the underlying psychology. It requires addressing to keep everyone—the person themself and others—physically and psychologically safe. And in clinical contexts, it tends to provoke either of two extreme and opposing reactions that it is all too easy to get trapped between: *rescue* and *blame*.

I was myself caught in this trap when I was new to clinical work. Suppose a group member was threatening to self-harm. Or suppose a group member was threatening toward another member or me. I very easily felt angry and scared—as well as inadequate. I routinely didn't know what to do. But although my senior and more experienced colleagues were ultimately responsible, I felt called upon to do something in virtue of my role. Initially, I could see only two options. The first was to adopt what I will call *a blaming mindset*. Although many of our group members were distrusting and a bit paranoid, they were not psychotic. Nothing in their behavior suggested they were not responsible when they did things like, say, issue threats. One option was therefore to hold them responsible for doing so. Threatening other people with self-harm or violence is wrong. If our group members were responsible, then they were to blame for doing wrong.

But even as someone new to clinical work and struggling to find her way, it was obvious that blaming our group members was inconsistent with my duty to care and undermining of the relationship between us—a relationship that was supposed to be of therapeutic value. I will say more in chapter 18 about how to understand the nature of blame and its impact on relationships. It is enough for now that we all have some understanding from our own experience of what it is like to be blamed. Even when you know you've done something wrong, blame stings. Because it stings, it is natural to try to deflect it and be defensive—not the ideal posture for therapy. But for our group members, the effects of blame were potentially much worse. Many of them already carried within them a sense of themselves as bad and worthless—as a lost cause, beyond hope. Blame exacerbated this sense, heightening both the risk that they would disengage from therapy, and the risk that they would carry out the threat and self-harm or act suicidally or violently. Why not, if you're a lost cause? If there's no hope that you or your relationships will ever change, you might as well do what you always do, thereby at least seizing control over the fact that other people judge you and blame you by ensuring it (see chapter 11).

All too aware of the perils of a blaming mindset, I would find myself swinging toward the other option and adopting what I will call *a rescuing mindset.* Our group members were all diagnosed with personality disorder and receiving treatment in a specialist mental health service. They suffered terribly. Notwithstanding the fact that little about their behavior suggested it, perhaps they were not in fact responsible. Maybe they couldn't help it, as we say. In which case, since they were not responsible, then they were not to blame. This mindset was—at least superficially—easier on our relationships. I could treat them as victims of their disorder and so deserving of care, rather than as people responsible for acting badly and so deserving of blame. But here's the rub: This mindset was also undermining of the therapeutic value of the relationships.

The behavior in question—behavior like threatening self-harm or violence—is diagnostic of personality disorder. From a formal, strictly diagnostic perspective, it needs to be addressed for the person to improve or recover. From an informal, more therapeutic perspective, it is terrible for the person that they are behaving like this. It is part of what is destroying their life and relationships. For, even if a rescuing mindset is superficially easier on relationships than a blaming mindset, it is hardly easy on relationships when people harm themselves and others. But, if the group member is not responsible— they genuinely can't help making threats, say, it's just not in their power to stop—then it is neither fair nor practical to hold them responsible and work to support their agency to do things differently. They simply can't be expected to undertake not to behave this way in future. What therapeutic tools are then left to address the behavior? Well, there is obviously sedation or, in the worst-case scenario, isolation and confinement. These are not good clinical outcomes. The point of therapy is to engage with people to support them to grow and change in ways that are lasting and lead to a better life. So, all too aware of the perils of a rescuing mindset, I would find myself swinging back toward seeing our group members as responsible—and would feel, in consequence, the pull of judgment and blame.

This is *the rescue-blame trap*: the experience of being caught between two stark and opposing mindsets when people act in ways that harm themselves and/or others. This behavior easily gives rise to feelings such as resentment, indignation, anger, outrage, disgust, and contempt—but also fear, anxiety, helplessness, inadequacy, grief, and despair. Meanwhile, although the reasons are different, the result of adopting either a blaming mindset or a rescuing mindset is the same. Neither is conducive to effective therapeutic engagement with people whose patterns of behavior form a significant part of the problems they face. This is obviously bad for patients. It is to be avoided first and foremost for that reason. But it is also bad for clinicians, who can easily become exhausted, hardened, and disillusioned as they struggle to deal with the toxicity of blame or the responsibility of working under the assumption that a patient can't help harming themself or others—and the impossibility of doing their job well either way.

I have articulated the rescue-blame trap in relation to my own experience as a philosopher embarking on clinical work in a UK therapeutic community for people with personality disorder. However, the trap resonates with the "split" within inpatient psychiatric staff teams that the psychoanalytic psychiatrist Thomas Main famously describes in his classic article "The Ailment." Main writes of how "two languages now grow up, one describing the patient as 'getting away with it,' 'playing up the staff,' 'hysterically demanding'; the other using terms like 'overwhelmed with psychotic anxieties,' 'showing the true illness she has hidden all her life,' 'seriously ill.'"[3] The staff members speaking the first language (in other words, expressing a blaming mindset) see the other staff as "collusive, unrealistic, over-indulgent."[4] The staff members speaking the second language (in other words, expressing a rescuing mindset) see the other staff as "suppressive, insensitive to the strains on an immature ego, lacking in proper feeling."[5] Whether the context is inpatient or outpatient, individual clinicians and staff teams as a whole can get caught in the rescue-blame trap. But in truth, any of us can. The trap can arise anywhere and in relation to anyone who harms themself and/or others—in families, among friends, at school, at work, in courtrooms, with strangers on the streets. In particular, it arises in relation to addiction—a pattern of behavior that is harmful to drug users and which can also wrong or hurt others.

Our thinking about addiction is mired in the rescue-blame trap. Consider the opposition between the moral model and the brain disease model. The moral model invites a blaming mindset. It treats drug use in addiction as no different from ordinary drug use apart from addiction. According to the moral model, both kinds of drug use are voluntary and morally wrong. People with addiction are therefore responsible for doing something—using drugs—that is wrong. In consequence, they deserve to be blamed.

As I argued in the introduction to this book: There are circumstances in which using drugs is morally wrong, namely those that straightforwardly involve or significantly risk seriously harming or violating the rights of others. There are also circumstances in which drug use, even if not wrong, is deeply upsetting to others in a way that hurts them and is in consequence damaging or threatening to the relationship. I will say more about this distinction—between wronging and hurting—in chapter 19. But there is nothing *intrinsically* morally wrong with using drugs. By assuming drug use is morally wrong and inviting a blaming mindset, the moral model stigmatizes all drug users and stifles reflection on the complexities surrounding the rights and wrongs of drug use and relationships. It therefore offers little help to anyone who has been wronged or hurt by someone in their life who is addicted to drugs, but who also cares about them and hopes to find a way forward that, ideally, repairs what has been lost between them as well as supporting the person to change their relationship with drugs.

By contrast, the brain disease model invites a rescuing mindset. It aims to address stigma and foster care for people with addiction by in effect providing them with a simple, blanket excuse. Contra the moral model, the brain disease model (in its orthodox version—but see chapter 8 for an alternative) claims that drug use is not voluntary in addiction because people with addiction have a brain disease that compels them to use drugs. *They can't help it.* The brain disease model can of course grant that people are responsible for using drugs prior to addiction. In consequence, there may be grounds for maintaining that they bear some degree of responsibility for becoming addicted in the first place. But drugs are supposed to "hijack" the brain, transforming ordinary, voluntary behavior into passive, involuntary symptoms of a brain disease. To follow through the ethical implications of the brain disease model: No one is responsible for using drugs once addicted; and, unless tremendous weight is given to whatever responsibility a person has for becoming addicted in the first place, no one addicted to drugs deserves blame for using in any circumstances. As I noted in the introduction to this book, this is arguably why large-scale surveys and experimental vignette studies suggest that a brain disease label can have a positive impact on relationships between people with addiction and families, friends, and colleagues[6]—just as I found that a rescuing mindset made it superficially easier for me to maintain relationships with the people in our group. By inviting a rescuing mindset, the brain disease model blocks attributions of responsibility and, with responsibility, blame.

But the brain disease model is not without costs. It blocks attributions of responsibility by denying agency. As argued in part II, this is inaccurate. Drug use in addiction is not compulsive but voluntary. For this reason alone, the brain disease model is a precarious way to maintain any relationship. But it also means that the possibility of engaging a person's agency to support them to change their relationship with drugs—and with it the way their relationship with drugs impacts their relationships with other people—is equally blocked. There is little for it but to resign oneself to live with it. Like the moral model, the brain disease model stifles reflection on the complexities surrounding the rights and wrongs of drug use and relationships with people with addiction. For it destroys the ground we need to stand on together to have conversations that find a better way forward for everyone's sake. This ground involves genuine recognition of each party's experience and agency alike, alongside their right to ask others to take responsibility for what they do. To put it bluntly: Denying agency undermines the possibility of engaging agency—in treatment and in relationships.

How to escape from the rescue-blame trap? The solution in a slogan is to adopt a stance of *responsibility without blame*. A blaming mindset slides from an attribution of responsibility to the idea that blame is deserved. A rescuing mindset rejects all attributions of responsibility to undermine the slide to the idea that blame is deserved. We should not reject attributions of responsibility. We should reject the slide from responsibility to blame.

When I was new to clinical work and myself caught in the rescue-blame trap, this is what I witnessed my colleagues—better and more experienced clinicians than I—doing. They took our group members to be responsible for their actions. If they behaved in ways that harmed themselves or others, they had to answer for doing so, they were expected to stop, and the group was empowered to hold them to account. But an attitude of concern and respect prevailed, and they were not blamed. Although responsibility-talk was an explicit part of the culture and language of the group, attributions of responsibility were not used to legitimate a blaming mindset. They were used as a condition for a set of answerability and accountability practices constructed to support individual change and positive, meaningful relationships between group members: to address any harm to self and/or others that had occurred, and to help people break the cycle and do things differently in future.[7]

These practices consist in at least two components, and sometimes a third. The first component is a frank conversation between the person and the group—a form of answerability to other people for any harm done. This gives other group members the opportunity to speak to their own feelings about what the person did—including not only the impact it had on them but what they see as its impact on the person themself and the group as a whole. In addition to the importance to other people of voicing their experience, this can also serve to make it more difficult for the person to avoid or deny the significance of their actions—a tendency we all have, but which may be especially strong in some cases of addiction (see chapter 13). It also gives them the chance to explain themself—and if appropriate, to apologize—and to begin the process of reflecting on why they acted as they did. These kinds of conversations can be heated, but they are part of most kinds of intensive group therapy and central to developing emotional intelligence and mentalizing skills. In a less direct and potentially heated form, they are also part of motivational interviewing—a very different therapeutic modality, but one that nonetheless aims to address problematic patterns of behavior by nonjudgmentally pointing out their consequences in the hope that increased awareness builds motivation to change.

The second component is a more focused, reflective exercise whereby the person is asked to take time outside of group to consider why they acted as they did and to produce a sketch of a plan for how to do things differently next time, which they then discuss with the group. This is designed to bring the "inner experience" driving the behavior and the person's history and life circumstances better into view, so that they can begin to get a handle on the question of why they behave as they do—what triggers it, but also what value the behavior has for them. This value may be hard to discern or painful to acknowledge—and so requires a dedicated process of reflection to articulate at all, let alone to share with the group. But once discerned, it can then inform their plan, increasing the chances that they succeed in carrying it out. Sometimes the plan is formalized as a contract between the person and the group, which will typically include an undertaking to get support—from other group members or friends and family—if the person is struggling to keep to it. The person publicly signs the contract and everyone else writes messages of support (see chapter 19). These kinds of reflective exercises and contracts can also be part of individual cognitive behavioral therapy. They constitute forms of answerability and accountability to oneself and other people alike.

The third, less standard component is the imposition of consequences over and above these conversations, tasks, and undertakings. Some of these consequences may be reparative—a question of making good. For example, if someone throws a chair in anger and it breaks, they might be required to fix it; if someone walks out when it's their turn to clean up thereby leaving others to pick up the work, they need to clean up next time. But some consequences impose a significant cost. For example, if someone comes to group drunk or high—an inviolable rule, if for no other reason than that you can't do your own therapy or help other people do theirs if you're drunk or high—they will be asked to leave and may in addition face a time-limited suspension from the group after they have returned sober and the conversation about what happened and why has begun. The imposition of consequences is a way of ensuring that the expectations of the group alongside their rationale—to facilitate therapy and to keep everyone physically and psychologically safe—are (and are seen to be) respected and upheld.

All three components—and no doubt especially the third—have the potential to feel punitive. But none is conceived as a form of punishment. The *Oxford English Dictionary* (OED) defines the primary meaning of "punishment" as "the infliction of a penalty or sanction in retribution for an offence or transgression; (also) that which is inflicted as a penalty; a sanction imposed to ensure the application and enforcement of a law";[8] secondary meanings include rough physical treatment or an unpleasant stimulus used to shape patterns of behavior.[9] There are certainly echoes of some of these elements in clinical practices of answerability and accountability. The imposition of consequences to uphold expectations—to "hold boundaries," as it's typically put—is perhaps akin to a sanction imposed to ensure the application and enforcement of a law; the therapeutic aspiration to help people do things differently in future is akin to shaping behavior—albeit not by the infliction of an "unpleasant stimulus" let alone rough physical treatment. Notwithstanding these echoes, these practices are not conceived as punishment because the motivation behind them is not retributive. They are not undertaken as a form of payback to make the person suffer for what they have done. They come from concern for the person and their relationship with the group—as well as concern for the group as a whole—and they are conducted with care and respect.

Part of what this means is that, even when things get heated, not every-thing goes. Any conversation veering toward a vengeful or disrespectful atti-tude will be halted and may itself become the topic of a further conversation in turn. There is, in other words, an expectation of self-reflexivity in place for all—including those who have been wronged or hurt, not just those who are the agents of the wrong or the hurt. To be clear, I am not suggesting that these expectations and norms are perfectly enacted. Group members (indeed, group therapists) can no doubt be retributive at times. And even when they aren't, other people may yet experience them as such. But the guiding ideal is caring rather than punitive, and the procedure to handle a situation that starts to feel punitive is clear: Talk about it, and be prepared to reflect on and take responsibility for your own part and to acknowledge the validity of di-vergent perspectives. Don't just get defensive or put the blame on the other person. This commitment to negotiating difficult relationships through con-versation and reciprocal self-reflexivity is part of how concern and respect are maintained within the group and how members are supported to take respon-sibility—as it's naturally put—for doing things differently in future. Every-one is treated as someone whose experience is important, who matters to the group, and who is capable of changing—and expected to change—for the better.

Summing up: In the therapeutic community where I worked, attributions of responsibility functioned to identify where a person had the capacity to do things differently and a relationship with them—a crucial mediator of psycho-logical and behavioral change—was likely to take shared work. Practices of answerability and accountability were constructed on the one hand to help people do things differently, and on the other to facilitate this relational work—to address any damage done, not for the sake of payback but for the sake of the future of the relationship.

The existence of this alternative, therapeutic culture shows that, in princi-ple and in practice, it is possible to reject the slide from responsibility to blame—that holding responsible without blaming is a viable aim within clini-cal relationships, even if it is of course perennially possible to fall short of achieving it. Our relationships with families, friends, colleagues, and people in our communities are not clinical. There are important differences—most obviously the fact that if you are a person's friend, family member, or col-league, you are not their therapist. Nonetheless, there is no sharp line between clinical and nonclinical contexts.[10] The practices of answerability and ac-countability I have described in this chapter are hardly recherché. They already have analogs in nonclinical relationships, and they can be further adapted to fit. Together with the idea of responsibility without blame that inheres in them, they are therefore tools we can use to shape our relationships to people with addiction and support them to change their relationships to drugs and us alike.

17

Responsibility

WITHIN BOTH MORAL philosophy and society at large, there is a tendency to model attributions of responsibility on what we might call a *juridical image*, to adapt a phrase from the philosopher Daniela Dover.[1] The image casts us in the roles of detective, judge, and executioner, walking the world rooting out wrongs, sitting on high and delivering judgment, apportioning blame and meting out punishment as deserved. On this conception, attributions of responsibility constitute a kind of moral verdict on a person and their actions—as good or bad, right or wrong. These attributions are like criminal findings of fault for wrongdoing. They give us a prima facie license to blame and punish in proportion to the wrong done, legitimating hostile attitudes and punitive treatment that would otherwise be morally questionable if not outright impermissible. The juridical image therefore serves as a prop for the slide from responsibility to blame by making an entitlement to blame and punish another person *the point* of determining whether they are responsible. Responsibility matters *because* it secures this entitlement.

What is responsibility, such that it can potentially secure this entitlement? Within moral philosophy, there are two broad classes of answer to this question.

The first class, found as early in the history of philosophy as Aristotle's *Ethics*, takes responsibility as flowing from a set of cognitive and volitional capacities.[2] With respect to *cognitive capacities*: To be responsible for wrongdoing, a person needs to know well enough what they are doing and have some inkling that it is wrong—or, if they don't actually know these things, then at the very least, they should. The terms "well enough," "inkling," and "should" are quagmires. When should you know what you don't? What if it never occurs to you that what you're doing is wrong, but had you stopped and seriously considered it, you'd have realized it was? What if you live in a culture that collectively fails to recognize the wrong—everyone is unreflectively perpetrating it, all around you? Do you need to know only what, minimally, you're doing, or do you also need to know why you're doing it? If the latter, how deep must your understanding be? What about the morally relevant outcomes of your actions, some of which may lie far in the future? How much do you need to know about these to be responsible for them? Come to think of it, can we even know the future at all?

With respect to *volitional capacities*: To be responsible for wrongdoing, a person needs at minimum to be acting voluntarily in an ordinary sense. Throughout this book, I have treated flexible, goal-directed behavior that is explained by beliefs and desires as voluntary in an ordinary sense. But the phrase "acting voluntarily in an ordinary sense" is also a quagmire. What if a person's beliefs, desires, and values are morally misshapen by brainwashing or gaslighting—or simply by their history and life circumstances, as chapter 4 intimates is possible? What if a person's options are severely and unjustly restricted, as described in chapter 10? What if they face problems of control, as described in chapter 14? Don't these and similar factors impact the ordinary sense in which actions are voluntary as relevant to attributions of responsibility? And, finally, what about free will and determinism? If physical determinism is true and free will is incompatible with it, then no one can ever act other than they do. Surely then we cannot think that our actions are voluntary in an ordinary sense, if no one can ever act other than they do?

These questions have generated a vast philosophical literature, with very little agreement or straightforward practical application. In chapter 19, I will return to some of them, insofar as they intersect with the various solutions to the puzzle of addiction presented in part III and so matter to questions of responsibility and relationships with people with addiction. But with the exception of one short comment about free will and determinism to follow, I will avoid them in general, and in particular at this level of abstraction. The reason is that whether they need to be answered depends on why we are asking them in the first place.

The juridical image with which I opened this chapter pushes us to ask such questions because attributions of responsibility are taken to legitimate hostile attitudes and punitive treatment that would otherwise be morally questionable if not outright impermissible. Taking responsibility for wrongdoing to flow from cognitive and volitional capacities can help explain why responsibility could in theory legitimate such attitudes and treatment. Put crudely, it is because a person knows what they are doing and does it voluntarily that they can be considered deserving of blame or punishment. By knowingly and voluntarily acting badly, they forsake their right that others *not* treat them with hostility and make them suffer. These are high stakes, requiring not only a high threshold for attributions of responsibility but a high degree of certainty both that our general theory of responsibility in all its details is correct, and that it has been correctly applied in the case at hand to deliver a moral verdict. If this is why you are interested in questions of responsibility—in order to secure a finding of fault and with it an entitlement to blame and punish—the quagmire of questions is pressing, in theory and in practice. If you get it wrong, *then you do wrong.* You blame and punish people who don't deserve it. For this reason, you'd better get it right. False positives must be avoided.

The idea of responsibility inherent in clinical practices of answerability and accountability belongs to this first class of answer in taking responsibility to flow from a set of cognitive and volitional capacities. But the clinical stance of responsibility without blame rejects the juridical image. The point of determining whether another person is responsible is to identify where they have the capacity to do things differently and a relationship with them can be expected to take shared work to repair and maintain in the face of damage. Do they have *agency for change*, as it is sometimes called?

This is why the idea of responsibility inherent in clinical practices is tied to cognitive and volitional capacities: The possibility of undertaking to change ourselves is tied to these capacities. On the one hand, we can *directly* work to change our behavior only in so far as we know what we are doing and are doing it voluntarily. On the other hand, we can *indirectly* work to change aspects of ourselves apart from such behavior—for example, our emotional temperament and tendencies, or our unbidden inner thoughts and impulses—only by deciding to behave in ways that we know stand a chance of influencing them (for example, by going to therapy; see chapter 18). In other words, whether they are deployed directly or indirectly, cognitive and volitional capacities—capacities to do things knowingly and voluntarily—are essential for working toward change of any sort, and hence for any idea of responsibility where change is the point.

But responsibility, understood as flowing from a set of cognitive and volitional capacities, can only be used as a practical tool for psychological and behavioral change and relational work if it is not at the same time used to legitimate hostile attitudes and punitive treatment. The point of determining whether another person is responsible is precisely *not* to establish an entitlement to blame and punish. Responsibility attributions must be conceived of

and enacted apart from blame and punishment, if they are to serve their purpose. In consequence, and by comparison with the role of attributions of responsibility according to the juridical image, the stakes are not high—the
possibility of doing wrong because you blame or punish a person who doesn't
deserve it is moot if you are not blaming or punishing at all—and the quagmire of questions is much less pressing.

Cognitive and volitional capacities—and therefore any idea of responsibility flowing from them—come in degrees. You can have some knowledge of
what you are doing and why, but your understanding of the nature of your
action and its outcomes—never mind your deeper motives—may be far from
complete. Your action may be voluntary to some extent yet compromised in
any number of ways—including restrictions of options and problems of
control—and so far from exemplifying the ideal of freedom of action or of will.
But so long as a person has some agency, there is reason to attribute responsibility to them if this is done as part of a practice designed to help their lives
and relationships improve and in which they voluntarily participate—rather
than as part of a practice of legitimating and inflicting hostile attitudes and
punitive treatment. It is much less important to get it right. Indeed, it is false
negatives rather than false positives that are better avoided. If you're unsure
whether someone is responsible *at all* because you're unsure that they have
any agency *at all*, you can still try acting as if they do and see what happens—
see if it helps. If it doesn't, then you need to change tack. But, if behavior really
is flexible and goal directed, then we should expect a self-conscious and self-
reflective being to have some power to affect it (pending a brief comment on
free will and determinism to follow). Indeed, having a conversation with a
person that digs into any questions from the quagmire of particular relevance
to them and their situation—a conversation that tries to figure out where their
knowledge of their behavior may be partial, their options restricted, their self-
belief, self-esteem, and self-control limited—is often an important part of the
process of helping them develop their agency and take responsibility for doing
things differently in future. In seeing where and how cognitive and volitional
capacities are compromised or less than ideal, we see where and how to try to
bolster them.

The clinical stance of responsibility without blame therefore shares with
the juridical image a commitment to an idea of responsibility as flowing from
cognitive and volitional capacities. It disagrees about what then flows from
attributions of responsibility. In place of seeing attributions of responsibility
as moral verdicts licensing blame and punishment for past wrongdoing, it

connects them to nonblaming and nonpunitive practices of holding responsible to help people and relationships flourish in future. In this respect, the clinical stance can be likened to what is called a "forward-looking account" of responsibility.[3] The stance does not flinch from looking at past damage and asking people to answer for it to others, but the point of doing so is the good of everyone involved and the future of the relationship. As the philosopher Victoria McGeer sums up the idea, in holding a person responsible we are ultimately saying to them: "You have what it takes!"[4]

But to be clear: Nothing in the clinical stance of responsibility without blame constitutes an argument against the idea contained in the juridical image that, in general, attributions of responsibility establish an entitlement to blame and punish. No doubt, if there is indeed such a general entitlement, it is in theory defeasible for any number of reasons and in practice defeated in clinical contexts by the duty of care that comes with the job (or in UK therapeutic communities, with membership of the group). But these are distinctive contexts and relationships. I take no view on whether attributions of responsibility establish an entitlement to blame and punish in general. My aim is more modest: to articulate an alternative way of thinking about responsibility and relationships with people who harm themselves and/or others. We can fail to recognize that this alternative is even possible because of how gripped we are by the juridical image and how easily we slide from responsibility to blame. Yet there are compelling reasons to adopt it in relation to the people in our lives who struggle with addiction (see chapters 16 and 19). Suppose, just for the sake of argument, that we are indeed entitled to blame and punish in many contexts and relationships where people wrong or hurt us—including in contexts of addiction. Do you believe we are required to take up this right? Surely, we have a choice about how we respond. Why choose to blame and punish, entitled or not, if there is indeed a better way forward for everyone involved?

This is why the responsibility without blame stance is not held hostage by the quagmire of questions about exactly what is required of a theory of responsibility. Its interest in responsibility is forward looking: a tool to help people and relationships flourish in future. Its interest is not backward looking: a license to blame and punish. But the final question raised about free will and determinism also offers an escape from the swamp. Skepticism about free will naturally invites skepticism about our entitlement to blame and punish. Very crudely, if determinism is true and free will is incompatible with it, then no one can ever act other than they do. In consequence, an important part of the idea that our actions are voluntary in any ordinary sense is potentially illusory, and any general entitlement to blame and punish when people are agents of wrongdoing looks like it rests on shaky ground. This is because it seems that no one is ever responsible for anything in such a way as to secure this entitlement.[5] In consequence, skepticism about free will also offers an escape from the burden of theorizing about responsibility. There is no point asking when exactly we are responsible for wrongdoing such as to license blame and punishment because we already know the answer. *Never.*

As we saw in the introduction to this book and throughout part II, the orthodox version of the brain disease model is routinely cast as the idea that addiction occurs when the kind of freedom of will that we normally take for granted is lost: Drug use becomes compulsive, transformed into a passive, involuntary symptom of a brain disease. It is therefore worth noting that what is lost to people with addiction according to the brain disease model is a world apart from what is lost to us all if determinism is true and free will is incompatible with it. If determinism is true and free will is incompatible with it—and we take this to mean that no one is ever responsible for anything in such a way as to license blame and punishment—then we are all in the same boat, those of us with addiction and those of us without, adrift together on a dead sea, none of us the agents or people we thought we were. There is nothing in this image that offers any resources to understand how addiction *in particular* might compromise or limit agency in a way that is relevant to responsibility. Nor is there anything to help us escape the rescue-blame trap and construct ethical and meaningful relationships with people with addiction. Skepticism about free will is therefore irrelevant to the questions driving this part of the book, which pertain to how we might best respond to and have relationships with people with addiction who harm not only themselves but others, and the relevance of ordinary agency, responsibility, and practices of answerability and accountability to our responses and relationships. Hence, just as I will avoid the quagmire of questions about our cognitive and volitional capacities in general and in the abstract, so too I will avoid questions about free will and determinism. Whether we are all stuck together in the same boat because there is no free will, or moored together on more fertile land because there is, we are still hoping for ideas and tools that can help people with addiction to change their relationships with drugs and help us sustain our relationships with people with addiction.

We started with a question pressed on us by the juridical image: What is responsibility, such that it can potentially secure an entitlement to blame and punish? The second broad class of answer also aims to avoid skeptical worries about free will. But to do so, it shifts the focus away from cognitive and volitional capacities, and onto one particular element of our ordinary practices of blame and punishment themselves—our "reactive attitudes" as they have come to be known, following the philosopher Peter Strawson. These are the hostile, negative emotions that are typically part and parcel of these practices, such as, for example, resentment, indignation, anger, outrage, disgust, and contempt. In his classic article "Freedom and Resentment," Strawson foregrounds the role of reactive attitudes in how we hold each other responsible.[6] For example, consider that you are likely to feel very differently about someone if they hurt you by accident than if they hurt you out of indifference or malevolence. Strawson's innovation is to use this observation both to sidestep skeptical worries about free will and to invert the original question: Rather than think that the idea of responsibility needs to explain our entitlement to blame and punish, we can instead see the idea of responsibility through the lens of our reactive attitudes and think of them as explaining it. Following the philosopher Gary Watson's influential interpretation of Strawson: What it is for a person to be responsible *just is* for them to be the appropriate object of our reactive attitudes.[7]

Thus interpreted, Strawson's picture is at odds with a responsibility without blame stance. If what it is to be responsible is to be the appropriate object of hostile, negative emotions—where these are part and parcel of our ordinary practices of blame and punishment—then there is limited space for an idea of responsibility without blame. The clinical practices of answerability and accountability that I outlined in the previous chapter would not straightforwardly count as ways of holding responsible, for they aim to proceed out of care and with concern and respect—that is, to keep these emotions at arm's length (but see chapter 18 for a fuller picture). The point of the responsibility without blame stance is precisely *not* to see responsibility through the lens of these reactive attitudes and our corresponding practices of blame and punishment. One way of putting this is that just as the juridical image slides from responsibility to blame, Strawson's picture slides from blame to responsibility. This is why—at least in its bare bones, without embellishment or refinement[8]—Strawson's picture is as inimical to the idea of responsibility inherent in clinical practices of answerability and accountability as the juridical image.

Again to be clear: I do not present the responsibility without blame stance as an argument against Strawson's picture any more than I present it as an argument against the juridical image. As I said, my aim is more modest: to articulate an alternative way of thinking about responsibility and relationships with people who harm themselves and/or others. But I nonetheless want to conclude this chapter by noting three concerns with Strawson's picture that are relevant to understanding the clinical idea of blame and the stance of responsibility without blame alike, and so prefigure the chapters to come. The first is more in the philosophical weeds; the second and third of broader relevance.

First concern. Strawson's account has been very influential within contemporary philosophy, but there is a philosophical challenge that it must meet. Many of our hostile, negative emotions are not appropriate. On the one hand, sometimes this is because we hold mistaken beliefs, justified or not, about their objects. Maybe you made a completely understandable mistake about who it is that did this to you or the nature of their intention toward you in doing it—a mistake that anyone could have made. Or maybe you made a mistake when others wouldn't have, because you are prone to paranoia or already disposed to be hostile to this person so you jumped to a false conclusion. Either way, the person is not an appropriate object of your hostile, negative emotions, for either they didn't do it at all, or they didn't do it out of indifference or malevolence. On the other hand, sometimes our hostile, negative emotions are not appropriate because they are irrational—by which I mean that they fly in the face of our judgments or beliefs about what we ought to feel—and yet we feel them nonetheless. Maybe you are at your wit's end with a pet or small child who won't stop being demanding and difficult. You find yourself seething with resentment—despite yourself. Neither pets nor small children are appropriate objects of resentment. You know this. But your knowledge that your resentment is inappropriate does nothing to make it abate—you just can't shake it off. I discuss these cases and their relevance to blame in the next chapter. For now, the point is that Strawson's picture requires a principle to separate the wheat from the chaff: the appropriate from the inappropriate reactive attitudes. And given that we are to explain the idea of responsibility by appeal to our reactive attitudes, this principle cannot state that our reactive attitudes are appropriately directed toward another only if they are responsible—on pain of circularity.[9]

The philosophical literature on reactive attitudes contains a number of proposals that attempt to address this challenge. For example, Jay Wallace has argued that the appropriateness of our entire suite of reactive attitudes is determined by a principle of fairness.[10] By contrast, Gideon Rosen limits his focus to resentment, arguing that implicit in resentment are the thoughts, however inchoate, that the person you resent has shown an objectionable pattern of concern toward you—for example, they really are acting out of indifference or malevolence—and deserves to suffer for it.[11] Rosen proposes that resentment is appropriate if these thoughts are true. Although he does not consider reactive attitudes other than resentment, a similar strategy could in theory be deployed in relation to each: Begin by determining which thoughts are implicit in the emotion in question; then the emotion is appropriate only if these thoughts are true. But for these proposals to be noncircular, a principle of fairness for the reactive attitudes, or what it is for a person to show an objectionable pattern of concern and deserve to suffer, will need to be elucidated without presupposing an idea of responsibility. It is certainly possible that this challenge can be met. But it will surely be challenging to meet without returning to the quagmire of questions about cognitive and volitional capacities—including free will and determinism—that Strawson hoped the appeal to reactive attitudes would shift our focus from. In which case, an idea of responsibility derived from the reactive attitudes is not ultimately an idea of responsibility divorced from cognitive and volitional capacities. This speaks to the centrality of these capacities to the idea of responsibility in our ordinary day-to-day practices. We can try to push them to one side, but they rebound.

Second concern. Strawson's picture is unduly conservative and narrow in focus. It is biased toward preserving selective aspects of the status quo. It doesn't ask: What should our practices of answerability and accountability ideally be like? What kinds of emotions do we want to shape our relationships with the people in our lives and communities who harm themselves and/or others? Rather, it takes a subset of our current practices and emotions for granted, and asks what idea of responsibility they contain, thereby leaving these practices and emotions more or less as they are while at the same time obscuring the existence and possibility of others.

Responsibility practices and associated emotions vary tremendously. For example, some cultures hold groups responsible for actions of individuals—a kind of guilt by association or, to borrow a term from the legal theorist Amy Sepinwall, *taint*.[12] Some cultures have radically different social norms for when to feel anger and when to feel shame as well as scripts for how to perform each—as the philosopher Owen Flanagan documents in his book *How to Do Things With Emotions* in the hope of persuading us to change our own cultural tendency to embrace anger and denigrate shame.[13] Some subcultures or groups like to point the finger more, some less—think, here, of the contrast between politicians and, say, teachers. And within any culture or subculture, some contexts bring out a blaming mindset while some bring out something strikingly akin to the stance of responsibility without blame—think, here, of the kinds of attitudes and practices toward wrongdoing that are typical of criminal proceedings by contrast with those typical of good parenting. Such cultural and contextual variety is evidence that it is possible to do things differently—for things *are* done differently. It can therefore encourage us to imagine more freely what shape our responsibility practices, emotions, and hence relationships could potentially have—no matter what culture or context we currently find ourselves in and what shape they actually do have. We should ask hard questions of the norms and scripts governing our reactive attitudes and our practices of holding responsible. Are they as we want them to be? Could they be better? What might we aspire to, were we constructing them from scratch?

Third concern. One of the virtues of Strawson's picture is its insistence on the importance of our emotional responses to each other. But it does so in the service of an idea of responsibility: Our reactive attitudes are cast under responsibility's net, as if the core of why they matter is that responsibility matters. But they matter also for other reasons. Our emotional responses to each other are, as I have just intimated, part of how we shape our relationships with each other—what these relationships mean, what they give and what they take, what they generously allow and what they will not stand. They also say something about who we are, as individuals and as society, which is part of why we should ask hard questions of them.

The idea of responsibility inherent in clinical practices of answerability and accountability and constitutive of a responsibility without blame stance takes responsibility as flowing from a set of cognitive and volitional capacities that these practices are in part designed to engage. The aim is to support a person who harms themself and/or others to do things differently in future—for their sake, for the sake of others, and for the sake of their relationships with others—and to recognize the experience and agency of all involved and each party's right to ask the others to take responsibility for what they do. The responsibility without blame stance sets aside the juridical image and the slide from responsibility to blame. It distances itself from the selective conservatism of Strawson's picture and the slide from blame to responsibility. It puts worries about free will and determinism into a boat and pushes it out to sea. It rejects blame—but it does not reject the importance of our emotions, including hostile, negative emotions, such as anger. What matters is what we do with them.

18

Blame

IN ROBERT BROWNING's epic poem *The Ring and the Book*, the Roman nobleman Guido Franceschini murders his wife, Pompilia, believing her to have had an affair with the young priest Giuseppe Caponsacchi. Caponsacchi defends himself against the accusation, saying: "Blame I can bear though not blameworthiness."[1] Suppose we take the word "blameworthiness" at face value to mean responsibility for wrongdoing such as to make a person *worthy of blame*—thereby providing a prima facie license to blame and punish, in keeping with the juridical image described in the previous chapter. Caponsacchi is claiming that he can bear for others to *actively blame* him—as I shall put it, borrowing a phrase from the philosopher Angela Smith.[2] By contrast, what would be unbearable to him is *to be blameworthy*. Caponsacchi is indeed actively blamed by many—by Franceschini, by half of the lawyers and people of Rome, and ultimately by the courts who banish him from the city. Being actively blamed can sting. This is why Caponsacchi's remark serves in his defense. If, for Caponsacchi, the sting of being actively blamed is *less* than the sting of being blameworthy, that is evidence that he couldn't have had an affair with Pompilia. For the implication is that the blameworthiness of committing adultery must *really* sting—so much that he wouldn't do it.

Blame-talk is loose. When we say that another is "to blame" or that we blame them, there are at least three different things we can mean:

1. They are blameworthy.
2. We should actively blame them.
3. We do actively blame them.

Statement 1 is *about the person* who is blameworthy—the blamee. Whatever exactly blameworthiness is, they've got it. By contrast, statements 2 and 3 are not about the blamee but rather *about us*—the actual or potential blamers. The infinitival verb phrase "to blame" can be synonymous with "to be blamed" akin to how, for example, food that is "to eat" is "to be eaten" or clothes that are "to wear" are "to be worn." In other words, by saying another is "to blame" we may be saying something about *what may be done to them.*

Statement 2 is about what we *should* all things considered be doing to them: actively blaming them. No doubt, for it to be true that we should blame a person, it is necessary for the person to be blameworthy. But it is not sufficient. Even if a person both is and is believed by us to be blameworthy, there can be any number of considerations that mean we shouldn't actively blame. Perhaps under the circumstances no one should. They are blameworthy, yes, but the wrong is long past, and they are now old, alone, dying. Or perhaps the relevant considerations are more particular to you. It might be hypocritical of you to blame them—a case of the pot calling the pan burnt-arse (as the traditional version of the saying goes).[3] Or you might be complicit in the wrongdoing. You did it together and so you have no right to blame them for what you yourself are equally to blame for. Or perhaps the nature of your relationship with them means that you shouldn't. You're not close enough, so it would be meddling. You're too close, so you should be loyal. You're their therapist, so to blame them would be to fail at your job. Alternatively, maybe it would exhaust you to blame them—it's just not worth the energy and the upset. Maybe it's as simple as that you just don't want to be that kind of person—*blamey.* These are some of the many considerations why a person can be blameworthy yet it not be the case that other people—whether all people or just some people—should actively blame them. The truth of statement 1 is no guarantee of the truth of statement 2. To continue with the above analogy: Just because a plate of food is to eat doesn't mean you should eat it. There can be any number of reasons— you're not hungry, you have an allergy, you just don't have the time—that you shouldn't.

But nor is the truth of statement 2 any guarantee of the truth of statement 3. Statement 3 is about what we *are* doing, for better or for worse. Suppose a person is blameworthy. Suppose too that you have the right kind of relationship for blame to be appropriate (and you aren't in on it and your arse isn't burnt). Suppose you are even confident that it would do them, you, and the world *good* for you to actively blame them. All things considered, you should actively blame them. Still, you may find that you don't. It's just not how you feel, not what you do. On the flip side, the truth of statement 3 is no guarantee of the truth of statement 2. We can sometimes find ourselves actively blaming someone even when we know that we shouldn't. Again by analogy: You can find yourself eating a plate of food even when you know that you shouldn't—you're not hungry, you have an allergy, you just don't have the time.

By way of illustration, consider an example that is both ordinary and familiar. A couple comes home from work after a long, hard day. Both are exhausted and stressed. Neither is at their best. And one has failed to see to a minor household duty they had promised to deal with, annoying and inconveniencing the other. The first partner has what, on another day, might be accepted as a reasonable excuse: their long, hard day. But their inconvenienced partner has also had a long, hard day. A critical remark—just slightly too sharp—is uttered and, once uttered, resented. A complaint is raised against the sharpness. The sharpness is defended—and a complaint against the complaint raised in turn. A blazing row ensues, in which each party takes their exhaustion and stress out on the other, becoming increasingly angry and upset as the other takes theirs out on them. The inconvenienced party blames their partner for failing to do what they promised, even though deep down, as we often put it, they know that their partner has a reasonable excuse. The partner who failed to deal with the minor household duty blames their partner for blaming them, even though deep down they too know that the background of stress and exhaustion might excuse their partner for failing to better manage their annoyance. As the fight develops, both parties become increasingly incensed, adamant, and self-righteous. Past wrongs and previous fights get dredged up. Things get said that, true or false or a bit of both, will be regretted. If the couple can't find a way to step back and resolve things, the blame, despite its irrationality, may linger in their relationship—a toxic background, yet another stamp in the collection of interpersonal wrongs. For now there is something additional to blame the other for—*this blazing row* where they were wrongly blamed.

Many of our go-to examples of active blame fit the juridical image. There is a good guy and a bad guy, no question which is which or who's in the right and who's in the wrong. The blamer is a model of justice: measured, proportionate, virtuous. The blamee is a model of vice: callous, selfish, negligent, indecent, cunning, and possibly harboring sexist, racist, classist, or otherwise objectionable attitudes and beliefs. The rowing couple is a different kind of example, less black-and-white as well as more revealing of the petty, darker side of all our natures. Yet it is an ordinary and familiar domestic tale. What does it reveal about active blame?

1. Active blame can be—indeed, arguably often is—irrational. It can float free of conscious, considered judgments or beliefs that another person is or is not blameworthy. We can judge a person blameworthy, but not actively blame them—maybe because we shouldn't, or maybe because even though we should, we just find that we don't. Or we can actively blame another person while judging them not to be blameworthy, as illustrated by the rowing couple (think too of the resentment we can feel toward a child or pet who won't stop being difficult, as noted in the previous chapter). Because of this irrationality, active blame is like an emotion.[4] Compare it to fear. It is one thing to judge that a situation is dangerous (compare: that a person is blameworthy). It is another to judge that we should feel fear (compare: that we should actively blame them). And it is another again actually to feel it (compare: that we do actively blame them). The classic idea of the brave soldier has it that they judge the battle to be dangerous so that they can think strategically and respond effectively. But supposedly they do not feel fear. Nor should they. Given their role and aim, probably better that they don't. By contrast, the arachnophobe feels fear even when looking at a nonpoisonous spider behind glass at the zoo. They know there is absolutely no danger. They wish they didn't feel it—it gets in the way of what would otherwise be a pleasant day's outing. Yet their heart pounds and they panic, desperate to leave. The brave solider shows that conscious, considered judgments or beliefs that something is dangerous are insufficient for fear; the arachnophobe shows that they are unnecessary for fear. Hence fear is something other than conscious, considered judgments or beliefs—something different, something distinct. Just so with active blame. Conscious, considered judgments or beliefs that a person is blameworthy are neither necessary nor sufficient for active blame.

2. Active blame is not only *like* an emotion. It seems to be in part *constituted by* emotions—in particular, reactive attitudes such as resentment, indignation, anger, outrage, disgust, and contempt. Some (even if not all) of these are the stuff from which the rowing couple's blame is made—the something different, something distinct from conscious considered judgments or beliefs. Like all emotions, these reactive attitudes can be irrational, in that they can exist and persist despite the knowledge that their object is not worthy of them. Like all emotions, they also capture attention and narrow our focus. Like all emotions, in their irrationality and their myopia, they feed themselves. Emotions find new features of

their object to latch on to, new reasons why they are the right way to feel.[5] Resentful that your partner failed to do a minor household duty, you then find yourself resenting the way they did do a different chore. Gripped by indignation, you are more likely to look for reasons why you are right to be indignant if presented with evidence that you aren't—rather than accept the evidence and let it go. Just so with anger, outrage, disgust, contempt, and their kin. These emotions are part and parcel of active blame, and they feed themselves and therefore it.

3. Notwithstanding its label, "active" blame and the emotions that constitute it can sometimes be dormant, waiting in the background. You can blame someone or feel resentment, indignation, anger, outrage, disgust, or contempt toward them for weeks, months, years—during which time you also sleep, eat, experience many other emotions and have long periods of time when you are busy with other things and don't think of them at all. What matters for it to be true that, during this time, you actively blame them or feel this way toward them is simply that these states really are there waiting—at the ready to be ignited as and when you remember or reencounter the person, and the stamp book you are collecting of interpersonal wrongs is opened again. (Of course, on other occasions, active blame and the emotions constituting it may be one-off or straightforwardly resolved rather than enduring.)

4. Blame and the emotions that constitute it can be active in the mind of the blamer without being overtly manifest to the blamee. Indeed, much of the activity of blame and these emotions lies in the inner workings of our minds. We dwell on things, returning repeatedly to whatever the other person did—incredulous, furious, scornful. We rant to ourselves—calling people names, saying derogatory things about them to ourselves. We ruminate about what we might say or do in response. We experience spiteful and retaliatory impulses to hurt, to wound, to get back at them. We feel waves of aggression and rage. We feel waves of coldness and contempt. These inner workings tend to out themselves one way or another. But it is surely not impossible for active blame to sometimes be kept entirely hidden from another's view.

5. For active blame to sting, it is necessary for it to be overtly manifest to the blamee, not kept entirely hidden from their view. Active blame can be overtly manifest to the blamee because the blamer consciously and voluntarily expresses and acts on it, or because it unconsciously or inadvertently seeps out. One reason why active blame tends to unconsciously

or inadvertently seep out is that it is constituted in part by emotions, which are associated with involuntary bodily expressions.[6] They can show in the tone of our voice, the cast of our face, our bodily posture and manner—whether or not we mean them to. So too can active blame, as constituted by these emotions.

6. Active blame stings at least in part because of the nature of the hostile, negative emotions that are part of its inner workings and that tend to come out one way or another. How they come out is no doubt varied. Active blame can be aggressive—expressed, for example, through heated words and violent threats. Or it can be passive-aggressive—expressed, for example, by the cold shoulder of rejection. But, whether manifest consciously and deliberately or unconsciously and inadvertently, it is unpleasant to be the object of another's hostile, negative emotions.

7. Because active blame stings, we tend to try to avoid it. No doubt, people have different degrees of resilience to active blame and different ways they try to avoid it. But a common defensive strategy is to blame the blamer. It matters less that someone thinks badly of you if you think the same of them. This is part of how blame escalates, and, once it has escalated, why it can be difficult to let go for reasons beyond the tendency of emotions to feed themselves. As with the rowing couple, we protect ourselves from the sting of another's active blame by actively blaming them in turn (see below).

Bringing these dimensions of active blame together: It can be irrational, floating free of conscious, considered judgments or beliefs that another person is or is not blameworthy. It is in part constituted by hostile, negative emotions. It can lie dormant, waiting in the background but ready to erupt. It captures attention and narrows our focus. It feeds itself. Much of its activity lies in the inner workings of our minds, but it also tends to come out, either consciously and voluntarily or unconsciously and inadvertently. When it comes out, it can sting. One way for the blamee to avoid blame's sting is to turn the tables and blame the blamer. In this, active blame is interactional and relational. It develops between people, shaping their relationship.

The responsibility without blame stance aims to attribute responsibility and hold people answerable and to account without *active blame*. I do not like to articulate this idea using the language of "blameworthiness" because doing so raises a question about what a person being *worthy of blame* could mean if not that we should actively blame them—which is exactly what the responsibility without blame stance aims to avoid.[7] It is therefore more in keeping with the stance to speak simply of responsibility for wrongdoing, understood as indicating the presence of cognitive and volitional capacities as described in the previous chapter. But if we put the worry about what "blameworthiness" could mean in this context momentarily to the side, we can articulate the idea by saying that a person who adopts an attitude of responsibility without blame toward another may yet have a conscious, considered judgment or belief that they are blameworthy. In other words, they do not flinch from looking squarely at the other person's responsibility for wrongdoing. The point is that neither in virtue nor in consequence of attributing this responsibility—of having a conscious, considered judgment or belief that the person is blameworthy—do they actively blame them.

In theory, the simplest and most straightforward way to adopt the responsibility without blame stance is to avoid feeling the hostile, negative emotions that are constitutive of active blame, replacing these with an attitude of concern and respect while yet attributing responsibility and holding answerable and to account. My own experience of working clinically was that over time, the pull of emotions like resentment, indignation, anger, outrage, disgust, and contempt significantly lessened. Slowly but surely, my emotional temperament and tendencies changed as I learned how to do my job. Thus far in this chapter, I have emphasized how active blame can be irrational. But it is important to note that it can also be rational, in the sense of responsive to what, on balance and all things considered, we judge we should under the circumstances ideally feel. As noted in the previous chapter, there is great cultural and contextual variation in our emotions. Making a serious attempt to change our emotional temperament and tendencies—by means such as going to therapy oneself, or by working to learn how to do one's job as a therapist, or simply by asking hard questions of ourselves about who we would ideally like to be and how we would ideally like to feel—can change them.

But change is never guaranteed. In practice, it is not possible to expect anyone to avoid feeling all hostile, negative emotions—no matter how convinced they are that they shouldn't and how hard they try to ensure that they don't. We cannot stop ourselves from feeling emotions (or alternatively make ourselves feel them) simply at will. They are things that happen to us, rather than things we do. And, even if we could simply will away our hostile, negative emotions, it is not obvious that it would be good for us and our relationships always to do so. These emotions signal that something is not right between us. For example, as the philosopher Amia Srinivasan—writing in a long tradition of feminism and political activism—has argued, anger and its allies can serve as a kind of affective protest: a recognition of wrongdoing, and a sign of concern and show of respect for those who have been wronged, whether that is oneself or another.[8] It is also a truism that personal relationships have most value when they are honest and authentic. We need to be able to communicate with each other and talk about how we feel and why we feel it—not just will our feelings away.

In consequence, it is neither realistic nor (if it was realistic) would it be obviously desirable to conceive of the responsibility without blame stance as demanding the avoidance of all hostile, negative emotions. Rather, the key is what we do with these emotions when they occur.

Think back to the rowing couple. At first, the inconvenienced party is annoyed—just a little bit angry—that their partner failed to do what they promised and see to the minor household duty. It would be an exaggeration to say that they actively blame their partner to start. It is as the row develops that both partners come to actively blame the other. How does this happen? No doubt part of the answer lies in the nature of hostile, negative emotions themselves—their irrationality, their myopia, their tendency to feed themselves. Meanwhile, the stronger the emotion, the more likely it will unconsciously or inadvertently seep out and sting; and the more it stings, the more likely it will feed and strengthen the other's reaction in turn. But what happens between the couple is not in the main unconscious and inadvertent. They *act* on their hostile, negative emotions—consciously and voluntarily.

Part of what is striking about the phenomenology of emotions like resentment, indignation, anger, outrage, disgust, and contempt is that they can involve *a sense of entitlement*—a feeling of being in the right in relation to another's wrong—that invites the subject to take them up. These emotions don't just happen to seep out. In their grip, we often consciously and voluntarily decide—or at the very least consciously and voluntarily allow ourselves—to intentionally act on them or to let them seep out. This is what the couple does, as they each become increasingly incensed, adamant, and self-righteous. Each acts as if they are in the right while the other is in the wrong—as if they are the good guy and the other is the bad guy—positioning themself in relation to the other as occupying the moral high ground. To position oneself as occupying the moral high ground just is to reject the idea of a shared ground for respectful and reflective conversation between equals. Recall the juridical image of attributions of responsibility as giving us a prima facie license to blame and punish, legitimating attitudes and treatment that would otherwise be morally questionable if not outright impermissible. We can see active blame as guided by this image: The blamer takes up the sense of entitlement that can be part and parcel of what it is like to be gripped by hostile, negative emotions, thereby allowing themself the freedom to vent, to berate, to inflict their emotions on the blamee who is cast as in the wrong and so deserving of what they get. Active blame develops in part through our agency. It is not itself an act of punishment, but it is a punishing state of mind that we actively embrace.

Summing up: In the ideal world, we would feel hostile, negative emotions less irrationally, less myopically, less obsessively—possibly, just *less*—than we do. That said, they nonetheless have an ineliminable place in our relationships, not just because we can't will them away, but because of the protest they embody and what they signal and mean. The responsibility without blame stance aims to attribute responsibility and hold people answerable and to account without actively embracing a sense of entitlement to hostile, negative emotions. This requires being open to hearing and considering another's perspective and mindful of the impact of our reactions on them—while not flinching from attributing responsibility for wrongdoing and holding answerable and to account. There is a reciprocal expectation of self-reflexivity: an expectation that we be willing to hold ourselves responsible for the impact on others of holding them responsible for their impact on us. This creates a shared ground for conversation between equals.[9] It also helps maintain concern and respect.

Three features of UK therapeutic communities as well as other clinical contexts support the responsibility without blame stance. None is unique to them and all three already exist within or can be adapted to nonclinical settings.

First, the relationships are caring. This is the nature of the role people play for each other within therapy groups. It is a clear expectation of therapists and group members—as it is with family and friends. But it is also genuine. (Most) therapists and group members really do value and hold concern for each other—as do (most) family and friends. Caring about a person typically involves wanting things to go well for them and for your relationship with them to flourish. It therefore gives you reason to do what you can to make it so, and hence to hold responsible without blame in so far as that is conducive to making it so (see chapter 19).

Second, there is a shared culture of expectations and a shared language for talking to each other when expectations are not met. The shared expectations include both that group members do not harm themselves or others *and* that there are very clear practices of answerability and accountability if they do (see chapter 16). This supports a responsibility without blame stance for a very simple reason. It is easier not to actively blame people when they take responsibility for what they do; and it is easier for people to take responsibility for what they do when they are part of a shared culture where this is expected of them and where they are held answerable and to account. The shared language includes ways of speaking designed to be less accusatory and inflammatory. For example, this can involve techniques as simple as using what are called "I-statements" and "what-questions." I-statements simply state what you feel rather than what you take to have made you feel that way. For example, rather than say "You've made me upset!" say instead "I feel upset." What-questions are replacements for why-questions when you are inquiring into another person's mental states or behavior. For example, instead of asking "Why are you feeling like that/Why are you doing that?" ask instead "What is your feeling about/What is making you do that?" These simple shifts in how we speak can help keep active blame at arm's length.

Third, the tendency toward active blame naturally diminishes in contexts that emphasize and value psychological explanation. As I noted in chapter 16 when introducing the rescue-blame trap, the deep question in any therapeutic context when people behave in ways that harm themselves and/or others is *why*. What is the inner experience driving the behavior and how has a person's history and life circumstances contributed to them feeling and acting as they do? Asking and answering this kind of question involves a process of coming to better understand another person. This typically induces empathy and compassion—a direct antidote to active blame—and deepens the relationship. It can also reveal where and how a person's cognitive and volitional capacities may be compromised or less than ideal—and so their responsibility reduced and their agency in need of scaffolding to develop. These kinds of conversations are obviously not limited to therapeutic contexts. In theory, they can take place anywhere, and it is open to us to have them more, and more seriously, within our relationships. The next chapter brings the solutions to the puzzle offered in part III—the various explanations of *why* a person is using drugs in a way that is profoundly counter to their own good—into contact with the responsibility without blame stance.

Browning's *The Ring and the Book* tells a complicated story. Pompilia is wed to Franceschini as a twelve-year-old girl. She endures a marriage of cruelty and rape. On his part, Franceschini believes he was misled by Pompilia's parents. He married for a dowry that was promised but not paid and a nobility that proved uncertain. In consequence, he petitions the courts early in their marriage for divorce, but his petition is denied. As Pompilia and Caponsacchi tell their story, they were never lovers, only friends: Caponsacchi took pity and helped her escape from Franceschini. In the aftermath of their flight, Franceschini again petitions the courts to uphold his honor, only to again feel that justice is denied him by the lightness of their sentences: Pompilia is sent to a convent and Caponsacchi is banished from Rome for three years. Then it is discovered that Pompilia is pregnant. Who is the father? Pompilia claims Franceschini. Franceschini believes Caponsacchi. Pompilia is sent back from the convent to live with her parents. Franceschini—believing he now faces even further dishonor—hires a group of hitmen to kill them. He is tried for murder and sentenced to die. He appeals the verdict to the Pope. The Pope concedes that he cannot be certain of all the facts, but nonetheless upholds Pompilia's innocence and condemns Franceschini. The poem is a series of books, each written from the differing perspectives of the narrator, the main characters, the lawyers in the case, the people of Rome, and the Pope himself. Remarkably, it is based on a true story.

Caponsacchi is right to imply that it is not only blame but blameworthiness that stings. Most of us struggle to face up to the ways we are responsible for wronging or hurting other people. Doing so is painful. It threatens our moral identity and sense of self-worth. So, we avoid taking responsibility. We minimize, deflect, deny. We look for excuses. We put the blame onto someone else. This is what Franceschini tries to do. Bitter and resentful, he blames Caponsacchi, Pompilia, and her parents for what he did. They tricked him, wronged him, dishonored him—it's their fault, he was left no choice. Even after the Pope condemns him, he remains self-righteous: "I lived and died a man, and take man's chance / Honest and bold: right will be done to such."[10] Only at death's door does he in any way repent, but not by taking responsibility for murdering Pompilia and her parents. Instead, Franceschini claims he was "just stark mad" and begs to be saved: "Abate,—Cardinal,—Christ,— Maria,—God, . . . / Pompilia, will you let them murder me?"[11]

Franceschini avoids the sting of blameworthiness to the end. As Browning tells the story, a modern reader cannot but be on Caponsacchi and Pompilia's side. Let us be plain: Franceschini is a rapist and a murderer. He is arrogant and unpleasant. But however paltry and insignificant the wrongs against him are compared to those he perpetrated, they are part of his story. And, like the Pope, we cannot be certain of all the facts. Should we really believe that Caponsacchi and Pompilia were just friends? Are we sure her parents did not mislead Franceschini to get him to marry their daughter? Might the courts have treated him unfairly? Has he been made the laughing stock of Rome? These things happen. People who claim to be friends are lovers. People lie to further their interests. The courts make mistakes. People gossip cruelly. Did these things happen to Franceschini? How black-and-white should we see this story, even while we refuse to waver from holding him responsible for cruelty, murder, and rape?

The sting of blameworthiness is why it can be important that others hold us answerable and accountable: Like Franceschini, we may refuse to so hold ourselves. But it is also part of why actively blaming others can be such an ineffective means of getting them to so hold themselves. For they will then have two things to try to avoid: the sting of blameworthiness, and the sting of active blame. If they can find a way to minimize, deflect, or deny their blameworthiness, that will also serve as a way to escape the sting of active blame. For if they are not blameworthy—or not *so* blameworthy—then active blame is inapt, unfair, undeserved. Indeed, it allows the tables to be all too easily turned: If they can convince themselves that they aren't in fact blameworthy, then those who actively blame them become blameworthy for wrongly doing so, and so deserve blame in turn. This is how blame escalates. Accusations abound. Protestations are issued. Accusations rebound. Each side becomes increasingly entrenched, embittered, righteous—refusing to hear or consider the other's perspective. Active blame rarely makes things better for people who want to maintain relationships with each other, and usually makes things worse. This is why we need an alternative.

19

Responsibility Without Blame for Addiction

IT IS A TRUISM that relationships bring meaning and joy to our lives—as well as pain. When people we care about wrong us or hurt us—or harm themselves—the pain can be deep. Many of us have people in our lives who have done this through drugs. Many of us have done this ourselves. There are no universal solutions to problems in relationships or answers to the question of whether people with addiction are responsible for using drugs. The heterogeneity of explanations of addiction makes for a corresponding heterogeneity of responsibility—as well as how best to make our relationships as good as possible under the circumstances and to support people with addiction to change their relationships with drugs. The clinical stance of responsibility without blame articulated in the previous three chapters can be used as an ethical framework—an interlocking set of ideas and practices—to help us think about responsibility and relationships in addiction. It offers an alternative to the black-and-white ethical thinking that both the brain disease model and the moral model invite, rejecting both a rescuing and a blaming mindset. But there should be no illusions. There are no quick fixes offered in place—no instruction manual for how to be with each other.

A note to readers: As this opening paragraph intimates, there are three limiting features of this chapter. First, the relationships it speaks to are between adults. It does not deal with relationships where either party is a child. Second, it is predominantly written to address people who are in relationships with people with addiction, not to address people with addiction themselves. Predominantly, but not entirely: The chapter's emphasis on conversation and mutual self-reflexivity precludes an entirely one-sided discussion—for these take two—even if it addresses one party in the relationship more than the other. Third, the chapter is written from a second-person standpoint. It aims to describe the ethical framework in relation to its application to another: to sketch some of what it can mean to hold others responsible without blame in contexts of addiction. But the framework can be taken up from a first-person standpoint. As a person with addiction, it is possible to hold yourself responsible for ways you harm yourself by using drugs—and ways you may also wrong or hurt others—without actively blaming yourself. Self-blame can be extraordinarily self-destructive. It can lead any of us to sabotage our attempts to do things differently—or, indeed, to refuse to make any such attempts at all—because we feel that we don't deserve anything better. Just as this chapter offers an alternative way of relating to others, so too it offers an alternative way of relating to ourselves. Very occasionally, I will point this out.

The pain of relationships. Let us begin with some general considerations. Relationships are structured by social roles, which come with expectations as well as rights and responsibilities. For example, when they are young, children have a right to be cared for by their parents, and parents have a responsibility to care for them. In most societies, these rights and responsibilities reverse as children grow up and parents grow old. No one has a right to another's friendship. But friends can expect certain things from each other—interest in each other's lives, concern for each other's well-being, enjoyment of each other's company, a degree of loyalty—on pain of not truly being friends at all. Similarly, many of us have relationships where we expect our partners to love us—but we can't claim their love by right. There is cultural variation in the expectations, rights, and responsibilities that come with role-based relationships. There is also tremendous freedom to shape their precise nature within individual relationships, as well as large tracts of these relationships that are not well-described in the language of expectations, rights, and responsibilities at all. How often do you call your parents? Are we going to be friends who exchange birthday gifts or not? How do we live together as partners—how much are our lives interwoven, how much are they independent?

When we fail to meet an agreed expectation or violate a right, we wrong the other person in the relationship. Sometimes, of course, we may have good reasons for what we do. If so—that is, if failing to meet the expectation or violating the right is, all things considered, the right thing to do under the circumstances—then, because we do not ourselves do wrong, it does not seem apt to say that we wrong the other. What we do is harm them, if justifiably so.

But sometimes we act in ways that hurt each other even when there is no expectation or right that we don't.[1] Your parents are hurt that you don't call them
more frequently, even though you do call regularly. There is no expectation let
alone duty for you to call more, nor do they think there is. They know you love
them. They just wish you called more frequently and feel hurt that you don't.
You give a friend a well-chosen birthday present that you put a lot of thought
into. They thank you, but explain that birthdays are fraught for them and ask
you not to buy anything again. When your birthday comes along later in the
year, there is no present for you. You not only don't believe that they owe you
a present. You also really understand why they haven't given you one. But you
are nonetheless hurt. You wanted the effort you put into their birthday to be
reciprocated and to share in the pleasures of birthdays together. Your partner
spends a lot of time at work and with their friends. Both are very important to
them. They have never misled you about this. You don't believe you have any
right to ask them to spend less time at work or with their friends, and more
time with you. Indeed, they really do spend plenty of time with you. But you
want more. You're hurt that they don't.[2]

Turning now to relationships with people with addiction: As emphasized
in the introduction to this book and throughout, there is nothing intrinsically
morally wrong with using drugs. Yet despite this fact—and despite the fact
that drugs have *social cachet* in some contexts (see chapter 12)—drug use is
nonetheless reliably stigmatized and moralized in our society. We therefore
need to guard against any tendency in us to think that a person is doing something wrong just because they are using drugs. But of course there are occasions when drug use is morally wrong—most obviously, when it involves or
significantly risks seriously harming or violating the rights of others. To
provide some interpersonal examples of varying degrees of severity and specificity: It is wrong to take money from friends to buy drugs under false
pretenses. It is wrong to use drugs having promised your partner that you
wouldn't. It is wrong to get drunk or high on an occasion when your family
wants and needs you to be fully present and part of things—letting them
down. And—this can be one of the most devastating and irreparable consequences of addiction—it is wrong to use drugs in ways and at times that compromise your ability to care for your children. But in addition, there is also the
fact that we can be hurt when people we care about use drugs *apart* from any
wrongdoing on their part. Suppose it isn't work or friends that takes your partner from you. It is drugs. Suppose they really do spend plenty of time with you.

But every day they use and get high. They want it. They say they need it. They have an attachment to drugs that rivals, you cannot help but feel, their attachment to you (see chapters 10 and 15). You hate that they want to get high every day. Perhaps you hate how they are—who they are—when they're high. You feel hurt. You might even say you feel betrayed.

The writer Augusten Burroughs tells of a conversation he had with the mother of a man who died alone in his apartment, drinking.[3] The son had struggled with alcohol for many years. The mother says that she desperately wishes she had been with him when he died, so he didn't die alone. Based on his own experience, Burroughs replies that the complete oblivion that comes from drinking that much is wonderful beyond words. He tells her that, given her son's history with alcohol, he probably died doing something he loved. Indeed, Burroughs goes even further, and says that her son may even have died doing what he loved most in all the world. The implication is that he didn't die alone—he had alcohol keeping him company. There is no way of knowing if what Burroughs says is true of this woman's son. As Burroughs tells the story, he clearly believes that it helped the mother to hear it said. Perhaps so. But imagine the pain of living with the fact that your child loved alcohol more than they loved their own life—including all the things they could have done and could have been. Indeed, if what Burroughs says is true, imagine the pain of living with the fact that your child loved alcohol more than they loved you. Recall what the addiction specialist Gabor Maté's patient Jake says: "Yeah, the coke's my life . . . I care more about the dope than my loved ones or anything else" (see chapter 4).[4] Jake's case is extreme. It is not true of most people with addiction that they love drugs *more* than their loved ones. But it is certainly true that people with addiction may love and value their relationships with drugs *alongside* the love they feel toward—and the value they find in—their relationships with people. This can be so despite the fact that drugs, unlike people, cannot love them back and—given that they are addicted—do not on balance do them good.

Are we wronged when people with addiction prefer to use drugs than to be with us? Are we wronged if they love drugs nearly as much as or perhaps even more than they love us? Is there something corrupt, misshapen, false about a set of values or conception of the good that treats love for drugs and the value of relationships with drugs akin to love for people and the value of relationships with people? I can see nothing here that is black-and-white. The answers to these questions will depend—on the particular people, the particular circumstances, and the particular nature of the relationships between them and with drugs. What social roles do these people occupy in relation to each other? What is owed? What has been promised? What have they agreed they can expect? Do they share an understanding of what they want and need from each other—as well as what they want and need apart from each other? Why in principle would drugs be so different from all the other things we devote ourselves to and get value from—thereby giving our lives meaning and shaping our identities—such as work, hobbies, projects, and indeed relationships not only with people but with things like nature, art, music, food, books? These questions are complicated. Even if sometimes their answers are obvious, other times they are far from certain. But the hurt of feeling second to drugs, as I am inclined to put it, is no less real for the complexity and uncertainty. Put aside questions of right and wrong. The pain of relationships matters regardless.

The philosopher Samuel Scheffler has argued that to value a relationship with another person just is to see yourself as having special responsibilities to them—to see the relationship as giving you reasons to act in distinctive ways toward them.[5] There can be no tidy list of ways we have reasons to act in relationships—no tidy list of our special responsibilities. But in so acting, we shape our relationships, and how we shape our relationships in turn shapes us and the people we are in relationship with. As Scheffler puts it:

> Whether we like it or not, such relations help to define the contours of our lives, and influence the ways that we are seen both by ourselves and by others. Even those who sever or repudiate such ties—insofar as it is possible to do so—can never escape their influence or deprive them of all significance, for to have repudiated a personal tie is not the same as never having had it, and one does not nullify social bonds by rejecting them. One is, in other words, forever the person who has rejected or repudiated those bonds; one cannot make oneself into a person who lacked them from the outset.[6]

Or, we might add, one is forever the person who was rejected or repudiated.

If you care about a person with addiction and value your relationship with them, then you can be wronged—and you can be hurt even if you are not wronged—in a way that people who do not care about them or have a relationship with them cannot. But you also have reason to hold hope for them and for your relationship, and to do what you can to help them and to sustain it—this is, to use Scheffler's language, a responsibility you have to them, in virtue of caring about them and valuing your relationship. But if they care about you, then they also have reason not to wrong or hurt you, and to sustain the relationship and do what they can to address any wrongs or hurts they have caused you—this is a responsibility they have to you, in virtue of caring about you and valuing your relationship.

Let me be very clear: I am not claiming that it is never right to reject the other person or repudiate the relationship. It may be. Arguably, this was true of the writer Cheryl Strayed: For her own sake, she had to leave Joe (see chapter 4).[7] In principle, this can be true of any of us, in any relationship—it can be true of a person with addiction, or of a person in a relationship with a person with addiction. The point is simply that if you care for a person, and they you, then there are reasons on both sides to try to sustain your relationship. This does not mean that it is never right to stop trying to make it work—or perhaps in some cases, not even to try at all.

The clinical stance of responsibility without blame aspires to make space for self-reflection and self-criticism on both sides, through conversations and practices that reckon with the pain of relationships while hoping to sustain them. When someone does something that is so upsetting to us personally that we can't go forward as if nothing is wrong, the first question is why we feel like this. Have they wronged us? Have they harmed us but not wronged us, because what they did was justifiable? Or is the truth of what matters just that we feel unbearably hurt? If so, what, exactly, is hurting us? Is there a clash of values? Are we being stigmatizing or moralizing about drugs? Do we feel disvalued? Do we feel betrayed? Or is it simply unbearable to us that they are doing this to themself—it is unbearable to watch them destroying their life— because of how much we care about them? What do we need from them? What do they need from us? What are they getting from drugs or what do drugs mean to them that would be lost if they quit? How can drugs be replaced and their meaning acknowledged and their loss made bearable if they quit? These questions are the context within which the further question of responsibility—without blame—can arise. For without answers to these questions, we don't know what we would be asking each other to take responsibility for and how best to find a way forward that doesn't let each other and the relationship down.

Duress and the tempering of active blame. The solutions to the puzzle of addiction are heterogeneous. The explanation of why a person is using drugs is specific to them. But there is nonetheless one respect in which all cases of addiction are the same. A life of addiction is not a good one. People live with terrible misery and suffering—even if they sometimes find a moment of peace or euphoria or shroud their pain in denial. They may not understand themselves. They may hate themselves. Their lives may be in ruins. They may despair at ever finding a way out. This simple fact can be a source of compassion that, like empathy, serves as an antidote to blame if we remain alive to it—a task no doubt made difficult when faced with pain of our own.

We are considering the situation where a person wrongs or hurts us by using drugs—inclining us, perhaps, to actively blame them. If only they would quit, we might think, our pain would be gone. But even though a life of addiction is not a good one, a life without drugs contains its own pain for people with addiction. They are caught in a double bind, a choice between our pain or theirs. For people who self-medicate, drugs offer relief from negative psychological states that are otherwise relentless and overwhelming. A life without drugs is a life with no respite from this pain, no moments, however fleeting, of peace or euphoria. For people who are attached to drugs, they need them to feel safe and secure in themselves and in the world. A life without drugs is like losing a friend or a lover—a cause for grief. For people who use drugs to self-harm, drugs are a way of grappling with the bad self within; of seizing ownership and control of their bodies and fates; possibly of finding a way to die. Drugs may not exactly relieve their pain, but they do allow them to have some mastery over it—or at least, some illusion of mastery. For people who identify as an "addict," drugs can provide community and meaningful relationships, structure and purpose in daily life, grounds for self-worth, and a sense of self when otherwise there would be emptiness within. Without drugs, they may not know how to live or who they would be.

When drugs have value to a person of this order of magnitude, the costs of not using are significant and real. They sit alongside the wrongs or hurt done to others by drug use. How to balance these competing costs and needs? How to choose between them?

We can think about this problem by analogy with duress. Duress can justify doing harm when otherwise what is done would be wrong. The classic example is the hold-up. A robber pulls a gun and threatens a bank teller, thereby constraining their options. *"The money or your life!"* The robber forces the teller to choose between handing over the money or giving up their life. Handing over the money is a harm to the bank. Giving up their life is a harm to them. In this case, the choice is obvious. No one thinks the responsibilities of a bank teller include laying down their life to protect the bank's money. Let us assume that the bank teller keeps a cool head. They are not scared or frantic. They are perfectly capable of refusing to hand over the money, thereby giving up their life. But they are entirely justified in choosing that the bank should bear the cost under the circumstances. They are under duress, so they don't wrong the bank in handing over the money even though they could have given up their life.

Tweak the example. A robber pulls a gun and threatens a bank teller. *"The money or your life!"* But it's a water pistol, and the teller knows it. The robber is slight in build and scared, while the teller is strong in build and undaunted. Handing over the money is still a cost to the bank. But what now is the cost to the teller of refusing? Perhaps it's not required for a teller to stand their ground against such a robber, but the fact that there is no credible threat to them changes the balance. It is less clear they are under duress. It is less obvious what they should do. If the teller hands over the money, no one would be surprised if the bank then complained that the teller wasn't justified and owed them the money—after all, it was a water pistol, and the teller knew it.

Whether or not a person is under duress and so justified in doing harm depends on the details of the case. What's the cost to the other party if they act? What's the cost to them if they don't? What's the nature of the relationship between the parties—the expectations, rights, and responsibilities? Now apply this to addiction. Let us assume for now that—like the imagined bank tellers—the cognitive and volitional capacities of people with addiction that are necessary for attributions of responsibility are intact (but see below). They know well enough what they are doing, and their drug use is voluntary in an ordinary sense. They could not use—just the way the tellers could not hand over the money. Nonetheless, the psychological breadth and depth of the value of drugs to people with addiction means that the costs of not using can be significant and real. Facing a choice between using and potentially wronging another person, or not using and bearing these costs themselves, is like being under duress. Depending on the details, sometimes the costs to people with addiction of not using might justify harming other people by using—so they do nothing wrong. If nothing is done that is wrong, then they are not responsible for wrongdoing. Hence, in such cases, we shouldn't blame them. Insofar as active blame can be rational—responsive to whether, on balance and all things considered, we judge or believe another responsible for wrongdoing—it can be tempered by recognition of duress.

But recognition of duress can temper active blame even when the details of the case do not justify the action chosen—the wrong to the other is too grave, or the cost to the person with addiction too small by comparison—and so a wrong is done and the person is responsible for it. To see this, consider how recognition of duress can affect us when we are hurt.

Suppose a person with addiction does not owe it to you not to use drugs. But they know that they are hurting you by using and it is within their power not to use. Recognizing the pain they would face by not using can help make sense of why they are using, thereby potentially mitigating your hurt and tempering any tendency you have to actively blame them for hurting you. This is because taking up their perspective and recognizing the value of drugs to them—and in consequence the double bind they find themself in—can help us empathize and maintain compassion even in the face of our own pain. But in just the same way, recognizing the pain they would face by not using can also help make sense of why they are using—and hence help us empathize and maintain compassion—if they have done wrong. Even if duress does not justify harm, it can mitigate how we feel about the person who does the wrong. Recognition of duress gives us reason to cut *affective slack* to people we care about when they hurt us *or* wrong us. Note that if you are a person with addiction, recognition of duress also gives you reason to cut yourself affective slack—to show yourself compassion rather than actively blaming yourself, while yet recognizing your capacity for agency and responsibility.

Social injustice and standing to blame. Thus far, I have confined my discussion of the duress of addiction to personal relationships. But it is also relevant to our collective attitudes toward people with addiction in our society. It is not only that recognition of pain can be reason to cut anyone affective slack, quite generally. Given the context in which addiction flourishes, we may collectively lack standing to blame in some cases. Recall that addiction is associated with backgrounds of severe adversity, limited socioeconomic opportunities, and the presence of additional mental health problems—which are often untreated (see chapters 10, 11, and 12). These circumstances reliably reflect injustice: failures of the state to respect basic rights and meet basic needs of its members and secure equal opportunities for all; failures of wider society to treat all its members with dignity and humanity. The use of drugs to self-medicate, to self-harm, to commit suicide, or to provide a social identity and sense of self can arise from such circumstances—from which there can be no realistic hope of escape. When this is so, the duress of addiction—of being caught in a double bind, between doing wrong to other members of society in relation to using drugs, or suffering one's own pain by not using drugs—arises in part from circumstances of social injustice. Insofar as we collectively tolerate social injustice, we are implicated in it. Insofar as we are implicated in it, our collective standing to blame may be compromised, for our hands are far from clean.[8]

Holding responsible. I turn now from how to temper active blame to how to hold responsible without it. As a brief reminder: The idea of responsibility constitutive of a responsibility without blame stance takes it to flow from a set of cognitive and volitional capacities that clinical practices of answerability and accountability are designed to engage. The point is not to license blame and punishment. The point is to identify where a person has the capacity to do things differently—for their sake, for the sake of others, for the sake of their relationships with others—and to support them to change. In consequence, clinical practices of answerability and accountability can be used even when cognitive and volitional capacities are compromised or less than ideal—so long as they are sensitive to why and how they are compromised and less than ideal. Indeed, this is part of the point of these practices: In seeing where and how cognitive and volitional capacities are diminished, we see where and how to bolster them.

Cognitive capacities. To be responsible for wrongdoing, a person needs to know well enough what they are doing and have some inkling that it is wrong—or, if they don't actually know these things, then at the very least, they should (see chapter 17). There is no question that such knowledge can be compromised or less than ideal in addiction. People may simply not realize how much they are wronging or hurting others—or alternatively harming themselves. Suppose the explanation of why a person is using drugs despite evident and severe costs is that they are ignorant of these costs or in denial. Now assume that these costs include wronging or hurting others, about whom they care. Then they don't know that, in using drugs, they are wronging or hurting others, and in consequence they are not responsible for doing so—unless, that is, they should know. Should they?

How should we go about answering this question? Were the point of attributing responsibility a license to punish and blame, false positives would need to be avoided. Since the point of attributing responsibility without blame is to support a person to do things differently in future and the associated practices of answerability and accountability are nonpunitive, false positives can be risked. What might we do to help them overcome their ignorance or denial? The answer is simple. *Talk to them.* Let them know what effect their drug use is having—that it is wronging another, that it is hurting you. Or let them know what, in your eyes, their drug use is doing to them. Tell them you're terrified for them, that you think they're just not seeing what they're doing to themself by using drugs. Tell them you're concerned (if indeed you are) that their values have been corrupted and misshapen by drugs—that you think they're too devoted, too emotionally dependent for their own good—whatever good they may themself feel that drugs offer. In other words, have the kind of hard conversation that I have repeatedly described over the course of this book as essential to diagnosis, treatment, and to the clinical practices of answerability and accountability that are constructed to support positive, meaningful relationships and help people do things differently (see chapters 4, 5, and 16). We know that many people with addiction are able to overcome whatever is blocking them from seeing the damage their drug use is doing to them and to others. Virtually all addiction memoirs tell this story. The effectiveness of techniques of motivational interviewing and cognitive behavioral therapy that target ignorance and denial testifies to it as well. And it is just plain common sense—people with addiction are just people, and the damage our actions do is something virtually all of us can learn, given time. Perhaps this is not true of everyone. There are exceptions to every rule. In which case, if a person is genuinely unable to acquire this knowledge, then it would be a mistake to say that they should have known, for they couldn't have known. But the best way to establish if they can come to know—that is, if they can learn what damage their actions are doing—is to talk to them and to treat them as a person who both can know and who would want to. This is a form of holding them answerable and to account for the costs of their drug use—the costs to them and to you.

Self-harm. In addition to ignorance and denial, a self-harming or suicidal mindset can stop people with addiction recognizing how their drug use is wronging or hurting others. These mindsets are like black holes. As the clinical psychologist Edwin Shneidman baldly states the point: "Never kill yourself while you are suicidal."[9] People are drawn into the hole, and their cognitive capacity to think clearly and rationally about life outside of it—about what reasons there might be to care about themselves, about what reasons there might be to live—is profoundly diminished.

As described in chapter 11, one characteristic feature of a self-harming or suicidal mindset is a sense of self as wrong, bad, evil—worthless. If you believe you are without value, it can be hard to believe that others value you. Rather than recognize that other people care about you and are devastated by the damage you are doing to yourself—that other people would be devastated were you to die—you think of yourself as a burden to them. You may even believe they would be better off without you. Here again, all we can do is our best to make sure the people we love know it. In this light, consider the following report from one of the philosopher and qualitative researcher Anke Snoek's subjects, describing a conversation with his son that marked a turning point in his addiction to alcohol. This is what he reports his son saying to him: "'Dad, if you drink or not I don't care. I will still come and visit you, because I know who you are, you are more than your drink. You are a positive person, and I will always love you. Only, if you continue drinking, you will have a smaller role in my life. Because, if you stay drinking, you only have a year or three left in life.'"[10] Notice how the son holds his father accountable for his drinking and its consequences simply by saying how he feels, and what will come to pass if his father doesn't quit.

Volitional capacities. To be responsible for wrongdoing, a person's actions need to be voluntary in an ordinary sense: flexible, goal-directed behavior explained by beliefs and desires (see chapter 17). Addiction is not compulsive but voluntary in this ordinary sense. Drug use is not directly controlled by stimuli but guided by representations of outcomes; drug desires are not irresistible (see chapters 6 and 7). But cravings and problems of control nonetheless impact volitional capacities. How could they not?

Cravings capture attention and have an immediate, felt, urgency. They pull people toward drugs. Problems of control explain why people with addiction heed the pull, acting against their better judgment or sincere intention to abstain—they explain what I have labeled "loss of control" (see chapter 14). Suppose cravings for drugs and problems of control together explain why a person is using despite wronging or hurting others, about whom they care. Are their volitional capacities sufficiently intact for responsibility to be appropriately attributed at all?

One kind of problem of control resolutely answers this question: *No.* Another resolutely answers: *Yes.* All others deliver the verdict: *Enough* (even if only marginally), given that the point of attributing responsibility without blame is to support a person to do things differently in future and sustain the relationship—meaning that false positives can be risked.

The problem of control that undercuts responsibility attributions alto-gether is the fallibility of the cognitive systems relevant to behavioral control (see chapters 7 and 14).[11] Suppose someone wrongs or hurts you by using, but the explanation for why they used is just bad luck, brute error. At the moment of action, their better judgment or sincere intention was to abstain. Indeed, they may have come to this judgment or formed this intention out of concern for what their drug use is doing to you. But there was a blip in the system, a kind of mechanical breakdown. There is no disregard for you expressed by their action, no failure on their part. They really couldn't help it, and there is nothing that they can do to ensure it doesn't happen again. This kind of fallibil-ity is immune to trying harder and taking precautions—it is immune to *agency*. It is just the nature of the human machine.

Contrast this with the problem of control that does the opposite of un-dercutting responsibility attributions: *Screw it*, in the words of Burroughs (see chapters 7 and 14).[12] Burroughs describes how wanting to drink but not drinking can lead to frustration, bitterness, resentment—emotions that make people decide to use drugs in defiance of their better judgment or sincere intention, because they get to a point where they just don't care enough anymore. If this is the explanation of why a person uses drugs de-spite wronging or hurting you, then what they didn't care enough about is *you*. This is to show blatant disregard, and in so doing "screw it" cannot but invite active blame, while hardly pointing to much reduction in the voli-tional capacities necessary for attributions of responsibility. Although we are not our best selves when frustrated, bitter, and resentful, these emotions by themselves neither justify nor excuse a decision to screw another person over for any reason, including drugs. To be clear, screwing another person over was not what I imagine Burroughs had in mind in describing the state that, for him, precipitates relapse. The person he imagined screwing over was surely himself. But sometimes people do, in the moment, knowingly and willingly wrong or hurt others, against their better judgment or (hitherto) sincere intention. If this is true of a person with addiction in relation to their drug use, it should be faced squarely. How can we do so, in keeping with the responsibility without blame stance so far as possible? How can we not be angry?

We don't need to be. Emotions like anger that serve to signal that some-thing is wrong between us and to protest against wrongdoing do not need to be suppressed to hold responsible without blame. It is what we do with them that matters (see chapter 18). The relationships we are considering in this chapter are between people who care for each other and hope for a relationship, even if one of them thinks: *Screw it*, and wrongs or hurts the other in the moment despite their better judgment or (hitherto) sincere intention not to use. This is why there is reason to reckon with the wrong and the hurt in a way that helps the person do things differently and sustains the relationship. A conversation that speaks to the wrong and voices the anger can yet hold back from a sense of entitlement to retribution and a moral righteousness, making room for questions that matter for the future of the relationship. That is, the conversation can focus more on anger, hurt, and repair, less on condemnation and revenge.[13] Does the person regret what they did? Are they sorry? Have they apologized? Do they care about us as they profess? Can they reassure us? Do they understand why they got so frustrated, bitter, and angry? Are there steps they could take to ward off these emotions in future, or, if not, then to stop their ill temper leading to ill will? Will they commit to not doing this again? Words can be cheap, so how might this commitment be made real?

Let us turn now to problems of control that leave volitional capacities intact *enough* for responsibility to be attributed. Cravings can combine with a depletion of self-control—whether that should be understood as a waning of the capacity or the motivation to exercise it. Bookkeeping can flip from global to local in the bat of an eye. Temporal myopia throws the future to the wind, making us blind to all considerations—including, alas, the future impact of our actions on others—except for the here and now. A history of drug use and failed attempts at abstinence can destroy self-efficacy, making us believe we will fail and so undercutting our efforts to succeed—even if, absent the belief we will fail, succeed we might. Any of these processes can sneak up on a person, causing them to change their mind or reappraise their intention to abstain in the moment. Are they responsible, if in doing so they wrong or hurt you? Could they have resisted, and stayed the course? How could we know?

Once again, given the point of attributing responsibility without blame, false positives can be risked. We do not need to know answers to these questions before we proceed. We can instead begin by asking: What might we do to help them resist in future? Or, if you are a person with addiction, you can begin by asking this of yourself. There are many simple clinical interventions and commonsense strategies that help people stay the course—despite the temptation not to. For example, avoid occasions for temptation and take concrete steps that make it harder to act on any cravings you feel (throw out all drugs and drug paraphernalia; delete your drug contacts from your phone). Commit to "personal rules"[14] surrounding drug use and find mechanisms to make them binding (contingency management treatment is such a mechanism). Make it a habit to stop and think before acting on impulse (count to a hundred, breathe). Promise other people (thereby making yourself accountable to other people) that you will reach out for support *prior* to using. Avail yourself of any of the vast array of tips, tricks, and ways of structuring the environment that render more salient the future rewards of abstinence and the future costs of drug use—including its impact on others—at the moment of choice (tape photos of the people you care about to your door, your dashboard, your wallet; learn to practice episodic future thinking;[15] make concrete, staged plans for exactly what you will do to resist using and how you will achieve your abstinence goals[16]). Lastly and most obviously, get help, access treatment, find a group, don't do all this alone. To insist that a person take some of these steps is to insist that they take responsibility for not using drugs in future—but in a way that bolsters their volitional capacities thereby increasing the likelihood they succeed in not using drugs in future.

None of these simple interventions and commonsense strategies are magic bullets, but they can help. If they do, that is evidence that the person is capable of behavioral control. But if you are a person who has been wronged or hurt by someone's failure not to use, you might yet feel the pull of the following question: If these interventions and strategies help, is that evidence that they *could* have resisted and stayed the course when they used drugs and wronged or hurt you in the past, prior to taking the steps to learn and implement these interventions and strategies? If you feel the pull of this question, ask yourself why. Is it because you want to know if they were responsible for wronging or hurting you in a way that is backward looking, that is, you want to know if you have license to blame and punish? This is not only to withdraw from the responsibility without blame stance but to wade right into the swamp (see chapter 17). Given that the interventions and strategies help them now, there is every reason to think they would have helped then, and so in one sense, yes, the person could have resisted. But in another sense, no, they couldn't have resisted, for they didn't have these interventions and strategies in their toolkit then, which is why it was right to insist they take steps to get them and how they have come to have them now. The bottom line is that we have reason to treat people with addiction we care about and who experience a loss of control—defined simply as acting against their better judgment or sincere

intention to abstain—as capable of exercising behavioral control and as wanting to do so. After all, however conflicted or indeed ambivalent the person is,
the hope for a different future is why they made an all-things-considered judgment that abstinence is best or formed a sincere intention to abstain in the first
place. They want, on balance, to abstain. And we want them to abstain. Abstinence is facilitated by a focus not on whether they were responsible in the past
but on how to hold them responsible now in such a way as to support them to
take responsibility and successfully abstain from drugs in future. Let me say
once again that this does not require pretending that you are not angry if you
are—what it requires is avoiding any tendency to self-righteousness and other-
denigration, that is, avoiding the punishing mindset of active blame.

Lastly, let us consider the effect of an extreme case of hyperbolic discounting, where loss of control as defined is beside the point. This is because the
person's judgments and intentions are insufficiently durable for adjectives like
"better" or "sincere" to get a grip at all—their preferences for use or abstinence
reverse on a dime. Hence, although we may want them to abstain, it is not
obvious that they want, on balance, to abstain. There is too much fickleness,
too much chaos. Some of the strategies described in this chapter may help
stabilize preferences, enabling talk of "better" judgments or "sincere" intentions to begin to stick. But, until some stability is achieved, there is no possibility of diachronic agency—of making plans, taking on projects, having life goals
of the sort that require commitment over time. This is because a person in this
state can't trust themselves to see anything through. Indeed, it may be unclear,
to them as much as to others, whether they really have a conception of their
own good—a set of values—guiding them at all. To quote him once again, the
philosopher Owen Flanagan describes himself in this stage of his addiction as
"a wretched, worsening train wreck of a person."[17] This cannot but be grounds
for compassion. It also means that the person's volitional capacities are profoundly diminished—responsibility can only be marginal, trained on the here
and now, as there is no real possibility of taking the bigger picture or longer
view. In consequence, practices of answerability and accountability must start
small to engage what agency there is: Don't worry about tomorrow, let's just
think about today, and how to get through it without drugs.

The shape of relationships. The clinical stance of responsibility without blame
is an alternative to the juridical image of responsibility as a license to blame and
punish. It comes into view once the idea of responsibility is separated from the

idea of blame and both are theorized independently, allowing us to escape the rescue-blame trap (see chapters 16, 17, and 18). It offers an ethical framework that can inform relationships with people with addiction. Seeing addiction by analogy with duress can remove responsibility for wrongdoing in some cases and potentially temper blame and promote empathy and compassion in all— this is true with respect to our collective attitudes toward people with addiction in our society as well as our personal relationships. Cognitive and volitional capacities can be less than ideal for a vast number of reasons, including ignorance and denial, a self-harming or suicidal mindset, brute fallibility, cravings, and the catalog of problems of control. This heterogeneity and complexity means that, just as there is no one treatment for addiction, there is no one solution when people are wronged or hurt and relationships founder because of addiction. It will depend on the specifics—of the people, their relationship, and the explanation of why one of them is using drugs. Meanwhile, a background assumption is that both parties care about each other and value the relationship and so are willing to work to sustain it. This, of course, will not always be the case.

The various considerations in this chapter that are relevant to the forward-looking idea of responsibility without blame are also relevant to a backward-looking idea of responsibility as a license to blame and punish. In theory, they can remove or diminish the quantity of active blame or punishment that would be proportionate and permissible in any particular case of drug-associated wrongdoing. I sometimes worry that the label "responsibility without blame" cannot help but invite a return to the juridical image, simply in virtue of containing the word "responsibility." The pull of the rescue-blame trap is real—no doubt especially when we are made weary by the pain of relating. Adopting either a rescuing mindset or a blaming mindset can feel reassuringly familiar—allowing us to read from a standard script. By contrast, the responsibility without blame stance offers no standard script and therefore takes a lot of work: to understand another person; to devise and use nonblaming and nonpunitive practices of answerability and accountability as tools to help them change their relationship to drugs and to us alike; simply to figure out how to be with each other. I hope that the articulation of the perils of the rescue-blame trap and the meaning and value of a responsibility without blame stance may encourage its adoption as a guiding ideal—or at least encourage a greater degree of mutual self-reflexivity and a critical eye for the influence of the juridical image on responsibility practices, emotions, and relationships. But if nothing else, the various considerations in this chapter impose some genuine limits on the permissibility of blame and punishment for drug-associated wrongdoing in many cases of addiction.

At the end of the day, what matters is how we go forward with people we care about who are addicted to drugs and whom we don't want to lose. We want to support them to stop harming themselves. To do so, we have to understand why they are using drugs in ways that are so profoundly counter to their own good, and not deny those parts of the explanation that may cause us pain—because of what they say about how they feel about themselves, or because of what they say about how they feel about us. We also want them to stop wronging or hurting us. To do so, we may need to "hold boundaries" (as it's often put in the clinic) and have conversations that are hard and no doubt often heated, while not losing sight of the fact that we care about them and want a relationship with them. The mix of emotions and what we do with them both shapes our relationships with each other and says something about who we are—and who we aspire to be. It is also one of the crucial means by which people with addiction whose lives and selves are in disarray see who they are and who they could be. People see themselves through the eyes of others: They see their own value as a reflection of the value that others see in them.[18] When responsibility practices sit alongside care, concern, respect—or even love—they can be expressions of belief in another's value and in their capacity to live a better life, while yet making it more rather than less likely that we ourselves feel able to continue to share their life.

In the therapeutic community where I worked, we often asked group members who were struggling with drugs to make a contract to quit. The person would take a blank piece of paper and write something like this: "I will not use drugs. If I find myself tempted, I will make a support call to another group member." They would date and sign the contract, and so would we, therapists and group members alike. We also wrote messages of support. "I know this is hard, but you can do it." "Call me whenever you need—don't hesitate." "You really deserve a better life—don't doubt it or yourself." "I will be thinking of you." Next week in group, we would check in with the person to see how it went. A breach of contract would trigger the kinds of conversations and focused, reflective exercises described in chapter 16. Not everyone quit, of course, but some people did. Some carried their contracts with them for months, until they were ragged and worn, barely legible. It was the power of these contracts that first made me question whether addiction was a brain disease of compulsion—at least in those cases where the contract worked—for surely no brain disease of compulsion could be cured by a piece of paper. How then do contracts work? A contract is a mechanism for answerability and forward-looking accountability. There is no better symbol of taking responsibility. But it is also a symbol of the care and support of the group that you can literally keep in your pocket and take with you wherever you go.

Marco Venniro

Conclusion

THE PARADIGM proposed over the course of this book is humanistic and heterogeneous. It is humanistic in its emphasis on the power of psychology to explain addiction—a power that is always to be understood relative to the circumstances of a person's life—and the importance of each person's understanding and evaluation of their own drug use to the nature and diagnosis of their addiction. It is heterogeneous in its insistence that there is no one-size-fits-all explanation or theory of addiction. Different psychological explanations of why a person is using drugs in a way that counts as addicted are true of different people. And, notwithstanding the power of psychology, some cases of addiction are best explained at least in part by the cognitive and brain sciences.

The paradigm is rooted in a simple observation: Drug use is pervasive across human civilization, a perfectly common, ordinary part of many of our lives. There is nothing puzzling—nor morally wrong—about the vast majority of drug use. We use drugs because of their benefits—the good they do us. By contrast, there is something puzzling about drug use in addiction. This is because whatever benefits a person is getting from drugs appear to be swamped by the costs. Yet they don't quit, thereby violating a basic, psychological assumption we make when explaining human behavior, namely an assumption of self-concern. Why would anyone keep using drugs when it no longer appears in any way worth it?

This is the puzzle of addiction. It is a question that drives much scientific inquiry into addiction, and which many models of addiction aspire to answer. And it can be used to explicate addiction by delineating it from ordinary drug use, thereby identifying the object of study. Addiction is a kind of behavior: a pattern of drug use that persists despite evident and severe costs such that it counts profoundly against a person's own good. In consequence, understanding and diagnosing addiction requires us to reckon with questions of values and a person's own good—answers to which cannot ignore their sincerely professed values and conception of their good.

The paradigm therefore represents a significant shift away from the currently dominant paradigm that identifies addiction with a brain disease causing compulsive drug use. On the one hand, addiction is not well characterized as compulsive. Desires for drugs are not irresistible and drug use in addiction is flexible and goal directed—voluntary in this ordinary sense. On the other hand, making good the claim that brain pathology is the cause of drug use in addiction—whether compulsive or not—has a theoretical and an empirical component. Theoretically, we need to clarify what brain pathology is and what counts as establishing causation; empirically, we need to determine whether brain pathology is present in a person with addiction and, if it is, whether it is causing them to use drugs. Although we should be open to the possibility that brain pathology is the cause of drug use in some cases, we should be clear that the evidence points against it in many others. Other factors matter tremendously to addiction and must not be sidelined.

These other factors include the lack of alternative reinforcers—goods in life that compete with drugs—especially (if by no means exclusively) when people live in conditions of hardship, coming from backgrounds of severe adversity and limited socioeconomic opportunities and suffering from poor mental health. But there are also a range of psychological states and processes—such as ignorance, denial, cravings, and problems of control—that are explanatory when set against a background that recognizes the *value* of drugs. This value is crucial. It includes self-medication, which can result in an attachment to drugs akin to the security-based attachments we have to people. Paradoxically, it also includes the very opposite: the use of drugs as a means to self-harm or to die. Lastly, drugs can provide goods such as relationships, community, daily structure and purpose, self-worth, and a sense of self. Sometimes drugs end up so deeply embedded in a person's life and identity that they no longer know how to live or who they would be without them. Let me ask one final variant of the titular question of this book: Alone in a cage with nothing but cocaine, what would drugs mean to you?

Understanding and addressing addiction requires us to keep all of this in view. Different factors will be salient in different cases. What is driving one person to use drugs may be a world away from what is driving another person to use; helping one person requires intervening in a completely different way from how to intervene to help another. But most people with addiction need help. If there is one universal truth about addiction, it is that recovery is not easy, especially on one's own. To help, we need to reach out. This requires putting stigma and blame to the side. There are ways we can work toward this collectively as a society, such as ensuring universal and unconditional access to health care, including evidence-based and individually tailored addiction treatment; socioeconomic initiatives that guarantee housing, education, and employment for all; and—although the issues here are highly complex—the decriminalization of drug possession, which, crucially, must proceed hand in hand with robust state regulation of drug markets and enforcement of crimes that are or can be drug associated, for example, driving under the influence or public disorder. But there are also ways we can work toward this individually, through our personal relationships with the people in our lives who struggle with addiction.

These relationships are often painful. The pull to moralize, stigmatize, and blame—possibly to reject a person we once cared for or repudiate a relationship—can be real. So too can be the pull in the opposite direction, toward a rescuing mindset. But it is possible to hold answerable and accountable without heeding the pull either way—which can both help the other person forge a different relationship with drugs and with us alike. This possibility is realized in the clinical stance of responsibility without blame—as adapted, so far as possible, to personal relationships—which draws a simple distinction between responsibility and blame. Responsibility is about the other person and the existence and extent of their agency. Blame is about us and how we respond to another person when they are the agent of wrongs, harms, and hurts. Although I have on the whole avoided the language of choice out of concern for the moralism it invites, we might put the idea thus: Just as other people have a choice in what they do, we have a choice in how we respond. There are choices on both sides.

Why choose to adopt a responsibility without blame stance within personal relationships? I have not tried to argue that we must, but only suggested why we might. The reason is that we care about the other person (and they us) and in consequence we want to support them to change their relationship with drugs as well as address and repair the damage done to their relationship with us. But theoretical considerations nonetheless frame this choice. On the one hand, we can see addiction by analogy with duress. The pain we feel because people with addiction use drugs must be balanced with the pain they feel if they don't. In consequence, their responsibility for wrongdoing may sometimes be removed or, even if it is not, our tendency to blame may be tempered. Duress is a reason to cut affective slack. On the other hand, the cognitive and volitional capacities relevant to agency and hence to attributions of responsibility may be significantly diminished in addiction. Knowledge may be lacking. Control may be marginal. Yet, so long as we hold answerable and accountable without blame, we have reason and right to engage what agency a person has in the hope that doing so will bolster it and support them to do things differently in future—for their sake, for our sake, and for the sake of the relationship.

However, "for their sake" must mean what it says. Just as the nature and diagnosis of addiction requires us to recognize the importance of a person's sincerely professed values and their conception of their good, so too does treating addiction and talking about it with the people in our lives. No one gets simply to decide for another person what is "for their sake." With respect to treatment, this is crucial to setting goals. With respect to relationships, it is relevant to when, why, and how we hold people answerable and accountable in a forward-looking way. Assuming that both people care about each other and want to sustain a relationship, there is common ground. But their values may yet conflict, their needs may yet compete. This is why conversations about values, needs, and differences are so important—and self-reflexivity on both sides so necessary—for establishing what it is right to ask people to take responsibility for and how to shape relationships together.

These kinds of conversations are also important for our society at large. To put the explication of addiction that is the foundation of the paradigm in a slogan: Addiction is drug use gone wrong. This slogan brings to light what has been lurking in the shadows all along: Drug use can go right. Our cultural discourse about both drug use and addiction is currently stifled by dogma, fear, and moralism. Our thinking is black-and-white. We need to break free of this, to have conversations that speak not only to the risks of drugs but also to their value—and the consequent need to create norms, expectations, and ways of thinking and being about drugs that take seriously the need to protect us from the risks while yet gifting us their value. My hope in writing this book and proposing a new paradigm for addiction has been to get us talking about the psychology of addiction and the heterogeneity of why and how drug use goes wrong—and how to address it when it does. But at some point, we must also wonder what it looks like when drug use goes right—and how to ensure that it does.

LIST OF ACRONYMS

AA	Alcoholics Anonymous
BPD	Borderline Personality Disorder
DSM	*Diagnostic and Statistical Manual of Mental Disorders*
EMA	Ecological Momentary Assessment
fMRI	functional Magnetic Resonance Imaging
LL	Larger, Later
MDMA	Methylenedioxymethamphetamine
NA	Narcotics Anonymous
NCS	Neurobiological Craving Signature
NHS	National Health Service
NIAAA	National Institute on Alcohol Abuse and Alcoholism
NIDA	National Institute on Drug Abuse
NIMBY	Not In My Backyard
OED	*Oxford English Dictionary*
PET	Positron Emission Tomography
rACC	rostral Anterior Cingulate Cortex
R-O	Response-Outcome
SCT	Self-Categorization Theory
SIMCM	Social Identity Model of Cessation Maintenance
SIMOR	Social Identity Model of Recovery
SIT	Social Identity Theory
S-R	Stimulus-Response
SS	Smaller, Sooner
SUD	Substance Use Disorder
TC	Therapeutic Community

ACKNOWLEDGMENTS

This book could not have been written without the decade that I spent working in a therapeutic community. I am grateful to all my colleagues and our group members for everything that they taught and shared with me. I would also like to take this opportunity to record my gratitude to Steve Pearce, then director of the service, and to recognize and grieve his loss. Steve took a punt on me, as people say in the UK: I was a junior philosopher from All Souls College with no training or experience to speak of, who showed up in his office offering to volunteer my time in order to get my foot in the clinical door. He gave me a chance when he didn't have to, and then he taught me and trained me and became not only a coauthor but a friend. Steve had an uncanny ability to say, in the simplest, most intuitive terms, what seemed unsayable until he spoke it—but was exactly what needed to be said. He was also a lot of fun. He helped so many people and did so much good. He died from cancer, far, far too early.

This book was written in large part while I was on sabbatical during the winter and spring months of 2024. I am grateful to Johns Hopkins University for its generous support, and to my colleagues from across the university for providing such an intellectually exciting and congenial community. I was lucky to be able to spend part of this sabbatical back at All Souls College, and I am grateful to the Warden, John Vickers, as well as all the Fellows and staff, for welcoming me so warmly.

Elizabeth Deng worked as my research assistant over the summer of 2024. Her attention to detail and professionalism was unmatched. Rob Tempio, my editor at Princeton University Press, guided me through the process of writing a book and was a pleasure to work with throughout. Natalie Jones was a superb copyeditor. Amia Srinivasan's fierce advocacy for the book's title gave me the courage to face the skeptics. Jeremy Goodman's support for my enthusiasm for rats brought me much cheer. Michael Smith told me to believe in myself when I most needed to hear it.

I have been thinking about addiction for a very long time, and many people have shaped my understanding of it, through conversations, their own writing, or a combination thereof. I would especially like to thank Peter Achinstein, Bruce Alexander, Marina Bedny, Kent Berridge, Aaron Bornstein, Stephen Darwall, Michael Della Rocca, David Epstein, Bennett Foddy, Genevieve Foddy, Carl Hart, Gene Heyman, Doug Husak, Rachana Kamtekar, Jeanette Kennett, Niki Lacey, Jenna Lange, Harvey Lederman, Doug McConnell, Tori McGeer, Shaun Nichols, Yael Niv, Laurie Paul, Richard Pettigrew, Sonya Ringer, Gideon Rosen, Kieran Setiya, Eldar Shafir, Yavin Shaham, Kirsten Smith, Michael Smith, Anke Snoek, Amia Srinivasan, Chandra Sripada, Eric Strain, Elanor Taylor, Youna Vandaele, Andrea Westlund, Monique Wonderly, Gideon Yaffe, and the participants at an NIH/Georgetown Joint Bioethics Colloquium in the fall of 2023 where I delivered an early version of the material in part I. Thank you also to the students in my first-year and master's seminars on addiction at Johns Hopkins University between 2019 and 2024. It was through teaching these seminars that the overarching narrative of this book came into view.

A number of people read and commented on parts of the manuscript. Lexie Frosh read the introduction and all the clinically relevant chapters, and I am grateful for her perceptive, compassionate clinical eye. Connie Rosati read chapter 4. Her deep knowledge of the area combined with her willingness to put aside her own views to help me develop mine was a true gift. Lee Hogarth, Ben Holguín, and Richard Holton gave me some of the most incisive comments I have ever received on early versions of the material in chapters 6, 7, and 15. It has been a joy to talk with all three of them about addiction over the years.

Marco Venniro welcomed me into his lab and transformed my understanding of animal models. His recognition of their limitations and his commitment to nonetheless making them as relevant as possible is inspirational. I am grateful for everything he has given to me, culminating in the incredible illustrations that grace this book.

In addition, a number of people read the entire manuscript.

When he was philosophy editor at Oxford University Press, Peter Momtchiloff encouraged me to write a book, waiting patiently for decades. Then he retired, and I wrote this one. With characteristic generosity, he nonetheless read it. His comments helped make the book so much more accessible to general readers.

Lucy Allais and I were in graduate school together, and then recently became colleagues. I did not believe her when she told me that she wanted to read the manuscript, but she said it consistently and insistently enough that I sent it to her anyway. She read all of it, and offered a wonderful, constructive set of comments. Beyond the call of friendship and collegiality.

Zach Pickard also went beyond the call—in his case of brotherhood—providing a raft of comments, both large and small, that were an immense help in crafting the writing and refining the cut and flow of ideas. Zach's support and excitement for the book has meant the world.

I have been in ongoing conversation about addiction with both Serge Ahmed and Owen Flanagan for many, many years now. Serge has always been a step ahead of me in his thinking, and I cannot thank him enough for his patience explaining the science to me and waiting for me to catch up. He has read and improved almost every paper on addiction that I've written, and he did the same for the manuscript of this book. Owen's integration of naturalism, pragmatism, and humanism has been a model for me in my own work—I want to say that it has kept me honest. Owen also read the manuscript and gave me a rich and detailed set of comments that made the book so much better—as well as supporting me in the writing of it every step of the way. I am grateful to Serge and Owen for everything I have learned from them and for their friendship.

Lastly, I wish to acknowledge my husband, Ian Phillips, who has been by my side throughout. Ian read the entire manuscript—and parts of it more than once—with a precision, creativity, and dedication that only someone who was at once a brilliant philosopher and a loving partner could possibly muster. As always, he makes everything better.

NOTES

Introduction

1. Bozarth and Wise, "Toxicity."
2. Wilde, *Picture of Dorian Gray*, 172.
3. Andreasen, *Broken Brain*; for a short history of the brain disease model, see Courtwright, "NIDA Brain Disease Paradigm."
4. Leshner, "Addiction Is a Brain Disease."
5. Leshner, 46.
6. For example, consider how Nora Volkow, current director of the US National Institute on Drug Abuse (NIDA), describes the brain disease model in her inaugural lecture "Addiction Is a Disease of Free Will": "To explain the devastating changes in behavior of a person who is addicted, such that even the most severe threat of punishment is insufficient to keep them from taking drugs—where they are willing to give up *everything they care for* in order to take a drug— it is not enough to say that addiction is a chronic brain disease. What we mean by that is something very specific and profound: that because of drug use, a person's brain is no longer able to produce something needed for our functioning and that healthy people take for granted, *free will.*" Similarly, for a typical example of how the brain disease model uses the idea of "hijacking," consider Volkow and Li, "Neuroscience of Addiction," 1430: "We have learned how some drugs and alcohol can disrupt volitional mechanisms by hijacking the brain mechanisms involved in seeking natural reinforcement and weakening brain mechanisms that inhibit these processes."
7. Field and Kersbergen, "Are Animal Models of Addiction Useful?"; Venniro et al., "Improving Translation of Animal Models."
8. Dole and Nyswander, "Diacetylmorphine (Heroin) Addiction"; Jasinski et al., "Treating Narcotic Addiction"; Jung and Kee, "Pharmacotherapy for Alcohol Dependence."
9. Kragh, "Disulfiram to Antabuse"; MacKillop et al., "Hazardous Drinking"; US Department of Health and Human Services, *Alcohol Pharmacotherapies.*
10. For early research on contingency management, see Higgins et al., "Outpatient Behavioral Treatment"; Higgins et al., "Behavioral Approach to Achieving Abstinence"; Higgins et al., "Incentives Improve Outcome in Outpatient Behavioral Treatment"; and Higgins et al., "Clinical Implications of Reinforcement." For reviews, see Ainscough et al., "Contingency Management Interventions"; and Zajac et al., "Contingency Management Approaches." For research on therapeutic workplaces, see Aklin et al., "Therapeutic Workplace for Long-Term Treatment"; Holtyn et al., "Therapeutic Workplace to Promote Treatment Engagement"; Silverman et al., "Therapeutic Utility of Employment"; and Toegel et al., "Abstinence Reinforcement."
11. Skinner, *Behavior of Organisms*; Skinner, "'Superstition' in the Pigeon"; Thorndike, "Animal Intelligence."
12. Ahmed, "Imbalance Between Drug and Non-drug Reward"; Ahmed, "Making Drug-Addicted Animals"; Ahmed, "Validation Crisis in Animal Models"; Lenoir et al., "Intense Sweetness Surpasses Cocaine."

13. Venniro et al., "Volitional Social Interaction Prevents Drug Addiction"; see also Fredriksson et al., "Animal Models of Drug Relapse and Craving"; Venniro et al., "Improving Translation of Animal Models"; and Venniro et al., "Operant Social Reward."

14. Papastrat et al., "Social Odor."

15. For an introduction to therapeutic communities, see Pearce and Haigh, *Democratic Therapeutic Community Treatment*; see also Pearce and Pickard, "How Therapeutic Communities Work."

16. For a classic philosophical defense of this claim, see Fodor, *Psychosemantics*.

17. Hamill, *Drinking Life*, introduction.

18. For example, see Burroughs, *Dry*; Burroughs, *This Is How*; Burroughs, *Junky*; Ditlevsen, *Copenhagen Trilogy*; Flanagan, *What Is It like to Be an Addict?*; Hamill, *Drinking Life*; Knapp, *Drinking*; and Smith, "Disease and Decision."

19. The idea is a cornerstone of talk therapies such as cognitive behavioral therapy, motivational interviewing, therapeutic communities, psychodynamic psychotherapy, Alcoholics Anonymous (AA) and Narcotics Anonymous (NA). See Dutra et al., "Psychosocial Interventions"; Kelly, "Is Alcoholics Anonymous Religious, Spiritual, Neither?"; and Miller and Wilbourne, "Analysis of Treatments."

20. Flanagan, *What Is It like to Be an Addict?*, 10.

21. For an ingenious experimental study investigating the surprising accuracy (as well as limitations) of introspective awareness of choice processes as measured against computational models, see Morris et al., "Introspective Access."

22. McConnell, "Narrative Self-Constitution"; McConnell and Snoek, "Self-Narration in Recovery."

23. For discussion, see Ahmed, "Relevance of Animal Studies"; Field and Kersbergen, "Are Animal Models of Addiction Useful?"; and Venniro et al., "Improving Translation of Animal Models."

24. Ismael, "Why (Study) the Humanities?," 185.

25. For a similar point, see Fenton and Wiers, "Free Will, Black Swans."

26. See especially Flanagan, *What Is It like to Be an Addict?*; also Carroll, "Profound Heterogeneity"; Fenton and Wiers, "Free Will, Black Swans"; Fingarette, *Heavy Drinking*; Heather et al., *Evaluating the Brain Disease Model*; Kendler, "Levels of Explanation"; Minhas et al., "Characterizing Clinical Heterogeneity"; Orford, *Excessive Appetites*; Peele, *Meaning of Addiction*; and Wiers, *New Approach to Addiction and Choice*. For a classic discussion of the heterogeneity of alcohol addiction and a corresponding effort to distinguish subtypes, see Edwards and Gross, "Alcohol Dependence"; and Jellinek, *Disease Concept of Alcoholism*; for a more recent discussion, see Litten et al., "Heterogeneity of Alcohol Use Disorder."

27. For discussion, see Zinberg, *Drug, Set, and Setting*.

28. Heilig et al., "Addiction as a Brain Disease Revised." Leshner hoped labeling addiction a brain disease would shift public perception from "bad person" to "chronic illness sufferer," thereby reducing stigma, improving funding for addiction neuroscience research and treatment, and eroding punitive attitudes and policies; see Leshner, "Addiction Is a Brain Disease."

29. For a proposal similar in spirit to the paradigm developed in this book, see Flanagan, *What Is It like to Be an Addict?*. Flanagan offers an "ecumenical" model of addiction that includes a method for integrating scientific and humanistic thinking about addiction alongside a discussion of responsibility, treatment, and policy.

30. Haslam and Kvaale, "Biogenetic Explanations."

31. Courtwright, "NIDA Brain Disease Paradigm."

32. Alexander, *New Jim Crow*; Hansen et al., *Whiteout*; Hart, "Don't Be Fooled"; Hart, *Drug Use for Grown-Ups*; Macy, *Dopesick*; Macy, *Raising Lazarus*.

33. Pescosolido et al., "Disease Like any Other?"

34. Haslam and Kvaale, "Biogenetic Explanations"; Kelly et al., "How to Reduce Stigma"; Pescosolido et al., "Disease like Any Other?"; Schomerus et al., "Evolution of Public Attitudes."

35. Haslam and Kvaale, "Biogenetic Explanations"; Kelly et al., "How to Reduce Stigma"; Mehta and Farina, "Is Being 'Sick' Really Better?"

36. Schomerus et al., "Stigma of Alcohol Dependence."

37. Killian et al., "Stigmatization"; McGinty et al., "Communication Strategies to Counter Stigma"; McGinty et al., "Public Support for Safe Consumption Sites"; Schomerus et al., "Evolution of Public Attitudes."

38. Haslam and Kvaale, "Biogenetic Explanations"; Kelly et al., "How to Reduce Stigma"; Pescosolido et al., "Disease like Any Other?"; Schomerus et al., "Evolution of Public Attitudes."

39. Flanagan, *What Is It like to Be an Addict?*; Lebowitz, "Biological Conceptualizations of Mental Disorders"; Wiens and Walker, "Chronic Disease Concept."

40. Morris et al., "Promoting Problem Recognition"; Morris et al., "Continuum Beliefs"; Morris et al., "'Alcoholic Other.'"

41. Haslam and Kvaale, "Biogenetic Explanations"; Kelly et al., "How to Reduce Stigma"; Lebowitz, "Biological Conceptualizations of Mental Disorders."

42. Miller et al., "What Predicts Relapse?"

43. Bandura, *Self-Efficacy*; Bandura, "Sociocognitive Analysis of Substance Abuse"; Lewis, *Biology of Desire*; Peele, *Meaning of Addiction*; Satel and Lilienfeld, "Brain-Disease Fallacy"; Wiens and Walker, "Chronic Disease Concept"; relatedly, see also Dar-Nimrod et al., "Learning About One's Own Genetic Susceptibility."

44. UNODC, "World Drug Report 2023."

45. Cooper, *Plato: Complete Works.*

46. Husak, *Drugs and Rights*; Husak, *Legalize This!* In addition to Husak, for discussion see Alexander, *New Jim Crow*; Earp et al., "Ending the War on Drugs"; and Pozen, *Constitution of the War on Drugs.*

47. For discussion, see Chiao, *Criminal Law*; Duff, *Realm of Criminal Law*; Farmer, *Modern Criminal Law*; Husak, *Drugs and Rights*; Husak, *Legalize This!*; and Lacey, *In Search of Criminal Responsibility.*

48. Kaplan, "Carrot Addiction."

49. Indeed, for a great many purposes, it can be useful to distinguish between classes of drugs more fully than I do here. See Nutt, *Drugs Without the Hot Air*; and Orford, *Excessive Appetites.*

50. *Oxford English Dictionary*, s.v. "drug (n.1)."

51. *Oxford English Dictionary*, s.v. "drug (n.1)."

52. For example, a classic two-by-two placebo laboratory study on consumption rates in people with alcohol addiction found not only an association between the belief that a drink contained alcohol (rather than the drink actually containing alcohol) and increased consumption rates, but also that some subjects report feeling a "buzz" or "a bit tipsy" when they falsely believed they were drinking alcohol; see Marlatt et al., "Loss of Control Drinking." Similarly, a more recent placebo study demonstrated that nicotine-deprived smokers report reduced craving upon smoking a nicotine cigarette only when they believe it contains nicotine; see Gu et al., "Belief About Nicotine."

Chapter One: The Puzzle of Addiction

1. For aberrant reinforcement learning/habit models, see Di Chiara, "Associative Learning Disorder"; Everitt and Robbins, "Actions to Habits to Compulsions"; Everitt and Robbins, "Neural Systems of Reinforcement"; Hyman, "Addiction"; Lüscher et al., "Transition to

Compulsion"; Redish, "Computational Process Gone Awry"; and Tiffany, "Cognitive Model." For emotional and motivational dysregulation models, see Koob et al., "Opponent Process Model"; Koob, "Brain Stress Systems"; Robinson and Berridge, "Incentive-Sensitization Theory"; Sinha, "Chronic Stress, Drug Use"; and Solomon and Corbit, "Opponent-Process Theory." For pathological decision-making models, see Bechara and Damasio, "Decision-Making (Part I)"; Bechara, "Decision Making, Impulse Control"; Heilig et al., "Addiction as a Brain Disease Revised"; Redish et al., "Unified Framework for Addiction"; Verdejo-Garcia et al., "Dysfunctional Decision-Making"; and Verdejo-Garcia, "Decision-Making Dysfunctions." For impaired cognitive control models, see Baler and Volkow, "Disrupted Self-Control"; Goldstein and Volkow, "Underlying Neurobiological Basis"; and Jentsch and Taylor, "Frontostriatal Dysfunction." For impaired self-awareness/interoception models, see Goldstein et al., "Neurocircuitry of Impaired Insight"; and Naqvi and Bechara, "Hidden Island of Addiction."

2. For a rational choice model, see Becker and Murphy, "Theory of Rational Addiction." For behavioral economic models, see Acuff et al., "Substance-Free Reinforcement"; Ainslie, *Breakdown of Will*; Ainslie, "Picoeconomics of Addiction"; Bickel et al., "Behavioral Economics of Substance Use Disorders"; Bickel and Marsch, "Delay Discounting Processes"; Bickel et al., "Temporal Discounting"; Herrnstein and Prelec, "Theory of Addiction"; Heyman, "Deriving Addiction"; Heyman, *Addiction*; Rachlin, "Four Teleological Theories of Addiction"; and Strickland and Lacy, "Behavioral Economic Demand." For nonpathological emotional and motivational self-regulation and psychological coping mechanism models, see Baumeister et al., *Losing Control*; Hogarth, "Excessive Goal-Directed Drug Choice"; Hogarth, "Persistence of Addiction"; Heather, "Disorder of Self-Regulation"; Khantzian, "Self-Medication Hypothesis: Heroin and Cocaine"; and Khantzian, "Self-Medication Hypothesis: A Reconsideration." For normal developmental learning models, see Lewis, *Biology of Desire*; Szalavitz, *Unbroken Brain*. For social identity models, see Becker, *Outsiders*; Buckingham and Best, *Addiction*; Lindgren et al., "Substance Self-Concept"; and Pickard, "Addiction and the Self." For models that see addiction as, metaphorically speaking, a *social* disease, see Alexander, *Globalization of Addiction*; Alexander, "Structural Problem of Modern Global Society"; Maté, *Hungry Ghosts*; and Room, "Addiction Is a Social Disease." For an integrative behavioral economic and social disease model, see Acuff et al., "Contextualized Reinforcer Pathology Approach." Some of these examples are less formal "models" than theories or approaches.

3. Flanagan, *What Is It like to Be an Addict?*, xiv.

4. Heyman, *Addiction*; Jay, *High Society*; Robinson and Adinoff, "Classification of Substance Use Disorder"; Salavert et al., "Early History of Opium Poppy"; Slingerland, *Drunk*.

5. UNODC, "World Drug Report 2023"; WHO, "Alcohol and Health 2018." Note that rates are typically higher in the US; see SAMHSA, "Key Substance Use Indicators 2022"; and SAMHSA, "National Survey on Drug Use 2022."

6. CDC, "Cigarette Smoking Among Adults"; Institute for Health Metrics and Evaluation, "Controlling the Tobacco Epidemic"; Ogawa and Ueki, "Caffeine Dependence and Abuse"; WHO, "Tobacco."

7. Müller and Schumann, "Drugs as Instruments"; SAMHSA, "Key Substance Use Indicators 2022"; UNODC, "World Drug Report 2023"; WHO, "Alcohol and Health 2018." Note that cigarette addiction may an exception to this general finding if operationalized as daily use; interestingly, electronic vaping appears not to be. See Birge et al., "What Proportion of People Who Try One Cigarette Become Daily Smokers?"; and SAMHSA, "Key Substance Use Indicators 2022."

8. Gladwell, "Drinking Games."

9. Grisel, *Never Enough*, 5.

10. Burroughs, *This Is How*; Flanagan, *What Is It like to Be an Addict?*; Hamill, *Drinking Life*; Knapp, *Drinking*.

11. Belser et al., "Psilocybin-Assisted Psychotherapy"; Griffiths et al., "Psilocybin Can Occasion Mystical-Type Experiences"; Müller and Schumann, "Drugs as Instruments."

12. Epstein et al., "Real-Time Electronic Diary Reports."

13. Ahmed et al., "Non-Pharmacological Factors"; Badiani et al., "Opiate Versus Psychostimulant Addiction."

14. For example, see Gladwell, "Drinking Games"; and Rohsenow and Marlatt, "Balanced Placebo Design."

15. Note that this is especially so if people abide by a suite of simple rules that make drug use more rather than less safe but that, in societies that moralize drugs and criminalize their possession, are all too rarely consistently and clearly communicated to the public. To take just a few examples: Don't use drugs from unknown sources. Don't share needles. Do use fentanyl test strips. Don't drink too much hard liquor—stick with beer and wine. Protect your drink from being spiked. Don't mix drugs. Start with small doses. Stick with small doses. If you increase your dose, do so gradually. Stay hydrated. Use with friends, in safe spaces. Don't leave your friends and go with strangers, to unsafe spaces. Never drink—or use any drug—and drive. And crucially: Make sure you have drug-free days regularly and use only when you're mentally in a good place—don't use when you're mentally in a bad place.

16. Knapp, *Drinking*, 8.

17. Burroughs, *Junky*, 4–5.

18. For discussion, see for example Ainslie, *Breakdown of Will*; Ainslie, "The Picoeconomics of Addiction"; Bickel et al., "Behavioral Economics of Substance Use Disorders"; Bickel and Marsch, "Delay Discounting Processes"; Bickel et al., "Temporal Discounting"; Herrnstein and Prelec, "Theory of Addiction"; Heyman, "Deriving Addiction"; Heyman, *Addiction*; Rachlin, "Four Teleological Theories of Addiction"; and Strickland and Lacy, "Behavioral Economic Demand."

19. Carnap, *Logical Foundations of Probability*.

20. For discussion of the nature of well-being and general theories of the good life, see Crisp, "Well-Being."

21. For discussion of the idea of a person's own good, see Darwall, *Welfare and Rational Care*; and Rosati, "Personal Good."

22. Kim, "Explanatory Knowledge and Metaphysical Dependence." For discussion, see McCain, *How Science Explains the World*; and Woodward and Ross, "Scientific Explanation."

23. APA, *DSM-5*.

Chapter Two: Diagnosing Disagreement

1. Kendler, "Levels of Explanation"; Murphy, "Disease as Pathology"; Murphy, "Disease and Health."

2. Kraepelin, *Psychiatry*.

3. APA, *DSM-5*, 20.

4. APA, 483.

Chapter Three: Heterogeneity

1. Epstein, "Let's Agree to Agree," 715.

2. For a classic philosophical discussion, see Dennett, *The Intentional Stance*; see also Ismael, "Why (Study) the Humanities?."

3. For example, see Carroll, "Profound Heterogeneity"; Litten et al., "Heterogeneity of Alcohol Use Disorder"; Minhas et al., "Characterizing Clinical Heterogeneity"; and Oslin, "Personalized Addiction Treatment."

4. Beetham et al., "Residential Addiction Treatment Programs"; for a comprehensive report on US addiction treatment and policy, see Interlandi, "48 Million Americans Live with Addiction." Note that this criticism should not be levied at Narcotics Anonymous (NA) and Alcoholics Anonymous (AA), which are free to access and have increasingly well-established theoretical and empirical foundations. See Kelly et al., "Alcoholics Anonymous"; and Kelly et al., "Behavior Change in Alcoholics Anonymous."

5. For discussion, see Collard et al., "Supportive Housing"; Mericle et al., "Role of Recovery Housing"; Roth et al., "Recovery Housing"; and SAMHSA, "Recovery and Recovery Support."

6. Fingarette, *Heavy Drinking*.

7. NIAAA, "Fiscal Year 2023 Congressional Budget Justification"; NIDA, "Fiscal Year 2024 Budget Information."

8. Waldorf et al., *Cocaine Changes*.

9. For discussion, see Acuff et al., "Contextualized Reinforcer Pathology Approach"; Acuff et al., "Substance-Free Reinforcement"; Banks and Negus, "Preclinical Determinants"; Banks and Negus, "Preclinical Choice Models"; Hogarth and Field, "Value of Drugs Versus Competing Rewards"; and Smith, "Disease and Decision."

10. See, for example, Aklin et al., "Therapeutic Workplace for Long-Term Treatment"; and Holtyn et al., "Therapeutic Workplace to Promote Treatment Engagement."

Chapter Four: Values and a Person's Own Good

1. Richards, *Life*.

2. For discussion of the importance of distinguishing psychological from physical dependence, see Szalavitz, *Unbroken Brain*.

3. This point was recognized by Leshner in his seminal 1997 article "Addiction Is a Brain Disease, and It Matters," who called the common overemphasis on physical dependence "outdated": "From both clinical and policy perspectives, it does not matter much what physical withdrawal symptoms, if any, occur. First, even the florid withdrawal symptoms of heroin addiction can now be easily managed with appropriate medication. Second, and more important, many of the most addicting and dangerous drugs do not produce severe physical symptoms upon withdrawal. Crack cocaine and methamphetamine are clear examples: Both are highly addicting, but cessation of their use produces few physical withdrawal symptoms, certainly nothing like the physical symptoms accompanying alcohol or heroin withdrawal." See Leshner, "Addiction Is a Brain Disease," 45–46.

4. Dowell et al., "CDC Guidelines for Prescribing Opioids for Pain 2022."

5. See Food and Drug Administration (FDA), "Sudden Discontinuation of Opioid Pain Medicines"; Keefe, *Empire of Pain*; Macy, *Dopesick*; and Macy, *Raising Lazarus*.

6. APA, *DSM-I*.

7. APA, *DSM-II*; APA, *DSM-III*.

8. APA, *DSM-III-R*.

9. APA, *DSM-IV*.

10. APA, *DSM-5*.

11. Strayed, "Heroin/e," 179.

12. Flanagan, *What Is It like to Be an Addict?*, 58.

13. For classic discussion, see Elster, *Sour Grapes*; Nussbaum, *Women and Human Development*; and Sen, *Commodities and Capabilites*.

14. Kennett, "Mental Disorder."

15. Sen, *Commodities and Capabilities*, 21.

16. Maté, *Hungry Ghosts*, 47.

17. Flanagan, *What Is It like to Be an Addict?*, 41.

18. Maté, *Hungry Ghosts*, 48.

19. Maté, 46.

20. A similar point is emphasized by Martha Nussbaum in her discussion of adaptive preferences; see Nussbaum, *Women and Human Development*. See too part IV.

Chapter Five: Comparisons and Objections

1. APA, *DSM-5*, 483.

2. APA, 483.

3. APA, 484.

4. APA, 20–21.

5. For reviews, see Murphy, "Disease and Health"; Murphy, "Philosophy of Psychiatry"; and Radden, "Mental Disorder (Illness)."

Introduction to Part II

1. Leshner, "Addiction Is a Brain Disease," 46.

2. Heather, "Concept of Compulsion."

3. Leshner, "Addiction Is a Brain Disease," 45.

4. Berridge, "Is Addiction a Brain Disease?"; Berridge, "Brain Disease? The Incentive-Sensitization View"; Heilig et al., "Addiction as a Brain Disease Revised"; Redish et al., "Unified Framework for Addiction."

Chapter Six: Compulsion in Rats and Humans

1. James, *Principles of Psychology*, 543; Rush, *Medical Inquiries and Observations*, 266.

2. Frankfurt, "Freedom of the Will," 12.

3. Wallace, "Defect of the Will"; Watson, "Disordered Appetites."

4. Watson, "Disordered Appetites."

5. Bozarth and Wise, "Toxicity." Note that this outcome is not observed when rats have unlimited access to heroin. Why not? Because cocaine is an anorexigenic that suppresses hunger and thirst, while heroin isn't. For discussion, see Ahmed, "Rodents' Drug Choice Behavior"; and Vandaele et al., "Choosing Under the Influence."

6. For classic statements in the philosophy of action, see Davidson, "Actions, Reasons, Causes"; and Smith, "Philosophy of Action"; in learning theory, see de Wit and Dickinson, "Associative Theories"; on their connection, see Heyes and Dickson, "Intentionality of Animal Action"; and, especially, Dretske, *Explaining Behavior*. Note that although I use "action" only for behavior that is explained by belief and desire, this is by convention only. There are many forms of animal behavior that are *active or agential* (and so therefore have a prima facie claim to be called "action") but are not explained by belief and desire (such as habitual or S-R behavior, to take an obvious example); see Burge, "Primitive Agency"; O'Shaughnessy, *The Will (Vol. I-II)*; and, again, especially Dretske, *Explaining Behavior*. What matters is not what we call animal behavior (including our own) that is explained by belief and desire, but that it is clearly delineated from behavior otherwise explained.

7. For animal model enthusiasts, note that these forms of outcome devaluation are therefore not identical. Reward-specific satiety affects desire for the reward only at the time of satiety, while aversion conditioning aims to eliminate desire for the reward altogether and requires generalization across contexts to be effective.

8. Adams and Dickinson, "Instrumental Responding."

9. Everitt and Robbins, "Actions to Habits to Compulsions"; Everitt and Robbins, "Neural Systems of Reinforcement"; Lüscher et al., "Transition to Compulsion."

10. Indeed, Steven Tiffany, one of the first to propose a role for S-R behavior in addiction, did so in part to explain the many cases of relapse *not* associated with craving; see Tiffany, "Cognitive Model."

11. Railton, "That Obscure Object, Desire," 28.

12. Neal et al., "Pull of the Past."

13. Hogarth, "Excessive Goal-Directed Drug Choice"; Hogarth, "Persistence of Addiction."

14. Vandaele and Janak, "Defining the Place of Habit."

15. De Wit et al., "Five Failures in Experimental Habit Induction."

16. Vandaele and Ahmed, "Habit, Choice, and Addiction."

17. Cushman and Morris, "Habitual Control of Goal Selection"; Kool et al., "Competition and Cooperation"; Vandaele and Ahmed, "Habit, Choice, and Addiction." Note that it is possible for a kind of mindlessness or acting out of habit to become a goal in itself. Drawing on studies of quinine-resistant drinking in mice, the addiction scientists Frederic Hopf and Heidi Lesscher propose that alcohol addiction may involve choosing to drink mindlessly, as a way of resolving conflict between the desire to drink and the desire not to incur the negative consequences of drinking, precisely by going into automatic pilot and thereby ignoring the negative consequences while drinking (Hopf and Lesscher, "Rodent Models for Compulsive Alcohol Intake").

18. Daw, "Of Goals and Habits."

19. For a similar idea, see Bargh and Ferguson, "Beyond Behaviorism," which proposes an automotive model of environmentally driven, unconscious, yet goal-directed behavior; for a critique of components of this model, see Newell and Shanks, "Unconscious Influences on Decision Making."

20. Elliott, "Who Holds the Leash?," 48.

21. Spragg, "Morphine Addiction in Chimpanzees."

22. Ahmed, "Imbalance Between Drug and Non-drug Reward"; Ahmed, "Making Drug-Addicted Animals"; Ahmed, "Validation Crisis in Animal Models"; Ahmed et al., "Neurobiology of Addiction"; Lenoir et al., "Intense Sweetness Surpasses Cocaine." For a fascinating recounting of the history of animal models, see Ahmed, "Walk on the Wild Side." For a classic review of findings from the history of drug choice studies across species, see Banks and Negus, "Preclinical Determinants."

23. Note that an important discovery is that delay of delivery of both rewards shifts choice from saccharin water to drug reward (Canchy et al., "Pharmacokinetics Trumps Pharmacodynamics"). The time between response and delivery is typically a matter of seconds for saccharin water; meanwhile intravenous drug reward appears to peak in the order of tens of seconds after responding. Rats do not like to wait. Delaying both rewards on average forty seconds appears to equalize the wait.

24. Venniro et al., "Volitional Social Interaction Prevents Drug Addiction"; see also Fredriksson et al., "Animal Models of Drug Relapse and Craving"; Venniro et al., "Improving Translation of Animal Models"; and Venniro et al., "Operant Social Reward."

25. Deroche-Gamonet et al., "Addiction-like Behavior in the Rat"; Piazza and Deroche-Gamonet, "Transition to Addiction."

26. At present, the evidence for this hypothesis is mixed. A 2019 forced-choice study found that responding for saccharin water over cocaine during extinction was unaffected by devaluation through satiety in rats—in sharp contrast to the human devaluation studies cited previously; see Vandaele et al., "Inflexible Habitual Decision-Making"; and Vandaele et al., "Habitual Preference." In contrast, a 2022 forced-choice study that was designed to engage more volitional behavior in rats (and hence to be more naturalistic) found conflicting evidence of sensitivity to devaluation through satiety; see Vandaele et al., "Cocaine Falls into Oblivion."

27. Acuff et al., "Substance-Free Reinforcement."

28. Banks and Negus, "Preclinical Determinants"; Banks and Negus, "Preclinical Choice Models"; Hogarth and Field, "Value of Drugs Versus Competing Rewards." See also Hart et al., "Alternative Reinforcers."

29. Heyman, *Addiction*; see also Tucker et al., "Epidemiology of Recovery"; and Witkiewitz et al., "Mechanisms of Behavior Change." For a summary and discussion of overall recovery rates and possible mechanisms, see Engeln and Ahmed, "Remission from Addiction."

30. For early research on contingency management, see Higgins et al., "Outpatient Behavioral Treatment"; Higgins et al., "Behavioral Approach to Achieving Abstinence"; Higgins et al., "Incentives Improve Outcome in Outpatient Behavioral Treatment"; and Higgins et al., "Clinical Implications of Reinforcement." For reviews, see Ainscough et al., "Contingency Management Interventions"; and Zajac et al., "Contingency Management Approaches." For research on therapeutic workplaces, see Aklin et al., "Therapeutic Workplace for Long-Term Treatment"; Holtyn et al., "Therapeutic Workplace to Promote Treatment Engagement"; Silverman et al., "Therapeutic Utility of Employment"; and Toegel et al., "Abstinence Reinforcement."

31. Regier and Redish, "Contingency Management."

32. Bickel and Marsch, "Delay Discounting Processes"; Bickel et al., "Behavioral Economics of Substance Use Disorders"; Bickel et al., "Temporal Discounting"; Heyman, *Addiction*.

33. Strain, "Meaning and Purpose in Opioid Overdose Deaths."

34. For a review, see Sripada, "Impaired Control"; and Sripada, "Loss of Control."

35. Goldstein et al., "Liking and Wanting of Drug and Non-Drug Rewards." Interestingly, the rating is reversed if subjects are asked to imagine how pleasant or desirable it would be to eat food, have sex, or take drugs, *were they under the influence of drugs.*

36. Koban et al., "Neuromarker for Drug and Food Craving."

Chapter Seven: The Idea of Irresistible Desire

1. The inspiration for this philosophical thought experiment lies in part with the moral philosopher Bernard Williams's famous discussion of whether a person who wants gin and falsely believes the glass of petrol in front of them is gin does or does not have a reason to drink it. See Williams, "Internal and External Reasons."

2. SAMHSA, "Key Substance Use Indicators 2022"; see also Engeln and Ahmed, "Remission from Addiction."

3. Indeed, in absence of a requirement that "irresistibility" be applicable to animals not susceptible to metacognitive psychological conflict, there are a range of ways to try to elucidate the idea; for example, the philosopher Al Mele argues that a desire is irresistible for a subject at a time if they do not have a *strategy* for effective resistance that meets a triad of epistemic, motivational, and agential conditions (Mele, "Irresistible Desires"); the philosopher Gary Watson, despite his skepticism at the idea of "irresistible" desires, nonetheless recommends a *normative* conception of "compulsive" desires that draws on resistibility (Watson, "Disordered Appetites"). For Watson, a desire is compulsive if it is sufficiently strong that it is unreasonable to expect even a strong-willed person to resist it under the circumstances.

4. Sripada, "Addiction and Fallibility"; Sripada, "Impaired Control"; Sripada, "Loss of Control."

5. Burroughs, *This Is How*, 141–42.

6. Watson, "Disordered Appetites," 13.

Chapter Eight: Brain Pathology

1. Ackerknecht, *Short History of Psychiatry.*

2. For a narrative review, see Kaur and Khana, "Neurosyphilis"; see also Nutile, "Neurosyphilis"; Rio and Pinto, "Hidden Neurosyphilis"; and Sarkar et al., "Schizophrenia-like Psychosis."

3. Berridge, "Is Addiction a Brain Disease?," 30; Heilig et al., "Addiction as a Brain Disease Revised," 6; see also Berridge, "Brain Disease? The Incentive-Sensitization View"; and Redish et al., "Unified Framework for Addiction."

4. For a review, see Engeln and Ahmed, "Remission from Addiction."

5. Lewis, *Biology of Desire*; Szalavitz, *Unbroken Brain*.

6. Heilig et al., "Addiction as a Brain Disease Revised."

7. Boorse, "Health as a Theoretical Concept"; Wakefield, "Concept of Mental Disorder."

8. Barnes, *Minority Body*; Murphy, "Disease and Health."

9. Boorse, "Health as a Theoretical Concept."

10. Raine, *Anatomy of Violence*.

11. Martinez and Castillo, "Imaging Dopamine Signaling."

12. Boorse, "Health as a Theoretical Concept."

13. Wright, "Functions"; Wright, *Teleological Explanations*.

14. Millikan, *Language, Thought, and Other Biological Categories*; Wakefield, "Concept of Mental Disorder."

15. Cummins, "Functional Analysis."

16. Godfrey-Smith, "Functions."

17. Bedny, "Evidence from Blindness."

18. Kipling, *Just So Stories for Little Children*.

19. Glover, *Alien Landscapes?*, part IV.

20. APA, *DSM-I*; APA, *DSM-III*; APA, *DSM-IV*; Bayer, *Homosexuality and American Psychiatry*.

21. Marr, *Vision*.

22. Andreasen, *Broken Brain*.

23. Wakefield, "Harmful Dysfunction Analysis of Addiction."

24. For discussion, see Shea, *Representation in Cognitive Science*.

25. Nesse and Berridge, "Psychoactive Drug Use in Evolutionary Perspective"; see also Levy, "Addiction Is Not a Brain Disease."

26. Hagen and Sullivan, "Evolutionary Significance of Drug Toxicity"; Hagen et al., "Neurotoxin Regulation Model."

27. Courtwright, *Age of Addiction*; Ross, "Socially Engineered Exploitation"; Schüll, *Addiction by Design*.

28. For discussion, see Pickard, "Denial in Addiction"; and Segal, "Ambiguous Terms and False Dichotomies."

Chapter Nine: The Cause

1. For a review, see Engeln and Ahmed, "Remission from Addiction"; see also Fenton and Wiers, "Free Will, Black Swans."

2. Berridge, "Is Addiction a Brain Disease?"; Robinson and Berridge, "Incentive-Sensitization Theory"; Samaha et al., "Dopamine 'Ups and Downs.'"

3. Ihssen et al., "Differentiating Heavy from Light Drinkers"; Leyton and Vezina, "Dopamine Ups and Downs"; Leyton and Vezina, "Striatal Ups and Downs"; Rachlin, "Four Teleological Theories of Addiction."

4. Noori et al., "Neuronal Substrates of Reactivity to Cues"; Starcke et al., "Cue-Reactivity in Behavioral Addictions."

5. Childress et al., "Prelude to Passion."

6. Moeller et al., "Neural Correlates of Drug-Biased Choice."

7. Vollstädt-Klein et al., "Initial, Habitual and Compulsive Alcohol Use."

8. Ihssen et al., "Differentiating Heavy from Light Drinkers."

9. Wrase et al., "Alcohol Craving in Detoxified Alcoholics."

10. Koban et al., "Neuromarker for Drug and Food Craving."

11. Volkow et al., "Cocaine Cues and Dopamine."

12. Moeller et al., "D2-Type Receptor Availability."

13. For a review, see Paul and Hall, *Causation*.

14. Woodward, *Making Things Happen*.

15. Kendler, "Levels of Explanation."

16. Acuff et al., "Substance-Free Reinforcement."

17. Banks and Negus, "Preclinical Determinants"; Banks and Negus, "Preclinical Choice Models"; Hogarth and Field, "Value of Drugs Versus Competing Rewards." See also Hart et al., "Alternative Reinforcers."

18. Ahmed, "Validation Crisis in Animal Models."

19. Heyman, *Addiction*; see also Tucker et al., "Epidemiology of Recovery"; Witkiewitz et al., "Mechanisms of Behavior Change." For a summary and discussion of overall recovery rates and possible mechanisms, see Engeln and Ahmed, "Remission from Addiction."

20. Smith, "Disease and Decision," 3. Reprinted from *Journal of Substance Abuse Treatment*, vol. 142, 108874. https://doi.org/10.1016/j.jsat.2022.108874. Copyright Elsevier (2022), with permission from Elsevier.

21. Burroughs, *This Is How*, 142.

22. Heyman, *Addiction*; Venniro et al., "Improving Translation of Animal Models."

23. For discussion of this line of reasoning, see Ahmed, "Validation Crisis in Animal Models"; Heather, "Concept of Compulsion"; Lüscher et al., "Transition to Compulsion"; and Segal, "Ambiguous Terms and False Dichotomies."

24. Epstein, "Let's Agree to Agree," 716 (italics in original).

25. Marr, *Vision*.

26. Krakauer et al., "Neuroscience Needs Behavior," 483. Also, Marr, *Vision*.

27. Niv, "Primacy of Behavioral Research," 601.

28. For example, see Goosens, "Values, Health, Medicine."

29. For example, see Engelhardt, "Concepts of Health and Disease"; and Kendell, "Concept of Disease."

30. For example, see Ross, "Socially Engineered Exploitation." For discussion of these various accounts, see Boorse, "Health as a Theoretical Concept"; and Murphy, "Disease and Health." Note, for comprehensiveness, that there is a model of mental disorder I have nowhere discussed in this book: the network model. For example, see Borsboom, "Network Theory of Mental Disorders"; for a brief discussion of one way the network model can illuminate addiction, see Pickard, "Addiction and the Meaning of Disease"; and Pickard, "Is Addiction a Brain Disease?."

31. Bandura, "Sociocognitive Analysis of Substance Abuse"; Bandura, *Self-Efficacy*; Dar-Nimrod et al., "Learning About One's Own Genetic Susceptibility"; Flanagan, *What Is It like to Be an Addict?*; Haslam and Kvaale, "Biogenetic Explanations"; Kelly et al., "How to Reduce Stigma"; Killian et al., "Stigmatization"; Lebowitz, "Biological Conceptualizations of Mental Disorders"; Lewis, *Biology of Desire*; McGinty et al., "Communication Strategies to Counter Stigma"; McGinty et al., "Public Support for Safe Consumption Sites"; Mehta and Farina, "Is Being 'Sick' Really Better?"; Miller et al., "What Predicts Relapse?"; Morris et al., "'Alcoholic Other'"; Morris et al., "Continuum Beliefs Associated with Higher Problem Recognition"; Morris et al., "Promoting Problem Recognition"; Peele, *Meaning of Addiction*; Pescosolido et al., "Disease like Any Other?"; Satel and Lilienfeld, "Brain-Disease Fallacy"; Schomerus et al.,

"Evolution of Public Attitudes"; Schomerus et al., "Stigma of Alcohol Dependence Compared"; Wiens and Walker, "Chronic Disease Concept."

32. Schüll, *Addiction by Design.*

33. Haslam and Kvaale, "Biogenetic Explanations"; Kelly et al., "How to Reduce Stigma"; Mehta and Farina, "Is Being 'Sick' Really Better?"

Chapter Ten: Self-Medication

1. Khantzian, "Self-Medication Hypothesis: A Reconsideration"; Khantzian, "Self-Medication Hypothesis: Heroin and Cocaine."

2. Lembke, "Time to Abandon the Self-Medication Hypothesis."

3. Homer, *The Odyssey: Book IV*, 42.

4. Knapp, *Drinking*, 111.

5. Knapp, 60–61.

6. Knapp, 266.

7. Strayed, "Heroin/e," 173.

8. Kingsolver, *Demon Copperhead*, 479.

9. Heyman, *Addiction*; see also Tucker et al., "Epidemiology of Recovery"; and Witkiewitz et al., "Mechanisms of Behavior Change." For a summary and discussion of overall recovery rates and possible mechanisms, see Engeln and Ahmed, "Remission from Addiction."

10. Compton et al., "Drug Abuse and Dependence"; Heyman, *Addiction*; Maté, *Hungry Ghosts.*

11. NIDA, "Comorbidity: Substance Use and Other Mental Disorders"; NIDA, "Common Comorbidities Research Report 2020"; NIDA, "Part 1: Substance Use Disorders and Mental Illness"; Regier et al., "Comorbidity of Mental Disorders"; Stewart and Conrod, *Anxiety and Substance Use Disorders.*

12. Hogarth, "Excessive Goal-Directed Drug Choice"; Hogarth, "Persistence of Addiction"; see also Garland et al., "Emotion Dysregulation in Addiction"; Hogarth et al., "Negative Mood-Induced Alcohol-Seeking"; and Hogarth et al., "Childhood Abuse and Substance Misuse."

13. Priester et al., "Treatment Access Barriers and Disparities."

14. Ainslie, *Breakdown of Will*; Ainslie, "Picoeconomics of Addiction"; Bickel and Marsch, "Delay Discounting Processes"; Bickel et al., "Behavioral Economics of Substance Use Disorders"; Bickel et al., "Temporal Discounting."

15. Snoek et al., "Managing Shame and Guilt in Addiction," 8.

16. Wonderly, "Affect of Security"; Wonderly, "Agency and Varieties"; Wonderly, "Attachment, Addiction, and Vices of Valuing"; Wonderly, "On Being Attached." For other theorists who characterize some elements of addiction in terms of a type of attachment, see Flores, *Addiction as an Attachment Disorder*; Orford, *Excessive Appetites*; and Watson, "Disordered Appetites."

17. Bowlby, *Attachment and Loss.*

18. Ainsworth, "Attachment and Other Affectional Bonds"; Bowlby, *Attachment and Loss.*

19. Hazan and Shaver, "Romantic Love Conceptualized"; Mikulincer and Shaver, *Attachment in Adulthood.*

20. Knapp, *Drinking*, xv.

21. Knapp, 5.

22. Strayed, "Heroin/e," 173.

23. Szalavitz, *Unbroken Brain*, 34.

24. For discussion, see Szalavitz, *Unbroken Brain.* Although she does not draw on attachment theory, the philosopher Zoey Lavallee has coined the phrase "addictive affective dependence" to introduce an idea that bears some similarity to security-based attachment to drugs: as

addiction progresses, drugs become an essential tool by which people emotionally self-regulate. See Lavallee, "Affective Scaffolding in Addiction."

Chapter Eleven: Self-Harm

1. Foulkes, *What Mental Illness Really Is.*
2. APA, *DSM-5*, 663–64.
3. BPD—Borderline Personality Disorder, "What Is Borderline Personality Disorder (BPD) at Its Core?." Quoted also in Glover, *Alien Landscapes*, 204–5.
4. APA, *DSM-5*, 663.
5. APA, 663.
6. Barker, *Sad and Sorry State of Disorder*, 9.
7. Barker, 20.
8. Barker, 21.
9. Barker, 25.
10. Barker, 25–26.
11. Barker, 26.
12. Hume, *Treatise*, 1.4.6.3, SBN 252.
13. Turner, "Self-Conception in Social Interaction," 98.
14. Melamed et al., "Relationship Between Negative Self-Concept"; Paris, "Psychosocial Adversity"; Vaidya et al., "Impact of Psychosocial Adversity."
15. APA, *DSM-5*, 663.
16. Motz, *Managing Self-Harm*, 47.
17. Freud, "Beyond the Pleasure Principle (1920)."
18. Schüll, *Addiction by Design*, 217–18.
19. Schüll, 231.
20. Schüll, 231.
21. Schüll, 232.
22. Snoek et al., "Managing Shame and Guilt," 7.
23. Knapp, *Drinking*, 106.
24. Strayed, "Heroin/e," 176.
25. Freud, "Beyond the Pleasure Principle (1920)."
26. Martin, *How Not to Kill Yourself*, 100.
27. Martin, 81.
28. The 27 Club is a group of famous musicians and artists who died at age twenty-seven.
29. A phrase coined by the economists Anne Case and Angus Deaton; see Case and Deaton, *Deaths of Despair*.
30. Martin, *How Not to Kill Yourself*, 81–82.
31. Sexton, "Wanting to Die."

Chapter Twelve: Self-Identity

1. West, *Theory of Addiction.*
2. Tombor et al., "Non-Smoker Identity."
3. Buckingham et al., "Group Membership and Social Identity"; Frings and Albery, "Social Identity Model of Cessation Maintenance."
4. Best et al., "Social Identity Model of Recovery"; Buckingham and Best, *Addiction*; Frings and Albery, "Social Identity Model of Cessation Maintenance."
5. Tajfel, "Social Psychology of Intergroup Relations"; Tajfel and Turner, "Integrative Theory of Intergroup Relations"; Turner, *Rediscovering the Social Group.*

6. Leslie, "'Hillary Clinton Is the Only Man in the Obama Administration'"; Leslie, "Original Sin of Cognition"; see also Knobe et al., "Dual Character Concepts."

7. Hacking, "Looping Effects of Human Kinds"; Turner, *Rediscovering the Social Group.*

8. Venniro et al., "Volitional Social Interaction Prevents Drug Addiction"; see also Fredriksson et al., "Animal Models of Drug Relapse and Craving"; Papastrat et al., "Social Odor"; Venniro et al., "Improving Translation of Animal Models"; and Venniro et al., "Operant Social Reward."

9. Bourgois and Schonberg, *Righteous Dopefiend,* 6.

10. Kennett et al., "Reactive Attitudes, Relationships, and Addiction," 447.

11. Kennett et al., 446.

12. Anonymous philosophy professor, email message to author, September 27, 2022.

13. Becker, *Outsiders*; see also Jay, *High Society.*

14. Bourgois and Schonberg, *Righteous Dopefiend,* 109.

15. Nelson, *On Freedom,* 146.

16. Flanagan, "Identity and Addiction"; Flanagan, *What Is It like to Be an Addict?.*

17. Hamill, *Drinking Life,* 57.

18. Goodman, "Outcasts Project"; see also Flanagan, "Identity and Addiction"; Flanagan, "Phenomenal Authority"; Flanagan, "Shame of Addiction"; and Flanagan, "Willing Addicts?." To cite just a few famous examples in literature: Burroughs, *Dry*; Burroughs, *Junky*; De Quincey, *Confessions of an English Opium Eater*; Gran, *Dope*; Karr, *Lit*; Wallace, *Infinite Jest*; Welsh, *Trainspotting.* For visual examples, see Clark, *Tulsa*; Richards, *Cocaine True, Cocaine Blue*; and the very many examples of "heroin chic" fashion photography that can be found in any major magazine.

19. Burroughs, *Junky,* 137. For further discussion of this point, see Flanagan, "Identity and Addiction"; Flanagan, "Phenomenal Authority"; Flanagan, "Shame of Addiction"; and Flanagan, "Willing Addicts?."

20. Knapp, *Drinking,* 279.

21. Burroughs, *Junky,* xix.

22. Burroughs, 6.

23. Zinberg, *Drug, Set, and Setting.*

24. Snoek, "Addiction, Self-Control and the Self," 145.

25. Snoek, 145.

26. Snoek, 147.

27. From Kate*, "Drugs Were the Only Life I Knew." Quoted also in McConnell, "Narrative Self-Constitution." *The author's surname has been withheld to protect her identity.

28. Kearney et al., "Mothering on Crack Cocaine."

29. Flanagan, "Identity and Addiction"; Flanagan, "Willing Addicts?."

30. Goffman, *Stigma*; see also Mackintosh and Knight, "Notion of Self."

31. Dingle et al., "Social Identities as Pathways."

32. McConnell and Snoek, "Self-Narration in Recovery," 37.

33. Macy, *Dopesick.*

34. Maté, *Hungry Ghosts,* 47.

35. Marušić, *Evidence and Agency.*

36. For further discussion of the nature and possible rationality of the process of becoming the ideal self that one imagines, see Velleman, "Motivation by Ideal"; Marušić, *Evidence and Agency*; and Callard, *Aspiration.* Strikingly, one of the examples Velleman uses to illustrate this point is of a colleague who reports quitting smoking by making-believe he was not a smoker. I am neutral about the issue of rationality; the point that matters to this chapter is rather that the process is only possible at all if the ideal self is imaginable.

37. Paul, *Transformative Experience.*

38. Agin-Liebes et al., "Psilocybin-Assisted Therapy"; Bogenschutz et al., "Psilocybin-Assisted Treatment for Alcohol Dependence"; Bogenschutz et al., "Psilocybin-Assisted Psychotherapy"; Johnson et al., "Pilot Study of the 5-HT 2A R Agonist Psilocybin"; van der Meer et al., "Therapeutic Effect of Psilocybin."

39. Other themes include experiences of interconnectedness, spiritual awe, and metaphysical curiosity; increased self-efficacy; decreased withdrawal symptoms and cravings; and the importance of their relationship with their therapist; see Nielson et al., "Psychedelic Debriefing"; and Noorani et al., "Psychedelic Therapy."

40. Noorani et al., "Psychedelic Therapy," 759.

41. Noorani et al., 759.

42. Noorani et al., 767.

43. Callard, *Aspiration*.

44. McConnell, "Narrative Self-Constitution"; McConnell and Snoek, "Self-Narration in Recovery."

45. Pickard, "Stories of Recovery."

Chapter Thirteen: Denial

1. Kruger, *Ashes to Ashes*; Proctor, "Cigarette–Lung Cancer Link."

2. Snoek, "Addiction, Self-Control and the Self," 149.

3. Freud, *Ego and the Mechanisms of Defense*; Freud, "Neuro-Psychoses of Defence"; see also Freud, "Further Remarks on the Neuro-Psychoses of Defence."

4. For example, see Cushman, "Rationalization Is Rational"; Gagnon et al., "Cognitive Control Processes"; McKay and Dennett, "Evolution of Misbelief"; and McKay et al., "'Sleights of Mind.'"

5. For discussion, see Mele, "Self-Deception and Delusions."

6. Knapp, *Drinking*, 149.

7. Knapp, 164–66.

8. Knapp, 165.

9. Knapp, 186.

10. Alcoholics Anonymous, *Alcoholics Anonymous*, 20.

11. Segal, "Alcoholism, Disease, and Insanity," 306.

12. Alcoholics Anonymous, *Alcoholics Anonymous*, 22.

13. Flanagan, *What Is It like to Be an Addict?*, 59; see in particular chapter 6; see also Flanagan, "Shame of Addiction."

14. For discussion, see Bayne and Fernández, "Delusion and Self-Deception." For some relevant reviews and findings, see Benjamin, "Errors in Probabilistic Reasoning"; Hazlett, *Luxury of the Understanding*, chapter 2; Kahneman et al., *Judgment under Uncertainty*; Kahneman, *Thinking, Fast and Slow*; Kurzban, *Why Everyone (Else) Is a Hypocrite*; and McKay and Dennett, "Evolution of Misbelief."

15. For some relevant review and findings, see Ditto, *Passion, Reason, and Necessity*; Hazlett, *Luxury of the Understanding*; and Mele, *Self-Deception Unmasked*.

16. Davidson, "Deception and Division."

17. For discussion, see Deweese-Boyd, "Self-Deception"; and Mele, *Self-Deception Unmasked*.

18. Knapp, *Drinking*, 154.

19. Johnston, "Self-Deception."

20. By way of orientation to some of the literature on self-deception: Mele, *Self-Deception Unmasked*, denies both that self-deception involves an intention to self-deceive and the simultaneous existence of two contradictory beliefs, offering a deflationary account of self-deception. Levy, "Self-Deception Without Thought Experiments," accepts the simultaneous existence of

two contradictory beliefs, but denies that there is a genuine intention to self-deceive as opposed to more garden-variety motivational influences on belief formation, perhaps alongside the presence of cognitive differences. Audi, "Self-Deception, Action, and Will," and Van Leeuwen, "Product of Self-Deception," deny the simultaneous existence of two contradictory beliefs, so that self-deception involves only one bona fide belief. In addition, more scientifically focused accounts of self-deception typically aim to address these puzzles by appeal to the possible evolutionary adaptiveness of self-deception alongside a modular view of mental architecture. For example, see Kurzban, *Why Everyone (Else) Is a Hypocrite*; Mijovi-Prelec and Prelec, "Self-Deception as Self-Signalling"; Trivers, *Folly of Fools*; Trivers, *Social Evolution*; Van Leeuwen, "Spandrels of Self-Deception"; and von Hippel and Trivers, "Evolution and Psychology of Self-Deception" who model self-deception on self-signaling.

21. Jean-Richard-Dit-Bressel et al., "Punishment Insensitivity"; McNally et al., "Persistence of Drug Use."

22. Goldstein et al., "Neurocircuitry of Impaired Insight"; Moeller and Goldstein, "Impaired Self-Awareness in Human Addiction"; Moeller et al., "Impaired Insight in Cocaine Addiction"; Moeller et al., "Metacognitive Impairment."

23. Boness et al., "Evaluation of Cognitive Behavioral Therapy"; Kang and Kim, "Efficacy of Motivational Interviewing with Cognitive Behavioral Treatment"; Riper et al., "Cognitive-Behavioural Therapy and Motivational Interviewing."

24. Knapp, *Drinking*, xv. For an operationalization of the construct of "hitting rock bottom," see Kirouac and Witkiewitz, "Identifying 'Hitting Bottom.'"

Chapter Fourteen: Problems of Control

1. Jellinek, *Disease Concept of Alcoholism*.

2. Jellinek.

3. Edwards and Gross, "Alcohol Dependence," 1060.

4. Edwards and Gross, 1060.

5. For discussion, see Stroud and Svirsky, "Weakness of Will."

6. For an alternative view, see Heather, "Addiction as a Form of Akrasia"; and Wiers, *New Approach to Addiction and Choice*.

7. Sripada, "Addiction and Fallibility"; Sripada, "Impaired Control"; Sripada, "Loss of Control."

8. Burroughs, *This Is How*.

9. Baumeister et al., "Ego Depletion"; Dewall et al., "Depletion Makes the Heart Grow Less Helpful"; Gailliot and Baumeister, "Self-Regulation and Sexual Restraint"; Mead et al., "Self-Control Resource Depletion"; Schmeichel et al., "Intellectual Performance and Ego Depletion"; Vohs et al., "Making Choices Impairs Subsequent Self-Control"; Vohs et al., "Self-Regulation and Self-Presentation"; for a review, see Dill and Holton, "Addict in Us All."

10. Baumeister et al., "Strength Model of Self-Control."

11. Inzlicht and Schmeichel, "What Is Ego Depletion?"; Inzlicht et al., "Why Self-Control Seems (but May Not Be) Limited"; Job et al., "Ego Depletion"; Kurzban, "Glucose During Self-Control Tasks"; Molden et al., "Effects of Carbohydrates on Self-Control."

12. Watson, "Disordered Appetites."

13. Berridge, "Is Addiction a Brain Disease?"; Wiers, *New Approach to Addiction and Choice*; Wiers et al., "Akrasia and Addiction."

14. Holton, "Addiction, Self-Signalling and the Deep Self."

15. Bandura, "Sociocognitive Analysis of Substance Abuse."

16. This is how organizations like Alcoholics Anonymous (AA) and Narcotics Anonymous (NA) conceive of addiction, but with the crucial caveat that people are powerless to abstain only without help from a *"Power greater than themselves."* With this help, abstinence is possible. See Alcoholics Anonymous, *Alcoholics Anonymous*, especially chapters II–IV.

17. Heyman, *Addiction*; Heyman, "Deriving Addiction."

18. Bornstein and Daw, "Model-Based Decisions"; Bornstein and Norman, "Sampling-Based Decisions"; Bornstein et al., "Past Choices Bias Decisions"; Wang et al., "Mixing Memory and Desire."

19. Bornstein and Pickard, "'Chasing the First High'"; see also Redish et al., "Vulnerabilities in the Decision Process."

20. Ainslie and Haslam, "Hyperbolic Discounting"; Ainslie, *Breakdown of Will*; Ainslie, "Intertemporal Bargaining in Addiction"; Ainslie, "Palpating the Elephant"; Ainslie, "Picoeconomics of Addiction."

21. Kennett, "Mental Disorder."

22. Flanagan, *What Is It like to Be an Addict?*, 41; see also chapter 4. "**P**" stands for any proposition and "~" stands for negation, so the statement expresses a contradiction by asserting a proposition and its negation in conjunction.

23. Coates, *In Praise of Ambivalence*.

Chapter Fifteen: Craving

1. Bergeria et al., "Multiple Dimensions of Opioid Craving."

2. Epstein et al., "Real-Time Electronic Diary Reports"; Preston et al., "Cocaine Craving and Use"; Serre et al., "Craving and Substance Use in Daily Life"; Suzuki and Kober, "Substance-Related and Addictive Disorders"; Vafaie and Kober, "Drug Cues and Craving."

3. Robinson and Berridge, "Incentive-Sensitization Theory."

4. Bergeria et al., "Multiple Dimensions of Opioid Craving."

5. Schroeder, "Desire."

6. Davis, "Two Senses of Desire." Davis argues that we must distinguish between volitive and appetitive desires to avoid contradiction. Suppose, for example, that I refrain from eating, even though I have a desire to eat, and you praise me for my self-restraint, saying that I could have eaten had I so desired, thereby implying that I didn't so desire. But, of course, I did so desire, which is why you praise me for my self-restraint. As Davis notes, this puzzle is apparent only. To make sense of your praise, all we need do is distinguish volitive and appetitive desires.

7. For discussion, see Wallace, "Defect of the Will"; Watson, "Disordered Appetites"; and Wonderly, "Agency and Varieties of Felt Necessity."

8. The evidence in relation to rats is mixed. Hutcheson et al., "Role of Withdrawal in Heroin Addiction" suggests that rats can learn to self-administer opioids to relieve withdrawal, but more recent studies suggest that this is true at most of a subset of rats, notwithstanding an intensive training procedure. See Shaham et al., "Relapse to Heroin-Seeking in Rats"; and Chow et al., "Rat Model of Operant Negative Reinforcement." This is yet another reason why the translational validity of animal models has its limits.

9. For a similar point, see Dretske, *Explaining Behavior*; and Dretske, "Reply to Reviewers."

10. Smith, "Philosophy of Action."

11. Drug priming refers to the administration of a small drug dose.

12. Hogarth, "Excessive Goal-Directed Drug Choice"; Hogarth, "Persistence of Addiction."

13. Dar et al., "Craving to Smoke in Flight Attendants."

14. Gu et al., "Belief About Nicotine."

15. Robinson and Berridge, "Incentive-Sensitization Theory."

16. For animal model enthusiasts: The attribution of excessive incentive salience to drug-associated stimuli in humans is hypothesized to connect to "sign-tracking" as opposed to "goal-tracking" in rats (Nasser et al., "Individual Variability in Behavioral Flexibility"; Robinson and Flagel, "Reward-Related Cues"; Tomie et al., "Pavlovian Sign-Tracking"). In animal models, a retractable lever is inserted into an experimental chamber; at the same time, food is delivered in a proximate cup. After training, sign-tracking rats will engage (for example, touch or bite) the lever when it is inserted into the chamber, while goal-tracking rats will approach the cup. Needle fixation (and similar states) in human addiction may appear analogous to sign-tracking in rats. However, qualitative studies suggest needle fixation is overlaid with multiple rewards and meanings, including, for example, the value of ritual, pride in skill, enjoyment of pain, desire to self-harm, and sexual fulfilment—once again complicating translation. See McBride et al., "Needle Fixation"; and Pates, "Case of Needle Fixation."

17. Holton and Berridge, "Addiction Between Compulsion and Choice."

18. See Robinson and Berridge, "Incentive-Sensitization Theory"; and Holton and Berridge, "Addiction Between Compulsion and Choice."

19. Flanagan, *What Is It like to Be an Addict?*, 41.

20. Ditlevsen, *Copenhagen Trilogy*, 356.

21. See also Grisel, *Never Enough*; Knapp, *Drinking*; and Szalavitz, *Unbroken Brain*.

22. Knapp, *Drinking*, 66–76.

23. Koob, "Brain Stress Systems"; Koob, "Neurobiology of Opioid Addiction"; Koob et al., "Opponent Process Model."

24. Hogarth, "Excessive Goal-Directed Drug Choice"; Hogarth, "Persistence of Addiction"; see also Garland et al., "Emotion Dysregulation in Addiction"; Hogarth et al., "Negative Mood-Induced Alcohol-Seeking"; and Hogarth et al., "Childhood Abuse and Substance Misuse Problems."

25. Bourgois and Schonberg, *Righteous Dopefiend*, 80.

26. Bourgois and Schonberg, 96.

27. Lewis, *Biology of Desire*, 74.

28. Nelson, *On Freedom*, 169.

29. Alexander, *New Jim Crow*; Earp et al., "Ending the War on Drugs"; Husak, *Drugs and Rights*; Husak, *Legalize This!*; Pozen, *Constitution of the War on Drugs*.

30. Hogarth, "Persistence of Addiction."

31. Strang et al., "Heroin on Trial."

32. Berridge, "Brain Disease? The Incentive-Sensitization View"; Berridge, "Is Addiction a Brain Disease?"; Holton and Berridge, "Addiction Between Compulsion and Choice."

33. Andrade et al., "Sensory Imagery in Craving"; Brose et al., "Effects of Standardised Cigarette Packaging"; Campbell et al., "Limiting Alcohol Outlet Density"; Hogarth, "Persistence of Addiction"; Langley et al., "Effect of Alcohol Marketing"; Martin et al., "On the Road to Addiction."

34. Acuff et al., "Substance-Free Reinforcement"; Banks and Negus, "Preclinical Choice Models"; Hogarth and Field, "Value of Drugs Versus Competing Rewards."

35. Burroughs, *Queer*, 60.

36. Holton and Berridge, "Addiction Between Compulsion and Choice"; Robinson and Berridge, "Incentive-Sensitization Theory."

37. Knapp, *Drinking*, 268.

38. McConnell, "Narrative Self-Constitution"; McConnell and Snoek, "Self-Narration in Recovery."

39. Kennett, "Mental Disorder."

Introduction to Part IV

1. Browning, *Ring and Book*.

Chapter Sixteen: The Rescue-Blame Trap

1. APA, *DSM-5*, 645.
2. For a classic discussion, see Main, "Ailment"; see also Bowers, *Dangerous and Severe Personality Disorder*; and Potter, *Mapping the Edges*.
3. Main, "Ailment," 138.
4. Main, 138.
5. Main, 138.
6. Haslam and Kvaale, "Biogenetic Explanations"; Kelly et al., "How to Reduce Stigma"; Mehta and Farina, "Is Being 'Sick' Really Better?"
7. For discussion, see Pearce and Haigh, *Democratic Therapeutic Community Treatment*; see also Pearce and Pickard, "How Therapeutic Communities Work."
8. *Oxford English Dictionary*, s.v. "punishment (n.)."
9. *Oxford English Dictionary*, s.v. "punishment (n.)."
10. For discussion, see Westlund, "Answerability Without Blame?."

Chapter Seventeen: Responsibility

1. Dover, "Criticism as Conversation"; for discussion, see also Lacey and Pickard, "Standing to Blame."
2. Aristotle, *Nicomachean Ethics*, Book III, Chapter 1.
3. Talbert, "Moral Responsibility." For other examples of forward-looking accounts, see McGeer, "Better Theory of Responsibility"; McGeer, "Mind-Making Practices"; McGeer, "Scaffolding Agency"; and Vargas, *Building Better Beings*.
4. McGeer, "Scaffolding Agency," 316.
5. For discussion, see Caruso, "Skepticism About Moral Responsibility." The philosopher Derk Pereboom is a long-standing skeptic of free will and moral responsibility, but seeks nonetheless to salvage elements of our practices of blame and punishment that serve forward-looking ends; see Pereboom, *Free Will, Agency, Meaning*; Pereboom, "Free Will Skepticism"; and Pereboom, *Living Without Free Will*.
6. Strawson, "Freedom and Resentment."
7. Watson, "Limits of Evil."
8. For discussion of some of the ways that Strawson's picture has been developed in the philosophical literature, see Talbert, "Moral Responsibility."
9. For a set of challenges that are similar in spirt, see Todd, "Order of Explanation."
10. Wallace, *Responsibility and the Sentiments*.
11. Rosen, "Alethic Conception of Responsibility."
12. Sepinwall, "Faultless Guilt." See also Sommers, *Relative Justice*.
13. Flanagan, *How to Do Things with Emotions*.

Chapter Eighteen: Blame

1. Browning, *Ring and Book*, Book iii, 1355.
2. Smith, "Being and Holding Responsible."
3. I owe this version to Dover, "Walk and Talk," 388.
4. For discussion, see Brady, "Irrationality of Recalcitrant Emotions."

5. For discussion, see Goldie, "Emotion, Feeling, Knowledge."
6. Darwin, *Expression of Emotions*; Ekman, "Basic Emotions."
7. For discussion of this concern, see Westlund, "Answerability Without Blame?."
8. Srinivasan, "Aptness of Anger"; see also Frye, *Politics of Reality*; Lorde, *Uses of Anger*.
9. For further discussion, see Westlund, "Answerability Without Blame?."
10. Browning, *Ring and Book*, Book xi, 2410–11.
11. Browning, Book xi, 2424–25.

Chapter Nineteen: Responsibility Without Blame for Addiction

1. For a classic philosophical discussion of the distinction between wrongs, harms, and hurts, see Feinberg, *Harm to Others*, chapter 1.
2. For discussion of the nature of "hurt feelings" in relation to a Strawsonian account of responsibility and other reactive attitudes, see Shoemaker, "Hurt Feelings."
3. Burroughs, *This Is How*, 174–77.
4. Maté, *Hungry Ghosts*, 47.
5. Scheffler, "Relationships and Responsibilities."
6. Scheffler, 204.
7. Strayed, "Heroin/e."
8. Note that standing to blame can be distinguished from standing to hold responsible, for example in criminal contexts. For general discussion, see Lacey and Pickard, "Dual Process Approach"; Lacey and Pickard, "From the Consulting Room to the Courtroom"; Lacey and Pickard; "To Blame or to Forgive?"; and Lacey and Pickard, "Standing to Blame"; for an application of responsibility without blame to drug courts in particular, see Nayfield, "Drug Courts."
9. Shneidman, *Suicidal Mind*, 166.
10. Snoek et al., "Managing Shame and Guilt," 9.
11. Sripada, "Addiction and Fallibility"; Sripada, "Impaired Control"; Sripada, "Loss of Control."
12. Burroughs, *This Is How*, 142.
13. For discussion of the value and paths to moral repair especially in contexts of political violence, see Walker, *Moral Repair*; for discussion of how anger in particular can be reconceived as a form of forward-looking protest, see Pereboom, *Wrongdoing and Moral Emotions*.
14. Ainslie, *Breakdown of Will*.
15. For discussion, see Rafei et al., "Imagining the Future to Reshape the Past."
16. For discussion, see Gollwitzer, "Implementation Intentions."
17. Flanagan, *What Is It like to Be an Addict?*, 59.
18. For discussion, see Kennett, "Mental Disorder."

BIBLIOGRAPHY

Ackerknecht, Erwin Heinz. *A Short History of Psychiatry*. 2nd rev. ed. Translated from German by Sula Wolff. Hafner Pub. Co., 1968.

Acuff, Samuel F., Ashley A. Dennhardt, Christopher J. Correia, and James G. Murphy. "Measurement of Substance-Free Reinforcement in Addiction: A Systematic Review." *Clinical Psychology Review* 70 (2019): 79–90. https://doi.org/10.1016/j.cpr.2019.04.003.

Acuff, Samuel F., James MacKillop, and James G. Murphy. "A Contextualized Reinforcer Pathology Approach to Addiction." *Nature Reviews Psychology* 2, no. 5 (2023): 309–23. https://doi.org/10.1038/s44159-023-00167-y.

Adams, Christopher D., and Anthony Dickinson. "Instrumental Responding Following Reinforcer Devaluation." *The Quarterly Journal of Experimental Psychology Section B* 33, no. 2 (1981): 109–21. https://doi.org/10.1080/14640748108400816.

Agin-Liebes, Gabrielle, Elizabeth M. Nielson, Michael Zingman, Katherine Kim, Alexandra Haas, Lindsey T. Owens, Ursula Rogers, and Michael Bogenschutz. "Reports of Self-Compassion and Affect Regulation in Psilocybin-Assisted Therapy for Alcohol Use Disorder: An Interpretive Phenomenological Analysis." *Psychology of Addictive Behaviors* 38, no. 1 (2024): 101–13. https://doi.org/10.1037/adb0000935.

Ahmed, Serge H., Magalie Lenoir, and Karine Guillem. "Neurobiology of Addiction Versus Drug Use Driven by Lack of Choice." *Current Opinion in Neurobiology* 23, no. 4 (2013): 581–87. https://doi.org/10.1016/j.conb.2013.01.028.

Ahmed, Serge H. "'A Walk on the Wild Side' of Addiction." In *The Routledge Handbook of Philosophy and Science of Addiction*, edited by Hanna Pickard and Serge H. Ahmed. 1st ed. Routledge, 2019.

Ahmed, Serge H. "Imbalance Between Drug and Non-drug Reward Availability: A Major Risk Factor for Addiction." *European Journal of Pharmacology* 526, no. 1 (2005): 9–20. https://doi.org/10.1016/j.ejphar.2005.09.036.

Ahmed, Serge H. "The Relevance of Animal Studies for Human Addiction." In *The Sage Handbook of Addiction Psychology*, edited by Ingmar H. A. Franken, Reinout Wiers, and Katie Witkiewitz. SAGE Publications, 2024.

Ahmed, Serge H. "The Science of Making Drug-Addicted Animals." *Neuroscience* 211 (2012): 107–25. https://doi.org/10.1016/j.neuroscience.2011.08.014.

Ahmed, Serge H. "Trying to Make Sense of Rodents' Drug Choice Behavior." *Progress in Neuro-Psychopharmacology and Biological Psychiatry* 87 (2017): 3–10. https://doi.org/10.1016/j.pnpbp.2017.09.027.

Ahmed, Serge H. "Validation Crisis in Animal Models of Drug Addiction: Beyond Non-Disordered Drug Use Toward Drug Addiction." *Neuroscience and Biobehavioral Reviews* 35, no. 2 (2010): 172–84. https://doi.org/10.1016/j.neubiorev.2010.04.005.

Ahmed, Serge H., Aldo Badiani, Klaus A. Miczek, and Christian P. Müller. "Non-Pharmacological Factors That Determine Drug Use and Addiction." *Neuroscience and Biobehavioral Reviews* 110 (2020): 3–27. https://doi.org/10.1016/j.neubiorev.2018.08.015.

Ainscough, Tom S., Ann McNeill, John Strang, Robert Calder, and Leonie S. Brose. "Contingency Management Interventions for Non-Prescribed Drug Use During Treatment for Opiate Addiction: A Systematic Review and Meta-Analysis." *Drug and Alcohol Dependence* 178 (2017): 318–39. https://doi.org/10.1016/j.drugalcdep.2017.05.028.

Ainslie, George. *Breakdown of Will.* 1st ed. Cambridge University Press, 2001.

Ainslie, George. "Intertemporal Bargaining in Addiction." *Frontiers in Psychiatry* 4 (2013): 63. https://doi.org/10.3389/fpsyt.2013.00063.

Ainslie, George. "Palpating the Elephant: Current Theories of Addiction in the Light of Hyperbolic Delay Discounting." In *Addiction and Choice: Rethinking the Relationship*, edited by Nick Heather and Gabriel Segal. Oxford University Press, 2017.

Ainslie, George. "The Picoeconomics of Addiction." In *The Routledge Handbook of Philosophy and Science of Addiction*, edited by Hanna Pickard and Serge H. Ahmed. 1st ed. Routledge, 2019.

Ainslie, George, and Nick Haslam. "Hyperbolic Discounting." In *Choice Over Time*, edited by G. Loewenstein and J. Elster. Russell Sage Foundation, 1992.

Ainsworth, Mary. "Attachment and Other Affectional Bonds Across the Life Cycle." In *Attachment Across the Life Cycle*, edited by Colin Murray Parkes, Joan Stevenson-Hinde, and Peter Marris. Routledge, 1991.

Aklin, Will M., Conrad J. Wong, Jacqueline Hampton, Dace S. Svikis, Maxine L. Stitzer, George E. Bigelow, and Kenneth Silverman. "A Therapeutic Workplace for the Long-Term Treatment of Drug Addiction and Unemployment: Eight-Year Outcomes of a Social Business Intervention." *Journal of Substance Abuse Treatment* 47, no. 5 (2014): 329–38. https://doi.org/10.1016/j.jsat.2014.06.013.

Aklin, Will M., PhD., Conrad J. Wong PhD., Jacqueline Hampton, Dace S. Svikis PhD., Maxine L. Stitzer PhD., George E. Bigelow PhD., and Kenneth Silverman PhD. "A Therapeutic Workplace for the Long-Term Treatment of Drug Addiction and Unemployment: Eight-Year Outcomes of a Social Business Intervention." *Journal of Substance Abuse Treatment* 47, no. 5 (2014): 329–38. https://doi.org/10.1016/j.jsat.2014.06.013.

Alcoholics Anonymous. *Alcoholics Anonymous: The Story of How Many Thousands of Men and Women Have Recovered from Alcoholism*, 4th ed. New York: Alcoholics Anonymous World Services, 2001.

Alexander, Bruce K. "Addiction: A Structural Problem of Modern Global Society." In *The Routledge Handbook of Philosophy and Science of Addiction*, edited by Hanna Pickard and Serge H. Ahmed, 1st ed. Routledge, 2019.

Alexander, Bruce K. *The Globalization of Addiction: A Study in Poverty of the Spirit.* 1st ed. Oxford University Press, 2010.

Alexander, Michelle. *The New Jim Crow: Mass Incarceration in the Age of Colorblindness.* The New Press, 2012.

American Psychiatric Association (APA). *Diagnostic and Statistical Manual of Mental Disorders: DSM-I.* American Psychiatric Publishing, Inc, 1952.

American Psychiatric Association (APA). *Diagnostic and Statistical Manual of Mental Disorders: DSM-II.* American Psychiatric Publishing, Inc, 1968.

American Psychiatric Association (APA). *Diagnostic and Statistical Manual of Mental Disorders: DSM-III.* American Psychiatric Publishing, Inc, 1980.

American Psychiatric Association (APA). *Diagnostic and Statistical Manual of Mental Disorders: DSM-III-R.* American Psychiatric Publishing, Inc, 1987.

American Psychiatric Association (APA). *Diagnostic and Statistical Manual of Mental Disorders: DSM-IV.* American Psychiatric Publishing, Inc, 1994.

American Psychiatric Association (APA). *Diagnostic and Statistical Manual of Mental Disorders: DSM-5*. 5th ed. American Psychiatric Publishing, Inc, 2013.

Andrade, Jackie, Jon May, and David Kavanagh. "Sensory Imagery in Craving: From Cognitive Psychology to New Treatments for Addiction." *Journal of Experimental Psychopathology* 3, no. 2 (2012): 127–45. https://doi.org/10.5127/jep.024611.

Andreasen, Nancy C. *The Broken Brain: The Biological Revolution in Psychiatry*. William Morrow Paperbacks, 1985.

Aristotle. *Aristotle: Nicomachean Ethics*. Edited by Roger Crisp. Cambridge University Press, 2000.

Audi, Robert N. "Self-Deception, Action, and Will." *Erkenntnis* 18, no. 2 (1982): 133–58. https://doi.org/10.1007/BF00227930.

Badiani, Aldo, Yavin Shaham, David Belin, David Epstein, and Donna Calu. "Opiate Versus Psychostimulant Addiction: The Differences Do Matter." *Nature Reviews. Neuroscience* 12, no. 11 (2011): 685–700. https://doi.org/10.1038/nrn3104.

Baler, Ruben D., and Nora D. Volkow. "Drug Addiction: The Neurobiology of Disrupted Self-Control." *Trends in Molecular Medicine* 12, no. 12 (2006): 559–66. https://doi.org/10.1016/j.molmed.2006.10.005.

Bandura, Albert. *Self-Efficacy: The Exercise of Control*. 1st ed. W. H. Freeman and Company, 1997.

Bandura, Albert. "A Sociocognitive Analysis of Substance Abuse: An Agentic Perspective." *Psychological Science* 10, no. 3 (1999): 214–17. https://doi.org/10.1111/1467-9280.00138.

Banks, Matthew L., and S. Stevens Negus. "Insights from Preclinical Choice Models on Treating Drug Addiction." *Trends in Pharmacological Sciences* 38, no. 2 (2017): 181–94. https://doi.org/10.1016/j.tips.2016.11.002.

Banks, Matthew L., and S. Stevens Negus. "Preclinical Determinants of Drug Choice Under Concurrent Schedules of Drug Self-Administration." *Advances in Pharmacological Sciences* (2012). https://doi.org/10.1155/2012/281768.

Bargh, John A., and Melissa J. Ferguson. "Beyond Behaviorism: On the Automaticity of Higher Mental Processes." *Psychological Bulletin* 126, no. 6 (2000): 925–45. https://doi.org/10.1037/0033-2909.126.6.925.

Barker, Tracy. *A Sad and Sorry State of Disorder: A Journey into Borderline Personality Disorder (and out the Other Side)*. Jessica Kingsley Publishers, 2017.

Barnes, Elizabeth. *The Minority Body: A Theory of Disability*. 1st ed. Oxford University Press, 2016.

Baumeister, Roy F., Ellen Bratslavsky, Mark Muraven, and Dianne M. Tice. "Ego Depletion: Is the Active Self a Limited Resource?" *Journal of Personality and Social Psychology* 74, no. 5 (1998): 1252–65. https://doi.org/10.1037/0022-3514.74.5.1252.

Baumeister, Roy F., Kathleen D. Vohs, and Dianne M. Tice. "The Strength Model of Self-Control." *Current Directions in Psychological Science* 16, no. 6 (2007): 351–55. https://doi.org/10.1111/j.1467-8721.2007.00534.x.

Baumeister, Roy F., Todd F. Heatherton, and Dianne M. Tice. *Losing Control: How and Why People Fail at Self-Regulation*. Academic Press, 1994.

Bayer, Ronald. *Homosexuality and American Psychiatry: The Politics of Diagnosis*. Princeton University Press, 1987.

Bayne, T., and J. Fernández. "Delusion and Self-Deception: Mapping the Terrain." In *Delusion and Self-Deception: Affective and Motivational Influences on Belief Formation*, edited by T. Bayne and J. Fernández. Taylor & Francis, 2009.

Bechara, A. "Decision Making, Impulse Control and Loss of Willpower to Resist Drugs: A Neurocognitive Perspective." *Nature Neuroscience* 8, 1458–63 (2005). https://doi.org/10.1038/nn1584

Bechara, Antoine, and Hanna Damasio. "Decision-Making and Addiction (Part I): Impaired Activation of Somatic States in Substance Dependent Individuals When Pondering

Decisions with Negative Future Consequences." *Neuropsychologia* 40, no. 10 (2002): 1675–89. https://doi.org/10.1016/S0028-3932(02)00015-5.

Becker, Gary S., and Kevin M. Murphy. "A Theory of Rational Addiction." *The Journal of Political Economy* 96, no. 4 (1988): 675–700. https://doi.org/10.1086/261558.

Becker, Howard S. *Outsiders: Studies in the Sociology of Deviance.* The Free Press, 1963.

Bedny, Marina. "Evidence from Blindness for a Cognitively Pluripotent Cortex." *Trends in Cognitive Sciences* 21, no. 9 (2017): 637–48. https://doi.org/10.1016/j.tics.2017.06.003.

Beetham, Tamara, Brendan Saloner, Marema Gaye, Sarah E. Wakeman, Richard G. Frank, and Lawrence Barnett Michael. "Admission Practices and Cost of Care for Opioid Use Disorder at Residential Addiction Treatment Programs in the US." *Health Affairs* 40, no. 2 (2021): 317–25. https://doi.org/10.1377/hlthaff.2020.00378.

Belser, Alexander B., Gabrielle Agin-Liebes, T. C. Swift, Sara Terrana, Neşe Devenot, Harris L. Friedman, Jeffrey Guss, Anthony Bossis, and Stephen Ross. "Patient Experiences of Psilocybin-Assisted Psychotherapy: An Interpretative Phenomenological Analysis." *The Journal of Humanistic Psychology* 57, no. 4 (2017): 354–88. https://doi.org/10.1177/0022167817706884.

Benjamin, Daniel J. "Errors in Probabilistic Reasoning and Judgment Biases." In *Handbook of Behavioral Economics - Foundations and Applications 2*, edited by B. Douglas Bernheim, Stefano DellaVigna, and David Laibson. Elsevier Science & Technology, 2019.

Bergeria, Cecilia L., Justin C. Strickland, Andrew S. Huhn, Eric C. Strain, and Kelly E. Dunn. "A Preliminary Examination of the Multiple Dimensions of Opioid Craving." *Drug and Alcohol Dependence* 219 (2021): 108473. https://doi.org/10.1016/j.drugalcdep.2020.108473.

Berridge, Kent C. "Is Addiction a Brain Disease? The Incentive-Sensitization View." In *Evaluating the Brain Disease Model of Addiction*, edited by N. Heather, M. Field, A. C. Moss, and S. Satel. Routledge, 2022.

Berridge, Kent C. "Is Addiction a Brain Disease?" *Neuroethics* 10, no. 1 (2017): 29–33. https://doi.org/10.1007/s12152-016-9286-3.

Best, David, Melinda Beckwith, Catherine Haslam, S. Alexander Haslam, Jolanda Jetten, Emily Mawson, and Dan I. Lubman. "Overcoming Alcohol and Other Drug Addiction as a Process of Social Identity Transition: The Social Identity Model of Recovery (SIMOR)." *Addiction Research & Theory* 24, no. 2 (2016): 111–23. https://doi.org/10.3109/16066359.2015.1075980.

Bickel, Warren K., and Lisa A. Marsch. "Toward a Behavioral Economic Understanding of Drug Dependence: Delay Discounting Processes." *Addiction* 96, no. 1 (2001): 73–86. https://doi.org/10.1046/j.1360-0443.2001.961736.x.

Bickel, Warren K., Matthew W. Johnson, Mikhail N. Koffarnus, James MacKillop, and James G. Murphy. "The Behavioral Economics of Substance Use Disorders: Reinforcement Pathologies and Their Repair." *Annual Review of Clinical Psychology* 10 (2014): 641–77. https://doi.org/10.1146/annurev-clinpsy-032813-153724.

Bickel, Warren K., Mikhail N. Koffarnus, Lara Moody, and A. George Wilson. "The Behavioral- and Neuro-Economic Process of Temporal Discounting: A Candidate Behavioral Marker of Addiction." *Neuropharmacology* 76 (2014): 518–27. https://doi.org/10.1016/j.neuropharm.2013.06.013.

Birge, Max, Stephen Duffy, Joanna Astrid Miler, and Peter Hajek. "What Proportion of People Who Try One Cigarette Become Daily Smokers? A Meta-Analysis of Representative Surveys." *Nicotine & Tobacco Research* 20, no. 12 (2018): 1427–33. https://doi.org/10.1093/ntr/ntx243.

Bogenschutz, Michael P., Alyssa A. Forcehimes, Jessica A. Pommy, Claire E. Wilcox, PCR Barbosa, and Rick J. Strassman. "Psilocybin-Assisted Treatment for Alcohol Dependence: A Proof-of-Concept Study." *Journal of Psychopharmacology* 29, no. 3 (2015): 289–99. https://doi.org/10.1177/0269881114565144.

Bogenschutz, Michael P., Stephen Ross, Snehal Bhatt, Tara Baron, Alyssa A. Forcehimes, Eugene Laska, Sarah E. Mennenga et al. "Percentage of Heavy Drinking Days Following Psilocybin-Assisted Psychotherapy vs Placebo in the Treatment of Adult Patients with Alcohol Use Disorder: A Randomized Clinical Trial." *Archives of General Psychiatry* 79, no. 10 (2022): 953–62. https://doi.org/10.1001/jamapsychiatry.2022.2096.

Boness, Cassandra L., Victoria R. Votaw, Frank J. Schwebel, David I. K. Moniz-Lewis, R. Kathryn McHugh, and Katie Witkiewitz. "An Evaluation of Cognitive Behavioral Therapy for Substance Use Disorders: A Systematic Review and Application of the Society of Clinical Psychology Criteria for Empirically Supported Treatments." *Clinical Psychology* 30, no. 2 (2023): 129–42. https://doi.org/10.1037/cps0000131.

Boorse, Christopher. "Health as a Theoretical Concept." *Philosophy of Science* 44, no. 4 (1977): 542–73. https://doi.org/10.1086/288768.

Bornstein, Aaron M., and Hanna Pickard. "'Chasing the First High': Memory Sampling in Drug Choice." *Neuropsychopharmacology* 45, no. 6 (2020): 907–15. https://doi.org/10.1038/s41386-019-0594-2.

Bornstein, Aaron M., and Kenneth A. Norman. "Reinstated Episodic Context Guides Sampling-Based Decisions for Reward." *Nature Neuroscience* 20, no. 7 (2017): 997–1003. https://doi.org/10.1038/nn.4573.

Bornstein, Aaron M., and Nathaniel D. Daw. "Cortical and Hippocampal Correlates of Deliberation During Model-Based Decisions for Rewards in Humans." *PLoS Computational Biology* 9, no. 12 (2013). https://doi.org/10.1371/journal.pcbi.1003387.

Bornstein, Aaron M., Mel W. Khaw, Daphna Shohamy, and Nathaniel D. Daw. "Reminders of Past Choices Bias Decisions for Reward in Humans." *Nature Communications* 8, no. 1 (2017): 15958. https://doi.org/10.1038/ncomms15958.

Borsboom, Denny. "A Network Theory of Mental Disorders." *World Psychiatry* 16, no. 1 (2017): 5–13. https://doi.org/10.1002/wps.20375.

Bourgois, Philippe, and Jeffrey Schonberg. *Righteous Dopefiend*. University of California Press, 2009.

Bowers, Len. *Dangerous and Severe Personality Disorder: Reactions and Role of the Psychiatric Team*. Routledge, 2002.

Bowlby, John. *Attachment and Loss, Vol. 1: Attachment*. Basic Books, 1969.

Bozarth, Michael A., and Roy A. Wise. "Toxicity Associated with Long-Term Intravenous Heroin and Cocaine Self-Administration in the Rat." *Journal of the American Medical Association (JAMA)* 254, no. 1 (1985): 81–83. https://doi.org/10.1001/jama.1985.03360010087032.

BPD—Borderline Personality Disorder. "What Is Borderline Personality Disorder (BPD) at Its Core?" Accessed July 12, 2024. https://www.bpd.org.uk/bpd-at-its-core/.

Brady, Michael S. "The Irrationality of Recalcitrant Emotions." *Philosophical Studies* 145, no. 3 (2009): 413–30. https://doi.org/10.1007/s11098-008-9241-1.

Brose, Leonie S., Chwen B. Chong, Emily Aspinall, Susan Michie, and Andy McEwen. "Effects of Standardised Cigarette Packaging on Craving, Motivation to Stop and Perceptions of Cigarettes and Packs." *Psychology & Health* 29, no. 7 (2014): 849–60. https://doi.org/10.1080/08870446.2014.896915.

Browning, Robert. *The Ring and the Book*. Yale University Press, 1981.

Buckingham, Sarah A., and David Best. *Addiction, Behavioral Change and Social Identity: The Path to Resilience and Recovery*. Routledge, 2016.

Buckingham, Sarah A., Daniel Frings, and Ian P. Albery. "Group Membership and Social Identity in Addiction Recovery." *Psychology of Addictive Behaviors* 27, no. 4 (2013): 1132–40. https://doi.org/10.1037/a0032480.

Burge, Tyler. "Primitive Agency and Natural Norms." *Philosophy and Phenomenological Research* 79, no. 2 (2009): 251–78. https://doi.org/10.1111/j.1933-1592.2009.00278.x.

Burroughs, Augusten. *Dry: A Memoir.* Picador, 2003.

Burroughs, Augusten. *This Is How: Surviving What You Think You Can't.* Picador, 2013.

Burroughs, William S. *Junky: The Definitive Text of "Junk".* Grove Press, 2003.

Burroughs, William S. *Queer: A Novel.* Viking Press, 1985.

Callard, Agnes. *Aspiration: The Agency of Becoming.* Oxford University Press, 2018.

Campbell, Carla Alexia, Robert A. Hahn, Randy Elder, Robert Brewer, Sajal Chattopadhyay, Jonathan Fielding, Timothy S. Naimi, Traci Toomey, Briana Lawrence, and Jennifer Cook Middleton. "The Effectiveness of Limiting Alcohol Outlet Density as a Means of Reducing Excessive Alcohol Consumption and Alcohol-Related Harms." *American Journal of Preventive Medicine* 37, no. 6 (2009): 556–69. https://doi.org/10.1016/j.amepre.2009.09.028.

Canchy, Ludivine, Paul Girardeau, Audrey Durand, Caroline Vouillac-Mendoza, and Serge H. Ahmed. "Pharmacokinetics Trumps Pharmacodynamics During Cocaine Choice: A Reconciliation with the Dopamine Hypothesis of Addiction." *Neuropsychopharmacology* 46, no. 2 (2021): 288–96. https://doi.org/10.1038/s41386-020-0786-9.

Carnap, Rudolf. *Logical Foundations of Probability.* University of Chicago Press, 1950.

Carroll, Kathleen M. "The Profound Heterogeneity of Substance Use Disorders: Implications for Treatment Development." *Current Directions in Psychological Science* 30, no. 4 (2021): 358–64. https://doi.org/10.1177/09637214211026984.

Caruso, Gregg. "Skepticism About Moral Responsibility." In *Stanford Encyclopedia of Philosophy* (Summer 2021 Edition), edited by Edward N. Zalta. Accessed October 17, 2024. https://plato.stanford.edu/archives/sum2021/entries/skepticism-moral-responsibility/.

Case, Anne, and Angus Deaton. *Deaths of Despair and the Future of Capitalism.* Princeton University Press, 2020.

Centers for Disease Control and Prevention (CDC). "Current Cigarette Smoking Among Adults in the United States." Accessed June 25, 2024. https://www.cdc.gov/tobacco/data_statistics/fact_sheets/adult_data/cig_smoking/index.htm.

Chiao, Vincent. *Criminal Law in the Age of the Administrative State.* Oxford University Press, 2019.

Childress, Anna Rose, Ronald N. Ehrman, Ze Wang, Yin Li, Nathan Sciortino, Jonathan Hakun, William Jens, et al. "Prelude to Passion: Limbic Activation by 'Unseen' Drug and Sexual Cues." *PloS One* 3, no. 1 (2008): e1506. https://doi.org/10.1371/journal.pone.0001506.

Chow, Jonathan J., Kayla M. Pitts, Jules M. Chabot, Rutsuko Ito, and Yavin Shaham. "A Rat Model of Operant Negative Reinforcement in Opioid-Dependent Males and Females." *Psychopharmacology*, 2024. https://doi.org/10.1007/s00213-024-06594-w.

Clark, Larry. *Tulsa.* Lustrum Press, 1971.

Coates, D. Justin. *In Praise of Ambivalence.* Oxford University Press, 2023.

Collard, Carol S., Terri Lewinson, and Karen Watkins. "Supportive Housing: An Evidence-Based Intervention for Reducing Relapse among Low Income Adults in Addiction Recovery." *Journal of Evidence-Based Social Work* 11, no. 5 (2014): 468–79. https://doi.org/10.1080/15433714.2013.765813.

Compton, Wilson M., Yonette F. Thomas, Frederick S. Stinson, and Bridget F. Grant. "Prevalence, Correlates, Disability, and Comorbidity of DSM-IV Drug Abuse and Dependence in the United States: Results from the National Epidemiologic Survey on Alcohol and Related Conditions." *Archives of General Psychiatry* 64, no. 5 (2007): 566–76. https://doi.org/10.1001/archpsyc.64.5.566.

Cooper, John M. *Plato: Complete Works.* Hackett, 1997.

Courtwright, David T. *The Age of Addiction: How Bad Habits Became Big Business.* Harvard University Press, 2019.

Courtwright, David T. "The NIDA Brain Disease Paradigm: History, Resistance and Spinoffs." *BioSocieties* 5, no. 1 (2010): 137–47. https://doi.org/10.1057/biosoc.2009.3.

Crisp, Roger. "Well-Being." In *Stanford Encyclopedia of Philosophy* (Winter 2021 Edition), edited by Edward N. Zalta. Accessed January 17, 2024. https://plato.stanford.edu/archives/win2021/entries/well-being/.

Cummins, R. "Functional Analysis." *The Journal of Philosophy* 72, no. 20 (1975): 741–65. https://doi.org/10.2307/2024640.

Cushman, Fiery. "Rationalization Is Rational." *The Behavioral and Brain Sciences* 43 (2020): e28. https://doi.org/10.1017/S0140525X19001730.

Cushman, Fiery, and Adam Morris. "Habitual Control of Goal Selection in Humans." *Proceedings of the National Academy of Sciences* 112, no. 45 (2015): 13817–22. https://doi.org/10.1073/pnas.1506367112.

Dar, R., N. Rosen-Korakin, O. Shapira, Y. Gottlieb, and H. Frenk. "The Craving to Smoke in Flight Attendants: Relations with Smoking Deprivation, Anticipation of Smoking, and Actual Smoking." *Journal of Abnormal Psychology* 119, no. 1 (2010): 248–53. https://doi.org/10.1037/a0017778

Dar-Nimrod, Ilan, Miron Zuckerman, and Paul R. Duberstein. "The Effects of Learning About One's Own Genetic Susceptibility to Alcoholism: A Randomized Experiment." *Genetics in Medicine* 15, no. 2 (2013): 132–38. https://doi.org/10.1038/gim.2012.111.

Darwall, Stephen L. *Welfare and Rational Care*. Princeton University Press, 2002.

Darwin, C. *The Expression of the Emotions in Man and Animals*. HarperCollins, 1998.

Davidson, D. "Actions, Reasons, and Causes." *The Journal of Philosophy* 60, no. 3 (1963): 685–700. https://doi.org/10.2307/2023177.

Davidson, Donald. "Deception and Division." In *Actions and Events*, edited by E. LePore and B. McLaughlin. Basil Blackwell, 1985.

Davis, Wayne A. "The Two Senses of Desire." *Philosophical Studies* 45, no. 2 (1984): 181–95. https://doi.org/10.1007/BF00372477.

Daw, Nathaniel D. "Of Goals and Habits." *Proceedings of the National Academy of Sciences* 112, no. 45 (2015): 13749–50. https://doi.org/10.1073/pnas.1518488112.

De Quincey, Thomas. *Confessions of an English Opium Eater*. Peter Harrington, 1821.

de Wit, Sanne, and Anthony Dickinson. "Associative Theories of Goal-Directed Behaviour: A Case for Animal–Human Translational Models." *Psychological Research* 73, no. 4 (2009): 463–76. https://doi.org/10.1007/s00426-009-0230-6.

de Wit, Sanne, Merel Kindt, Sarah L. Knot, Aukje A. C. Verhoeven, Trevor W. Robbins, Julia Gasull-Camos, Michael Evans, Hira Mirza, and Claire M. Gillan. "Shifting the Balance Between Goals and Habits: Five Failures in Experimental Habit Induction." *Journal of Experimental Psychology: General* 147, no. 7 (2018): 1043–65. https://doi.org/10.1037/xge0000402.

Dennett, Daniel C. *The Intentional Stance*. MIT Press, 1987.

Deroche-Gamonet, Véronique, David Belin, and Pier Vincenzo Piazza. "Evidence for Addiction-like Behavior in the Rat." *Science (American Association for the Advancement of Science)* 305, no. 5686 (2004): 1014–17. https://doi.org/10.1126/science.1099020.

Dewall, C. N., Baumeister, R. F., Gailliot, M. T., and Maner, J. K. "Depletion Makes the Heart Grow Less Helpful: Helping as a Function of Self-Regulatory Energy and Genetic Relatedness." *Personality & Social Psychology Bulletin* 34, no. 12 (2008): 1653–62. https://doi.org/10.1177/0146167208323981.

Deweese-Boyd, Ian. "Self-Deception." In *Stanford Encyclopedia of Philosophy* (Fall 2023 Edition), edited by Edward N. Zalta and Uri Nodelman. Accessed July 17, 2024. https://plato.stanford.edu/archives/fall2023/entries/self-deception/.

Di Chiara, G. "Drug Addiction as Dopamine-Dependent Associative Learning Disorder." *European Journal of Pharmacology* 375, no. 1–3 (1999): 13–30. https://doi.org/10.1016/s0014-2999(99)00372-6.

Dill, Brendan, and Richard Holton. "The Addict in Us All." *Frontiers in Psychiatry* 5 (2014): 139. https://doi.org/10.3389/fpsyt.2014.00139.

Dingle, Genevieve A., Tegan Cruwys, and Daniel Frings. "Social Identities as Pathways into and out of Addiction." *Frontiers in Psychology* 6 (2015): 1795. https://doi.org/10.3389/fpsyg.2015 .01795.

Ditlevsen, Tove. *The Copenhagen Trilogy: Childhood; Youth; Dependency*. Farrar, Straus and Giroux, 1971.

Ditto, P. "Passion, Reason, and Necessity: A Quantity-of-Processing View of Motivated Reasoning." In *Delusion and Self-Deception*, edited by T. Bayne and J. Fernandez. Psychology Press, 2009.

Dole, Vincent P., and Marie Nyswander. "A Medical Treatment for Diacetylmorphine (Heroin) Addiction: A Clinical Trial with Methadone Hydrochloride." *Journal of the American Medical Association (JAMA)* 193, no. 8 (Aug. 1965): 646–50. http://dx.doi.org/10.1001/jama.1965 .03090080008002.

Dover, Daniela. "Criticism as Conversation." *Philosophical Perspectives* 33, no. 1 (2019): 26–61. https://doi.org/10.1111/phpe.12125.

Dover, Daniela. "The Walk and the Talk." *The Philosophical Review* 128, no. 4 (2019): 387–422. https://doi.org/10.1215/00318108-7697850.

Dowell, Deborah, Kathleen R. Ragan, Christopher M. Jones, Grant T. Baldwin, and Roger Chou. "CDC Clinical Practice Guideline for Prescribing Opioids for Pain - United States, 2022." *MMWR. Recommendations and Reports* 71, no. 3 (2022): 1–95. https://doi.org/10 .15585/mmwr.rr7103a1.

Dretske, F. *Explaining Behavior: Reasons in a World of Causes*. MIT Press, 1988.

Dretske, Fred. "Reply to Reviewers." *Philosophy and Phenomenological Research* 50, no. 4 (1990): 819–39. https://doi.org/10.2307/2108244.

Duff, Antony. *The Realm of Criminal Law*. 1st ed. Oxford University Press, 2018.

Dutra, Lissa, Georgia Stathopoulou, Shawnee L. Basden, Teresa M. Leyro, Mark B. Powers, and Michael W. Otto. "A Meta-Analytic Review of Psychosocial Interventions for Substance Use Disorders." *The American Journal of Psychiatry* 165, no. 2 (2008): 179–87. https://doi.org/10 .1176/appi.ajp.2007.06111851.

Earp, Brian D., Jonathan Lewis, and Carl L. Hart. "Racial Justice Requires Ending the War on Drugs." *American Journal of Bioethics* 21, no. 4 (2021): 4–19. https://doi.org/10.1080 /15265161.2020.1861364.

Edwards, G., and M. M. Gross. "Alcohol Dependence: Provisional Description of a Clinical Syndrome." *British Medical Journal* 1, no. 6017 (1976): 1058–61. https://doi.org/10.1136/bmj .1.6017.1058.

Ekman, P. "An Argument for Basic Emotions." *Cognition and Emotion* 6, no. 3–4 (1992): 169–200. https://doi.org/10.1080/02699939208411068.

Elliott, Carl. "Who Holds the Leash?" *American Journal of Bioethics* 2, no. 2 (2002): 48. https://doi.org/10.1162/152651602317533695.

Elster, John. *Sour Grapes: Studies in the Subversion of Rationality*. Cambridge University Press, 1983.

Engelhardt, H. T., Jr. "The Concepts of Health and Disease." In *Evaluation and Explanation in the Biomedical Sciences*, edited by H. T. Engelhardt and S. F. Spicker. Reidel, 1975.

Engeln, Michel, and Serge H. Ahmed. "Remission from Addiction: Erasing the Wrong Circuits or Making New Ones?" *Nature Reviews Neuroscience*, December 11, 2024. https://doi.org/10 .1038/s41583-024-00886-y.

Epstein, David H. "Let's Agree to Agree: A Comment on Hogarth (2020), with a Plea for Not-so-Competing Theories of Addiction." *Neuropsychopharmacology* 45, no. 5 (2020): 715–16. https://doi.org/10.1038/s41386-020-0618-y.

Epstein, David H., Jessica Willner-Reid, Massoud Vahabzadeh, Mustapha Mezghanni, Jia-Ling Lin, and Kenzie L. Preston. "Real-Time Electronic Diary Reports of Cue Exposure and

Mood in the Hours Before Cocaine and Heroin Craving and Use." *Archives of General Psychiatry* 66, no. 1 (2009): 88–94. https://doi.org/10.1001/archgenpsychiatry.2008.509.

Everitt, Barry J., and Trevor W. Robbins. "Drug Addiction: Updating Actions to Habits to Compulsions Ten Years On." *Annual Review of Psychology* 67 (2016): 23–50. https://doi.org/10.1146/annurev-psych-122414-033457.

Everitt, Barry J., and Trevor W. Robbins. "Neural Systems of Reinforcement for Drug Addiction: From Actions to Habits to Compulsion." *Nature Neuroscience* 8, no. 11 (2005): 1481–89. https://doi.org/10.1038/nn1579.

Farmer, Lindsay. *Making the Modern Criminal Law.* Oxford University Press, 2016.

Fenton, Ted, and Reinout W. Wiers. "Free Will, Black Swans and Addiction." *Neuroethics* 10, no. 1 (2017): 157–65. https://doi.org/10.1007/s12152-016-9290-7.

Feinberg, Joel. *Harm to Others.* Oxford University Press, 1984.

Field, Matt, and Inge Kersbergen. "Are Animal Models of Addiction Useful?" *Addiction* 115, no. 1 (Jan. 2020): 6–12. https://doi.org/10.1111/add.14764.

Fingarette, Herbert. *Heavy Drinking: The Myth of Alcoholism as a Disease.* University of California Press, 1989.

Flanagan, Owen. *How to Do Things with Emotions: The Morality of Anger and Shame Across Cultures.* Princeton University Press, 2023.

Flanagan, Owen. "Identity and Addiction." In *The Routledge Handbook of Philosophy and Science of Addiction,* 1st ed. Routledge, 2019. https://doi.org/10.4324/9781315689197-8.

Flanagan, Owen. "Phenomenal Authority: The Epistemic Authority of Alcoholics Anonymous." In *Addiction and Self-Control,* edited by N. Levy, 67–93. Oxford University Press, 2013.

Flanagan, Owen. "The Shame of Addiction." *Frontiers in Psychiatry* 4 (2013): 120. https://doi.org/10.3389/fpsyt.2013.00120.

Flanagan, Owen. "Willing Addicts? Drinkers, Dandies, Druggies, and Other Dionysians." In *Addiction and Choice: Rethinking the Relationship,* edited by N. Heather and G. Segal. Oxford University Press, 2016.

Flanagan, Owen. *What Is It like to Be an Addict?.* Oxford University Press, 2025.

Flores, Philip J. *Addiction as an Attachment Disorder.* Jason Aronson, 2011.

Fodor, Jerry A. *Psychosemantics.* MIT Press, 1989.

Food and Drug Administration (FDA). "FDA Identifies Harm Reported from Sudden Discontinuation of Opioid Pain Medicines and Requires Label Changes to Guide Prescribers on Gradual, Individualized Tapering." Accessed June 20, 2024. https://www.fda.gov/drugs/drug-safety-and-availability/fda-identifies-harm-reported-sudden-discontinuation-opioid-pain-medicines-and-requires-label-changes.

Foulkes, Lucy. *What Mental Illness Really Is . . . (and What It Isn't).* Penguin Books, 2021.

Frankfurt, H. "Freedom of the Will and the Concept of a Person." In *Free Will,* edited by G. Watson. Oxford University Press, 1971.

Fredriksson, Ida, Marco Venniro, David J. Reiner, Jonathan J. Chow, Jennifer M. Bossert, and Yavin Shaham. "Animal Models of Drug Relapse and Craving After Voluntary Abstinence: A Review." *Pharmacological Reviews* 73, no. 3 (2021): 1050–83. https://doi.org/10.1124/pharmrev.120.000191.

Freud, Anna. *The Ego and the Mechanisms of Defense.* Hogarth Press and the Institute of Psychoanalysis, 1937.

Freud, Sigmund. "Beyond the Pleasure Principle (1920)." In *The Standard Edition of the Complete Psychological Works of Sigmund Freud Vol.18,* edited by James Strachey. Vintage Random House, 2001.

Freud, Sigmund. "Further Remarks on the Neuro-Psychoses of Defence." In *The Standard Edition of the Complete Psychological Works of Sigmund Freud,* 3. Translated by James Strachey. Hogarth Press, 1994.

Freud, Sigmund. "The Neuro-Psychoses of Defence." In *The Standard Edition of the Complete Psychological Works of Sigmund Freud*, 3. Translated by James Strachey. Hogarth Press, 1994.

Frings, Daniel, and Ian P. Albery. "The Social Identity Model of Cessation Maintenance: Formulation and Initial Evidence." *Addictive Behaviors* 44 (2015): 35–42. https://doi.org/10.1016/j.addbeh.2014.10.023.

Frye, Marilyn. *The Politics of Reality: Essays in Feminist Theory*. Crossing Press, 1983.

Gagnon, Jean, Joyce Emma Quansah, and Paul McNicoll. "Cognitive Control Processes and Defense Mechanisms That Influence Aggressive Reactions: Toward an Integration of Socio-Cognitive and Psychodynamic Models of Aggression." *Frontiers in Human Neuroscience* 15 (2022): 751336. https://doi.org/10.3389/fnhum.2021.751336.

Gailliot, Matthew T., and Roy F. Baumeister. "Self-Regulation and Sexual Restraint: Dispositionally and Temporarily Poor Self-Regulatory Abilities Contribute to Failures at Restraining Sexual Behavior." *Personality & Social Psychology Bulletin* 33, no. 2 (2007): 173–86. https://doi.org/10.1177/0146167206293472.

Garland, Eric L., Spencer Bell, Rachel M. Atchley, and Brett Froeliger. "Emotion Dysregulation in Addiction." In *The Oxford Handbook of Emotion Dysregulation*, edited by Theodore P. Beauchaine and Sheila E. Crowell. Oxford University Press, 2020.

Gladwell, Malcolm. "Drinking Games." *New Yorker*, February 7, 2010. https://www.newyorker.com/magazine/2010/02/15/drinking-games.

Glover, Jonathan. *Alien Landscapes?: Interpreting Disordered Mind*. Harvard University Press, 2014.

Godfrey-Smith, P. "Functions: Consensus Without Unity." *Pacific Philosophical Quarterly* 74, no. 3 (1993): 196–208. https://doi.org/10.1111/j.1468-0114.1993.tb00358.x.

Goffman, Erving. *Stigma: Notes on the Management of Spoiled Identity*. Touchstone, 1986.

Goldie, Peter. "Emotion, Feeling, and Knowledge of the World." In *Thinking About Feeling: Contemporary Philosophers on Emotions*, edited by Robert C. Solomon. Oxford University Press, 2004.

Goldstein, Rita Z., and Nora D. Volkow. "Drug Addiction and Its Underlying Neurobiological Basis: Neuroimaging Evidence for the Involvement of the Frontal Cortex." *The American Journal of Psychiatry* 159, no. 10 (2002): 1642–52. https://doi.org/10.1176/appi.ajp.159.10.1642.

Goldstein, Rita Z., A. D. Craig, Antoine Bechara, Hugh Garavan, Anna Rose Childress, Martin P. Paulus, and Nora D. Volkow. "The Neurocircuitry of Impaired Insight in Drug Addiction." *Trends in Cognitive Sciences* 13, no. 9 (2009): 372–80. https://doi.org/10.1016/j.tics.2009.06.004.

Goldstein, Rita Z., P. A. Woicik, S. J. Moeller, F. Telang, M. Jayne, C. Wong, G. J. Wang, J. S. Fowler, and N. D. Volkow. "Liking and Wanting of Drug and Non-Drug Rewards in Active Cocaine Users: The STRAP-R Questionnaire." *Journal of Psychopharmacology* 24, no. 2 (2010): 257–66. https://doi.org/10.1177/0269881108096982.

Gollwitzer, Peter M. "Implementation Intentions: Strong Effects of Simple Plans." *The American Psychologist* 54, no. 7 (1999): 493–503. https://doi.org/10.1037/0003-066X.54.7.493.

Goodman, Aaron. "The Outcasts Project: Humanizing Heroin Users Through Documentary Photography and Photo-Elicitation." In *The Routledge Handbook of Philosophy and Science of Addiction*, 1st ed. Routledge, 2019.

Goosens, William K. "Values, Health, and Medicine." *Philosophy of Science* 47, no. 1 (1980): 100–15. https://doi.org/10.1086/288912.

Gran, Sara. *Dope: A Novel*. Penguin Books, 2007.

Griffiths, R. R., W. A. Richards, U. McCann, and R. Jesse. "Psilocybin Can Occasion Mystical-Type Experiences Having Substantial and Sustained Personal Meaning and Spiritual

Significance." *Psychopharmacology* 187, no. 3 (2006): 268–83. https://doi.org/10.1007/s00213-006-0457-5.

Grisel, Judith. *Never Enough: The Neuroscience and Experience of Addiction*. Scribe UK, 2019.

Gu, Xiaosi, Terry Lohrenz, Ramiro Salas, Philip R. Baldwin, Alireza Soltani, Ulrich Kirk, Paul M. Cinciripini, and P. Read Montague. "Belief About Nicotine Modulates Subjective Craving and Insula Activity in Deprived Smokers." *Frontiers in Psychiatry* 7 (2016): 126. https://doi.org/10.3389/fpsyt.2016.00126.

Hacking, I. "The Looping Effects of Human Kinds." In *Causal Cognition: A Multidisciplinary Debate*, edited by D. Sperber, D. Premack and A. James Premack. Oxford University Press, 1996.

Hagen, Edward H., and Roger J Sullivan. "The Evolutionary Significance of Drug Toxicity Over Reward." In *The Routledge Handbook of Philosophy and Science of Addiction*, 1st ed. Routledge, 2019.

Hagen, Edward H., Casey J. Roulette, and Roger J. Sullivan. "Explaining Human Recreational Use of 'Pesticides': The Neurotoxin Regulation Model of Substance Use vs. the Hijack Model and Implications for Age and Sex Differences in Drug Consumption." *Frontiers in Psychiatry* 4 (2013): 142. https://doi.org/10.3389/fpsyt.2013.00142.

Hamill, Pete. *A Drinking Life: A Memoir*. Back Bay Books, 1995.

Hansen, Helena, Jules Netherland, and David Herzberg. *Whiteout: How Racial Capitalism Changed the Color of Opioids in America*. 1st ed. University of California Press, 2023.

Hart, C. L., M. Haney, R. W. Foltin, and M. W. Fischman. "Alternative Reinforcers Differentially Modify Cocaine Self-Administration by Humans." *Behavioural Pharmacology* 11, no. 1 (2000): 87–91. https://doi.org/10.1097/00008877-200002000-00010.

Hart, Carl L. "Don't Be Fooled by the Euphemistic Language Attesting to a Gentler War on Drugs." In *The Routledge Handbook of Philosophy and Science of Addiction*, edited by Hanna Pickard and Serge H. Ahmed, 1st ed. Routledge, 2019.

Hart, Carl L. *Drug Use for Grown-Ups: Chasing Liberty in the Land of Fear*. Penguin Press, 2021.

Haslam, Nick, and Erlend P. Kvaale. "Biogenetic Explanations of Mental Disorder: The Mixed-Blessings Model." *Current Directions in Psychological Science: A Journal of the American Psychological Society* 24, no. 5 (2015): 399–404. https://doi.org/10.1177/0963721415588082.

Hazan, Cindy, and Phillip Shaver. "Romantic Love Conceptualized as an Attachment Process." *Journal of Personality and Social Psychology* 52, no. 3 (1987): 511–24. https://doi.org/10.1037/0022-3514.52.3.511.

Hazlett, Allan. *A Luxury of the Understanding: On the Value of True Belief*. Oxford: Oxford University Press, 2013.

Heather, Nick. "Addiction as a Form of Akrasia." In *Addiction and Choice: Rethinking the Relationship*, edited by Nick Heather and Gabriel Segal. Oxford, 2016.

Heather, Nick. "Alcohol Addiction: A Disorder of Self-Regulation but Not a Disease of the Brain." In *The Handbook of Alcohol Use: Understandings from Synapse to Society*, edited by Daniel Frings and Ian P. Albery. Elsevier, 2021.

Heather, Nick. "Is the Concept of Compulsion Useful in the Explanation or Description of Addictive Behaviour and Experience?" *Addictive Behaviors Reports* 6 (2017): 15–38. https://doi.org/10.1016/j.abrep.2017.05.002.

Heather, Nick, Matt Field, Antony C. Moss, and Sally Satel. *Evaluating the Brain Disease Model of Addiction*. Routledge, 2022.

Heilig, Markus, James MacKillop, Diana Martinez, Jürgen Rehm, Lorenzo Leggio, and Louk J. M. J. Vanderschuren. "Addiction as a Brain Disease Revised: Why It Still Matters, and the Need for Consilience." *Neuropsychopharmacology* 46, no. 10 (2021): 1715–23. https://doi.org/10.1038/s41386-020-00950-y.

Herrnstein, Richard J., and Drazen Prelec. "A Theory of Addiction." In *Choice Over Time*, edited by George Loewenstein and Jon Elster. Russell Sage Foundation, 1992.

Heyes, Cecilia, and Anthony Dickson. "The Intentionality of Animal Action." *Mind & Language* 5, no. 1 (1990): 87–103. https://doi.org/10.1111/j.1468-0017.1990.tb00154.x.

Heyman, Gene M. *Addiction: A Disorder of Choice*. Harvard University Press, 2010.

Heyman, Gene M. "Deriving Addiction: An Analysis Based on Three Elementary Features of Making Choices." In *The Routledge Handbook of Philosophy and Science of Addiction*, edited by Hanna Pickard and Serge H. Ahmed, 1st ed. Routledge, 2019.

Higgins, Stephen T., Alan J. Budney, Warren K. Bickel, Florian E. Foerg, Robert Donham, and Gary J. Badger. "Incentives Improve Outcome in Outpatient Behavioral Treatment of Cocaine Dependence." *Archives of General Psychiatry* 51, no. 7 (1994): 568–76. http://dx.doi.org/10.1001/archpsyc.1994.03950070060011.

Higgins, Stephen T., Alan J. Budney, Warren K. Bickel, Gary J. Badger, Florian E. Foerg, and Doris Ogden. "Outpatient Behavioral Treatment for Cocaine Dependence: One-Year Outcome." *Experimental and Clinical Psychopharmacology* 3, no. 2 (1995): 205–12. https://doi.org/10.1037/1064-1297.3.2.205.

Higgins, Stephen T., Dawn D. Delaney, Alan J. Budney, Warren K. Bickel, John R. Hughes, Florian Foerg, and James W. Fenwick. "A Behavioral Approach to Achieving Initial Cocaine Abstinence." *The American Journal of Psychiatry* 148, no. 9 (1991): 1218–24. https://doi.org/10.1176/ajp.148.9.1218.

Higgins, Stephen T., Sarah H. Heil, and Jennifer Plebani Lussier. "Clinical Implications of Reinforcement as a Determinant of Substance Use Disorders." *Annual Review of Psychology* 55, no. 1 (2004): 431–61. https://doi.org/10.1146/annurev.psych.55.090902.142033.

Hogarth, Lee. "Addiction Is Driven by Excessive Goal-Directed Drug Choice Under Negative Affect: Translational Critique of Habit and Compulsion Theory." *Neuropsychopharmacology* 45, no. 5 (2020): 720–35. https://doi.org/10.1038/s41386-020-0600-8.

Hogarth, Lee. "The Persistence of Addiction Is Better Explained by Socioeconomic Deprivation-Related Factors Powerfully Motivating Goal-Directed Drug Choice than by Automaticity, Habit or Compulsion Theories Favored by the Brain Disease Model." In *Evaluating the Brain Disease Model of Addiction*, edited by Nick Heather, Matt Field, Antony Moss, and Sally Satel, 1st ed. Routledge, 2022.

Hogarth, Lee, and Matt Field. "Relative Expected Value of Drugs Versus Competing Rewards Underpins Vulnerability to and Recovery from Addiction." *Behavioural Brain Research* 394 (2020): 112815. https://doi.org/10.1016/j.bbr.2020.112815.

Hogarth, Lee, Lindi Martin, and Soraya Seedat. "Relationship Between Childhood Abuse and Substance Misuse Problems Is Mediated by Substance Use Coping Motives, in School Attending South African Adolescents." *Drug and Alcohol Dependence* 194 (2019): 69–74. https://doi.org/10.1016/j.drugalcdep.2018.10.009.

Hogarth, Lee, Lorna Hardy, Amanda R. Mathew, and Brian Hitsman. "Negative Mood-Induced Alcohol-Seeking Is Greater in Young Adults Who Report Depression Symptoms, Drinking to Cope, and Subjective Reactivity." *Experimental and Clinical Psychopharmacology* 26, no. 2 (2018): 138–46. https://doi.org/10.1037/pha0000177.

Holton, Richard. "Addiction, Self-Signalling and the Deep Self." *Mind & Language* 31, no. 3 (2016): 300–13. https://doi.org/10.1111/mila.12107.

Holton, Richard, and Kent Berridge. "Addiction Between Compulsion and Choice." In *Addiction and Self-Control*, edited by N. Levy. Oxford University Press, 2013. https://doi.org/10.1093/acprof:oso/9780199862580.003.0012.

Holtyn, August F., Mikhail N. Koffarnus, Anthony DeFulio, Sigurdur O. Sigurdsson, Eric C. Strain, Robert P. Schwartz, Jeannie-Marie S. Leoutsakos, and Kenneth Silverman. "The

Therapeutic Workplace to Promote Treatment Engagement and Drug Abstinence in Out-of-Treatment Injection Drug Users: A Randomized Controlled Trial." *Preventive Medicine* 68 (2014): 62–70. https://doi.org/10.1016/j.ypmed.2014.02.021.

Homer. *The Odyssey*. Translated by Butcher, S. H. and A. Lang. Edited by W. Eliot, Charles. Harvard Classics, Vol. 22. Collier & Son, 1909–14.

Hopf, F. Woodward, and Heidi M. B. Lesscher. "Rodent Models for Compulsive Alcohol Intake." *Alcohol* 48, no. 3 (2014): 253–64. https://doi.org/10.1016/j.alcohol.2014.03.001.

Hume, David. *A Treatise of Human Nature*. Edited by L. A. Selby-Bigge. Clarendon Press, 1978.

Husak, Douglas N. *Drugs and Rights*. Cambridge University Press, 1992.

Husak, Douglas N. *Legalize This!: The Case for Decriminalizing Drugs*. Verso Books, 2002.

Hutcheson, D. M., B. J. Everitt, T. W. Robbins, and A. Dickinson. "The Role of Withdrawal in Heroin Addiction: Enhances Reward or Promotes Avoidance?" *Nature Neuroscience* 4, no. 9 (2001): 943–47. https://doi.org/10.1038/nn0901-943.

Hyman, Steven E. "Addiction: A Disease of Learning and Memory." *The American Journal of Psychiatry* 162, no. 8 (2005): 1414–22. https://doi.org/10.1176/appi.ajp.162.8.1414.

Ihssen, Niklas, W. Miles Cox, Alison Wiggett, Javad Salehi Fadardi, and David E. J. Linden. "Differentiating Heavy from Light Drinkers by Neural Responses to Visual Alcohol Cues and Other Motivational Stimuli." *Cerebral Cortex* 21, no. 6 (2011): 1408–15. https://doi.org/10.1093/cercor/bhq220.

Institute for Health Metrics and Evaluation. "Preventing New Smokers Is Key to Controlling the Tobacco Epidemic." Accessed June 17, 2024. https://www.healthdata.org/research-analysis/library/preventing-new-smokers-key-controlling-tobacco-epidemic.

Interlandi, Jeneen. "48 Million Americans Live with Addiction. Here's How to Get Them Help That Works." *New York Times*, December 13, 2023. https://www.nytimes.com/2023/12/13/opinion/addiction-policy-treatment-opioid.html?smid=url-share.

Inzlicht, Michael, and Brandon J. Schmeichel. "What Is Ego Depletion? Toward a Mechanistic Revision of the Resource Model of Self-Control." *Perspectives on Psychological Science* 7, no. 5 (2012): 450–63. https://doi.org/10.1177/1745691612454134.

Inzlicht, Michael, Brandon J. Schmeichel, and C. Neil Macrae. "Why Self-Control Seems (but May Not Be) Limited." *Trends in Cognitive Sciences* 18, no. 3 (2014): 127–33. https://doi.org/10.1016/j.tics.2013.12.009.

Ismael, Jenann. "Why (Study) the Humanities?: The View from Science." In *Making Sense of the World: New Essays on the Philosophy of Understanding*, edited by Stephen R. Grimm. Oxford University Press, 2017.

James, W. *Principles of Psychology*. Henry Holt and Company, 1890.

Jasinski, Donald R., Jeffrey S. Pevnick, and John D. Griffith. "Human Pharmacology and Abuse Potential of the Analgesic Buprenorphine: A Potential Agent for Treating Narcotic Addiction." *Archives of General Psychiatry* 35, no. 4 (Apr. 1978): 501–16. https://doi.org/10.1001/archpsyc.1978.01770280111012.

Jay, Mike. *High Society: Mind-Altering Drugs in History and Culture*. Thames & Hudson, 2012.

Jean-Richard-Dit-Bressel, Philip, Jessica C. Lee, Shi Xian Liew, Gabrielle Weidemann, Peter F. Lovibond, and Gavan P. McNally. "A Cognitive Pathway to Punishment Insensitivity." *Proceedings of the National Academy of Sciences* 120, no. 15 (2023): e2221634120. https://doi.org/10.1073/pnas.2221634120.

Jellinek, E. M. *The Disease Concept of Alcoholism*. Hillhouse Press, 1960.

Jentsch, J. D., and J. R. Taylor. "Impulsivity Resulting from Frontostriatal Dysfunction in Drug Abuse: Implications for the Control of Behavior by Reward-Related Stimuli." *Psychopharmacology* 146, no. 4 (1999): 373–90. https://doi.org/10.1007/pl00005483.

Job, Veronika, Carol S. Dweck, and Gregory M. Walton. "Ego Depletion—Is It All in Your Head? Implicit Theories About Willpower Affect Self-Regulation." *Psychological Science* 21, no. 11 (2010): 1686–93. https://doi.org/10.1177/0956797610384745.

Johnson, Matthew W., Albert Garcia-Romeu, Mary P. Cosimano, and Roland R. Griffiths. "Pilot Study of the 5-HT 2A R Agonist Psilocybin in the Treatment of Tobacco Addiction." *Journal of Psychopharmacology* 28, no. 11 (2014): 983–92. https://doi.org/10.1177/0269881114548296.

Johnston, Mark. "Self-Deception and the Nature of Mind." In *Perspectives on Self-Deception*, edited by Brian P. McLaughlin and Amélie Oksenberg Rorty. University of California Press, 1988.

Jung, Young-Chul, and Kee Namkoong. "Pharmacotherapy for Alcohol Dependence: Anticraving Medications for Relapse Prevention." *Yonsei Medical Journal* 47, no. 2 (Apr. 2006): 167–78. https://doi.org/10.3349/ymj.2006.47.2.167.

Kahneman, Daniel, Paul Slovic, and Amos Tversky. *Judgment Under Uncertainty: Heuristics and Biases*. Cambridge University Press, 1982.

Kahneman, David. *Thinking, Fast and Slow*. Farrar, Straus and Giroux, 2013.

Kang, Kyonghwa, and Sungjae Kim. "The Efficacy of Motivational Interviewing with Cognitive Behavioral Treatment on Behavior Changes in Heavy Drinkers." *Sustainability* 13, no. 3 (2021): 1338. https://doi.org/10.3390/su13031338.

Kaplan, Robert. "Carrot Addiction." *Australian and New Zealand Journal of Psychiatry* 30, no. 5 (1996): 698–700. https://doi.org/10.3109/00048679609062670.

Karr, Mary. *Lit: A Memoir*. HarperCollins, 2010.

Kate*. "Drugs Were the Only Life I Knew." Accessed July 15, 2024. https://www.stuff.co.nz/stuff -nation/assignments/how-have-drugs-affected-your-life/9513619/Drugs-were-the-only -life-I-knew.

Kaur, Baneet, and Deepesh Khanna. "A Narrative Review of the Many Psychiatric Manifestations of Neurosyphilis: The Great Imitator." *Curēus* 15, no. 9 (2023): e44866. https://doi.org /10.7759/cureus.44866.

Kearney, Margaret H., Sheigla Murphy, and Marsha Rosenbaum. "Mothering on Crack Cocaine: A Grounded Theory Analysis." *Social Science & Medicine* (1982) 38, no. 2 (1994): 351–61. https://doi.org/10.1016/0277-9536(94)90405-7.

Keefe, Patrick Radden. *Empire of Pain: The Secret History of the Sackler Dynasty*. Picador, 2022.

Kelly, John F. "Is Alcoholics Anonymous Religious, Spiritual, Neither? Findings from 25 Years of Mechanisms of Behavior Change Research." *Addiction* 112, no. 6 (2017): 929–36. https:// doi.org/10.1111/add.13590.

Kelly, John F., Keith Humphreys, and Marica Ferri. "Alcoholics Anonymous and Other 12-Step Programs for Alcohol Use Disorder." *Cochrane Database of Systematic Reviews* no. 3 (2020). https://doi.org//10.1002/14651858.CD012880.pub2.

Kelly, John F., M. C. Greene, and Alexandra Abry. "A US National Randomized Study to Guide How Best to Reduce Stigma When Describing Drug-Related Impairment in Practice and Policy." *Addiction* 116, no. 7 (2021): 1757–67. https://doi.org/10.1111/add.15333.

Kelly, John Francis, Molly Magill, and Robert Lauren Stout. "How Do People Recover from Alcohol Dependence? A Systematic Review of the Research on Mechanisms of Behavior Change in Alcoholics Anonymous." *Addiction Research & Theory* 17, no. 3 (2009): 236–59. https://doi.org/10.1080/16066350902770458.

Kendell, R. E. "The Concept of Disease and Its Implications for Psychiatry." *British Journal of Psychiatry* 127, no. 4 (1975): 305–15. https://doi.org/10.1192/bjp.127.4.305.

Kendler, K. S. "Levels of Explanation in Psychiatric and Substance Use Disorders: Implications for the Development of an Etiologically Based Nosology." *Molecular Psychiatry* 17, no. 1 (2012): 11–21. https://doi.org/10.1038/mp.2011.70.

Kennett, Jeanette, Doug McConnell, and Anke Snoek. "Reactive Attitudes, Relationships, and Addiction." In *The Routledge Handbook of Philosophy and Science of Addiction*, 1st ed. Routledge, 2019.

Kennett, Jeanette. "Mental Disorder, Moral Agency, and the Self." In *The Oxford Handbook of Bioethics*, edited by Bonnie Steinbock. Oxford University Press, 2009.

Khantzian, E. J. "The Self-Medication Hypothesis of Addictive Disorders: Focus on Heroin and Cocaine Dependence." *The American Journal of Psychiatry* 142, no. 11 (1985): 1259–64. https://doi.org/10.1176/ajp.142.11.1259.

Khantzian, E. J. "The Self-Medication Hypothesis of Substance Use Disorders: A Reconsideration and Recent Applications." *Harvard Review of Psychiatry* 4, no. 5 (1997): 231–44. https://doi.org/10.3109/10673229709030550.

Kilian, Carolin, Jakob Manthey, Sinclair Carr, Franz Hanschmidt, Jürgen Rehm, Sven Speerforck, and Georg Schomerus. "Stigmatization of People with Alcohol Use Disorders: An Updated Systematic Review of Population Studies." *Alcoholism, Clinical and Experimental Research* 45, no. 5 (2021): 899–911. https://doi.org/10.1111/acer.14598.

Kim, Jaegwon. "Explanatory Knowledge and Metaphysical Dependence." In *Essays in the Metaphysics of Mind*. Oxford University Press, 2010.

Kingsolver, Barbara. *Demon Copperhead*. HarperCollins, 2022.

Kipling, R. *Just So Stories for Little Children*. Macmillan, 1902.

Kirouac, Megan, and Katie Witkiewitz. "Identifying 'Hitting Bottom' Among Individuals with Alcohol Problems: Development and Evaluation of the Noteworthy Aspects of Drinking Important to Recovery (NADIR)." *Substance Use & Misuse* 52, no. 12 (2017): 1602–15. doi:10.1080/10826084.2017.1293104.

Knapp, Caroline. *Drinking: A Love Story*. Dial Press Trade Paperback, 1997.

Knobe, Joshua, Sandeep Prasada, and George E. Newman. "Dual Character Concepts and the Normative Dimension of Conceptual Representation." *Cognition* 127, no. 2 (2013): 242–57. https://doi.org/10.1016/j.cognition.2013.01.005.

Koban, Leonie, Tor D. Wager, and Hedy Kober. "A Neuromarker for Drug and Food Craving Distinguishes Drug Users from Non-Users." *Nature Neuroscience* 26, no. 2 (2023): 316–25. https://doi.org/10.1038/s41593-022-01228-w.

Koob, George F. "Neurobiology of Opioid Addiction: Opponent Process, Hyperkatifeia, and Negative Reinforcement." *Biological Psychiatry* (1969) 87, no. 1 (2020): 44–53. https://doi.org/10.1016/j.biopsych.2019.05.023.

Koob, George F. "A Role for Brain Stress Systems in Addiction." *Neuron* 59, no. 1 (2008): 11–34. https://doi.org/10.1016/j.neuron.2008.06.012.

Koob, George F., S. B. Caine, Loren Parsons, Athina Markou, and Friedbert Weiss. "Opponent Process Model and Psychostimulant Addiction." *Pharmacology, Biochemistry and Behavior* 57, no. 3 (1997): 513–21. https://doi.org/10.1016/S0091-3057(96)00438-8.

Kool, W., F. A. Cushman, and S. J. Gershman. "Competition and Cooperation Between Multiple Reinforcement Learning Systems." In *Goal-Directed Decision Making*, edited by R. Morris, A. Bornstein, and A. Shenhav. Academic Press, 2018.

Kraepelin, Emil. *Psychiatry: A Textbook for Students and Physicians*. Science History Publications, 1990.

Kragh, Helge. "From Disulfiram to Antabuse: The Invention of a Drug." *Bulletin for the History of Chemistry* 33, no. 2 (2008): 82–88.

Krakauer, John W., Asif A. Ghazanfar, Alex Gomez-Marin, Malcolm A. MacIver, and David Poeppel. "Neuroscience Needs Behavior: Correcting a Reductionist Bias." *Neuron* 93, no. 3 (2017): 480–90. https://doi.org/10.1016/j.neuron.2016.12.041.

Kruger, Richard. *Ashes to Ashes: America's Hundred-Year Cigarette War, the Public Health and the Unabashed Triumph of Philip Morris*. New York: Vintage Books, 1996.

Kurzban, Robert. "Does the Brain Consume Additional Glucose During Self-Control Tasks?" *Evolutionary Psychology* 8, no. 2 (2010): 244–59. https://doi.org/10.1177/147470491000800208.

Kurzban, Robert O. *Why Everyone (Else) Is a Hypocrite: Evolution and the Modular Mind*. Princeton University Press, 2012.

Lacey, Nicola, and Hanna Pickard. "Why Standing to Blame May Be Lost but Authority to Hold Accountable Retained: Criminal Law as a Regulative Public Institution." *The Monist* 104, no. 2 (2021): 265–80. https://doi.org/10.1093/monist/onaa028.

Lacey, Nicola, and Hanna Pickard. "A Dual Process Approach to Criminal Law: Victims and the Clinical Model of Responsibility Without Blame." *Journal of Political Philosophy* 27, no. 2 (2019): 229–51. https://doi.org/10.1111/jopp.12160.

Lacey, Nicola, and Hanna Pickard. "From the Consulting Room to the Courtroom? Taking the Clinical Model of Responsibility Without Blame into the Legal Realm." *Oxford Journal of Legal Studies* 33, no. 1 (2013): 1–29. https://doi.org/10.1093/ojls/gqs028.

Lacey, Nicola, and Hanna Pickard. "To Blame or to Forgive? Reconciling Punishment and Forgiveness in Criminal Justice." *Oxford Journal of Legal Studies* 135, no. 4 (2015): 665–96. https://doi.org/10.1093/ojls/gqv012.

Lacy, Nicola M. *In Search of Criminal Responsibility: Ideas, Interests and Institutions*. Oxford University Press, 2016.

Langley, T., J. Leonardi-Bee, A. Barker, O. Brown, and R. Murray. "The Effect of Alcohol Marketing on People with, or at Risk of, an Alcohol Problem: A Rapid Review." *European Journal of Public Health* 32 (2022). https://doi.org/10.1093/eurpub/ckac131.327.

Lavallee, Zoey. "Affective Scaffolding in Addiction." *Inquiry* (2023): 1–29. https://doi.org/10.1080/0020174X.2023.2194321.

Lebowitz, Matthew S. "Biological Conceptualizations of Mental Disorders Among Affected Individuals: A Review of Correlates and Consequences." *Clinical Psychology* 21, no. 1 (2014): 67–83. https://doi.org/10.1111/cpsp.12056.

Lembke, Anna. "Time to Abandon the Self-Medication Hypothesis in Patients with Psychiatric Disorders." *The American Journal of Drug and Alcohol Abuse* 38, no. 6 (2012): 524–29. https://doi.org/10.3109/00952990.2012.694532.

Lenoir, Magalie, Fuschia Serre, Lauriane Cantin, and Serge H. Ahmed. "Intense Sweetness Surpasses Cocaine Reward." *PloS One* 2, no. 8 (2007): e698. https://doi.org/10.1371/journal.pone.0000698.

Leshner, Alan I. "Addiction Is a Brain Disease, and It Matters." *Science* 278, no. 5335 (Oct. 1997): 45–47. https://doi.org/10.1126/science.278.5335.45.

Leslie, Sarah-Jane. "'Hillary Clinton Is the Only Man in the Obama Administration': Dual Character Concepts, Generics, and Gender." *Analytic Philosophy* 56, no. 2 (2015): 111–41. https://doi.org/10.1111/phib.12063.

Leslie, Sarah-Jane. "The Original Sin of Cognition: Fear, Prejudice, and Generalization." *The Journal of Philosophy* 114, no. 8 (2017): 393–421. https://doi.org/10.5840/jphil2017114828.

Levy, Neil. "Addiction Is Not a Brain Disease (and It Matters)." *Frontiers in Psychiatry* 4 (2013): 24. https://doi.org/10.3389/fpsyt.2013.00024.

Levy, Neil. "Self-Deception Without Thought Experiments." In *Delusion and Self-Deception*, edited by T. Bayne and J. Fernandez. Psychology Press, 2009.

Lewis, Marc. *The Biology of Desire: Why Addiction Is Not a Disease*. Perseus Books Group, 2015.

Leyton, Marco, and Paul Vezina. "Dopamine Ups and Downs in Vulnerability to Addictions: A Neurodevelopmental Model." *Trends in Pharmacological Sciences* 35, no. 6 (2014): 268–76. https://doi.org/10.1016/j.tips.2014.04.002.

Leyton, Marco, and Paul Vezina. "Striatal Ups and Downs: Their Roles in Vulnerability to Addictions in Humans." *Neuroscience and Biobehavioral Reviews* 37, no. 9 (2013): 1999–2014. https://doi.org/10.1016/j.neubiorev.2013.01.018.

Lindgren, Kristen P., Clayton Neighbors, Melissa L. Gasser, Jason J. Ramirez, and Dario Cvencek. "A Review of Implicit and Explicit Substance Self-Concept as a Predictor of

Alcohol and Tobacco Use and Misuse." *Early Childhood Research Quarterly* 43, no. 3 (2017): 237–46. https://doi.org/10.1080/00952990.2016.1229324.

Litten, Raye Z., Megan L. Ryan, Daniel E. Falk, Matthew Reilly, Joanne B. Fertig, and George F. Koob. "Heterogeneity of Alcohol Use Disorder: Understanding Mechanisms to Advance Personalized Treatment." *Alcoholism: Clinical and Experimental Research* 39, no. 4 (2015): 579–84. https://doi.org/10.1111/acer.12669.

Lorde, Audre. "The Uses of Anger: Women Responding to Racism." *Women and Language* 11, no. 1: 4. Crossing Press, 1987.

Lüscher, Christian, Trevor W. Robbins, and Barry J. Everitt. "The Transition to Compulsion in Addiction." *Nature Reviews. Neuroscience* 21, no. 5 (May 2020): 247–63. https://doi.org/10.1038/s41583-020-0289-z.

MacKillop, James, Roberta Agabio, Sarah W. Feldstein Ewing, Markus Heilig, John F. Kelly, Lorenzo Leggio, Anne Lingford-Hughes, et al. "Hazardous Drinking and Alcohol Use Disorders." *Nature Reviews. Disease Primers* 8, no. 1 (2022): 80. https://doi.org/10.1038/s41572-022-00406-1.

Mackintosh, Valerie, and Tess Knight. "The Notion of Self in the Journey Back from Addiction." *Qualitative Health Research* 22, no. 8 (2012): 1094–1101. https://doi.org/10.1177/1049732312450325.

Macy, Beth. *Dopesick: Dealers, Doctors, and the Drug Company That Addicted America.* Little, Brown and Company, 2018.

Macy, Beth. *Raising Lazarus: Hope, Justice, and the Future of America's Overdose Crisis.* Little, Brown and Company, 2022.

Main, T. F. "The Ailment." *British Journal of Medical Psychology* 30, no. 3 (1957): 129–45. https://doi.org/10.1111/j.2044-8341.1957.tb01193.x.

Marlatt, G. A., Barbara Demming, and John B. Reid. "Loss of Control Drinking in Alcoholics: An Experimental Analogue." *Journal of Abnormal Psychology* 81, no. 3 (1973): 233–41. https://doi.org/10.1037/h0034532.

Marr, David. *Vision: A Computational Investigation into the Human Representation and Processing of Visual Information.* MIT Press, 2010.

Martin, Clancy. *How Not to Kill Yourself: A Portrait of the Suicidal Mind.* Pantheon Books, 2023.

Martin, Ingrid M., Michael A. Kamins, Dante M. Pirouz, Scott W. Davis, Kelly L. Haws, Ann M. Mirabito, Sayantani Mukherjee, Justine M. Rapp, and Aditi Grover. "On the Road to Addiction: The Facilitative and Preventive Roles of Marketing Cues." *Journal of Business Research* 66, no. 8 (2013): 1219–26. https://doi.org/10.1016/j.jbusres.2012.08.015.

Martinez, Diana, and Felipe Castillo. "Imaging Dopamine Signaling in Addiction." In *The Routledge Handbook of Philosophy and Science of Addiction,* 1st ed. Routledge, 2019.

Marušić, Berislav. *Evidence and Agency: Norms of Belief for Promising and Resolving.* Oxford University Press, 2015.

Maté, Gabor. *In the Realm of Hungry Ghosts: Close Encounters with Addiction.* North Atlantic Books, 2010.

McBride, Andrew J., Richard M. Pates, Karin Arnold, and Nicola Ball. "Needle Fixation, the Drug User's Perspective: A Qualitative Study." *Addiction* 96, no. 7 (2001): 1049–58. https://doi.org/10.1046/j.1360-0443.2001.967104914.x.

McCain, Kevin. *Understanding How Science Explains the World (Understanding Life).* New ed. Cambridge University Press, 2022.

McConnell, Doug, and Anke Snoek. "The Importance of Self-Narration in Recovery from Addiction." *Philosophy, Psychiatry & Psychology* 25, no. 3 (2018): E-31–E-44. https://doi.org/10.1353/ppp.2018.0022.

McConnell, Doug. "Narrative Self-Constitution and Vulnerability to Co-authoring." *Theoretical Medicine and Bioethics* 37, no. 1 (2016): 29–43. https://doi.org/10.1007/s11017-016-9356-x.

McGeer, Victoria. "Building a Better Theory of Responsibility." *Philosophical Studies* 172, no. 10 (2015): 2635–49. https://doi.org/10.1007/s11098-015-0478-1.

McGeer, Victoria. "Mind-Making Practices: The Social Infrastructure of Self-Knowing Agency and Responsibility." *Philosophical Explorations* 18, no. 2 (2015): 259–81. https://doi.org/10.1080/13869795.2015.1032331.

McGeer, Victoria. "Scaffolding Agency: A Proleptic Account of the Reactive Attitudes." *European Journal of Philosophy* 27, no. 2 (2019): 301–23. https://doi.org/10.1111/ejop.12408.

McGinty, Emma E., Colleen L. Barry, Elizabeth M. Stone, Jeff Niederdeppe, Alene Kennedy-Hendricks, Sarah Linden, and Susan G. Sherman. "Public Support for Safe Consumption Sites and Syringe Services Programs to Combat the Opioid Epidemic." *Preventive Medicine* 111 (2018): 73–77. https://doi.org/10.1016/j.ypmed.2018.02.026.

McGinty, Emma, Bernice Pescosolido, Alene Kennedy-Hendricks, and Colleen L. Barry. "Communication Strategies to Counter Stigma and Improve Mental Illness and Substance Use Disorder Policy." *Psychiatric Services* 69, no. 2 (2018): 136–46. https://doi.org/10.1176/appi.ps.201700076.

McKay, Ryan, Robyn Langdon, and Max Coltheart. "'Sleights of Mind': Delusions, Defences, and Self-Deception." *Cognitive Neuropsychiatry* 10, no. 4 (2005): 305–26. https://doi.org/10.1080/13546800444000074.

McKay, Ryan T., and Daniel C. Dennett. "The Evolution of Misbelief." *The Behavioral and Brain Sciences* 32, no. 6 (2009): 493–510. https://doi.org/10.1017/S0140525X09990975.

McNally, Gavan P., Philip Jean-Richard-Dit-Bressel, E. Zayra Millan, and Andrew J. Lawrence. "Pathways to the Persistence of Drug Use Despite Its Adverse Consequences." *Molecular Psychiatry* 28, no. 6 (2023): 2228–37. https://doi.org/10.1038/s41380-023-02040-z.

Mead, Nicole L., Roy F. Baumeister, Francesca Gino, Maurice E. Schweitzer, and Dan Ariely. "Too Tired to Tell the Truth: Self-Control Resource Depletion and Dishonesty." *Journal of Experimental Social Psychology* 45, no. 3 (2009): 594–97. https://doi.org/10.1016/j.jesp.2009.02.004.

Mehta, Sheila, and Amerigo Farina. "Is Being 'Sick' Really Better? Effect of the Disease View of Mental Disorder on Stigma." *Journal of Social and Clinical Psychology* 16, no. 4 (1997): 405–19. https://doi.org/10.1521/jscp.1997.16.4.405.

Melamed, Daniela M., Jessica Botting, Katie Lofthouse, Laura Pass, and Richard Meiser-Stedman. "The Relationship Between Negative Self-Concept, Trauma, and Maltreatment in Children and Adolescents: A Meta-Analysis." *Clinical Child and Family Psychology Review* 27, no. 1 (2024): 220–34. https://doi.org/10.1007/s10567-024-00472-9.

Mele, Alfred. "Self-Deception and Delusions." In *Delusion and Self-Deception*, edited by T. Bayne and J. Fernandez. Psychology Press, 2009.

Mele, Alfred. *Self-Deception Unmasked*. Princeton University Press, 2001.

Mele, Alfred R. "Irresistible Desires." *Noûs* 24, no. 3 (1990): 455–72. https://doi.org/10.2307/2215775.

Mericle, Amy A., Valerie Slaymaker, Kate Gliske, Quyen Ngo, and Meenakshi S. Subbaraman. "The Role of Recovery Housing During Outpatient Substance use Treatment." *Journal of Substance Abuse Treatment* 133 (2022). https://doi.org/10.1016/j.jsat.2021.108638.

Mijovi-Prelec, Danica, and Dražen Prelec. "Self-Deception as Self-Signalling: A Model and Experimental Evidence." *Philosophical Transactions of the Royal Society of London. Series B. Biological Sciences* 365, no. 1538 (2010): 227–40. https://doi.org/10.1098/rstb.2009.0218.

Mikulincer, Mario, and Phillip R. Shaver. *Attachment in Adulthood: Structure, Dynamics, and Change*. 2nd ed. Guilford Press, 2016.

Miller, William R. and Paula L. Wilbourne. "Mesa Grande: A Methodological Analysis of Clinical Trials of Treatments for Alcohol Use Disorders." *Addiction* 97, no. 3 (2002): 265–77. https://doi.org/10.1046/j.1360-0443.2002.00019.x.

Miller, William R., Verner S. Westerberg, Richard J. Harris, and J. S. Tonigan. "What Predicts Relapse? Prospective Testing of Antecedent Models." *Addiction* 91, no. 12 (1996): 155–72. https://doi.org/10.1046/j.1360-0443.91.12s1.7.x.

Millikan, Ruth Garrett. *Language, Thought, and Other Biological Categories: New Foundations for Realism.* MIT Press, 1984.

Minhas, Meenu, Alysha Cooper, Sarah Sousa, Jean Costello Mary, and James MacKillop. "Characterizing Clinical Heterogeneity in a Large Inpatient Addiction Treatment Sample: Confirmatory Latent Profile Analysis and Differential Levels of Craving and Impulsivity." *Substance Abuse: Research and Treatment* 16 (2022). https://doi.org/10.1177/11782218221126977.

Moeller, Scott J., and Rita Z. Goldstein. "Impaired Self-Awareness in Human Addiction: Deficient Attribution of Personal Relevance." *Trends in Cognitive Sciences* 18, no. 12 (2014): 635–41. https://doi.org/10.1016/j.tics.2014.09.003.

Moeller, Scott J., Anna B. Konova, Muhammad A. Parvaz, Dardo Tomasi, Richard D. Lane, Carolyn Fort, and Rita Z. Goldstein. "Functional, Structural, and Emotional Correlates of Impaired Insight in Cocaine Addiction." *JAMA Psychiatry (Chicago, Ill)* 71, no. 1 (2014): 61–70. https://doi.org/10.1001/jamapsychiatry.2013.2833.

Moeller, Scott J., Anna Zilverstand, Anna B. Konova, Prantik Kundu, Muhammad A. Parvaz, Rebecca Preston-Campbell, Keren Bachi, Nelly Alia-Klein, and Rita Z. Goldstein. "Neural Correlates of Drug-Biased Choice in Currently Using and Abstinent Individuals With Cocaine Use Disorder." *Biological Psychiatry: Cognitive Neuroscience and Neuroimaging* 3, no. 5 (2018): 485–94. https://doi.org/10.1016/j.bpsc.2017.11.001.

Moeller, Scott J., Kyoji Okita, Chelsea L. Robertson, Michael E. Ballard, Anna B. Konova, Rita Z. Goldstein, Mark A. Mandelkern, and Edythe D. London. "Low Striatal Dopamine D2-Type Receptor Availability Is Linked to Simulated Drug Choice in Methamphetamine Users." *Neuropsychopharmacology* 43, no. 4 (2018): 751–60. https://doi.org/10.1038/npp.2017.138.

Moeller, Scott J., Stephen M. Fleming, Gabriela Gan, Anna Zilverstand, Pias Malaker, Federico d'Oleire Uquillas, Kristin E. Schneider, et al. "Metacognitive Impairment in Active Cocaine Use Disorder Is Associated with Individual Differences in Brain Structure." *European Neuropsychopharmacology* 26, no. 4 (2016): 653–62. https://doi.org/10.1016/j.euroneuro.2016.02.009.

Molden, Daniel C., Chin Ming Hui, Abigail A. Scholer, Brian P. Meier, Eric E. Noreen, Paul R. D'Agostino, and Valerie Martin. "Motivational Versus Metabolic Effects of Carbohydrates on Self-Control." *Psychological Science* 23, no. 10 (2012): 1137–44. https://doi.org/10.1177/0956797612439069.

Morris, Adam, Ryan W. Carlson, Hedy Kober, and Molly Crockett. 2023. "Introspective Access to Value-Based Multi-attribute Choice Processes." PsyArXiv. October 12. https://doi.org/10.31234/osf.io/2zrfa.

Morris, J., A. C. Moss, I. P. Albery, and N. Heather. "The 'Alcoholic Other': Harmful Drinkers Resist Problem Recognition to Manage Identity Threat." *Addictive Behaviors* 124, (2022): 107093. https://doi.org/10.1016/j.addbeh.2021.107093.

Morris, J., I. P. Albery, N. Heather, and A. C. Moss. "Continuum Beliefs Are Associated with Higher Problem Recognition than Binary Beliefs Among Harmful Drinkers Without Addiction Experience." *Addictive Behaviors* 105 (Jun. 2020): 106292. https://doi.org/10.1016/j.addbeh.2020.106292.

Morris, James, Ian P. Albery, Antony C. Moss, and Nick Heather. "Promoting Problem Recognition Amongst Harmful Drinkers: A Conceptual Model for Problem Framing Factors." In *The Handbook of Alcohol Use*, edited by Daniel Frings and Ian P. Albery. Elsevier, 2021.

Motz, A. *Managing Self-Harm.* Routledge, 2009.

Müller, Christian P. and Gunter Schumann. "Drugs as Instruments: A New Framework for Non-addictive Psychoactive Drug Use." *The Behavioral and Brain Sciences* 34, no. 6 (2011): 293–310. https://doi.org/10.1017/S0140525X11000057.

Murphy, Dominic. "Concepts of Disease and Health." In *Stanford Encyclopedia of Philosophy* (Spring 2021 Edition), edited by Edward N. Zalta. Accessed January 18, 2024. https://plato .stanford.edu/archives/spr2021/entries/health-disease/.

Murphy, Dominic. "Philosophy of Psychiatry." In *Stanford Encyclopedia of Philosophy* (Fall 2020 Edition), edited by Edward N. Zalta. Accessed January 18, 2024. https://plato.stanford.edu /archives/fall2020/entries/psychiatry/.

Murphy, Dominic. "Psychiatry and the Concept of Disease as Pathology." In *Psychiatry as Cognitive Neuroscience: Philosophical Perspectives*, edited by Matthew Broome and Lisa Bortolotti. Oxford University Press, 2009.

Naqvi, Nasir H., and Antoine Bechara. "The Hidden Island of Addiction: The Insula." *Trends in Neurosciences* 32, no. 1 (2009): 56–67. https://doi.org/10.1016/j.tins.2008.09.009.

Nasser, Helen M., Yu-Wei Chen, Kimberly Fiscella, and Donna J. Calu. "Individual Variability in Behavioral Flexibility Predicts Sign-Tracking Tendency." *Frontiers in Behavioral Neuroscience* 9 (2015): 289. https://doi.org/10.3389/fnbeh.2015.00289.

National Institute on Alcohol Abuse and Alcoholism (NIAAA). "FY 2023 Congressional Budget Justification." Accessed June 18, 2024. https://www.niaaa.nih.gov/about-niaaa/our -funding/congressional-budget-justification/fy-2023-congressional-budget-justification.

National Institute on Drug Abuse (NIDA). "Common Comorbidities with Substance Use Disorders Research Report 2020." Accessed August 7, 2024. https://www.ncbi.nlm.nih.gov /books/NBK571451/.

National Institute on Drug Abuse (NIDA). "Comorbidity: Substance Use and Other Mental Disorders." Accessed August 7, 2024. https://nida.nih.gov/research-topics/comorbidity /comorbidity-substance-use-other-mental-disorders-infographic.

National Institute on Drug Abuse (NIDA). "Fiscal Year 2024 Budget Information - Congressional Justification for National Institute on Drugs and Addiction." Accessed June 18, 2024. https://nida.nih.gov/about-nida/legislative-activities/budget-information/fiscal-year -2024-budget-information-congressional-justification-national-institute-drug-abuse.

National Institute on Drug Abuse (NIDA). "Part 1: The Connection Between Substance Use Disorders and Mental Illness." Accessed August 7, 2024. https://nida.nih.gov/publications /research-reports/common-comorbidities-substance-use-disorders/part-1-connection -between-substance-use-disorders-mental-illness.

Nayfield, Nicolas. "Drug Cours and the 'Responsibility Without Blame' Approach." *Journal of Applied Philosophy* 40, no. 3 (2023): 488–504. https://doi.org/10.1111/japp.12640.

Neal, David T., Wendy Wood, Mengju Wu, and David Kurlander. "The Pull of the Past: When do Habits Persist Despite Conflict with Motives?" *Personality and Social Psychology Bulletin* 37, no. 11 (2011): 1428–37. https://doi.org/10.1177/0146167211419863.

Nelson, Maggie. *On Freedom: Four Songs of Care and Constraint.* Graywolf Press, 2021.

Nesse, Randolph M., and Kent C. Berridge. "Psychoactive Drug Use in Evolutionary Perspective." *Science (American Association for the Advancement of Science)* 278, no. 5335 (1997): 63–66. https://doi.org/10.1126/science.278.5335.63.

Newell, Ben R., and David R. Shanks. "Unconscious Influences on Decision Making: A Critical Review." *Behavioral and Brain Sciences* 37, no. 1 (2014): 1–19. https://doi.org/10.1017/ S0140525X12003214.

Nielson, Elizabeth M., Darrick G. May, Alyssa A. Forcehimes, and Michael P. Bogenschutz. "The Psychedelic Debriefing in Alcohol Dependence Treatment: Illustrating Key Change Phenomena Through Qualitative Content Analysis of Clinical Sessions." *Frontiers in Pharmacology* 9 (2018): 132. https://doi.org/10.3389/fphar.2018.00132.

Niv, Yael. "The Primacy of Behavioral Research for Understanding the Brain." *Behavioral Neuroscience* 135, no. 5 (2021): 601–9. https://doi.org/10.1037/bne0000471

Noorani, Tehseen, Albert Garcia-Romeu, Thomas C. Swift, Roland R. Griffiths, and Matthew W. Johnson. "Psychedelic Therapy for Smoking Cessation: Qualitative Analysis of Participant Accounts." *Journal of Psychopharmacology* 32, no. 7 (2018): 756–69. https://doi.org/10.1177/0269881118780612.

Noori, Hamid R., Alejandro Cosa Linan, and Rainer Spanagel. "Largely Overlapping Neuronal Substrates of Reactivity to Drug, Gambling, Food and Sexual Cues: A Comprehensive Meta-Analysis." *European Neuropsychopharmacology* 26, no. 9 (2016): 1419–30. https://doi.org/10.1016/j.euroneuro.2016.06.013.

Nussbaum, Martha. *Women and Human Development: The Capabilities Approach.* Cambridge University Press, 2001.

Nutile, Lauren M. "Neurosyphilis with Psychosis as the Primary Presentation." *American Journal of Psychiatry Residents' Journal* 16, no. 3 (2021): 6–8. https://doi.org/10.1176/appi.ajp-rj.2021.160304.

Nutt, David. *Drugs Without the Hot Air: Minimising the Harms of Legal and Illegal Drugs.* UIT Cambridge, 2012.

Ogawa, Naoshi, and Hirofumi Ueki. "Clinical Importance of Caffeine Dependence and Abuse." *Psychiatry and Clinical Neurosciences* 61, no. 3 (2007): 263–68. https://doi.org/10.1111/j.1440-1819.2007.01652.x.

Orford, Jim. *Excessive Appetites: A Psychological View of Addictions.* 2nd ed. Wiley, 2001.

O'Shaughnessy, B. *The Will (Vol. I-II).* Cambridge University Press, 1980.

Oslin, David. "Personalized Addiction Treatment: How Close Are We?" *Alcohol and Alcoholism* 46, no. 3 (2011): 231–32. https://doi.org/10.1093/alcalc/agr030.

Oxford English Dictionary, s.v. "drug (n.1)." March 2024, https://doi.org/10.1093/OED/3784863498.

Oxford English Dictionary, s.v. "punishment (n.)." July 2023, https://doi.org/10.1093/OED/4688245746.

Papastrat, Kimberly M., Cody A. Lis, Daniele Caprioli, Hanna Pickard, Adam C. Puche, Leslie A. Ramsey, and Marco Venniro. "Social Odor Choice Buffers Drug Craving." *Neuropsychopharmacology* 49, no. 4 (2024): 731–39. https://doi.org/10.1038/s41386-023-01778-y.

Paris J. "Psychosocial Adversity." In *Handbook of Personality Disorders*, edited by W. J. Livesley. Guilford, 2001.

Pates, R. "A Case of Needle Fixation." *Journal of Substance Use* 6, no. 3 (2001): 202–6.

Paul, L. A. *Transformative Experience.* Oxford: Oxford University Press, 2014.

Paul, L. A., and N. Hall. *Causation: A User's Guide.* 1st ed. Oxford University Press, 2013.

Pearce, Steve, and Hanna Pickard. "How Therapeutic Communities Work: Specific Factors Related to Positive Outcome." *International Journal of Social Psychiatry* 59, no. 7 (2013): 636–45. https://doi.org/10.1177/0020764012450992.

Pearce, Steve, and Rex Haigh. *The Theory and Practice of Democratic Therapeutic Community Treatment.* Jessica Kingsley, 2017.

Peele, Stanton. *The Meaning of Addiction: Compulsive Experience and its Interpretation.* Lexington Books, 1985.

Pereboom, Derk. "Free Will Skepticism, Blame, and Obligation." In *Blame: Its Nature and Norms,* edited by Coates, D. Justin, and Neal A. Tognazzini. Oxford Academic, 2013. https://doi.org/10.1093/acprof:oso/9780199860821.003.0010.

Pereboom, Derk. *Free Will, Agency, and Meaning in Life.* Oxford University Press, 2016.

Pereboom, Derk. *Living Without Free Will.* Cambridge University Press, 2001.

Pereboom, Derk. *Wrongdoing and the Moral Emotions.* 1st ed. Oxford University Press, 2021.

Pescosolido, Bernice A., Jack K. Martin, J. S. Long, Tait R. Medina, Jo C. Phelan, and Bruce G. Link. "A Disease Like any Other? A Decade of Change in Public Reactions to Schizophrenia, Depression, and Alcohol Dependence." *The American Journal of Psychiatry* 167, no. 11 (2010): 1321–30. https://doi.org/10.1176/appi.ajp.2010.09121743.

Piazza, Pier Vincenzo, and Véronique Deroche-Gamonet. "A Multistep General Theory of Transition to Addiction." *Psychopharmacology* 229, no. 3 (2013): 387–413. https://doi.org/10.1007/s00213-013-3224-4.

Pickard, Hanna. "Addiction and the Meaning of Disease." In *Evaluating the Brain Disease Model of Addiction*, 1st ed. Routledge, 2022.

Pickard, Hanna. "Addiction and the Self." *Noûs* 55, no. 4 (2021): 737–61. https://doi.org/10.1111/nous.12328.

Pickard, Hanna. "Denial in Addiction." *Mind & Language* 31, no. 3 (2016): 277–99. https://doi.org/10.1111/mila.12106.

Pickard, Hanna. "Is Addiction a Brain Disease? A Plea for Agnosticism and Heterogeneity." *Psychopharmacology* 239, no. 4 (2022): 993–1007. https://doi.org/10.1007/s00213-021-06013-4.

Pickard, Hanna. "Stories of Recovery: The Role of Narrative and Hope in Overcoming PTSD and PD." In *The Oxford Handbook of Psychiatric Ethics*, edited by J. Z. Sadler, W. C. W. Staden, and K. W. M. Oxford University Press, 2015.

Pickard, Hanna. "What We're Not Talking About When We Talk About Addiction." *The Hastings Center Report* 50, no. 4 (2020): 37–46. https://doi.org/10.1002/hast.1172.

Potter, N. *Mapping the Edges and In-Between: A Critical Analysis of Borderline Personality Disorder.* Oxford University Press, 2009.

Pozen, David. *The Constitution of the War on Drugs.* Oxford University Press, 2024.

Preston, Kenzie L., Massoud Vahabzadeh, John Schmittner, Jia-Ling Lin, David A. Gorelick, and David H. Epstein. "Cocaine Craving and Use During Daily Life." *Psychopharmacologia* 207, no. 2 (2009): 291–301. https://doi.org/10.1007/s00213-009-1655-8.

Priester, Mary Ann, Teri Browne, Aidyn Iachini, Stephanie Clone, Dana DeHart, and Kristen D. Seay. "Treatment Access Barriers and Disparities Among Individuals with Co-occurring Mental Health and Substance Use Disorders: An Integrative Literature Review." *Journal of Substance Abuse Treatment* 61 (2016): 47–59. https://doi.org/10.1016/j.jsat.2015.09.006.

Proctor, Robert N. "The History of the Discovery of the Cigarette–Lung Cancer Link: Evidentiary Traditions, Corporate Denial, Global Toll." *Tobacco Control* 21, no. 2 (2012): 87–91. https://doi.org/10.1136/tobaccocontrol-2011-050338.

Rachlin, Howard. "Four Teleological Theories of Addiction." *Psychonomic Bulletin & Review* 4, no. 4 (1997): 462–73. https://doi.org/10.3758/BF03214335.

Radden, Jennifer. "Mental Disorder (Illness)." In *Stanford Encyclopedia of Philosophy* (Fall 2023 Edition), edited by Edward N. Zalta and Uri Nodelman. Accessed January 18, 2024. https://plato.stanford.edu/archives/fall2023/entries/mental-disorder/.

Rafei, Parnian, Tara Rezapour, Warren K. Bickel, and Hamed Ekhtiari. "Imagining the Future to Reshape the Past: A Path to Combine Cue Extinction and Memory Reconsolidation with Episodic Foresight for Addiction Treatment." *Frontiers in Psychiatry* 12 (2021): 692645. https://doi.org/10.3389/fpsyt.2021.692645.

Railton, Peter. "That Obscure Object, Desire." *Proceedings and Addresses of the American Philosophical Association* 86, no. 2 (2012): 22–46. http://www.jstor.org/stable/43661297.

Raine, Adrian. *The Anatomy of Violence: The Biological Roots of Crime.* Vintage Books, 2014.

Redish, A. D. "Addiction as a Computational Process Gone Awry." *Science (American Association for the Advancement of Science)* 306, no. 5703 (2004): 1944–47. https://doi.org/10.1126/science.1102384.

Redish, A. David, Steve Jensen, Adam Johnson, and Zeb Kurth-Nelson. "Reconciling Reinforcement Learning Models with Behavioral Extinction and Renewal: Implications for

Addiction, Relapse, and Problem Gambling." *Psychological Review* 114, no. 3 (2007): 784–805. https://doi.org/10.1037/0033-295X.114.3.784.

Redish, A. David, Steve Jensen, and Adam Johnson. "A Unified Framework for Addiction: Vulnerabilities in the Decision Process." *The Behavioral and Brain Sciences* 31, no. 4 (2008): 415–37. https://doi.org/10.1017/S0140525X0800472X.

Redish, A. David, Steve Jensen, and Adam Johnson. "Addiction as Vulnerabilities in the Decision Process." *The Behavioral and Brain Sciences* 31, no. 4 (2008): 461–87. https://doi.org/10.1017/S0140525X08004986.

Regier, Darrel A., Mary E. Farmer, Donald S. Rae, Ben Z. Locke, Samuel J. Keith, Lewis L. Judd, and Frederick K. Goodwin. "Comorbidity of Mental Disorders with Alcohol and Other Drug Abuse: Results from the Epidemiologic Catchment Area (ECA) Study." *Journal of the American Medical Association (JAMA)* 264, no. 19 (1990): 2511–18. https://doi.org/10.1001/jama.1990.03450190043026.

Regier, Paul S., and A. David Redish. "Contingency Management and Deliberative Decision-Making Processes." *Frontiers in Psychiatry* 6 (2015): 76. https://doi.org/10.3389/fpsyt.2015.00076.

Richards, Eugene. *Cocaine True, Cocaine Blue.* Aperture, 2005.

Richards, Keith. *Life.* Little, Brown and Company, 2011.

Rio, C., and H. C. Pinto. "1479—Schizophrenialike Psychosis—a Case of a Hidden Neurosyphilis." *European Psychiatry* 28 (2013): 1. https://doi.org/10.1016/S0924-9338(13)76505-2.

Riper, Heleen, Gerhard Andersson, Sarah B. Hunter, Jessica de Wit, Matthias Berking, and Pim Cuijpers. "Treatment of Comorbid Alcohol Use Disorders and Depression with Cognitive-Behavioural Therapy and Motivational Interviewing: A Meta-Analysis." *Addiction (Abingdon, England)* 109, no. 3 (2014): 394–406. https://doi.org/10.1111/add.12441.

Robinson, Sean M., and Bryon Adinoff. "The Classification of Substance Use Disorders: Historical, Contextual, and Conceptual Considerations." *Behavioral Sciences* 6, no. 3 (2016): 18. https://doi.org/10.3390/bs6030018.

Robinson, Terry E., and Kent C. Berridge. "The Neural Basis of Drug Craving: An Incentive-Sensitization Theory of Addiction." *Brain Research Reviews* 18, no. 3: 247–91. https://doi.org/10.1016/0165-0173(93)90013-P.

Robinson, Terry E., and Shelly B. Flagel. "Dissociating the Predictive and Incentive Motivational Properties of Reward-Related Cues Through the Study of Individual Differences." *Biological Psychiatry* 65, no. 10 (2009 [1969]): 869–73. https://doi.org/10.1016/j.biopsych.2008.09.006.

Rohsenow, Damaris J., and G. A. Marlatt. "The Balanced Placebo Design: Methodological Considerations." *Addictive Behaviors* 6, no. 2 (1981): 107–22. https://doi.org/10.1016/0306-4603(81)90003-4.

Room, Robin. "No Level Has Primacy in What Is Called Addiction: 'Addiction Is a Social Disease' Would Be Just as Tenable." *Neuropsychopharmacology* 46, no. 10 (2021): 1712. https://doi.org/10.1038/s41386-021-01015-4.

Rosati, Connie. "Personal Good." In *Metaethics After Moore*, edited by Terry Horgan and Mark Timmons. Clarendon Press, 2006.

Rosen, Gideon. "The Alethic Conception of Moral Responsibility." In *The Nature of Moral Responsibility.* Oxford University Press, 2015.

Ross, Don. "Addiction Is Socially Engineered Exploitation of Natural Biological Vulnerability." In *Evaluating the Brain Disease Model of Addiction*, 1st ed. Routledge, 2022.

Roth, Sarah E., Kyle G. Jones, and Keri B. Vartanian. "Assessing the Impact of Recovery Housing on Healthcare Utilization in Portland, Oregon." *Drug and Alcohol Dependence Reports* 9 (2023): 100192. https://doi.org/10.1016/j.dadr.2023.100192.

Rush, B. *Medical Inquiries and Observations, Upon the Diseases of the Mind.* Kimber and Richard-son, 1812.

Salavert, Aurélie, Antoine Zazzo, Lucie Martin, Ferran Antolín, Caroline Gauthier, François Thil, Olivier Tombret, et al. "Direct Dating Reveals the Early History of Opium Poppy in Western Europe." *Scientific Reports* 10 (2020): 20263. https://doi.org/10.1038/s41598-020-76924-3.

Samaha, Anne-Noël, Shaun Y. S. Khoo, Carrie R. Ferrario, and Terry E. Robinson. "Dopamine 'Ups and Downs' in Addiction Revisited." *Trends in Neurosciences* 44, no. 7 (2021): 516–26. https://doi.org/10.1016/j.tins.2021.03.003.

Sarkar, Sharmila, Malay Ghosal, Sudip Ghosh, and Goutam Guha. "Schizophrenia-like Psycho-sis as the Presenting Feature of Neurosyphilis in a Non-Human Immunodeficiency Virus-Infected Indian Man: A Reminder of a Forgotten Complication." *Indian Journal of Psychiatry* 61, no. 2 (2019): 213–16. https://doi.org/10.4103/psychiatry.IndianJPsychiatry_330_18.

Satel, Sally, and Scott O. Lilienfeld. "Addiction and the Brain-Disease Fallacy." *Frontiers in Psy-chiatry* 4 (2014): 141. https://doi.org/10.3389/fpsyt.2013.00141.

Scheffler, Samuel. "Relationships and Responsibilities." *Philosophy & Public Affairs* 26, no. 3 (1997): 189–209. https://doi.org/10.1111/j.1088-4963.1997.tb00053.x.

Schmeichel, Brandon J., Kathleen D. Vohs, and Roy F. Baumeister. "Intellectual Performance and Ego Depletion: Role of the Self in Logical Reasoning and Other Information Pro-cessing." *Journal of Personality and Social Psychology* 85, no. 1 (2003): 33–46. https://doi.org/10.1037/0022-3514.85.1.33.

Schomerus, G., C. Schwahn, A. Holzinger, P. W. Corrigan, H. J. Grabe, M. G. Carta, and M. C. Angermeyer. "Evolution of Public Attitudes About Mental Illness: A Systematic Review and Meta-Analysis." *Acta Psychiatrica Scandinavica* 125, no. 6 (2012): 440–52. https://doi.org/10.1111/j.1600-0447.2012.01826.x.

Schomerus, Georg, Michael Lucht, Anita Holzinger, Herbert Matschinger, Mauro G. Carta, and Matthias C. Angermeyer. "The Stigma of Alcohol Dependence Compared with Other Mental Disorders: A Review of Population Studies." *Alcohol and Alcoholism* 46, no. 2 (2011): 105–12. https://doi.org/10.1093/alcalc/agq089.

Schroeder, Tim. "Desire." In *Stanford Encyclopedia of Philosophy* (Summer 2020 Edition), edited by Edward N. Zalta. Accessed July 18, 2024. https://plato.stanford.edu/archives/sum2020/entries/desire/.

Schüll, Natasha Dow. *Addiction by Design: Machine Gambling in Las Vegas.* Princeton University Press, 2014.

Segal, Gabriel. "Alcoholism, Disease, and Insanity." *Philosophy, Psychiatry, and Psychology* 20, no. 4 (2013): 297–315. https://doi.org/10.1353/ppp.2013.0059.

Segal, Gabriel. "Ambiguous Terms and False Dichotomies." In *Addiction and Choice: Rethinking the Relationship.* Oxford University Press, 2017.

Sen, Amartya. *Commodities and Capabilities.* North-Holland, 1985.

Sepinwall, Amy J. "Faultless Guilt: Toward a Relationship-Based Account of Criminal Liability." *The American Criminal Law Review* 54, no. 2 (2017): 521.

Serre, Fuschia, Melina Fatseas, Joel Swendsen, and Marc Auriacombe. "Ecological Momentary Assessment in the Investigation of Craving and Substance Use in Daily Life: A Systematic Review." *Drug and Alcohol Dependence* 148 (2015): 1–20. https://doi.org/10.1016/j.drugalcdep.2014.12.024.

Sexton, Anne. "Wanting to Die." In *The Complete Poems: Anne Sexton.* Houghton Mifflin, 1981.

Shaham, Y., H. Rajabi, and J. Stewart. "Relapse to Heroin-Seeking in Rats Under Opioid Main-tenance: The Effects of Stress, Heroin Priming, and Withdrawal." *The Journal of Neuroscience* 16, no. 5 (1996): 1957–63. https://doi.org/10.1523/jneurosci.16-05-01957.1996.

Shea, N. *Representation in Cognitive Science*. Oxford University Press, 2018.

Shneidman, Edwin S. *The Suicidal Mind*. Oxford University Press, 1996.

Shoemaker, David. "Hurt Feelings." *The Journal of Philosophy* 116, no. 3 (2019): 125–48. https://doi.org/10.5840/jphil201911638.

Silverman, Kenneth, August F. Holtyn, and Reed Morrison. "The Therapeutic Utility of Employment in Treating Drug Addiction: Science to Application." *Translational Issues in Psychological Science* 2, no. 2 (2016): 203–12. https://doi.org/10.1037/tps0000061.

Sinha, Rajita. "Chronic Stress, Drug Use, and Vulnerability to Addiction." *Annals of the New York Academy of Sciences* 1141, no. 1 (2008): 105–30. https://doi.org/10.1196/annals.1441.030.

Skinner, B. F. "'Superstition' in the Pigeon." *Journal of Experimental Psychology* 121, no. 3 (1992): 273–74. https://doi.org/10.1037/0096-3445.121.3.273.

Skinner, B. F. *The Behavior of Organisms: An Experimental Analysis*. Appleton-Century-Crofts, 1966.

Slingerland, Edward. *Drunk: How We Sipped, Danced, and Stumbled Our Way to Civilization*. Little, Brown and Company, 2021.

Smith, Angela M. "On Being Responsible and Holding Responsible." *The Journal of Ethics* 11, no. 4 (2007): 465–84. https://doi.org/10.1007/s10892-005-7989-5.

Smith, Kirsten E. "Disease and Decision." *Journal of Substance Abuse Treatment* 142 (2022): 108874. https://doi.org/10.1016/j.jsat.2022.108874.

Smith, M. "The Possibility of Philosophy of Action." In *Human Action, Deliberation and Dausation*, edited by J. Bransen and S. Cuypers. Kluwer Academic Publishers, 1998.

Snoek, Anke. "Addiction, Self-Control and the Self: An Empirical, Ethical Study." *Macquarie University*, November 21, 2017. https://doi.org/10.25949/19427693.v1.

Snoek, Anke, Victoria McGeer, Daphne Brandenburg, and Jeanette Kennett. "Managing Shame and Guilt in Addiction: A Pathway to Recovery." *Addictive Behaviors* 120 (2021): 106954. https://doi.org/10.1016/j.addbeh.2021.106954.

Solomon, Richard L., and John D. Corbit. "An Opponent-Process Theory of Motivation: I. Temporal Dynamics of Affect." *Psychological Review* 81, no. 2 (1974): 119–45. https://doi.org/10.1037/h0036128.

Sommers, Tamler. *Relative Justice: Cultural Diversity, Free Will, and Moral Responsibility*. Princeton University Press, 2012.

Spragg, S. D. S. "Morphine Addiction in Chimpanzees." *Comparative Psychology Monographs* 15, no. 7 (1940): 132.

Srinivasan, Amia. "The Aptness of Anger." *The Journal of Political Philosophy* 26, no. 2 (2018): 123–44. https://doi.org/10.1111/jopp.12130.

Sripada, Chandra. "Addiction and Fallibility." *The Journal of Philosophy* 115, no. 11 (2018): 569–87. https://doi.org/10.5840/jphil20181151133.

Sripada, Chandra. "Impaired Control in Addiction Involves Cognitive Distortions and Unreliable Self-Control, Not Compulsive Desires and Overwhelmed Self-Control." *Behavioural Brain Research* 418 (2022): 113639. https://doi.org/10.1016/j.bbr.2021.113639.

Sripada, Chandra. "Loss of Control in Addiction: The Search for an Adequate Theory and the Case for Intellectual Humility." In *The Oxford Handbook of Moral Psychology*. Oxford University Press, 2022.

Starcke, Katrin, Stephanie Antons, Patrick Trotzke, and Matthias Brand. "Cue-Reactivity in Behavioral Addictions: A Meta-Analysis and Methodological Considerations." *Journal of Behavioral Addictions* 7, no. 2 (2018): 227–38. https://doi.org/10.1556/2006.7.2018.39.

Stewart, Sherry H., and Patricia Conrod. *Anxiety and Substance Use Disorders: The Vicious Cycle of Comorbidity*. 1st ed. Springer, 2007.

Strain, Eric C. "Meaning and Purpose in the Context of Opioid Overdose Deaths." *Drug and Alcohol Dependence* 219 (2021): 108528. https://doi.org/10.1016/j.drugalcdep.2021.108528.

Strang, John, Teodora Groshkova, Ambros Uchtenhagen, Wim van den Brink, Christian Haasen, Martin T. Schechter, Nick Lintzeris, et al. "Heroin on Trial: Systematic Review and Meta-Analysis of Randomised Trials of Diamorphine-Prescribing as Treatment for Refractory Heroin Addiction." *British Journal of Psychiatry* 207, no. 1 (2015): 5–14. https://doi.org/10.1192/bjp.bp.114.149195.

Strawson, P. F. *Freedom and Resentment, and Other Essays*. Routledge, 2008.

Strayed, Cheryl. "Heroin/e." In *The Best American Essays 2000 (The Best American Series)*, edited by Robert Atwan and Alan Lightman. HarperCollins, 2000.

Strickland, Justin C., and Ryan T. Lacy. "Behavioral Economic Demand as a Unifying Language for Addiction Science: Promoting Collaboration and Integration of Animal and Human Models." *Experimental and Clinical Psychopharmacology* 28, no. 4 (2020): 404–16. https://doi.org/10.1037/pha0000358.

Stroud, Sarah, and Larisa Svirsky. "Weakness of Will." In *Stanford Encyclopedia of Philosophy* (Winter 2021 Edition), edited by Edward N. Zalta. Accessed January 10, 2025. https://plato.stanford.edu/archives/win2021/entries/weakness-will/.

Substance Abuse and Mental Health Services Administration (SAMHSA). "Key Substance Use and Mental Health Indicators in the United States: Results from the 2022 National Survey on Drug Use and Health." Accessed June 18, 2024. https://www.samhsa.gov/data/sites/default/files/reports/rpt42731/2022-nsduh-nnr.pdf.

Substance Abuse and Mental Health Services Administration (SAMHSA). "Recovery and Recovery Support." Accessed June 26, 2024. https://www.samhsa.gov/find-help/recovery.

Substance Abuse and Mental Health Services Administration (SAMHSA). "Results from the 2022 National Survey on Drug Use and Health: A Companion Infographic." Accessed June 18, 2024. https://www.samhsa.gov/data/sites/default/files/reports/rpt42730/2022-nsduh-infographic-report.pdf.

Suzuki, Shosuke, and Hedy Kober. "Substance-Related and Addictive Disorders." In *APA Handbook of Psychopathology: Vol. 1. Psychopathology: Understanding, Assessing, and Treating Adult Mental Disorders*. American Psychological Association, 2018.

Szalavitz, M. *Unbroken Brain: A Revolutionary New Way of Understanding Addiction*. New Picador Press, 2016.

Tajfel, H. "Social Psychology of Intergroup Relations." *Annual Review of Psychology* 33, no. 33, 1982. https://doi.org/10.1146/annurev.ps.33.020182.000245.

Tajfel, H., and J. C. Turner. "An Integrative Theory of Intergroup Relations." In *The Social Psychology of Intergroup Relations*, edited by S. Worchel and W. G. Austin. Brooks/Cole, 1979.

Talbert, Matthew. "Moral Responsibility." In *Stanford Encyclopedia of Philosophy* (Fall 2024 Edition), edited by Edward N. Zalta and Nodelman, Uri. Accessed October 17, 2024. https://plato.stanford.edu/archives/fall2024/entries/moral-responsibility/.

Thorndike, Edward L. "Animal Intelligence: An Experimental Study of the Associative Processes in Animals." *Psychological Monographs* 2, no. 4 (1898): i–109. https://doi.org/10.1037/h0092987.

Tiffany, Stephen T. "A Cognitive Model of Drug Urges and Drug-Use Behavior: Role of Automatic and Nonautomatic Processes." *Psychological Review* 97, no. 2 (1990): 147–68. https://doi.org/10.1037/0033-295X.97.2.147.

Todd, Patrick. "Strawson, Moral Responsibility, and the 'Order of Explanation': An Intervention." *Ethics* 127, no. 1 (2016): 208–40. https://doi.org/10.1086/687336.

Toegel, Forrest, August F. Holtyn, Shrinidhi Subramaniam, and Kenneth Silverman. "Effects of Time-Based Administration of Abstinence Reinforcement Targeting Opiate and Cocaine Use." *Journal of Applied Behavior Analysis* 53, no. 3 (2020): 1726–41. https://doi.org/10.1002/jaba.702.

Tombor, Ildiko, Lion Shahab, Jamie Brown, Caitlin Notley, and Robert West. "Does Non-smoker Identity Following Quitting Predict Long-Term Abstinence? Evidence from a Population Survey in England." *Addictive Behaviors* 45 (2015): 99–103. https://doi.org/10.1016/j .addbeh.2015.01.026.

Tomie, Arthur, Kathryn L. Grimes, and Larissa A. Pohorecky. "Behavioral Characteristics and Neurobiological Substrates Shared by Pavlovian Sign-Tracking and Drug Abuse." *Brain Research Reviews* 58, no. 1 (2008): 121–35. https://doi.org/10.1016/j.brainresrev.2007.12 .003.

Trivers, Robert. *Social Evolution.* Benjamin/Cummings, 1985.

Trivers, Robert. *The Folly of Fools: The Logic of Deceit and Self-Deception in Human Life.* Basic Books, 2013.

Tucker, Jalie A., Susan D. Chandler, and Katie Witkiewitz. "Epidemiology of Recovery from Alcohol Use Disorder." *Alcohol Research: Current Reviews* 40, no. 3 (2020): 2. https://doi.org /10.35946/arcr.v40.3.02.

Turner, John C. *Rediscovering the Social Group: A Self-Categorization Theory.* Blackwell, 1987.

Turner, R. H. "Psychosocial Adversity." In *Handbook of Personality Disorders*, edited by W. J. Livesly. Guilford Press, 2001.

Turner, R. H. "The Self-Conception in Social Interaction." In *The Self in Social Interaction*, edited by C. Gorden and K. J. Gergen. Wiley, 1968.

United Nations Office on Drugs and Crime (UNODC). "World Drug Report 2023." Accessed June 10, 2024. https://www.unodc.org/unodc/en/data-and-analysis/world-drug-report -2023.html.

US Department of Health and Human Services. *Alcohol Pharmacotherapies.* Substance Abuse and Mental Health Services Administration, 2009.

Vafaie, Nilofar, and Hedy Kober. "Association of Drug Cues and Craving With Drug Use and Relapse: A Systematic Review and Meta-Analysis." *Journal of the American Medical Association (JAMA) Psychiatry* 79, no. 7 (2022): 641–50. https://doi.org/10.1001/jamapsychiatry .2022.1240.

Vaidya, Nilakshi, Andre F. Marquand, Frauke Nees, Sebastian Siehl, and Gunter Schumann. "The Impact of Psychosocial Adversity on Brain and Behaviour: An Overview of Existing Knowledge and Directions for Future Research." *Molecular Psychiatry*, 2024. https://doi.org /10.1038/s41380-024-02556-y.

van der Meer, Pim B., Juan J. Fuentes, Ad A. Kaptein, Jan W. Schoones, Marleen M. de Waal, Anneke E. Goudriaan, Kees Kramers, et al. "Therapeutic Effect of Psilocybin in Addiction: A Systematic Review." *Frontiers in Psychiatry* 14 (2023): 1134454. https://doi.org/10.3389 /fpsyt.2023.1134454.

Van Leeuwen, D. S. Neil. "The Product of Self-Deception." *Erkenntnis* 67, no. 3 (2007): 419–37. https://doi.org/10.1007/s10670-007-9058-x.

Van Leeuwen, D. S. Neil. "The Spandrels of Self-Deception: Prospects for a Biological Theory of a Mental Phenomenon." *Philosophical Psychology* 20, no. 3 (2007): 329–48. https://doi.org /10.1080/09515080701197148.

Vandaele, Youna, and S. H. Ahmed. "Habit, Choice, and Addiction." *Neuropsychopharmacology* 46, no. 4 (2021): 689–98. https://doi.org/10.1038/s41386-020-00899-y.

Vandaele, Youna, and Patricia H. Janak. "Defining the Place of Habit in Substance Use Disorders." *Progress in Neuro-Psychopharmacology and Biological Psychiatry* 87, (2018): 22–32. https://doi.org/10.1016/j.pnpbp.2017.06.029.

Vandaele, Youna, Caroline Vouillac-Mendoza, and Serge H. Ahmed. "Inflexible Habitual Decision-Making During Choice Between Cocaine and a Nondrug Alternative." *Translational Psychiatry* 9, no. 1 (2019): 109. https://doi.org/10.1038/s41398-019-0445-2.

Vandaele, Youna, Eric Augier, Caroline Vouillac-Mendoza, and Serge H. Ahmed. "Cocaine Falls into Oblivion During Volitional Initiation of Choice Trials." *Addiction Biology* 27, no. 6 (2022): https://doi.org/10.1111/adb.13235.

Vandaele, Youna, Karine Guillem, and Serge H. Ahmed. "Habitual Preference for the Nondrug Reward in a Drug Choice Setting." *Frontiers in Behavioral Neuroscience* 14 (2020): 78. https://doi.org/10.3389/fnbeh.2020.00078.

Vandaele, Youna, Lauriane Cantin, Fuschia Serre, Caroline Vouillac-Mendoza, and Serge H. Ahmed. "Choosing Under the Influence: A Drug-Specific Mechanism by Which the Setting Controls Drug Choices in Rats." *Neuropsychopharmacology* 41, no. 2 (2016): 646–57. https://doi.org/10.1038/npp.2015.195.

Vargas, Manuel. *Building Better Beings: A Theory of Moral Responsibility.* 1st ed. Oxford University Press, 2013.

Velleman, J. David. "Motivation by Ideal." *Philosophical Explorations* 5, no. 2 (2002): 89–103. https://doi.org/10.1080/10002002058538724.

Venniro, Marco, Leigh V. Panlilio, David H. Epstein, and Yavin Shaham. "The Protective Effect of Operant Social Reward on Cocaine Self-Administration, Choice, and Relapse Is Dependent on Delay and Effort for the Social Reward." *Neuropsychopharmacology* 46, no. 13 (2021): 2350–57. https://doi.org/10.1038/s41386-021-01148-6.

Venniro, Marco, Matthew L. Banks, Markus Heilig, David H. Epstein, and Yavin Shaham. "Improving Translation of Animal Models of Addiction and Relapse by Reverse Translation." *Nature Reviews Neuroscience* 21, no. 11 (2020): 625–43. https://doi.org/10.1038/s41583-020-0378-z.

Venniro, Marco, Matthew L. Banks, Markus Heilig, David H. Epstein, and Yavin Shaham. "Improving Translation of Animal Models of Addiction and Relapse by Reverse Translation." *Nature Reviews. Neuroscience* 21, no. 11 (2020): 625–43. https://doi.org/10.1038/s41583-020-0378-z.

Venniro, Marco, Michelle Zhang, Daniele Caprioli, Jennifer K. Hoots, Sam A. Golden, Conor Heins, Marisela Morales, David H. Epstein, and Yavin Shaham. "Volitional Social Interaction Prevents Drug Addiction in Rat Models." *Nature Neuroscience* 21, no. 11 (2018): 1520–29. https://doi.org/10.1038/s41593-018-0246-6.

Verdejo-Garcia, Antonio, Trevor T.-J Chong, Julie C. Stout, Murat Yücel, and Edythe D. London. "Stages of Dysfunctional Decision-Making in Addiction." *Pharmacology Biochemistry and Behavior* 164 (2018): 99–105. https://doi.org/10.1016/j.pbb.2017.02.003.

Verdejo-Garcia, Antonio. "Decision-Making Dysfunctions in Addiction." In *The Routledge Handbook of Philosophy and Science of Addiction*, edited by Hanna Pickard and Serge H. Ahmed. 1st ed. Routledge, 2019.

Vohs, Kathleen D., Roy F. Baumeister, and Natalie J. Ciarocco. "Self-Regulation and Self-Presentation: Regulatory Resource Depletion Impairs Impression Management and Effortful Self-Presentation Depletes Regulatory Resources." *Journal of Personality and Social Psychology* 88, no. 4 (2005): 632–57. https://doi.org/10.1037/0022-3514.88.4.632.

Vohs, Kathleen D., Roy F. Baumeister, Brandon J. Schmeichel, Jean M. Twenge, Noelle M. Nelson, and Dianne M. Tice. "Making Choices Impairs Subsequent Self-Control: A Limited-Resource Account of Decision Making, Self-Regulation, and Active Initiative." *Journal of Personality and Social Psychology* 94, no. 5 (2008): 883–98. https://doi.org/10.1037/0022-3514.94.5.883.

Volkow, Nora. "Addiction Is a Disease of Free Will," *Nora's Blog* (blog), National Institute on Drug Abuse, June 12, 2015, https://archives.nida.nih.gov/news-events/noras-blog/2015/06/addiction-disease-free-will.

Volkow, Nora, and Ting-Kai Li. "The Neuroscience of Addiction." *Nature Neuroscience* 8 (2005): 1430. https://doi.org/10.1038/nn1105-1429.

Volkow, Nora D., Gene-Jack Wang, Frank Telang, Joanna S. Fowler, Jean Logan, Anna-Rose Childress, Millard Jayne, Yeming Ma, and Christopher Wong. "Cocaine Cues and Dopamine in Dorsal Striatum: Mechanism of Craving in Cocaine Addiction." *The Journal of Neuroscience* 26, no. 24 (2006): 6583–88. https://doi.org/10.1523/JNEUROSCI.1544-06.2006.

Vollstädt-Klein, Sabine, Svenja Wichert, Juri Rabinstein, Mira Bühler, Oliver Klein, Gabriele Ende, Derik Hermann, and Karl Mann. "Initial, Habitual and Compulsive Alcohol Use Is Characterized by a Shift of Cue Processing from Ventral to Dorsal Striatum." *Addiction* 105, no. 10 (2010): 1741–49. https://doi.org/10.1111/j.1360-0443.2010.03022.x.

von Hippel, William, and Robert Trivers. "The Evolution and Psychology of Self-Deception." *The Behavioral and Brain Sciences* 34, no. 1 (2011): 1–16. https://doi.org/10.1017/S0140525X10001354.

Wakefield, Jerome C. "The Concept of Mental Disorder: On the Boundary Between Biological Facts and Social Values." *The American Psychologist* 47, no. 3 (1992): 373–88. https://doi.org/10.1037/0003-066X.47.3.373.

Wakefield, Jerome C. "The Harmful Dysfunction Analysis of Addiction: Normal Brains and Abnormal States of Mind." In *The Routledge Handbook of Philosophy and Science of Addiction*, 1st ed. Routledge, 2019.

Waldorf, Dan, Craig Waldorf, and Sheigla Murphy. *Cocaine Changes: The Experience of Using and Quitting*. Temple University Press, 1992.

Walker, Margaret Urban. *Moral Repair: Reconstructing Moral Relations after Wrongdoing*. Cambridge University Press, 2006.

Wallace, David Foster. *Infinite Jest*. Little, Brown and Company, 1996.

Wallace, R. J. "Addiction as Defect of the Will: Some Philosophical Reflections." *Law and Philosophy* 18, no. 6 (1999): 621–54. https://doi.org/10.1023/A:1006315614953.

Wallace, R. J. *Responsibility and the Moral Sentiments*. Harvard University Press, 1996.

Wang, Shaoming, Samuel F. Feng, and Aaron M. Bornstein. "Mixing Memory and Desire: How Memory Reactivation Supports Deliberative Decision-Making." *Wiley Interdisciplinary Reviews. Cognitive Science* 13, no. 2 (2022): e1581. https://doi.org/10.1002/wcs.1581.

Watson, G. "Disordered Appetites: Addiction, Compulsion, and Dependence." In *Addiction: Entries and Exits*, edited by J. Elster. Russell Sage Foundation, 1999.

Watson, Gary. "Responsibility and the Limits of Evil: Variations on a Strawsonian Theme." In *Responsibility, Character, and the Emotions*. Cambridge University Press, 1988.

Welsh, Irvine. *Trainspotting*. Vintage, 1994.

West, Robert. *Theory of Addiction*. 1st ed. Wiley, 2006.

Westlund, Andrea C. "Answerability without Blame?." In *Social Dimensions of Moral Responsibility*. Oxford University Press, 2018.

Wiens, Thomas K., and Lawrence J. Walker. "The Chronic Disease Concept of Addiction: Helpful or Harmful?" *Addiction Research & Theory* 23, no. 4 (2015): 309–21. https://doi.org/10.3109/16066359.2014.987760.

Wiers, Reinout W. *A New Approach to Addiction and Choice: Akrasia and the Nature of Free Will*. Routledge, 2024.

Wiers, Reinout W., Simon van Gaal, and Mike E. Le Pelley. "Akrasia and Addiction: Neurophilosophy and Psychological Mechanisms." In *Social Neuroeconomics*, 1st ed. Routledge, 2021.

Wilde, Oscar. *The Picture of Dorian Gray*. Alma Classics, 2014.

Williams, Bernard. "Internal and External Reasons." In *Moral Luck: Philosophical Papers, 101–13*. Cambridge University Press, 1981.

Witkiewitz, Katie, Rory A. Pfund, and Jalie A. Tucker. "Mechanisms of Behavior Change in Substance Use Disorder with and Without Formal Treatment." *Annual Review of Clinical Psychology* 18 (2022): 497–525. https://doi.org/10.1146/annurev-clinpsy-072720-014802.

Wonderly, Monique. "Agency and Varieties of Felt Necessity." *Ethics* 132, no. 1 (2021): 155–79. https://doi.org/10.1086/715290.

Wonderly, Monique. "Attachment, Addiction, and Vices of Valuing." In *Attachment and Character: Attachment Theory, Ethics, and the Developmental Psychology of Vice and Virtue*, edited by Edward Harcourt. Oxford University Press, 2021.

Wonderly, Monique. "On Being Attached." *Philosophical Studies* 173, no. 1 (2016): 223–42. https://doi.org/10.1007/s11098-015-0487-0.

Wonderly, Monique. "On the Affect of Security." *Philosophical Topics* 47, no. 2 (2019): 165–82. https://doi.org/10.5840/philtopics201947221.

Woodward, James. *Making Things Happen: A Theory of Causal Explanation*. Oxford University Press, 2003.

Woodward, James, and Lauren Ross. "Scientific Explanation." In *Stanford Encyclopedia of Philosophy* (Summer 2021 Edition), edited by Edward N. Zalta. Accessed January 17, 2024. https://plato.stanford.edu/archives/sum2021/entries/scientific-explanation/.

World Health Organization (WHO). *Global Status Report on Alcohol and Health 2018*. Accessed June 10, 2024. World Health Organization, 2018.

World Health Organization (WHO). "Tobacco." Accessed June 17, 2024. https://www.who.int/news-room/fact-sheets/detail/tobacco.

Wrase, Jana, Florian Schlagenhauf, Thorsten Kienast, Torsten Wüstenberg, Felix Bermpohl, Thorsten Kahnt, Anne Beck, et al. "Dysfunction of Reward Processing Correlates with Alcohol Craving in Detoxified Alcoholics." *NeuroImage* 35, no. 2 (2007): 787–94. https://doi.org/10.1016/j.neuroimage.2006.11.043.

Wright, L. "Functions." *The Philosophical Review* 82, no. 2 (1973): 139–68. https://doi.org/10.2307/2183766.

Wright, L. *Teleological Explanations*. University of California Press, 1976.

Zajac, Kristyn, Sheila M. Alessi, and Nancy M. Petry. "Contingency Management Approaches." In *The Routledge Handbook of Philosophy and Science of Addiction*, edited by Hanna Pickard and Serge H. Ahmed. 1st ed. Routledge, 2019.

Zinberg, Norman. *Drug, Set, and Setting: The Basis for Controlled Intoxicant Use*. Yale University Press, 1986.

INDEX

Page numbers in *italics* refer to figures.

abstinence: active blame and, 266; commitment to, 164–65; costs of, 135–36, 185–86, 258–59; definition of addiction and, 41–42; denial and, 186–87; nonaddict identities and, 153–54; relapse and, 96–98, 183–86, 208, 263; time discounting and, 188–90; violation effect, 186. *See also* behavior; withdrawal

accountability, 223–26, 230, 234–37, 248, 260–61

active blame, 241–46, 256–59, 266

adaptive preferences, 55. *See also* good life; values

addict, as term, 153

addict identity, 152–58, 162–65, 192, 203–4. *See also* identity

addiction: asymptomatic, 41–42; behavioral, 17–18; community in, 156–58; definitions of, 36–38, 297n16; descriptions of, 56, 131–32, 157–58, 199–200, 266; diagnosis of, 63–64; disposition to, 31, 41–42, 68–70; duress of, 257–59; environmental factors for, 33–34, 90, 115–18, 132–36, 145, 156–57, 167–68, 259–60; factors of, 271–72; gambling, 110, 120–21, 146–47; heroin, 26, 27, 159, 172–73, 202–3, 286n3; human vs. rat, 9, 98–100, 182–83; necessary and sufficient conditions for, 36–37; ordinary drug use vs., 24–25, 58, 79; origins of, 24–27; physical dependence vs., 49–51; polydrug, 3, 26, 48, 152; puzzle of, 28–35, 37–38, 169–70, 270–71; self-harm and, 147–51; smoking, 91, 153–54, 164–65, 169–70, 283n52; stigma of, 11–12, 14, 16–17, 156–57, 208–9, 218, 253, 282n28. *See also* abstinence; addiction studies; alcohol addiction; brain disease model; control; costs; cravings; drug use; memoirs; models of addiction; opioid addiction; theories of addiction; treatments

"Addiction as a Brain Disease Revised: Why It Still Matters" (Heilig), 12

Addiction by Design (Schüll), 121, 146–47

"Addiction Is a Brain Disease, and It Matters" (Leshner), 1, 12, 286n3

addiction studies: clinical practice and, 45–46; epidemiological data and, 90; human, 86–87, 90–91, 93–94, 112–14, 178, 283n52. *See also* rat experiments

affective slack, 259, 273

agency, 190, 223, 231, 263. *See also* responsibility

Ahmed, Serge H., 3–4, 88–89

"Ailment, The" (Main), 221

Ainslie, George, 188

alcohol addiction: Alcoholics Anonymous (AA) and, 41–42, 173–74, 297n16; attitudes towards alcohol and, 9, 24, 159; as coping strategy, 141; cravings in, 81–82; denial and, 173–74; descriptions of, 7, 25, 27, 97–98, 148, 200, 208, 254; mindlessness of, 288n17; National Institute on Alcohol Abuse and Alcoholism (NIAAA) and, 46–47; Neurobiological Craving Signature (NCS) and, 91; plurality of causes of, 114–15; relapse and, 183–84; strong disease model and, 114–15; studies on, 46, 93–94, 112–13, 180–81, 283n52; suicide and, 149; treatments for, 3, 206, 262; withdrawal and, 49. *See also* addiction

154–55; loss of, 155, 160–61; sense of self and, 142–45, 161–64
ignorance, 72, 169–70, 178–79
imaging studies, 112–14
immediacy, 135, 184, 188
imprinting parable, 107–9
In the Realm of Hungry Ghosts (Maté), 55–56. *See also* Maté, Gabor
incentive salience theory, 198–201, 206, 298n16
interventionist model of causation, 113–14
interventions. *See* treatments
intrinsic desire, 67–68, 195, 199. *See also* desire
irresistibility, 81–83, 88, 93, 95–97, 99, 206, 289n3. *See also* cravings
Ismael, Jenann, 10
I-statements, 248

Jake (patient of Gabor Maté), 55–58, 163, 254. *See also* Maté, Gabor
James, Williams, 81, 91, 100
Jean-Richard-Dit-Bressel, Philip, 178
Jellinek, E. Morton, 180
Joe (Cheryl Strayed's ex-boyfriend), 51, 53–54, 57, 148, 172–73, 256. *See also* Strayed, Cheryl
Johnson, Samuel, 148
Johnston, Mark, 177
Junky (Burroughs), 27, 159. *See also* Burroughs, Augusten
juridical image, 228–31, 233–34, 241–47, 266–68
"just-so stories," 105, 108

Kate (addict in recovery), 160–63
Kendler, Kenneth, 38, 114, 117
Kennett, Jeanette, 55, 190, 208
Khantzian, Edward, 131
Kim, Jaegwon, 35
Kingsolver, Barbara, 131–32
Knapp, Caroline: on cravings, 208; on denial, 138, 173, 177, 187; description of addiction by, 27, 131, 148, 200; *Drinking: A Love Story*, 27, 137; on rock bottom, 179; on social cachet, 159
Koban, Leonie, 91
Kober, Hedy, 91
Koob, George, 201
Kraepelin, Emil, 35

Krakauer, John, 118
Kurlander, David, 86

lapses vs. relapses, 186
larger, later (LL) rewards, 135. *See also* rewards
Leshner, Alan, 1, 12, 78, 282n28, 286n3
Leslie, Sarah-Jane, 155
levels of explanation, 105–9
Lewis, Marc, 103
Life (Richards), 48, 51. *See also* Richards, Keith
life circumstances. *See* environmental factors; values
lived experiences, 199–201. *See also* memoirs
local bookkeeping, 185–86. *See also* control
loss of control, 96–100, 180, 181, 262–63. *See also* control
Lüscher, Christian, 86

Main, Thomas, 221
Marr, David, 106–7, 118
Martin, Clancy, 149–50
Marušić, Berislav, 164
mastery, 146–47
Maté, Gabor, 55–56, 57, 58, 163, 254
"maturing out," 90, 115, 132
McConnell, Doug, 9, 167
McGeer, Victoria, 232
McNally, Gavin, 178
medication-assisted treatments, 3, 49, 72–73, 205–6. *See also* treatments
memoirs: *Drinking: A Love Story* (Knapp), 27, 137; *A Drinking Life* (Hamill), 7; *Heroin/e* (Strayed), 51; *How Not to Kill Yourself* (Martin), 149–50; *Junky* (Burroughs), 27, 159; *Life* (Richards), 48, 51; *A Sad and Sorry State of Disorder: A Journey into Borderline Personality Disorder (and Out the Other Side)* (Barker), 143–44; self-harming mindset in, 147–48; *This Is How: Surviving What You Think You Can't* (Burroughs), 97–98, 183; tropes in, 158–59; *Unbroken Brain* (Szalavitz), 137–38; *What Is It like to Be an Addict?* (Flanagan), 53. *See also* Burroughs, Augusten; Flanagan, Owen; Knapp, Caroline; Strayed, Cheryl
memory sampling, 187
"mental blank," 174

A NOTE ON THE TYPE

This book has been composed in Arno, an Old-style serif typeface in the
classic Venetian tradition, designed by Robert Slimbach at Adobe

GPSR Authorized Representative: Easy Access System Europe - Mustamäe tee
50, 10621 Tallinn, Estonia, gpsr.requests@easproject.com

www.ingramcontent.com/pod-product-compliance
Lightning Source LLC
Chambersburg PA
CBHW032016020426
42338CB00039B/2010/J